One Job Town

Work, Belonging, and Betrayal in Northern Ontario

There's a pervasive sense of betrayal in areas scarred by mine, mill, and factory closures. Steven High's *One Job Town* delves into the long history of one such town located on Canada's resource periphery. Much like hundreds of other towns and cities across North America and Europe, Sturgeon Falls, Ontario, lost its primary source of industry, resulting in the displacement of workers and their families, when its century-old paper mill closed in 2002.

Through stories shared by mill workers, managers, and city officials, *One Job Town* takes us into the making of a culture of industrialism and the significance of industrial work and its loss for mill-working families. It approaches deindustrialization as a long-term economic, political, and cultural process, which did not simply begin and end with the closure of the local mill. Oral history and memory are at the heart of *One Job Town*, challenging us to rethink the relationship between the past and the present in what was formerly known as the industrialized world.

STEVEN HIGH is a professor of history at Concordia University and the author of *Industrial Sunset: The Making of North America's Rust Belt, 1969–1984*.

ONE JOB TOWN

WORK, BELONGING, AND BETRAYAL IN NORTHERN ONTARIO

Steven High

UNIVERSITY OF TORONTO PRESS
Toronto Buffalo London

© University of Toronto Press 2018
Toronto Buffalo London
utorontopress.com
Printed and bound by CPI Group (UK) Ltd, Croydon, CR0 4YY

ISBN 978-1-4426-4083-2 (cloth)   ISBN 978-1-4426-1023-1 (paper)

Printed on acid-free paper with vegetable-based inks.

Title page and chapter opening image: junjie/shutterstock

Library and Archives Canada Cataloguing in Publication

High, Steven C., author
One job town : work, belonging, and betrayal in Northern Ontario / Steven High.

Includes bibliographical references and index.
ISBN 978-1-4426-4083-2 (cloth). ISBN 978-1-4426-1023-1 (paper)

1. Paper mills – Ontario – Sturgeon Falls.   2. Mills and mill-work – Ontario –
Sturgeon Falls.   3. Paper industry – Ontario – Sturgeon Falls – Employees.
4. Deindustrialization – Ontario – Sturgeon Falls.   5. Sturgeon Falls (Ont.) –
Economic conditions – 20th century.   6. Sturgeon Falls (Ont.) –
Social conditions – 20th century. I. Title.

HD9834.C23S78 2018   338.7'67609713147   C2017-908046-6

This book has been published with the help of a grant from the Federation for the Humanities
and Social Sciences, through the Awards to Scholarly Publications Program, using funds
provided by the Social Sciences and Humanities Research Council of Canada.

University of Toronto Press acknowledges the financial assistance to its publishing program of the
Canada Council for the Arts and the Ontario Arts Council, an agency of the government of Ontario.

 Canada Council   Conseil des Arts
for the Arts   du Canada

 ONTARIO ARTS COUNCIL
CONSEIL DES ARTS DE L'ONTARIO
an Ontario government agency
un organisme du gouvernement de l'Ontario

Funded by the   Financé par le
Government   gouvernement
of Canada   du Canada | Canadä

Class is something beneath your clothes, under your skin,
in your reflexes, in your psyche, at the very core of your being.
– Annette Kuhn, historian

CONTENTS

PREFACE

This book represents a coming home of sorts for me. It tells the story of Sturgeon Falls, a former mill town of six thousand people in Ontario's Northland, my home region, which lost its century-old paper mill in December 2002. Actually, it was not so much "lost" as it was suddenly ripped away. Anything that could be sold by the departing company was put onto trucks and shipped out. Everything else was pulverized into dust. A century's worth of production records and blueprints were shredded. Walking along the chain-link fence today, one finds only small reminders of what once stood there. It is an all-too-familiar scenario, repeated in towns and cities across the region and around the world.

The genesis of this book grew out of my own geographic and social proximity to the unfolding story. The mill closed shortly after I took up a new teaching position at Nipissing University, and like everyone else in the area, I followed the story in the local newspaper. I strongly identified with the mill workers, their community, and their struggle. It also hit home for a number of my students who were from Sturgeon Falls itself. Eventually my stance as an interested, but passive, bystander shifted when several of my students encouraged me to investigate. After all, my PhD thesis focused on the deindustrialization of North America's industrial heartland in the 1970s and 1980s, so it seemed logical to respond to events unfolding twenty-five minutes down the Trans-Canada Highway.

With the help of local students David Hunter and Louise Bidal, I met Bruce Colquhoun, one of two worker-historians in the mill, at the union-run Action Centre, where those displaced could get help with their job search or just be together.[1] Interviewees such as Pierre Hardy regularly dropped into the Action Centre to "just talk to the guys."[2] His wife, Jane, noted how much it helped him: "You're all in the same boat there. And you can go cry on each other's shoulder. Or get pissed off. And just vent somewhere."[3] Sitting at a table, Bruce and I flipped through the mill history binder, the biggest binder you have ever seen; he and Hubert Gervais had put it together over the years. The binder, which is the focus of Chapter 11, was chock full of photocopied materials going back to the mill's beginnings. This initial conversation convinced me that the project had to be a book-length study.

The first round of oral history interviews was conducted within two years of the mill's closure, as efforts to reopen it petered out and the facility was demolished. This rapidly changing context strongly influenced what was said and how it was said. Accordingly each interview records the changing moment. A second round of interviewing was conducted in 2005 and 2006, tracking change over the first four years. Oral interviews therefore offered people a space to share their thoughts and feelings and a place to try to make sense of what was happening to them. The emotions were often raw, with peaks and valleys of anger, defiance, and despair.

I cannot pretend to be a disinterested observer of this unfolding story. As a Northerner, I saw in Sturgeon Falls a microcosm of the economic and political crisis facing the region as a whole. I was (and remain) deeply frustrated by the failure of politicians in Ottawa and Toronto to acknowledge the crisis or to respond in some meaningful way. It is clear to me that peripheral regions are politically and economically disposable. As we will see, self-proclaimed "thought leaders" in the "creative class," such as Richard Florida, have provided intellectual cover for this mass abandonment. Whole areas have been written off. Northern Ontario might as well be on the moon, so great is its distance from the centres of economic, social, political, and cultural power.

Permit me to share something of my own roots in the region and its culture. I grew up in Thunder Bay, an isolated resource town on the North Shore of Lake Superior. As a Northerner, I had a strong sense of being on the political and geographic periphery. Growing up next to the railway yard where my father worked, one of my earliest memories is of being led with other children into the front room of a neighbour who then rolled up his pant leg to reveal the jagged stump where his leg used to be. He had tried to cut through the rail yard one day and had been dragged by a passing train. A lesson learned. Industrial spaces had to be respected. In elementary school, my classmates and I visited a working mine, a working grain elevator, and a working paper mill. We visited the woods operations to see how trees were harvested. We even learned how to make paper. Then one day in high school my economics teacher dramatically flung open the classroom window to let the mill's rotten egg smell into the room: "Smell that," he said, "that's the smell of money. That smell puts food on the table." Another lesson learned. It was the same one once taught to children across the industrialized world, where the "smell of money" was regularly used to justify the uneven environmental consequences of industrial development.[4]

Anthropologist Tom Dunk, also from Thunder Bay, has called my hometown a quintessential "working man's town," a place where male proletarians made their living cutting trees, making paper, or moving grain. My father, a railway haustler – essentially, a switchman between two of the city's rail yards – moved grain. He worked night shift until I was in high school; by then he had accumulated enough seniority to work steady days and get Saturdays and Sundays off. Formerly our family had been in temporal flux, as my mother was a primary school teacher and had the weekends off. She would later become a local union leader.

My parents worked hard and saved their money. After a few years they bought a small home in the central city area. Six or seven years later we moved into a suburban home farther away from the sounds and smells of industry, although the daily rhythms of industry continued to structure our lives. My family's trajectory mirrored that of the blue-collar middle class that emerged in the second half of the twentieth century, a period historian Jefferson Cowie calls the "great exception." Unionization and hard work had brought prosperity and new opportunities for the next generation.

Much of this industrial world has unravelled since my childhood, not only in Thunder Bay but across North America and Europe. Deindustrialization has ruptured the lives of tens of millions of working-class families, including my own. Three of the city's four paper mills are shuttered, as are most of the city's grain terminal elevators – a number have been demolished. The railway no longer employs many people, and my father was "bridged" into retirement at age fifty-one. It was not an easy transition.

This book project began with some seed money from Nipissing University that was then matched by Ontario student employment funding. This was enough to hire a local undergraduate student to conduct interviews. Kristen O'Hare proved to be outstanding, and this project would have been impossible without her. With a grant from the Social Sciences and Humanities Research Council of Canada (SSHRC), I was able to hire two additional undergraduate students from the area – Kayla Bilton and Nina Di Sabatino – during the summer of 2005. Since then, having relocated to Concordia University in Montreal, I have benefited from the assistance of Eve-Lyne Cayouette Ashby, Piyusha Chatterjee, Sue Doro, William Hamilton, Michael Klassen, Jessica Silva, David Sworn, and Simon Vickers. A number of others helped with transcription, including Kristoffer Archibald, Afsaneh Hojabri, Lara Lavelle, Lachlan MacKinnon, and Miranda O'Connor. Ron Harpelle was good enough to offer me the use of his office at Lakehead University one summer. For its part the Centre for Oral History and Digital Storytelling at Concordia has been instrumental in expanding and deepening my oral history practice since these interviews were conducted. Fred Burrill, Lachlan MacKinnon, and Tim Strangleman read the entire manuscript just before it was submitted for publication, as did Ed Hatton and Gerry Stevens, who worked at the mill itself.

I want to thank my friends for the many conversations we have had, often over food and drink, about this project over the years: Kees Botterbloem, Anne Clendinning, Cynthia Hammond, Ted Little, Arthur McIvor, Liz Miller, Dana Murphy, Françoise Noel, Larry Patriquin, Andrew Perchard, Ronald Rudin, Jarrett Rudy, Duane Schippers, Helen and Vic Smith, Kathleen Vaughan, John Walsh, Jean-Philippe Warren, and Jeff Webb. I also want to thank my partner in life, Barbara Lorenzkowski, and our children Sebastian and Leanna, who have filled my life with so much hearty laughter as well as inspiration.

I was again incredibly fortunate to work with photographer David W. Lewis, who visually documented the dismantling of the interior of the mill. To this we added individual portraits of a half-dozen former mill workers as well as from around town. Some of these early photos appeared in our 2007 book, *Corporate Wasteland*, which includes a chapter on the Sturgeon Falls closure, and were featured in a photo exhibition that travelled to various cities. A permanent exhibition of David's Sturgeon Falls photographs, entitled *Le Moulin*, funded by my SSHRC grant, was inaugurated at the Sturgeon House Museum in 2007. At that time, all of the oral history interview recordings were donated to the museum to ensure that area residents could have immediate access to their recorded history.

Special mention also goes out to University of Toronto Press, which brought this book to publication in record time. It was great to work with Len Husband again and with freelance copy editor Barry Norris for the first time. The anonymous reviewers also helped make this a better book.

Most of all, however, I want to thank all those who agreed to share their stories with us. Their generosity in a very difficult moment in their lives indicated their desire to speak truth to power. For a full listing of interviewees, see the bibliography. I particularly want to thank those who shared historic documents and photographs, as well as the three interviewees who served as local guides and mentors throughout the process. Bruce Colquhoun, Hubert Gervais, and Wayne LeBelle generously shared materials, provided leads, and commented on draft chapters. They also checked in with me from time to time to make sure I was still plugging away on this project. I regret it has taken so long. That said, I believe the book has benefited from a little more distance from the events being recounted.

I dedicate *One Job Town* to my father Gerald High, who died as this book was going to press. This kind and gentle man was a constant presence in my life. I am proud to be his son.

One Job Town

INTRODUCTION

The Shield, the enormous irregular triangle of rocky, ravaged upland, had been both a barrier to economic progress and a bulwark of economic development. These ancient, worn-down rocks, with their vast stretches of towering conifers, their elaborate mazes of lakes, lakelets, rivers, falls, rapids, and spillways, had been the basis of both the fur trade and the timber trade. There had been two great "crops" in the Precambrian Shield. Men had exploited its animals and forests; but now they were to tear out wealth and power from its soils, and rocks, and waters. The north became the great new impulse of Canadian life. It filled men's pockets and fired their imaginations. Its massive forms, its simple, sweeping rhythms, its glittering and sombre colours, inspired in Tom Thompson and the members of the Group of Seven the most distinctive group of painters which the country had yet produced.

– Donald Creighton[1]

Once known as "New Ontario," a mythic land of seemingly infinite wealth and promise, Northern Ontario is now associated with hard times, out-migration, and declining industries.[2] The region's resource-based economy is in a prolonged state of crisis with the closure of dozens of area mines, sawmills, paper mills, railway shops, and grain elevators. Tens of thousands have lost their well-paying union jobs in my lifetime. The decline of the region's primary and manufacturing industries has been dramatic, falling from 28 per cent of the overall workforce in 1981 to just 16 per cent in 2001. Employment in mining and forestry plummeted 47 per cent over the same period,[3] and it has fallen further since then. Arguably, the region's resource industries no longer represent its economic future, but a polluting past. Place names such as Sudbury, Grassy Narrows, and Temagami have become synonymous with environmental destruction or conflict with and disregard for Indigenous peoples.[4] Northern Ontario, Canada's largest provincial north, comprising seven-eighths of the province's total land surface and one-quarter of the entire length of the Trans-Canada Highway, has become an economic backwater, a forgotten place.[5]

Yet not so very long ago, the Precambrian (or Canadian) Shield stood at the symbolic centre of Canadian history and identity. Writing in 1929, historian Arthur Lower proclaimed: "There is no element in the present Dominion of greater significance than the so-called Canadian Shield or Laurentian Barrier. This vast region of lakes, rocks, and forests, which occupies all but a few thousand square miles of eastern Canada and which interposes the most formidable of obstacles between the usable regions of the East and the fertile areas of the West, has determined the direction and rate of the country's growth in the past, and doubtless will continue to be a decisive actor in its expansion in the future."[6] Then, in 1937, historian Donald Creighton argued that the Shield exercised an "imperious domination over the northerners, for though it was a harsh and exacting country, it offered lavish prizes to the restless, the ambitious and the daring."[7] Freehold grants for agricultural purposes proved impossible in much of the Shield except for the clay belts and a few other pockets of marginal farmland. The region's inhospitality to farming helped insure that the Crown retained ownership of its lands and waters. In time this grew into a point of principle: that a portion of the wealth produced from the country's lands and water should be retained by its people.[8] The provincial government therefore was integrally involved in promoting and shaping regional industrialization and in establishing a regime of forest management.

Throughout the twentieth century, the single-industry resource town was the "backbone" of staples production in Canada.[9] In 1987 the Canadian Association of Single-Industry Towns calculated that there were over one thousand resource-dependent communities in the country.[10] An estimated 348 of these towns were tied to the forestry industry.[11] In his classic 1971 study of Canada's towns of single industry, sociologist Rex Lucas presented them as "twentieth century products of an age of industry and technology," and he cast the inhabitants of these "communities of today" as "men, women, and children of the twentieth century."[12] Lucas might still be right in his assessment, but not in the way he probably meant at the time. Much has changed in the ensuing decades. The social distance between global cities and their hinterlands is growing, and these remote communities are no longer central to the national conversation. Resource towns do not occupy the attention of scholars, who have turned their gaze to a handful of global cities and to ruined heartland areas where nothing has filled the economic or cultural vacuum: Detroit looms particularly large in the study and representation of deindustrialization.[13]

One Job Town considers the particular significance of deindustrialization on the industrial frontier of Northern Ontario, my home region – but in a wider temporal frame than is usually taken into consideration. The chapters that follow take us into this resource hinterland, revealing the extent to which the culture of industrialism was a product of wider processes of Euro-Canadian colonization and the racial exclusion of Indigenous peoples. Historically, the mine and mill towns of Ontario's northland were white settlements: employers hired few Indigenous people except in their seasonal woods operations or as occasional labourers.[14] Anishnabe and Cree people were expected to live on the lands reserved for them by treaties.[15] Even today, Indigenous people are underrepresented in the region's wage labour force, and suffer persistent occupational segregation. Hence, when anthropologist Tom Dunk suggests that, "[f]rom the perspective of the male working class, this is an area where men go to work in work clothes, and hard hats, and carry a lunch box," he is speaking of an industrial working class that is overwhelmingly white.[16]

The region's mills and mines were thus an integral part of the wider colonization project that sought to extend white civilization and industrial modernity northward. Historian Adele Perry has noted that dispossession and settlement were "not discrete processes: they were mutually dependent and deeply intertwined."[17] Euro-Canadian settlers and workers moving into Ontario's northland brought with them a "mental map" that assumed that white people were the "apex of civilized achievement."[18] Accordingly the social structure that mill colonialism supported was profoundly racialized.

Although the region's culture of industrialism validated the worklives of my own family, and instilled in me many of the feelings and sensibilities that continue to define me as a person, I nevertheless have grappled with how to write about working-class history on the resource frontier, as this industrial culture was bound up in the larger processes of racial exclusion and dispossession. Unlike in the fur trade, Indigenous people were employed at the margins of these extractive industries, and relatively few found employment in the mines or mills themselves. Although this situation is changing, thanks in large part to the activism and agency of Indigenous people, racial segregation and a stark gendered division of labour remain hallmarks of social relations in the region. In Ontario's Northeast, mill towns were also marked by a profound linguistic and social divide between a mainly French-speaking (and Catholic) workforce recruited locally and non-resident English-speaking (and often Protestant) managers. Anglo-power was therefore an integral part of mill colonialism in the region, much as it was in Quebec before the Quiet Revolution of the 1960s swept aside the old social and political order.

Spanish River Pulp and Paper, Sturgeon Falls, 1920s. Courtesy of Sturgeon River House Museum.

This book focuses on the history of Sturgeon Falls, a Franco-Ontarian town of six thousand inhabitants located midway between Sudbury and North Bay in Northeastern Ontario. Initial white settlement and municipal incorporation both preceded the town's paper mill, which began to operate in 1898 and for more than a century was the town's major employer. The mill harnessed the water power of the Sturgeon River to drive the wood downstream and turn the mill's turbines. The Nipissing lowlands, in which the town is situated, is one of the few areas where agriculture was able to take root in the region, and local farmers supplied the mill with much of its wood supply and labour force.[19] After a stuttering start, the industrial site was owned by a series of large companies, starting with the Spanish River Pulp and Paper Company (1912–29), then Abitibi Pulp and Paper (1929–79), MacMillan Bloedel (1979–99), and, finally, Weyerhaeuser (1999–2002).[20] Although Sturgeon Falls was not a quintessential company town like Spanish River's Espanola or Abitibi's Iroquois Falls, it was no less dependent on its mill for much of this time.[21]

Many writers have noted that the central fact of life in single-industry towns is one of dependence.[22] Forest-reliant communities have always faced uncertainty in regard to wood supply, foreign competition, global markets, technological change, and environmental concerns.[23] Specialization, and external ownership, exposes remotely located single-industry towns "to a greater extent to external actions than are larger, more economically diversified communities."[24] As a result, resource-dependent communities such as Sturgeon Falls are more "susceptible to global upturns and downturns" than are places with a more diversified economy.[25] There were many such periods of crisis in the century-long history of the Sturgeon Falls mill, but it was most prolonged during its seventeen-year closure between 1930 and 1947. During that time, most of the town relied on poor relief, and Abitibi stripped the mill of two of its three paper machines. These were devastating years, which improved only after the Second World War, when Abitibi reactivated the site with massive new investment to convert the mill from newsprint to producing corrugated paper medium – the wavy, middle fluting material in corrugated boxes – and, later, other product lines.

The town's population trends mirrored the mill's ups and downs. In 1901 Sturgeon Falls was a predominantly English-speaking community of nearly one thousand five hundred inhabitants; by 1961 more than four in five were French-speaking.[26] The cause of this demographic shift were the prolonged mill closures from 1907 to 1912 and again from 1930 to 1947, when English-speaking residents were far more likely than French-speaking ones to leave. The single biggest jump in the town's population, from 2,199 to 4,125, occurred between 1911 and 1921, after a major expansion of the mill by the Spanish River Company. With the reopening of the mill in 1947, the town's population began to grow again, but even by 1951 it had reached only 4,962. With a further expansion of the mill in the 1950s, Sturgeon Falls's population reached 6,288 inhabitants in 1961.[27]

Working at the mill became a family affair for generations of Sturgeon Falls people, as young men followed their fathers, uncles, older brothers, and occasionally mothers into the mill. Virtually everyone we interviewed in Sturgeon Falls had a similar story. Claude Lortie's father, for example, was a welder in the mill and two of his brothers were millwrights. Working the "production end" at the mill, he thought of himself as something of an outlier in the family.[28] Harold Stewart, for his part, had a cousin and four uncles working with him at the mill. One ran the crane in the wood yard, while Harold and his cousin worked production.[29] It is therefore useful to think of the mill workers not simply as individuals, but as belonging to "mill families" with a multigenerational connection to the workplace.[30]

This thick web of familial association and social reproduction was facilitated, no doubt, by the mill's longstanding policy of hiring the offspring of mill employees as summer students – the first step towards permanent employment. Students were hired on the basis of their father's or mother's mill seniority, no matter if that parent was a production worker, office worker, superintendent, or even the mill manager

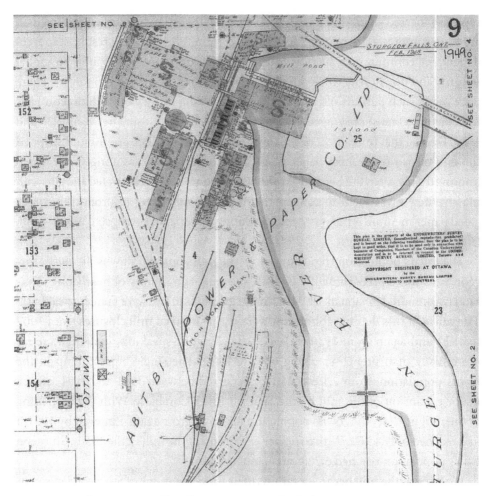

Fire insurance plan, Sturgeon Falls mill, 1949. Courtesy of Risk Management Services.

himself. The mill was very much a closed shop, and one that got smaller and smaller after the 1960s, when it peaked at six hundred employees. At its height, the operation was a diversified industrial complex with a corrugated paper machine, two hardboard mills, and a platewood mill. By the time the mill closed in December 2002, only 140 employees were left and only the corrugated paper machine remained in operation. The story of Sturgeon Falls is thus best understood as a slow-death closure as one production line after another fell silent.

Still, in the early 1990s, the mill got a new lease on life when the Ontario government funded its conversion to recycled paper. The community also raised a million dollars, which helped make the mill's new recycled pulping operation a formal public-private partnership. Henceforth its wood fibre would come from old boxes trucked in from southern cities, rather than from "virgin wood" cut from nearby Crown forests and private lands. New environmental regulations had made this conversion necessary, as the mill's then owner, MacMillan Bloedel, was unwilling to make any major new investments in the production facility. The presence of local managers – particularly mill manager Wally Shisko – and other local leaders who were committed to the mill's future proved vital. Given the devastation wrought by the unfolding forestry crisis in boreal forest areas, Sturgeon Falls stood as a success story for years to come, joining a handful of other area mill towns such as Kapuskasing (Ontario) and Temiscaming (Quebec) that refused to die.[31]

This positive storyline was overturned, however, in 2002, when US-based Weyerhaeuser, which had acquired the mill three years earlier as part of its purchase of MacMillan Bloedel, announced its closure after a century of production. My research makes clear that the company closed the mill because it could: it was small and old, and the company could easily cover its modest output of corrugated paper at its newer and bigger US-based plants. In the era of free trade, national borders no longer mattered much. It is a familiar story, of course – one repeated tens of thousands of times across North America. What was different this time, however, was that vague corporate assertions that the mill was "losing money" proved untenable. In fact, as the recycling facility was co-owned by the community, its financial books were a matter of public record.[32] The mill was not only making money; it had a firm order for its entire output of corrugated paper for another nine months. The timing of the mill's closure thus surprised and infuriated many of the people we interviewed. The company's refusal to pay more than the bare minimum required by its legal and contractual obligations further embittered long-service workers who were only a few years away from early retirement. The mill's final shutdown marked a "crucial rupture" for the remaining mill families, tearing asunder "a social structure that had sustained generations."[33] Marcel Boudreau, who used to work on the paper machine, one of the best-paying jobs in the mill, recalled: "I can remember lying in bed and wondering what the hell I was going to do. I mean, I basically have a grade 12 education."[34] This was the immediate context in which I initiated this project.

For the book, a cross-section of mill employees was interviewed, including unionized production workers, skilled trades, office workers, superintendents, and managers. Four of the interviewees were women who worked in the mill's offices, and at least one interviewee was Anishnabe. Reflecting the mill colonialism of Ontario's Northeast, the mill's workforce was overwhelmingly white and male, with a historic linguistic divide between largely English-speaking managers and mainly French-speaking production workers. Interviewing began within a year of the mill's

Interior of the closed mill, 2004. Warehouse area as seen from the old corrugated cardboard pulping area.

The paper machine. Photographs by David W. Lewis.

closure and continued for the next two years. During that time, efforts to reopen the mill fizzled out, and the facility was demolished by the departing company, which also shredded a century's worth of production records. Accordingly, each interview is effectively time-stamped, as the changing present profoundly shaped what we heard and saw. In early interviews, for example, displaced workers expressed residual hope that the mill would reopen. This hope faded, then disappeared altogether in subsequent interviews as Weyerhaeuser began to demolish the mill and the grim reality of the need to start over took hold. By then, the mill's centrality to the local community had steadily declined.

To suggest that deindustrialization began and ended with the final closure of the mill in December 2002 is therefore to miss much. It was a long and uneven process, and the product of a specific time and place. Deindustrialization first emerged as an explanatory framework for such closures in the early 1970s, when left-nationalists in the New Democratic Party sought to blame Canadian plant closings on US-controlled companies anxious to keep factories running at home. By the early 1980s, a variant of the "deindustrialization thesis" had taken hold in the United States, popularized by Barry Bluestone and Bennett Harrison in their influential book, *The Deindustrialization of America*. In this American formulation, deindustrialization pitted local communities against outside capital. As Blustone and Harrison wrote, "At the root of all this is a fundamental struggle between capital and community."[35] Since then, the global study of deindustrialization has revealed the devastating personal consequences of mill and factory closures for industrial workers, their families, and communities. As Jefferson Cowie has noted, the corporate command of spatial relations was a "crucial weapon in management's arsenal."[36] The spatial restructuring of industrial production has meant the shift of industrial labour from North America to low-wage areas elsewhere in the world.[37] Automation has also continued to replace workers with machines. In the aftermath of deindustrialization, the old culture of industrialism withers and dies or a new, post-industrial culture supplants it, pushing manual workers to the cultural and economic periphery.[38] Fundamentally, these are not their places anymore.

Canadian scholars of the "new economic geography" have challenged what they call the "blinkered thinking" that "peripheralizes" resource hinterlands in the study of globalization and economic change.[39] I find a great deal of inspiration in their work. For Roger Hayter, Trevor J. Barnes, and Michael J. Bradshaw, globalization has "different meanings, implications and history for resource peripheries than for cores"[40] – that is, the meanings derived from economic change at the core and on the periphery are not necessarily the same. The same point can be made about deindustrialization. With few exceptions, the study of deindustrialization has been applied almost exclusively to core economic sectors such as autos and steel and

An old fence surrounds an empty field after the mill's demolition in 2004; the railway switch is a small reminder of a thriving past. Photograph by David W. Lewis.

usually located in heartland regions. However, a more flexible understanding of deindustrialization is in order: we can learn a great deal if we push the field to engage with economic change on the resource periphery.[41]

Historically the meaning of economic change at the core and on the periphery has been structured by two explanatory frameworks. In the first instance, industrial decline in heartland areas has been governed by the life course analogy: a linear slide into industrial oblivion and, perhaps, economic rebirth as a new post-industrial place. Not surprisingly, the meanings derived from this post-industrial transformation are hotly contested. Enthusiasts herald the rise of a new post-industrial era, while critics argue that capital divestment has led to the death of industry and the destruction of communities. By contrast, the meaning of economic change in the resource sector is premised on the idea that the normal economic cycle on the periphery is one of extremes. The dependence of resource towns on staples exports makes them vulnerable to changing prices and market demand on the one hand and resource exhaustion on the other. The "boom and bust" metaphor has thus been used to explain hard times in good times. However, although both explanatory frameworks emphasize loss of local control and the inevitability of hard times, the prolonged crisis in forestry in recent years has rendered this bifurcated understanding largely redundant.

One Job Town considers mill workers' shop-floor memories and what Bob Russell calls the "political apparatuses of production,"[42] which he defines as "the norms, rules, and laws that regulate the employment relation more generally; and the spatial organization of production."[43] At a basic level this political apparatus includes a range of procedures involving job assignment, layoff, bumping rights, overtime, and safety. As historian Gordon Hak notes, the "everyday world of work [is] thus governed by conflict and accommodation."[44] The history of Sturgeon Falls as a unionized workplace is a long one, stretching back to 1907. Early battles for union recognition, though no longer remembered locally, are preserved in the archival records of the paper mill unions. As we will see, industrial work is, over the long term, culturally generative and socially constitutive. In speaking of class formation, historian E.P. Thompson suggests that "we are thinking of a very loosely defined body of people who share the same categories of interest, social experiences, traditions and value-systems."[45] Deindustrialization in Sturgeon Falls, as elsewhere, therefore caused the fragmentation of relatively stable class formations.[46]

To some extent *One Job Town* is also a history of "men as men."[47] Historian Stephen Meyers has written extensively on the masculine identities of industrial workers in the United States, both respectable and rough. Although the chapters that follow reveal the boylike playfulness of shop-floor hijinks and camaraderie, as well as the restlessness of young men entering the mill's workforce in the late 1960s and early 1970s, we do not hear the kinds of rough masculinity or bravado that others have found. To my surprise respectable manhood looms largest in the interviews. There are a number of reasons for this. First, as interviewees' were in their fifties, sixties, and seventies, their "rough" youth had long since faded in their memories. More important, perhaps, the plant's closing had dampened working-class bravado: the interviews occurred at a time when the mill workers were being politically defeated. The prevailing mood among interviewees was therefore a sombre one with flashes of raw anger, their hurt often expressed in terms of masculine pride in hard work and shop-floor knowledge.

In thinking about working-class subjectivities, I have been particularly influenced by the extraordinary work of historian John Kirk in the United Kingdom. For Kirk, class is a sensibility grounded in "experiences and practices."[48] Like a growing number of researchers of industrial work or working-class culture, Kirk has turned to the theoretical ideas of Raymond Williams to help understand culture and identity. For Williams, culture is a "constitutive social process, creating specific and different ways of life."[49] Class is found in sentiment and thought, which over time together form a "structure of feeling" – which Williams says "are

André Cartier and his son inside the paper machine room. Courtesy of André Cartier.

products of socio-historic contexts of change and continuity, conflict and struggle."[50] Change over time is thus understood in terms of residual, dominant, and
emergent structures of feeling. Dominant ones, for Williams, might be understood
as a time's "official consciousness."[51] This book speaks to the making of a culture
of industrialism in one locality and its subsequent undoing with the mill's decline
and eventual closure.

It is no coincidence that, at this critical juncture, when class inequality has
become extreme economic polarization, we have seen a retreat from class as a category of analysis or identification.[52] In a cutting critique of academic research, sociologist Beverley Skeggs notes that the "retreat from class is just the expression of the
class interest of a group of relatively powerfully placed professional intelligentsia."[53]
For example, wanting some sage advice, the Ontario government commissioned
Richard Florida, author of the bestselling book, *The Rise of the Creative Class*, to
study the changing composition of the province's economy and workforce as well
as its historical changes and "projected futures." His 2009 report declared: "The
current economic transformation is as big and as challenging as the transformation

from agriculture to industry. Our economy is shifting away from jobs based largely on physical skills or repetitive tasks to ones that require analytical skills and judgement ... The change is inexorable. We cannot turn away from it; nor can we slow it. The clock of history is always ticking."[54] Florida went on to urge the Ontario government to resist public calls to "protect the past," advising that these changes are "inevitable." To prosper in the new global economy, he wrote, "we must create new jobs in high-value industries and occupations, and shift our employment from routine-oriented to creativity-oriented occupations."

In this report, as in much of his writing, Florida categorizes the workforce as either "creative" or "routine." On the one hand, creative-oriented jobs in business, engineering, information technology, science, finance, law, and the arts are highly autonomous and require workers to think. Everyone else, on the other hand, is employed in routine-oriented jobs in which they merely "carry out tasks" in a prescribed order. According to Florida, these workers do not think: "In essence, they run an algorithm – a specific set of procedures that will produce the desired result." The resulting geography of rise and decline mirrors Florida's bifurcated view of the world. The future is found in large post-industrial cities – New York, Boston, Toronto – while "older" industrial areas must radically retool if they are to survive in the creative age. As for Northern Ontario, its only chance is a vague "connectivity" with Toronto. At its core, Florida's argument blames rural areas, industrial towns, and resource-dependent regions for their own decline. In effect, the industrial working class, once viewed as dangerously mobile, is now understood to be immobilized by history.[55] In a post-industrial era, industrial workers are assigned to the past, not to the present.

The eleven chapters that follow – organized into three sections, moving from tentative beginnings to shop-floor realities to slow-death closing – are built from the ground up using worklife oral histories and textual documents found in people's garages and basements. As historian Luisa Passerini has suggested, if one takes memory seriously, it means "letting it organize the story."[56] Public archives in the United States, Canada, and the United Kingdom also proved important in filling some of the gaps. *One Job Town* reminds us that every place has a long and varied history, and that these layers of history are "sedimented over time."[57]

The political aftershocks of deindustrialization have been felt throughout the writing of this book. The election of Donald Trump as US president, the British vote to exit the European Union, and the rise of right-wing populism in continental Europe have revealed the depth of working-class anger over the ravages of globalization, unfair trade deals, and the failure of social democratic or centrist parties to defend working people. A sense of betrayal is pervasive in deindustrialized

Workers wrote their names on the last roll of paper produced in Sturgeon Falls, in December 2002; several interviewees' names are legible here, including those of Randy Restoule and Raymond Marcoux. Photograph by Bruce Colquhoun.

communities. Mill and factory closings are rituals of status degradation that strip industrial workers of their pride and validation as well as their wages and benefits. Such workers have become "yesterday's people,"[58] "mocked and derided and ... coded as all that is wrong."[59] In *Chavs: The Demonization of the Working Class*, Owen Jones makes the case that the "new liberal bigotry" has led middle-class people to view the working class as a "lost tribe on the wrong side of history, disoriented by multiculturalism and obsessed with defending their identity from the cultural ravages of mass immigration."[60] This was certainly evident in the immediate aftermath of Trump and Brexit, as my social media feed was filled with sarcasm and vitriol against working-class voters. Any suggestion that the white working class had any reason to protest was met with sharply worded responses or a quick dismissal. For myself, I believe that, until we recognize why so many people in the US Rust Belt voted for Barack Obama twice, only to switch to Trump, liberals and social democrats risk more of the same. Sturgeon Falls is not located in the US Rust Belt or in northeast England, but its underlying socio-economic issues are much the same. So is the heartfelt sense of having been betrayed – by one's company, one's political party, one's union, and even one's own community. The "community versus capital" formulation does not begin to capture the political messiness of deindustrialization and its poisoned legacy. *One Job Town* offers an in-depth look at the deindustrialization of one small town, largely as experienced and understood by working people themselves.

TENTATIVE BEGINNINGS

THE INDUSTRIAL FRONTIER

Sturgeon Falls is extremely fortunate to have secured the location of this company here. For years past our legislators have allowed the Americans to take our wood without duty, manufacturing it into paper, and sell that paper manufactured from Canadian wood in the English market. This system must be changed. The raw material must be manufactured at home. This is Canada's opportunity.

– newspaper, Sturgeon Falls, 1898[1]

Speaking on behalf of the Sturgeon Falls Pulp Company, Ernest A. Bremner welcomed the sizable crowd that had gathered "within the walls of this mill, which, though comparatively small in itself is, I believe, destined to become the forerunner and beginning of an immense industry."[2] Turning to the town's mayor, he continued: "When you open the gates of these Wheels, Mr. Mayor, you open the first act in a long drama of prosperity to this town and community, an era of seven times seven years of plenty succeeding a long period of waiting for the necessary first expenditure." Bremner ended his rousing speech with a wish: "May your town's prosperity go to and increase until it becomes an object lesson to the whole Province of Ontario." After an appreciative reply from Mayor Cockburn, the gates of the water wheels were thrown open and the "massive shafts began to revolve, at first slowly, and then, as the gates opened wider, more rapidly and with a smoothness that spoke well for the character of the work of construction." Even Reverend Father Gingras had a role, placing the first block of wood in the grinders. The presence of a journalist from the Toronto *Globe* ensured that the day's events in October 1898 were performed on a national stage, rather than on a strictly local one.

The wider political significance of the ceremony, and the reason the *Globe* ran such an extensive front page story, was that it provided clear evidence that the province's controversial new manufacturing condition regarding spruce pulpwood was working. That year the Ontario government, which retained property rights and controlled the exploitation of minerals, forests, and water power on Crown land – had required that pulpwood and pine timber cut on public lands be sawn into lumber or pulped in the province. As part of its control of such land and resources, the province had established an elaborate system of licences, royalties, and rents that was a legacy of British and French monarchical traditions. The rocky terrain of much of the province made it nearly impossible to pursue a homesteading policy of distributing land in fee simple[3] – in Northern Ontario, especially, except in pockets, farming was a marginal undertaking. The manufacturing condition imposed on pulpwood and pine resulted in many US sawmill operations crossing the border into Canada, accelerating the industrialization of the province's northland.

Pulp and paper mills required massive fixed capital investments and a continuous flow of wood, however, so the Ontario government provided additional incentives, signing a series of long-term wood concessions encompassing huge swathes of the region, starting with the area near Sault Ste Marie. Industrialist Francis Clergue had used his political connections to build and control a vast complex in the Sault, including a steel mill, mines, a railway, city utilities, and a new pulp and paper mill.[4] This pulp concession agreement served as the model for ones that followed in Sturgeon Falls (1898) and Espanola (1899). In return for a monopoly over pulpwood covering large areas, the companies agreed to build substantial pulp and paper operations employing a minimum number of Canadians.[5] The new mills were to be located on the industrial frontier, near the wood supply, rather than close to the southern cities. Access to plentiful water power and the use of rivers to carry logs to the mills made this system attractive. In Sturgeon Falls Ernest A. Bremner and the British investors he represented – a syndicate which included the "foremost British capitalists" – were given the right to cut spruce, poplar, tamarac, jackpine, and other hardwood trees over an ill-defined area five miles on either side of the Sturgeon River and its tributaries amounting to 75 square miles for twenty-one years.[6] In return, the company agreed to spend a million dollars on the mill and employ no fewer than 240 people.

The industrialization of Northern Ontario was made possible by the building of railway lines through the region, which opened up the Nipissing lowlands and the clay belts to mixed farming development. Nearby farming families provided the new mills with both wood and labour, particularly in their seasonal woods operations. The first forestry towns developed at the intersections of southward-flowing rivers and the Canadian Pacific Railway (CPR). Fully 85 per cent of the towns in

The caption for this illustration from the Sturgeon River House Museum describes it as: "Hudson Bay Post, Indian Houses and First Steam Boat on the Sturgeon River. Bottom first log cabin along side the present-day John Street Bridge. Inset first home of James Holditch." Courtesy of Sturgeon River House Museum.

Northern Ontario were incorporated between 1880 and 1920, mostly along the railway lines slicing through the Precambrian Shield.[7] The discovery of silver at Cobalt and other precious minerals confirmed the region as "New Ontario": a land of wealth and opportunity. It is in this context of northward expansion and industrial optimism that Ontarians understood and celebrated the opening of the Sturgeon Falls mill. After the pomp and ceremony of its opening, the *Globe* proclaimed that the mill "will make Canada a mighty competitor in the British market with the American paper exporters and will at the same time give employment to a large number of Canadians."[8]

This history is the stuff of which local origin stories are made. Every village or town in the region has an origin story, or founding myth. Mostly, the point of origin is located in the appearance of European explorers or missionaries, or the first prominent white settler or white industrialist, who then plays the part of founding

Sturgeon Falls, 1907. Courtesy of West Nipissing Public Library.

father in a story of settlement and progress. These foundational stories can be understood as part of what historian Kerry Abel calls the "cult of the pioneer."[9] Sometimes, as in the nearby mining town of Cobalt, community origin is located in a mythic moment, such as when a railway worker threw his hammer at a fox that stole his food, only to hit silver, and a boom town was born.[10] In the decades that follow, these foundational stories are told and retold in community histories, local museums, newspaper retrospectives, and other commemorative activities. Mention of Indigenous people, if any, is only as a prelude to white settlement and industrial progress; they are usually located sometime before or somewhere else.

The constitutive narrative of Sturgeon Falls fits comfortably in this wider pattern. Wayne LeBelle, a community-based historian, begins his popular 1995 centennial history of Sturgeon Falls with the story of the first white settler, James Holditch, who was later elected the town's first mayor.[11] Anishnabe or Cree people once lived in the area and traded at the nearby Hudson's Bay Company post, but they were not credited with living in the same locality as white settlers; rather, references to their transit, rather than home-place, predominate. Instead the white settler narrative of survival and resilience frames the telling of local history.

Yet the ceremonial opening of the mill in 1898 is not a story that has been remembered locally: nobody we interviewed shared it, nor does it appear in any of the commemorative books or articles consulted for this project. This historical moment and the industrialist who promised "a long drama of prosperity" have been all but forgotten. As we will see, the mill's uncertain early history was punctuated by lawsuits, layoffs, changing absentee ownership, and industrial conflict. No local larger-than-life personalities emerged in Sturgeon Falls. But it was the mill's association with Anglo economic power that caused the most discomfort, particularly given the town's emergence as a Franco-Ontarian community. The mill thus holds a contentious place in the town's memory and history. Not simply the outcomes of global processes, localities are the "products of long and varied histories."[12]

Mill Colonialism and the Politics of Racial Exclusion

Treaty-making and Canada's Indian Act provided the legal basis for the Euro-Canadian occupation and exploitation of the region's natural wealth as well as for the legal segregation of Indigenous communities. "Maintaining the colonial," notes historian Frederick Cooper, "required coercive and administrative work and cultural work – to define hierarchies and police social boundaries."[13] We can see the northward march of white colonization in the six Northern Ontario treaties. Of most relevance here are the two Robinson Treaties of 1850, which were signed as a direct result of Indigenous resistance to mining exploration and development. It was the Anishnabe who petitioned to have a treaty, and in 1849 a delegation travelled to Montreal and threatened to remove trespassing miners unless royalties were paid to them.[14] Conflict erupted that same year when fifty Anishnabek, Métis, and white allies seized the mine of the Quebec Mining Company at Mica Bay on Lake Superior. This act of resistance sparked a national debate about Indigenous rights and brought William Benjamin Robinson, a politician and mine manager, to the area to negotiate treaties.

The chief and headmen of Nipissing First Nation were signatories to the 1850 Robinson-Huron Treaty. However, the lands reserved for the Anishnabe between present-day Sturgeon Falls and North Bay on the north shore of Lake Nipissing – amounting to 80,640 acres – were not surveyed until 1880, which gave the timber interests the time needed to cut over the area. The CPR then sliced through these lands in 1885, followed by the right-of-way for the Canadian National Railway and, considerably later, the Trans-Canada Highway. In its online history, the Nipissing First Nation rightly notes that the Indian Act was used to "colonize the Nipissing District and diminish the land base."[15] Slightly more than 73,000 acres of Nipissing lands was surrendered in 1904 to facilitate the operations of the mill and in 1907 to open up the area between Sturgeon Falls and North Bay to white settlement.[16] A journalist at the time observed that, "for many years the citizens of both towns have been working to have it thrown open."[17] These efforts finally "bore fruit" when the Nipissing First Nation agreed to "retire" to the shores of Lake Nipissing and to surrender its land north of the CPR tracks.

In the meantime the Canadian government actively sought to limit the economic activity of Nipissing First Nation members, who were unable to obtain off-reserve commercial timber-cutting licences but were restricted on-reserve to pulp extraction, a policy confirmed by annual reports of the local Indian Agent between 1900 and 1918. Generally, Indian Agents reported that Indigenous people in the area hunted, fished, guided, and assisted survey parties. Many men were employed cutting spruce, pulpwood, and telegraph poles or went to work in the lumber camps during the winter months.[18] Other sources confirm this pattern, particularly after the decline of the area's fur trade and the closure of the local Hudson's Bay Company post in 1879.[19] There was no early mention of Nipissing First Nation people working in the Sturgeon Falls mill itself, even though Garden Village, their largest community, physically adjoined the town.[20]

The generation coming of age on Nipissing First Nation territory in the 1960s and 1970s was much more equipped to undertake industrial wage labour than earlier generations had been. According to Lise C. Hansen, Garden Village's sixty-four households included heavy equipment operators, boilermakers, iron workers, smelter workers, machinists, year-round labourers of various kinds, and at least two pulp and paper mill workers.[21] Its labour force, therefore, much like that of Sturgeon Falls itself, was highly industrialized. It is difficult to know the full extent to which Indigenous people worked in the paper mill and how long they worked there, as the mill's production records were shredded by the departing company after the mill closed in 2002. Asked how many Indigenous people were working in the mill, interviewees replied uncertainly anywhere between two and a dozen. Brian Laflèche recalled that he used to work with someone who later became the chief of Nipissing First Nation.

The only interviewee who self-identified as Indigenous was Randy Restoule. His parents grew up on the Garden Village and Dokis reserves, but he grew up in town. Restoule's father was a bushworker and his mother a waitress in one of the town's restaurants. In his oral narrative, Restoule noted that at school there was a group of people who "looked down on us" but he felt some distance from other Anishnabe students, as he "didn't have the same attitude as people from the reserve."[22] Significantly, during our interview, Restoule's heritage surfaced only when he recalled his childhood and youth, not during his account of working in the mill. His workplace memories were otherwise indistinguishable from those of other mill workers we interviewed. In the mill's final years, no hard line appears to have been

Expansion of the Sturgeon Falls mill, 1912. Courtesy of West Nipissing Public Library.

drawn between white and Indigenous workers – indeed, several Anishnabe workers belonged to the same extended families as their "white" co-workers. Language, not race, loomed largest in the interviews.

Mill colonialism took hold in Sturgeon Falls only haltingly in the early years. Far from being a showcase for Ontario's new manufacturing condition, the early development of the Sturgeon Falls mill and the exploitation of its accompanying pulpwood concession was marred by undercapitalization, speculation, litigation, and liquidation. The traces of this sad and uninspiring story can be found in the major newspapers of Canada, the United States, and the United Kingdom, as well as in documentary records found in the British National Archives. As we will see, six companies owned the mill between 1898 and 1912, a period when mill expansion and operation was sporadic and halting. It was only when the Spanish River Pulp and Paper Company arrived on the scene in 1912 that the mill had sufficient capitalization and management stability to deliver on some of the optimism on display in October 1898.

Logging began in the area in the 1880s, as Ottawa Valley lumbermen worked their way inland to Lake Nipissing and up the Sturgeon River. In 1882 J.R. Booth built the first timber camps upriver. The following year, Martin L. Russell, a well-known Ottawa Valley lumberman from Renfrew, built a sawmill in what would become Sturgeon Falls. When he died in 1898, Russell had an estate worth $100,000 and extensive timber limits on the Sturgeon River, as well as water power at Sturgeon Falls and back in Renfrew.[23] In 1884 James Holditch purchased the lands on the east side of the Sturgeon River and subdivided them as the town site. The following year Rinaldo McConnell acquired land on the west side of the river, but kept it as a block in the hope of developing the water power there. A number of white travellers passing through the area commented on these early developments. In 1896 R.S. Cassels, paddling up the Sturgeon River, passed a "small village" on the CPR's main line, and noted that the "incomers seem to be chiefly French-Canadians, the most admirable settlers, hard-working, hopeful and enduring. Very interesting is it to mark in all its stages the conquering progress of axe-bearing civilization."[24]

In these early days, Sturgeon Falls was frequently in the news. A search of the Toronto *Globe* and the *New York Times* and trade journals such as the *Canada Lumberman* reveals a great deal of business interest in the town's early developments. Reports of a new pulp mill being built at Sturgeon Falls appeared in *Canada Lumberman* as early as March 1891.[25] First on the scene was a group of investors headed by George Paget of Huntsville, Ontario.[26] In 1894 Paget convinced a large majority of the ratepayers in the Township of Springer to vote for a by-law that accorded his company a $7,000 bonus (or public subsidy) to erect a small pulp mill at Sturgeon Falls.[27] Paget made little progress, however, and could not meet the conditions attached to the bonus – namely, to erect a mill costing no less than $29,000 and to employ at least thirty people.[28] As a result, Paget sold out to a British syndicate incorporated as the Sturgeon Falls Pulp Company.

The June 1898 agreement saw the Sturgeon Falls Pulp Company purchase Paget's pulp mill properties, water power rights, machinery, and harvested wood for £5,600.[29] The incorporation records of the company, dated 20 July 1898 and filed in London, England, reveal that its initial capitalization was a modest £25,000.[30] Officially it was established to carry on the business of pulp and paper manufacturing in Canada, as well as sawmilling, but the only property it acquired was located in Sturgeon Falls.[31] Indeed, 1898 proved a momentous year for the town, as the Ontario government granted Bremner and the British investors he represented the right to cut spruce over 75 square miles alongside the Sturgeon River.[32]

With everything seemingly in place, the Sturgeon Falls Pulp Company invested up to $500,000 in the paper mill over the next two years.[33] The *Canada Lumberman* reported that daily pulp production had reached 20 tons per day by mid-1899.[34] In August 1899 the trade journal observed that a "large pulp mill has been built and is now in operation and that daily shipments of large quantities of pulp are being made. Preparations are under way for the erection of paper mills; the intention being to manufacture completely the raw material in the near future."[35] If these plans had been fully realized, the company would have expended the required million dollars on the site. This was not to be, however, as it instead sold the mill in December 1899 to Edward Lloyd, Limited, of London, the owner of the popular British newspaper *Daily Chronicle*.[36]

Almost immediately, however, the new owners grew dissatisfied with the terms of their purchase and refused to meet their obligations.[37] Edward Lloyd charged that the water power and timber limits were not nearly as great as the former owners had stated, and work at the Sturgeon Falls mills had to be suspended for two years due to the resulting litigation.[38] Meanwhile the US media, already angered by Ontario's manufacturing condition, had a field day, blaming the Canadian and Ontario governments for the controversy. The legal dispute went to arbitration, and a settlement was finally reached in late 1901 vindicating the Sturgeon Falls Pulp Company. An inspection tour of the mill, water power, and timber limits proved to be the turning point. Travelling in ten canoes and assisted by thirty sets of hired hands, the inspection party reached the pulp concession. It was a remarkable sight: "Although only the actual necessities were carried, the amount of baggage was so large that the touring party appeared when camped to be the advance guard of the army." The group included a London-based banker and woolen merchant, a representative of the Sydney (Australia) *Morning Herald*, a pulp investor, and a legal advisor. "In the brief history of new Ontario," wrote the correspondent for the Toronto *Globe*, "few of the efforts at the exploitation of its resources have been so completely successful and far-reaching in their results as those which will follow the journey of inspection made by several directors of the Sturgeon Falls Paper Company and a number of representatives of British and American capital in the district of Nipissing during the past month."[39]

As part of the arbitration settlement, Edward Lloyd agreed to return the whole property to the Sturgeon Falls Paper Company and pay damages of £102,417.[40] The British firm also agreed to guarantee an issue of bonds amounting to £25,000 and to purchase the entire paper output of the Sturgeon Falls Pulp Company for the first two years at fair market value.[41] After the settlement, the company proceeded to finish construction. It was a good thing, too, as the case had caused British investors to question Canada as a place for investment.[42] The *Globe* went even further, telling its readers that the "history of the property of the company is somewhat remarkable, and for a time it appeared that the concession granted by the Government would be the means of almost entirely destroying the confidence of investors in Great Britain in the resources of new Ontario."[43]

Inevitably the investment prospectus for the Sturgeon Falls Pulp Company, issued in the aftermath of the legal dispute, emphasized the size and importance of the Crown concession and its "close proximity" to the Sturgeon Falls mill.[44] L.P. Andrews, vice-president of the British Wood Pulp Association of London, attested that the lands were "entirely occupied by timber," that there were "no burnt lands or barren lands," and, accordingly, that the location "seems an ideal one for manufacturing paper at lowest possible cost." The company's pulp concession was conditional, however, on its spending certain sums on construction and equipment by 1 July 1904, and it struggled to find the money to do so. Perhaps, as a result, its assets and liabilities were taken over in 1903 by Imperial Paper Mills of Canada Limited for a price of £500,000 in preferred stock and £2 million in common stock.[45] The archival evidence suggests this was essentially the same ownership group, with the addition of the Occidental Syndicate. Operations resumed, and Imperial Paper Mills decided to add two new paper machines and a sulphite pulp mill.[46] In 1903 the mill was producing 100 tons of pulp daily,[47] and when the paper mills were completed in 1904, Sturgeon Falls could produce 40 to 50 tons of newsprint per day.[48] With the litigation behind it, Sturgeon Falls boomed briefly, but the company finally went into receivership, causing production of paper to halt for a time.[49] Without question, the first fifteen years of the mill's existence were more bust than boom.

Then, in 1912, the mill facilities were purchased by The Good Old Spanish River Pulp and Paper Company, which already operated a mill at Espanola and would soon acquire Lake Superior Paper, the paper mill Francis Clergue founded in Sault Ste Marie.[50] Spanish River now controlled huge blocks of land as timber concessions at Sault Ste Marie (6,801,280 acres), Espanola (2,742,400 acres), and Sturgeon Falls (1,976,320 acres).[51] With its new owner, the Sturgeon Falls mill finally had the capitalization it needed to flourish.[52] The timing was good. The elimination of US tariffs on Canadian newsprint between 1911 and 1913 led to the rapid growth of Canadian pulp and paper production from 350,000 tons in 1913 to 876,000 tons in 1920.[53] "Canada is to-day one of the greatest paper producing countries in the world," proclaimed one observer.[54]

What followed was a period of rapid expansion. Spanish River modernized the mill, introducing new paper-making technology and installing a third paper machine in 1921 at a cost of $1 million. Machine No. 3 proved ideal for wallpaper, or "hanging paper" as it was then known. The company's wood operations were also extensive.[55] A new concrete dam was completed in 1924, and the company sought to better control the flow of the river itself with a network of storage dams upriver.[56]

Dam construction. Courtesy of Sturgeon River House Museum.

During this early phase of industrialization, the mill depended on water power to turn the turbines and grinders. Highly variable seasonal water levels, however, limited the industrial output of the mill. In their study of the Temagami area, north of Sturgeon Falls, Bruce Hodgins and Jamie Benidickson show how competing industrial interests in Sturgeon Falls and Cobalt to the east sought to control the outflow of water from Lake Temagami to benefit their own localities. The Cobalt Hydraulic Power Company and Imperial Mills/Spanish River "contended for advantage," manipulating water levels and even the direction of water flow to their benefit.[57] The industrialization of the Sturgeon River and Lake Temagami, like the forests, had stark environmental consequences. As historian William Boyd has noted in another context, "[p]oor and minority communities all too often bore the brunt of the pollution problems."[58] This was certainly the case here, as Anishnabe found their traditional hunting and fishing areas altered, levelled, or poisoned. Historical photographs included in this chapter record the mill's expansion during these boom years.

Early Trade Unionism and Industrial Conflict

Soon after pulp production began in 1898, mill managers in Sturgeon Falls ran into trouble with their employees and the wider community. Tensions got so bad locally that the town council wrote to the attorney general of Ontario in August 1899 to complain that "[f]oreigners, or workmen from the United States, are now employed by the Sturgeon Falls Paper Company, at this place to the detriment of our own people."[59] Town officials even asked Ontario to investigate the company's compliance with the Alien Labour Act.[60]

Another point of tension involved complaints that the company regularly violated the province's Lord's Day Act, which barred Sunday operations. One Sunday in November 1903 the mayor and chief constable toured the mill's works. They "found the refuse burner being fed by three men. Five or six men at Carpenter work. Machinery being moved, and wood hauled. On Monday, at least six men were dismissed because they refused to work on Sunday." Writing to the Crown attorney in North Bay, they noted that this "unnecessary Sunday work" had been going on for the past two summers "and it ought to be checked. I wish you would take measures as would remedy the matter. Might I suggest that you instruct the town Constable Mr. William Raynor to visit the Works next Sunday and take the names of those at work, which had the appearance of being unnecessary." This complaint was then forwarded to the Lord's Day Alliance of Canada, which then sent it to the attorney general's office in Toronto. Reverend J.G. Shearer, the group's general secretary, asked the government to respond "at once."[61] The matter was

Inside the paper machine room, Sturgeon Falls, 1920s. Courtesy of West Nipissing Public Library.

then raised with the company. C.W. Rantoul, the general manager, responded that no such work was under way "in the sense you speak of, i.e. 'work of their ordinary calling.'" Indeed, he continued, "[o]ur mills are not operated on Sunday, but certain necessary and essential repairs are made every Sunday in every paper mill in the Continent. Were it otherwise it would prevent 170 men from earning wages on Monday, as the repairs can be done by 20 or 30 men and must be done when the rest of the machinery is idle."[62] In all likelihood, these early conflicts contributed to the organization of local mill workers into trade unions.

The Brotherhood of Paper Makers – the "Paper Makers union" – was formed in the United States in 1893 to represent skilled workers and paper machine tenders. The union's American Federation of Labor (AFL) charter was expanded in 1897 to include all classes of workers on the paper machine itself.[63] Soon thereafter, other pulp and paper mill workers sought to unionize, and the AFL directed them to the Paper Makers union. In a "daring move," however, these workers withdrew in 1906 to form the International Brotherhood of Pulp and Sulphite Mill Workers – the "Pulp & Sulphite Workers."[64] For the next three years the two unions fought bitterly, breaking each other's strikes and raiding rival locals. Peace was re-established only in 1909. Both unions followed American capital to Canada, as the rapid expansion of newsprint production in this country "caused considerable unemployment and disrupted wage rates in the United States."[65]

The Paper Makers union was the first to organize workers in Sturgeon Falls. After a short strike in 1906, the union won the eight-hour workday and limited work on Sundays. Management also agreed to hire only union paper makers, but reserved the right to hire anyone they pleased elsewhere in the mill. A second walk-out, however, on 10 June 1907 was provoked by the company's apparent disregard of the deal.[66] Mill manager John Craig took exception to the strike, claiming that the union had violated the agreement's no-strike clause. In a 26 July letter to the Department of Labour, Craig maintained:

> The cause is obscure – the mills had an agreement with the International Brotherhood of Paper Makers which contained a clause providing that there should be no strikes and no lockouts. In spite of their agreement the paper makers walked out without giving any reason. The bulk of the paper makers thereafter left town. The pulp mills continued to operate until the management endeavored to start the paper machines with non-union men whereupon the man in charge of the generator shut down the mill probably instigated thereto by some of the Union officials. The Manager has repeatedly offered to receive a committee of the men. This by reason of instructions from the headquarters in Watertown, NY of the Union that no committee was to be sent unless the Union was recognized has not been appointed. The opinion of the management here is that the sole cause of the trouble is the determination of the American Union to control the management of a Canadian mill.[67]

Continuing, Craig noted that, when the company turned to non-union labour, other mill workers refused to stay on the job: "As union help all left the mills and the town even under this agreement, non-union paper makers could be employed." What began as a Paper Makers union dispute thus quickly escalated into a plant-wide confrontation between management and labour.

The 1907 strike was sparked by the company's insistence that union members work on Sundays. At least 141 mill workers struck, including four women – reminding us that women worked inside the mill. By 25 July the number of strikers had risen to 350, mostly "heads of families," as the "[m]en refused to work on Sundays also refused to give up the 8-hour day and work 12 hours per day."[68] The company responded by importing foreign labour. Another report from the mill manager, dated 10 August, indicated that the sulphite plant was reopened on 29 July "and has been running continuously since that date, although not to its full capacity."[69] The mill's finishing room partially reopened on 2 August.

Sturgeon Falls mill, 1920s. Courtesy of West Nipissing Public Library.

It was at this point in the strike that John Craig received a list of demands from Lodge 57 of the Pulp & Sulphite Workers, conveyed to the company by a local merchant sympathetic to the union. Their main demand was union recognition, and to "be treated as such." The union also insisted that it would not "furnish stock for non-Union paper makers."[70] This expression of solidarity occurred at a time when the two unions were locked in a bitter confrontation. The Pulp & Sulphite Workers' message also indicated that union men had been fired that spring for not agreeing to work on Sundays, and were promptly replaced by immigrants from Italy and Poland. In response the company insisted that the Pulp & Sulphite Workers union "has not been recognized by the Management, its existence has never been brought officially to the knowledge of the Management." Indeed, Craig concluded, "[s]o far as the Management of the mill is concerned the first official knowledge of this Union's existence was when they entered into conspiracy to shut down the mills, for which we prosecuted one man, who was convicted and fined and we have summoned several others for entering into illegal conspiracy."[71] Imperial Mills was resolved to run Sturgeon Falls as an "open mill," rather than as a closed union shop, refusing to negotiate "with outsiders."[72]

It is unclear from the fragmentary archival evidence if the unions survived the strike, but the company went into receivership and the mill ceased to operate soon thereafter. The mill's reopening in 1912 under the ownership of Spanish River did not immediately reactivate the union locals. Only with the coming of the First

Labour Day parade, Sturgeon Falls, 1922. Courtesy of West Nipissing Public Library.

World War did the balance of power in the workplace shift temporarily. The Paper Makers union reorganized the mill in 1915 into Local 57, and Local 71 of the Pulp & Sulphite Workers union was resuscitated shortly thereafter. At the end of his worklife, decades later, Alvin Chellew, who served as president of Local 57 for seventeen years and as master of the Loyal Orange Lodge Branch 1709, recalled the return of trade unionism to the mill: "Joe Wilson was chief engineer at that time and he was a good one. The mill had been shut down for some time. There were two paper machines and two digesters … In those days, we worked for 15 cents an hour, and believe me, we really worked. In 1914, Bill Lord, Marcel L'Heroux and I got together and had a union organizer come to organize the men. Joe Grant was elected the first president and he proved a good one. At our first conference with the Company we got a raise to 35 cents per hour."[73] Chellew also recalled that times were tough before the outbreak of war: "many men were travelling by freight trains looking for work. They would jump off when they saw the mill and come to the boiler house to get warm. I used to hide them on top of the boilers."[74]

For its part, with a charter dated 30 November 1914, Local 71 in Sturgeon Falls was the second-oldest Pulp & Sulphite Workers local in Canada. Robert Dickson, the union's international treasurer, based in upstate New York, travelled to Sturgeon Falls in 1914 and is said to have organized the local there. When Maurice LaBelle was elected the local union's first recording and corresponding secretary, the company promptly fired him.[75] Undeterred, LaBelle went on to help the union organize Spanish River's mill in Espanola, then led an organizing drive in Quebec during the 1930s. He eventually became vice-president of the International Union.[76]

The tight wartime labour market forced the company's hand, and it signed an agreement with the Paper Makers union in 1917 that covered its mills in Sault Ste Marie, Espanola, and Sturgeon Falls.[77] A sharp post-war business recession in 1921, with declining newsprint prices and production volumes, and continuing employer demands for an "open shop" led to renewed conflict. Sparked by a demand to roll back wages by 20, even 30, per cent, the 1921 strike closed most of the paper mills in Canada and the United States.

The Pulp & Sulphite Workers union was highly centralized: locals across North America reported to headquarters in Fort Edward, a Hudson River mill town located north of Albany, New York. The union's historical records, held at Cornell University, offer a vivid inside look at the 1921 strike from the perspective of John P. Burke, international president, and A. Wagner, the secretary of Local 71 in Sturgeon Falls.[78] There does not appear to have been much opportunity for the local union to provide input into negotiations, except when two Sturgeon Falls representatives travelled down to New York City for a consultation. In February 1921, Wagner asked if the "signing of new agreements this year will be like it was two years ago [with] each Company separate. We have some classifications and changes to make and we would like to take these up with the Company when the new agreement is drawn up."[79] Burke's response reveals the extent to which collective bargaining was centralized:

> I am unable to state at this time whether or not we shall have separate conferences with the different manufacturers. We just held a conference in New York, Thursday February 24, at which thirteen Companies were represented, including the Spanish River Company. About the only thing done at this conference was the notification given to the various Companies as to the wage increases the men were expecting at the expiration of the agreements. The manufacturers stated that they wanted time to consider these matters and would notify us when they could meet us again. I shall endeavor to keep all the locals notified as to the progress we make in our conferences with the manufacturers.[80]

On 17 April, 350 union members in Sturgeon Falls voted unanimously against the company's proposed wage cuts.[81] With so much at stake, local union membership soared, leading Local 71 urgently to request two hundred more dues books and French-language copies of the union's constitution.[82] The company, meanwhile, was visibly preparing for a long strike: it had stopped its logs from coming down river and sent a manager to Sturgeon Falls to tell the men "how sorry [company president Colonel C.H.L.] Jones was in regard to being on that [central employer's] committee in regards to wages this year. He said if it wasn't for him being on the committee representing those 19 Companys [*sic*] we would likely be having our wage question settled in the Soo. He has a great line of Bull."[83] The International Union leadership, too, braced for a long fight. According to Burke, "[i]t does not seem reasonable to me that they could expect the men to accept any such proposition as they submitted. For the information of your members I wish to say that the members of our organization in this vicinity are strongly opposed to accepting any wage reductions. I hope that the men in Canada feel the same about it."[84]

The strike at Spanish River's three Northern Ontario mills began on 11 May and continued until 6 July, when workers returned pending an arbitration ruling. When the strike began, Spanish River's president, Colonel Jones, telephoned Burke from New York City to ask that the slasher mill in Sturgeon Falls be allowed to continue operating. Jones reasoned that it was necessary to permit the mill construction to proceed, and so differed from regular mill operations. Burke agreed, and sent a telegram to Local 71 asking it to give the company special dispensation to do so.[85]

He thought it was in the "future interests" of the union to let it operate, "so you may allow enough men to remain at work to do this. It should be distinctly understood, however, that they are to get the regular schedule of wages and are not to work for the 30% reduction. It should also be understood that these men can be pulled off the job at any time should the local union so decide."[86] This recommendation proved complicated, however, as the operation of the slasher mill required that fifty or sixty cars of wood be unloaded per day. Ongoing construction also obligated men to operate both the powerhouse and the machine shop.[87]

At a meeting on 10 May, the local decided to let the slasher mill run, but only for a few days. Wagner, the secretary, communicated the local's concern that the company would abuse the goodwill gesture. As he explained, the company "has three weeks cutting in the river after that they can shut the slasher mill down and not be in the way of other Companys [sic] who are driving logs down this river. In regards to construction work which is now going on at this mill there is work our carpenters and mechanics have been doing that is now going on under construction work. If this keeps on the whole mill will soon be running by construction. The Strike Committee would like you to let us know whether C.H.L. Jones said anything where it will benefit us in the final settlement by allowing all this work to continue." No such assurances were given. After meeting with Jones in New York City, Burke again justified this special consideration, as striking union members could get some wage work on the construction side of things: "The only way the Companies can beat us in this strike is by producing paper," he insisted. "If we can keep the paper mills from operating there is no question but what they will eventually have to give in."[88] Burke sought to build bridges with one of the more moderate employers, perhaps trying to drive a wedge between them.

Everything remained quiet in Sturgeon Falls as the strike dragged on into June. The local strike committee, evenly divided between the two unions, managed the effort. Finances were tight, so the committee asked for help from the Pulp & Sulphite Workers' defence fund. In one of several such payments, Burke sent the local union a cheque for $200, to be paid out as strike benefits. He then reminded them that the situation was dire everywhere.[89] In mid-June, the union local remained defiant, saying that "the men are all out to win."[90]

Throughout the strike, the Spanish River Pulp and Paper Company sought to maintain direct communications with its striking employees by distributing a monthly bulletin. In June, Colonel Jones reported that the "meetings leading up to this arbitration proposal were held in New York City on Friday and Saturday, June 17th and 18th. These were joint meetings between the chief executives of the two unions and the committee representing the manufacturers."[91] Both sides

Spanish River Company Labour Day float, 1922. Courtesy of West Nipissing Public Library.

Labour Day festivities, Sturgeon Falls, 1920. Courtesy of West Nipissing Public Library.

recommended arbitration. Jones therefore took the opportunity to sell his employ-ees on the idea of arbitration, noting that, if striking employees approved, "then the mills of the Spanish River Company can be immediately set into operation, thus putting an end to the present situation." However, "[i]f arbitration is rejected by the votes of members of the locals, then the responsibility for the continuation of the present shut-down and the idleness of our mills will rest entirely upon the individual workers who so rejected it." Jones then emphasized the steep financial cost of the strike for the company: In a "world-wide depression," wages were greatly "reduced in every trade." Continuing, Jones said: "Harder times are inevitable and must be faced by the Spanish River Company, both management and men, just as they must be faced by everybody else in the world. The condition is a world-wide one, and employers and employees in the paper trade are not immune from it."[92]

On 23 June the international vice-president of the Paper Makers union visited Sturgeon Falls, prompting a joint meeting of union members to decide on whether or not to agree to compulsory arbitration.[93] They voted in favour, on the understanding that only wages, not working conditions, would be arbitrated. Local secretary Wagner admitted, however, that attendance was "not very large," as only 206 members were present, with 171 voting for arbitration. Times were tough for striking families: "We are in sore need of finances here. I wish you would try and send us what you can."[94] Still, the strike dragged on into July. "Everything is very quiet here," wrote Wagner. "The Company has stopped all work."[95] But he noted that Spanish River was taking a census of employees' families, perhaps hoping to minimize the numbers for the sake of the binding arbitration.[96] While the union's own census figures of 411 local mem-bers arrived too late to be used in arbitration, they do provide a unique snapshot of the mill's workforce at this critical juncture.[97] All told, there were 253 married union members with children, 56 married without children, 104 unmarried, and five wid-owers. Union members had 861 children, or an average of 5.4 per member.[98]

The Arbitration Board ruled in the company's favour, rolling back wages. Labour-ers earning less than sixty cents per hour saw their wages rolled back sixteen and two-thirds per cent. Skilled workers came out slightly better, their wages declining only ten per cent. A minimum wage of forty cents an hour was also established.[99] International president Burke defended the result by noting that common labour at some non-union mills in New York State had fallen to a "trifle over" thirty cents an hour: "When the recent changes and drastic reductions which have been made in other industries are taken into consideration we believe that the members will not consider that they have fared quite so badly as might have been the case had they not had the organization to back them."[100] It was a hard sell, however, with Burke conceding that forty cents an hour was a "low rate of wages for any one at the present time. However, where can a man go and get any more than that? In fact, most industries are paying less. The steel industry has just reduced wages to thirty cents an hour. The men work ten hours a day for $3.00. I'd rather work eight hours for $3.20 than work ten hours for $3.00. The railroads are only paying thirty-eight cents an hour for common labor. We must take all these things into consideration when considering the award of the Arbitration Board."[101]

The arbitration award proved to be a bitter pill to swallow for low-wage workers in Sturgeon Falls. Wagner acknowledged receipt of the telegram, admitting that wages went down "more than we expected." He reported that there had been "an awful cry from the common labor" locally. But, he too, went on to put the award into a wider context: "But the shape of the country is in today I don't know where they are going to better themselves. Factories and Mines in this part of the country are closing down nearly every day. Lumber companys [sic] are hiring men for the camps at pre-war wages from 20 to 30 dollars a month. Where last year they were getting from 75–90 dollars a month. When we look around and see conditions are these, we certainly did not lose anything by going on strike for seven weeks."[102]

Not surprisingly, these appeals to logic did not resonate with those with the most to lose. In the months that followed, the local union reported it was now having "a lot of trouble" getting common and unskilled labour to pay union dues.[103] Wagner noted that "we have done nearly all we can do and some of our oldest and best members are beginning to lose interest."[104] In response, Burke reminded Wagner of the "great crisis" facing the International Union as a whole. Thousands of union members remained off the job, and they "will starve before they will go back on the open shop."[105] The International Union was trying to support twenty-eight striking local unions, sending out $5,000 a week in strike benefits. Twenty-two of these mills were owned by the International Paper Company.[106] Burke expressed his frustration, even disgust, about members who didn't wish to help the wider cause:

> I certainly am disgusted with the way some of our members are acting. Everything was all lovely when we were getting big wage increases every year, but now when the tide has turned they do not seem to want to act the part of men. I want to say to our members at Sturgeon Falls that they are mighty lucky compared to the workers in many other places. There are men here at Fort Edward who have not done a day's work for six months. Look at the wage reductions that have been given the workers in other industries. The steel workers are only getting 30 cents an hour. I want to tell the men at Sturgeon Falls something more, and I hope you will convey this information to them Brother Wagner, that but for the fight that I made on the Arbitration Board they would have got a much larger slash in wages.[107]

Spanish River employees (probably salaried) in front of the mill, 1920. Courtesy of West Nipissing Public Library.

All the evidence indicates, however, that the 1921 strike proved disastrous for the Pulp & Sulphite Workers union.[108] The union's Canadian vice-president was later quoted as saying, "the last few years have been more or less peaceful, our demands have been conservative, and when refused, our policy has been to take what we could get without disturbance."[109]

Conclusion

These early developments in the economic and labour history of Sturgeon Falls remind us of the extent to which resource peripheries are highly susceptible to global forces. The process of capital investment and disinvestment was an uneven one in the mill's first forty years of existence, decades that saw periods of rapid growth and of closure. There were also three strikes, two of which were locally rooted. Spanish River was purchased by Abitibi Power & Paper in 1929, placing the Sturgeon Falls mill in new corporate hands just in time for the Great Depression. Prior to 1928, Abitibi operated only a newsprint mill at Iroquois Falls and a pulpwood mill at Smooth Rock Falls. The company then purchased five other paper makers, including the Spanish River Pulp and Paper

Mills Limited with newsprint mills at Sault Ste Marie, Espanola, and Sturgeon Falls.[110] The timing of these acquisitions could not have been worse, and Abitibi itself was pushed into receivership in 1932.[111]

2

A TOWN ON TRIAL

The life blood of Sturgeon Falls has been this mill and over the years many different owners have taken the town on a roller coaster. The most difficult time was from 1930 until the mill reopened again in 1947.

– Wayne LeBelle[1]

The Great Depression arrived in Sturgeon Falls on 12 November 1930 when the Abitibi Power & Paper Company shut its local mill. It stayed closed for seventeen long years – the "hell years," as Ken Colquhoun recalled.[2] Life was rough; nearly everyone subsisted on poor relief.[3] Sturgeon Falls probably had the worst unemployment rate in Ontario, and the joblessness persisted longer there than in other places.[4] Even seventy-five years later, people still remembered how "everything emptied."[5] Hundreds of residents left; those who remained lived in "very poor circumstances."[6] Many houses stood "black and empty, stripped of everything movable, windows broken, doors swinging in the wind, roofs leaking, floors heaving."[7] It was a period of protracted crisis marked by protest and scandal.

Oral interviews speak to the hardships, revealing vivid details and deeper meaning, but little economic or political context. The memory of this period also lives on in community histories. In her booklet produced for Canada's centennial, Jeanine Beauchemin spoke of how the Depression "settled slowly over the town destroying initiative, energy and pride in honest work." The town's reputation "suffered."[8] This allusion to scandal surfaces in other histories. The history of the local Masonic Temple, for example, notes that Sturgeon Falls "was considered an easy place to get government assistance and the system became abused."[9] A much more nuanced account is given in Wayne LeBelle's commemorative book published to mark the town's first century: "Up to 75 percent of the residents of Sturgeon Falls were on welfare in the late 1930s with no jobs, and little hope ... It was not unusual to see long lines of people waiting to get into the town hall in Sturgeon Falls to get welfare. They were not proud times. The Ontario government carried out an investigation into welfare fraud in Sturgeon Falls during these hard times."[10]

In each of these recollections, the scandal is cast in individualized or moral terms. The archival records and newspaper accounts from the 1930s reveal, however, a much more interesting story anchored in community resistance to the minimalist response of the provincial and federal governments to this unprecedented crisis. In Sturgeon Falls this resistance took the form of an elaborate scheme to defraud senior levels of government. When this was met with a forceful response in the form of a public inquiry, people on relief turned to direct action and protest. The chapter ends by looking at the retirement notices of "old timers" in the 1950s and early 1960s, which reveals the extent to which working lives were ruptured by the seventeen-year shutdown. These were truly lost years.[11]

Remembering the Hard Times

Each spring hundreds of thousands of logs were driven down the Sturgeon River, right past the closed mill to still-operating sawmills in Cache Bay and Calendar. One could still hear a hint of anger in our interviewees' voices as they recalled this sight and the mountain of rotting wood that sat in the mill yard. Wood, long the town's lifeblood, took on a new significance in the 1930s. Ken Colquhoun recalled how his neighbours secreted out pulp logs from the mill yard to heat their stoves. There was a great deal of petty theft, but "nothing big." As children, to help make ends meet, Ed Fortin and his friends would swim out to the logs being driven down river to pick the "flimwood" and cut it for firewood, splitting it and letting it dry. He would then deliver it in a wheelbarrow to the old age pensioners. He got a couple of quarters for a cord of wood, and turned the money over to his father, who had lost his job as a teamster at the mill "like everybody else."[12]

The mill closure struck the community hard:

> [It was] sad for a lot of people. Meals were very limited in many households. Brown sugar was a favourite sugar, but rarely available to whip down and put on your bread. So, we struggled and my older brother managed to get a bit of work. And my dad, well, you see the Depression came along and I think my mother died in 1927, and the

Depression was right up until 1940, '41 with the war. And my dad was unemployed all of those years and we were on the welfare. And, I would say probably 80 per cent of the people of Sturgeon Falls were on welfare. And you never had any goodies for free … I remember I was the second youngest of the family and there was a sister slightly older than me, and I recall on Easter weekend, my dad going downtown and Easter Morning all we had was a Sweet Marie chocolate bar and he had to cut it, he paid a nickel for it, and he had to cut it in three pieces so C. and L. and I would each have a bite.

They would pick blueberries and poach fish. Ed Fortin recalled that "[w]e ate lots of fish that were illegal, but they were plentiful. That was the upbringing in Sturgeon Falls."

Childhood memories of the Depression years also turned to play. Our interviewees remembered the closed mill as a place of exploration, and several got to know the mill's watchmen, some of whom were apparently more forgiving of young trespassers than others. Ben Lajeunesse, born in April 1935, who grew up next to the mill site, remembered playing in and around the empty "mill houses" on Cache Bay Road that had been built to house mill superintendents and other middle managers. Children would play "on the verandas of those houses. They were big houses and verandas. Most of the kids in this end of town would play there." A few of the children would also

go and play in the mill yard. But the watchman at the time, one of them would get very angry at the children, at the kids. The other ones really didn't care, as long as they didn't do any damage. It was just a place to play. As a matter of fact, before the mill reopened, most of the children in town would bring their skates to the mill gate and one fella come out and picked them up and brought them down to the powerhouse, where they had a grinder, and would sharpen all the skates. There was two of them that did that. Roch Laflèche and E. Stack would do that. Often, you'd see the kids lined up at the gate. Except when Mr […] was there. He wouldn't allow it. It didn't take long for the people to know when he was on and when he wasn't.

We heard similar stories from other interviewees. Merna Nesbitt, whose father and grandfather both worked at the mill,[13] was born in 1929 and grew up near the mill site on Cache Bay Road. She recalled a "big old building" across the road from the mill that stood "empty, no windows or doors or anything. We'd run through and then when we went to town … And it had a curved front. I remember that as, I don't know why, maybe it's because something we didn't see, and we'd run through

Pulpwood at Sturgeon Falls, 1923–24. Courtesy of Library and Archives Canada, PA-031333.

Mill offices, Cache Bay Road. Courtesy of West Nipissing Public Library.

there in one door and out the other, on the way down to the show." Generally the mill watchmen left Nesbitt and her childhood friends alone. One time, years later, she had the chance to go to the top of the tallest building of the closed mill. The view was spectacular: "If you've seen any old pictures of the mill you will have seen this especially tall building stood out … And there was a circular stairway in there and, a friend of mine, her father was one of the men who worked at the mill as a watchman before the mill reopened. And we went around with him one time and he let us go up the circular stair, went right up to the top of the building. We could see the lake from up there, I remember that, and I would have been a teenager. A young teenager. Yeah." Merna Nesbitt's father was laid off from the mill when she was just a year old. He then went west looking for work, riding the rails, eventually finding a job in Sudbury and returning home on weekends. When Merna was six, her mother died. At first, she and her brother were kept by a housekeeper and then boarded with a local couple. Sometime later, Nesbitt's father brought them to live with him in Sudbury until the outbreak of the war, when they returned to Sturgeon Falls together.

With the war, Ken Colquhoun recalled that "anybody of the right age was gone." He had tried to enlist near war's end, but he was still too young. To make sure it didn't happen, his mother went down to the recruitment office. "She got to them before they got to me," he recalled. She was adamant: "no, no, no, you're not going there." Colquhoun's friend, Sidney Armitage, was killed in Normandy. Before the shutdown, Sidney's father, Harry, had been responsible for collecting the union dues: "He collected in church. He collected anywhere he could get it [chuckles]."

This story is one of the few moments when interviewees spoke of industrial or union life before the 1930 closure. Several vaguely recalled that women once made "hanging paper" (wallpaper) inside the mill, but the story remained obscure. This forgetfulness surprised me – in the Northern Ontario town in which I grew up, the old union and socialist stories were very much in circulation in the 1970s and 1980s. Perhaps I had come to Sturgeon Falls too late to record these memories – timing is everything in oral history, and all of the interviewees had gone to work in the mill only after it reopened in 1947. Or perhaps Sturgeon Falls did not have the same tradition of left-wing activism that exists elsewhere in Northern Ontario. Certainly the institutional memory in the local union did not seem to reach back past 1947. I can only speculate, but my suspicion is that the mill's seventeen-year closure ruptured local memory, causing mill workers to lose their former connection to this earlier activist history. The rest of this chapter explores these years of rupture from the vantage point of the surviving archival and newspaper evidence.

Shutting the Mill

The Depression came relatively late to Sturgeon Falls, as a sense of normality persisted into 1930. In April that year, *Abitibi Magazine* featured the fishing and sporting activities of Sturgeon employees. Bob Vardin's participation in a union meeting in Montreal as local representative of the Pulp & Sulphite Workers was also mentioned.[14] A month later, it was reported that a new athletics association had been formed at the mill. The Abitibi Athletics Association of Sturgeon Falls intended to organize a variety of sporting activities that summer.[15] A softball league was formed, pitting grouped departments against one another. Fun was apparently had by all.[16] Reading these articles so many years later, one is surprised by the sense of normality. There is no mention of the disaster unfolding in the country nor any sign of the immanent closing of the Sturgeon Falls mill itself.

Once closed on 12 November 1930, the mill began physically to deteriorate.[17] By 1937 the company's receivers reported that the mill was "not in good physical condition" and that major expenditures would have to be made before operations could resume. The mill's hydro plant, however, continued to generate electricity for the town.[18] The company also owned forty-two workmen's dwellings, "some are in poor condition and vacant, and others are occupied." As early as 1932, ten of these houses were deemed uninhabitable, twenty required repairs, and the rest were in only "fair" condition.[19] The mill had a huge quantity of wood on hand: an estimated 74,716 cords, with a gross book value of $689,269, piled high in the wood yard.[20] During those years, fifteen to eighteen men continued to work at the closed mill. When the mill's pulpwood concession – an area of 2,525 square miles accorded to it in 1898 – expired in 1932, it was not renewed.[21] Given this state of affairs, the receivers warned that the reorganized company might dispose of the mill, move its paper-making equipment to other Abitibi mills, or consider the "possible conversion of the property to other manufacturing purposes."[22]

For its part, the Pulp & Sulphite Workers union was devastated by the collapse of the North American forestry industry. International Union president John P. Burke reported in 1931 that virtually the "whole paper industry" was "facing bankruptcy."[23] He observed that Abitibi was fully operating only three of its mills. Four years later, Burke reported that the union had lost "some of our finest locals," mentioning the Sturgeon Falls local in particular.[24] The International Union was not optimistic about its future. Despite a strike wave in many industrial cities, associated with the rise of the militant Congress of Industrial Organizations (CIO), Burke pessimistically noted: "To throw a picket line around abandoned mills is neither very heroic, nor very intelligent." It would be a "gesture of futility."[25] Seventy-two

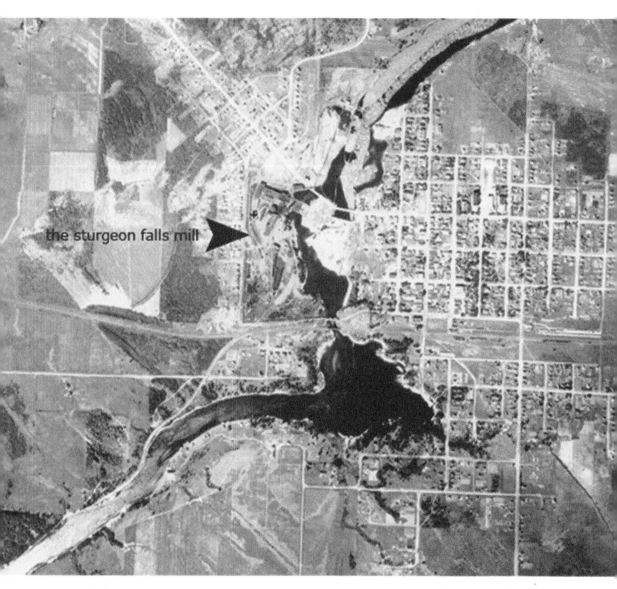

the sturgeon falls mill

Sturgeon Falls from the air, 1929; the mill's location is identified. Courtesy of Government of Canada.

years later, Sturgeon Falls mill workers would know the bitter truth of this statement as they walked the picket line in front of their closed mill. As we will see, a
similarly stubborn resistance marked the history of Sturgeon Falls in the 1930s.

"The Sturgeon Falls Vaudeville Show"[26]

When the Depression struck, Ontario did not have a province-wide public welfare
system. Only impoverished widows with two or more children and the elderly
over seventy years of age were eligible for a mother's allowance or old age pension,
respectively.[27] Direct relief for food, clothing, fuel, and shelter was administered
by the municipalities. Only in 1932 did Ontario establish province-wide standards
and a measure of uniformity in relief administration and payments. It therefore
did not take long after the Depression struck for hard-hit towns to be thrown
into crisis.[28] By 1934 more than forty municipal and school boards had defaulted
in Ontario, including many mill towns such as Sturgeon Falls.[29] It was a messy
business.

The mill's closure made people desperate, prompting an "epidemic of loot-
ing and burglary" in some areas. "Sturgeon Falls facing anarchy, say petitioners," shouted a front-page story in the Toronto *Globe* published on 15 April 1931:
"Faced with an unemployment situation so critical that members of Council fear
a state of anarchy is in the offing, Sturgeon Falls citizens turned out en masse to
protest against the inactivity of the local plant of the Abitibi Power and Paper
Company and to discuss the employment situation generally."[30] Mayor Zotique
Mageau, a former Liberal member of the provincial parliament, read a lengthy
petition calling for "drastic action" from the Ontario Conservative government to
reopen the mill: "The petition charges that the Abitibi Power & Paper Company
opposed the establishment of a sawmill at Sturgeon Falls by refusing to waive its
riparian rights. As a result of the closing down of the Abitibi mill 365 families
wholly dependent on the paper industry for their employment are destitute, and,
in the words of the petition, 'facing starvation in the near future.'" The signatories urged the province to confiscate Abitibi's timber limits and concessions, and
demanded that Abitibi divest itself of the mill, allowing someone else to operate
it. It would not be the last time that local residents demanded that the company
free their mill. What was particularly galling this time was that the wood yard
remained full. "The hoarding of pulpwood until it rots is classed as 'shameful
waste,'" noted the *Globe*.

Two weeks after this mass meeting, a delegation of twenty-five prominent citizens from Sturgeon Falls travelled to Toronto to present their case to the premier

Table 2.1 Municipal Revenues, Town of Sturgeon Falls, 1930–2

Year	Collected ($)	In Arrears ($)
1930	98,926.42	29,880.08
1931	82,077.64	42,135.90
1932	78,604.27	55,935.22

Source: Ontario, Royal Commission on the Enquiry as to the Handling of Unemployment and Direct Relief at Sturgeon Falls, Ontario, *Report* (Toronto, 1933), RG 18, Series B-81, Archives of Ontario, Toronto.

of Ontario.[31] Their visit prompted the *Globe* to publish another page-one story, this one entitled "Tale of distress." Here we learn that workers were given only twenty-four hours advance notice of the mill's closing. Mayor Mageau reported that 250 families were now in arrears in paying their water and light bills. Another $12,000 was owed in overdue rents.[32] Even the *New York Times* ran a story about destitute school children in the town when parents asked the school board for permission to send their children to school barefoot.[33] As a "one-mill town," Sturgeon Falls was in a "hopeless situation."[34]

Almost three-quarters of the population of Sturgeon Falls – 2,851 people, comprising 561 heads of households, 2,295 dependents, and 25 single men – was on poor relief by November 1932. Growing numbers of property owners were falling in arrears with their taxes (see Table 2.1). As a result Sturgeon Falls found itself saddled with $350,000 in debentured debt and a "growing mountain" of unpaid tax levies.[35] To make matters worse, the problem persisted considerably longer than elsewhere. In 1937 48.8 per cent of the town's population remained on poor relief, the worst rate by far in Northern Ontario.[36] The rate actually worsened in 1938 when 54.4 per cent were on relief, declining in 1939 to 45.2 per cent.[37] Only the war ameliorated the situation, with those on relief dropping to 27.8 per cent in 1940 and to 9.5 percent in 1941.[38] In response to the unfolding crisis, the Ontario government agreed in November 1930 to cover one-third of the cost of local relief, with an additional third coming from the federal government. A year later this agreement was amended to cover 80 per cent of the cost of poor relief, with the municipality picking up the remainder. Then, in July 1932, to "stave off municipal default," the provincial and federal governments assumed 85 per cent of the expenditure of poor relief in Sturgeon Falls.[39] On the basis of these agreements, the town received $42,806.53 between November 1930 and April 1931 and another $65,720 between September 1931 and April

1932.[40] How this money was then distributed by the town became the subject of a public inquiry.

On 9 January 1993, Judge James McNairn Hall was directed by the Ontario government to enquire into the "handling of unemployment and direct relief" in Sturgeon Falls. Specifically, he was asked to examine the receipts, expenditures, and methods of handling unemployment relief in the town and to report back. In the course of the hearings that followed, it was established that the mayor, town councillors, the local relief officer, and much of the local community conspired to defraud the provincial and federal governments. Vouchers for food, clothing, and rent were misappropriated on a massive scale. Amounts were charged that were never expended and other amounts increased or otherwise changed. Notably, "items that should have been paid by the Town for regular general Town expenses were disguised and charged as direct relief."[41]

Before the federal and provincial governments were pushed unwillingly into providing poor relief in 1931, the St Vincent de Paul Society distributed local charity in Sturgeon Falls. But the practice of making grants to local charities continued and expanded in the years that followed. The public inquiry found that the municipality colluded with members of the Society as well as the Knights of Columbus, the Rotary Club, and the Sewing Circle in a "vicious scheme" of subterfuge. In a typical example, the Knights of Columbus received a $600 cheque from the town for the purpose of direct relief. Once it was cashed, the charity retained $100 and returned $500 to the town as "donation relief." The town was then eligible for an additional $1,000, as the provincial government paid two dollars for every dollar subscribed by private individuals towards poor relief. It was an ingenious if dishonest scheme. The judge noted that local councillors "openly and freely" admitted that they sought to "save the Town from any relief expenditures, and get as much as possible for the people."[42]

Other irregularities in town disbursements were also flagged. Public hearings revealed that permanent town employees were paid, in part, in relief vouchers out of provincial government funds. The town's teamsters were thus paid in food and clothing vouchers, as were those who repainted the town hall. Even the chief of police received $40 a month in relief vouchers in addition to his regular monthly salary of $85, as did several municipal employees. According to J.L. Malcolm, chief investigator for the provincial government, "for some months relief vouchers were used as scrip and accepted as cash. Given for food, they were used for all sorts of things" such as "buying hay and oats for horses."[43]

Several hundred people managed to squeeze into the council chamber for the public hearings. Joseph Côté, relief officer and a former blacksmith at the mill, was on the stand for much of one day. He was asked to produce a list of all those who received firewood from the town's wood lot, the amount of firewood delivered to the homes of town councillors, and the amount of rent subsidy these same councillors received. The inquiry next turned its attention to the method of giving out clothing to persons on relief. On the whole, this scheme was designed to support local merchants and landowners – not unlike the bailout of US banks in more recent times. Many food and clothing vouchers signed by the relief officer and given to merchants were left blank. The merchant would later write in the cost of the items purchased. In general, Judge Hall found that "the prices were high for the class of article furnished, and in many cases of finer quality than the nature of each case warranted." There was apparently no limits on the amount a person on relief could get for clothing. W.H. William described one case as particularly "fishy," as the recipient was supposed to have a family of nine children ages four, six, eight, ten, twelve, fourteen, sixteen, eighteen, and twenty. "Is he a railroader, in stick to a schedule like that?" The town clerk solemnly replied: "No, he's a paper maker."[44]

It was determined that relief-funded clothing was given to 122 "employed" persons in Sturgeon Falls – although some were on old age pension, mother's allowance, or worker's compensation.[45] The Relief Committee had invited all the town's school children to the town hall, where they were given vouchers for new school clothes. The wife of one prominent local merchant had even obtained relief clothing valued at $122, using her maiden name. In all 277 ineligible people were named as having received "relief clothing."

The final week of public hearings probed the matter of relief rents, with many prominent local landlords called to speak to their actions. It was established that Mayor Mageau had met with local landlords in January 1931, where it was agreed that the rent of those on relief would be paid directly to landlords. In return landlords agreed to take only two-thirds of the full rent billed to the Ontario government, covertly handing the remaining third over to the municipality.[46] Landlords submitted their statements of account of rents in arrears, "in some cases for a year or more"; the claims were then scrutinized by the mayor, who paid landlords what they thought they were owed. In this way the town paid landlords an estimated $8,448. Not surprisingly, there were abuses: "In many cases the landlords were not entitled and the tenants were not on relief, or entitled to either relief or rent." In some cases, parents were treated as landlords and their sons and daughters as tenants; in others, "parents became the tenants of their children, while all living together." Some landlords also double-dipped.[47] On the stand for a second time, Mageau insisted that "we did nothing dishonest;" indeed, "every cent we got from the Government was spent on relief."[48]

In reality, so extensive was the ruse that Justice Hall concluded that regular town expenses were being "deliberately and fraudulently charged to relief account."[49] Local merchants and others cooperated in this scheme. According to one prominent local merchant, so great was the crisis facing the residents, that "the Town had to have the money and there did not appear to be any other way to get it."[50] The public inquiry found that the system put in place in Sturgeon Falls by municipal officials seemed to "have been to include in each monthly claim, every possible item that could be charged up." The generalized nature of these abuses was made abundantly clear in the report. Accordingly Judge Hall could not "too strongly condemn, not only these practices, but those guilty of them." The Toronto media had a field day, with the *Globe* declaring that "even" the horses were paid in Sturgeon Falls.[51] Virtually everyone in the community was implicated to some degree.

Judge Hall was scathing in his indictment of town officials and townsfolk who "fraudulently received relief."[52] In his final report he named all those found to have received relief illegally. It was a who's who of Sturgeon Falls. In some instances residents with "substantial assets" accepted relief payments and "some even withdrew their bank balances to place themselves in a position to truthfully say they had no bank balances." One person had a balance of $1,021, only to withdraw it all on the day he signed a statement attesting to the fact that he had no money in the bank. Alphonse, a local barber and proprietor of a pool room with seven tables, received a relief order for clothing valued at $92.70 in September 1932 after repeated application to local officials.

But the "Sturgeon Falls Vaudeville Show" was not so much about corrupt practices – in the sense of personal benefit, though this certainly happened – as it was a public conspiracy to defy upper-level governments in the face of an unprecedented crisis. The old ways of doing things were clearly inadequate, and the provincial and federal governments were slow in responding. Going into the third week of hearings, the town remained defiant. A 22 January 1933 meeting of merchants and councillors called on the Ontario government to take over all relief costs, threatening to put the town into bankruptcy proceedings. Local merchants dared not take any more relief vouchers out of fear that the government would no longer honour them.[53] It was suggested in the press that some local merchants held $10,000 worth of these vouchers. Deploring the negative publicity, the meeting also called on Judge Hall to employ an interpreter for the duration of the hearings, as some of the Franco-Ontarian witnesses were having difficulty understanding the questions put to them. The mayor reminded the media that only 75 persons out of a population of 4,605 "are engaged in gainful occupations."[54]

Local defiance was not limited to public officials and community leaders. On 27 January 1933 it was reported that people on relief in the town who owned cows

General yard, Sturgeon Falls mill, 1920; Ed Fortin's father was a teamster at the mill. Courtesy of West Nipissing Public Library.

were threatening to kill their cattle at four o'clock the next day "unless the Government agrees to supply them with hay and fodder."[55] Previously they had been able to "exchange vouchers for cash with which to buy hay, but a stricter check on relief vouchers now prevents that."[56] In the end Judge Hall found that Sturgeon Falls was overpaid $18,246.40 from January 1931 to August 1932.[57]

In the midst of this extended act of public shaming, the financial position of the Town of Sturgeon Falls deteriorated. In February 1933, W.L. Fortier, the town's clerk and treasurer, warned that "it will be impossible to carry on much longer under the present conditions" unless it issued more debentures.[58] Otherwise the town would have no choice but to declare bankruptcy: "Owing to the very unfavourable publicity which this Municipality has had for the past six months, it is absolutely out of the question to attempt to market debentures unless they are guaranteed by the Province."[59] Under the circumstances, Fortier admitted that the town

has not behaved in a way to induce your Government to sympathize. Besides being humiliated as it is, it is going to suffer and stand the consequences of the mistakes of a few. There is but one excuse which can be advanced, and although it does not justify the errors, it is a logical excuse; and this is that Sturgeon Falls is in a desperate situation owing to the fact that only 30% of its population has to carry the burden and it was receiving the same help as many other towns who had 75 to 80% of its population in a position to help carry the load. Sturgeon Falls could probably carry on for another year if it can issue debentures as stated above and in the meantime conditions may change so that the situation would be saved and permit this Municipality to carry on.[60]

To this appeal, Fortier received a short, rudimentary response denying the request.[61] On 9 May 1933, Fortier wrote the minister of public works and labour:

It seems to me, that you do not realize the seriousness of the consequences which result from this unreasonable prolonged delay. Everyday intensifies the difficulties which will ultimately have to be overcome if we are going to rescue our financial organization from the desperate situation in which it finds itself at present … Our bank will not assist us for the logical reason that they must be furnished with a financial statement which we have been unable to do and with our finances so upset, it would be unreasonable to insist in getting further assistance. Our merchants who are the only few ratepayers, who are able to assist this Municipality in carrying on, are being starved and their struggling business are seriously affected by the fact that we owe them considerable money and unable to pay them.[62]

The municipality hobbled on until a bank demanded the immediate repayment of its loan in February 1934, tipping Sturgeon Falls into bankruptcy and provincial government supervision.[63]

With the town under the direct financial administration of the province, civil servants scrambled to raise funds from ratepayers. But Abitibi's refusal to pay its local municipal and school taxes exacerbated the situation. With a debt load of $918,218 in 1935, the mill rate for local public schools was raised from 8.6 to 23.[64] Even this failed to provide sufficient funds. Then, in 1936, four elected members of the Sturgeon Falls town council were unseated by a court ruling – disbarred because one was bankrupt, another was in arrears in the payment of taxes, and the other two were on the welfare rolls. The town complained as late as February 1939 of the strict enforcement of relief, treating the town council "like a bunch of slaves." With relief payments under Ontario government control, things quickly came to a head.[65]

The Relief Strike of 1933

If the Depression years proved disastrous for the local government, conditions were even worse for those on relief. In response to the scandal, the Ontario government appointed a three-person committee to run relief in Sturgeon Falls: Walter Cockburn, the local Indian agent; A. Bourgault, a businessman; and Peter Levis, an agent of Abitibi Power & Paper.[66] Levis' appointment must have been particularly galling given the company's refusal to pay its own local taxes.

Matters came to a head on 1 December 1933, when 508 relief recipients refused to work in protest against reductions in their food allowance ranging from 18 to 20 per cent and the elimination of their clothing allowance altogether.[67] Under the new schedule, a family of six would receive a food allowance of $17 a month. The district relief officer, James McCluskey, introduced the cuts without warning. "Recipients first learned of the change when they applied for weekly vouchers" that very morning. Striking relief workers sought to convince the Ontario government to rescind the new regulations. Both Mayor J.P. Marchildon and the local MPP, A.Z. Aubin, sided with the strikers. "All recipients are required to give labor in return for aid and the moment they decline to comply relief in all forms ceases," responded McCluskey.[68]

The next day the *Toronto Star* reported that the town hall was filled to capacity with "unemployed strikers" who insisted that they would not return to "work" until their allowance was restored. Robert Verdun, a leading union activist inside the mill, stood up and spoke at the mass meeting: "'Before the cut, lots of families had just enough to eat on ... Seventy-five per cent, have not enough to buy meat. The most we've been able to get is porridge, bread, and butter." Another young man told the reporter that he and his wife and baby could barely get by on $2.45 per week when it cost fifty cents per week for the baby's milk alone. "When this is taken off, I have just a little over a dollar week left to buy food," he said.[69] Reportedly, one father of fourteen children was simply told by relief inspectors not to have so many. According to the *Toronto Worker*, "It is stated that this official has berated and bullied heads of family on such occasions and has issued the dictum: 'Unemployed people who cannot feed the babies should not have them.'"[70] For his part Mayor Marchildon warned that the new schedule meant starvation. In all, some 500 families (or 2,734 people) were affected by the strike. Fearing the worst, the *Toronto Star* indicated that the relief strike in Sturgeon Falls "may spread to other points" and that the local struggle had "assumed the aspect of an endurance contest."[71]

James McCluskey's initial reaction was one of defiance, warning that, if the relief strikers should persist in "refusing to work, it will mean a discontinuance of relief issues. All recipients are required to give labour in return for aid." He defended his actions by saying that "[e]ven under the new schedule the people of Sturgeon Falls will receive more than is issued in any other part of Nipissing and North Parry Sound districts"[72] – for example, Springer Township, a rural area adjoining Sturgeon Falls, had a rate that was fully 20 per cent less. Under the instructions of a town official, the local relief officer in Sturgeon Falls ignored McCluskey's orders and provided relief anyway during the first week of the strike. "Ten days after it began, the strike ended when McCluskey offered to meet the men "half-way" and postpone the reductions until after Christmas.[73] The *Toronto Worker* claimed that the authorities had been forced to "stage a partial retreat,"[74] and reported that the Workmen's Protective Association was "determined" to strike again if the cutbacks were re-imposed. The leftist newspaper saw in this strike a sign that the "French-Canadian masses are ready for struggle for their right to live."[75]

Traces of continued unemployed activism can be found in the papers of William Lyon Mackenzie King, Canada's prime minister. Robert Verdun wrote to King on 9 April 1936, on behalf of the Unemployed and Workers Union of Sturgeon Falls, seeking a response to a resolution requesting permission for those who were on relief to fish with lines and nets in the Sturgeon River during the spring run. King's office simply forwarded the letter to the Ontario Ministry of Fishery, as the matter was under provincial jurisdiction.[76] This fragmentary archival evidence nicely dovetails Ed Fortin's own childhood recollections of illegal fishing.

Rumours of the mill's reopening or its impending sale were in constant circulation during these years, producing renewed hope and despair. Writing in the *North Bay Nugget* in May 1944, Madeleine Parks noted that the town was once again "busy" with rumours that the mill was set to reopen.[77] Apparently "something is 'cooking' behind the silent walls of the mill." Some thought that the mill was about to be purchased by a US-based company, but few believed it: "Hardened to disappointments as the result of recurring rumors of the mill's reopening in past years, however, all town officials are regarding the stories with distinct pessimism, determined to avoid the usual let-down." Madeline Parks told her readers that Sturgeon Falls had once been a "busy, thriving little town" where "unemployment was practically unknown." But "[t]hen disaster struck." Those who stayed, she wrote, were "struck by a helpless apathy and clinging to the hope that somehow, someday, operations would be resumed. That was 14 years ago, and that hope has long since been dimmed by discouragement and repeated rumors of the type now circulating." By 1944 more than one hundred residential homes stood empty: "their paint peeled off, windows boarded up or staring like, broken sightless eyes, every sagging line an epitaph to failure and heartbreak. Scores more have been sold and torn down for salvage." Only the logs destined for the Gordon Lumber mill in Cache Bay continued to slide down the timber chute alongside the Abitibi dam. "No," Parks concluded, "Sturgeon Falls isn't clutching at any straw this time. Too often in the past they have broken off in its hopeful grasp. Maybe there's just a little glimmer of hope, but no one is counting on it."[78]

Life Returns

The long-awaited reopening of the Sturgeon Falls Mill in September 1947 was a moment of community rebirth. For some, this ended seventeen long years of contingent work and government relief. Lives had been put on hold. In 1948 *Abitibi Magazine* noted that it seemed "like old times to see the Paper Makers coming to town. Some of them are former employees of Abitibi and a few are new, but it's good to see the gang around."[79] New homes were built and old ones renovated. In the months to come the Sturgeon Falls Curling Club held its first bonspiel since the mill's closing and the "Abitibi League" for bowling was inaugurated. And in short order, the new Odeon Theatre opened on King Street.[80] There was suddenly much to celebrate.

There was a huge and boisterous turnout for the 1948 Labour Day Parade, organized by the two mill unions as well as the Agricultural Society.[81] Parade floats, agricultural exhibitions, softball matches, children's races, horse racing, amusement games, and refreshment booths – all marked the new beginning. The day ended with boxing bouts and two dances. *Abitibi Magazine* congratulated the "Paper Mill Union" for an enjoyable day and for "reviving the Labor Day celebrations."[82] It was as if the town had reawakened after a nightmarish night. As *Abitibi Magazine* reported, "once again, Sturgeon Falls Plant is on the 'map' as an operating mill."[83]

But the social impact of the shutdown proved to be long-lasting. The working lives of many of those returning to work in the mill were short lived, as a large number reached retirement age in the 1950s. Much of their working lives had been spent doing odd jobs or collecting relief. This sixteen-year rupture was apparent in the retirement notices published in *Abitibi Magazine* over the coming years. Beginning with the retirement of Ernest W. Innes in June 1949, we see the extent to which lives were put on hold during these lost years. Innes started at the mill in 1915 as a powerhouse operator, and remained in the same position for thirty-three years except his "years non-service on account of mill shutdown."[84] George Cole, for his part, started at the mill in 1922 as a pipefitter's helper. During the shutdown, "he was employed temporarily at various times, returning permanently when [the] mill

Abitibi bowling party, 1954. Courtesy of West Nipissing Public Library.

re-opened in 1946, first with Foundation [construction] Company and then with Abitibi, where he has been watchman since."[85] Joseph Rudolphe Serre, known to his friends as "Duff," was described in his retirement notice as "another of our real old-timers." Born in Sturgeon Falls, he started to work at the mill in 1913, working various positions in the wood room, wet press, the acid plant, and as cook's helper and a pipefitter "until shutdown." During the years when the mill was shut, he "worked from time to time keeping the mill buildings in good repair, in Sudbury for a spell, a log driver on the river and for contractors in town. He rejoined the Company in 1946, first in the wood yard then wrapping hardboard – his job when he left."[86]

The retirement notices for other "old timers" told similar stories. Ezra Carswell, born in Madawaska, came to Sturgeon Falls with his parents. He started first with Gordon Lumber in Cache Bay as a bush worker and log driver before starting at the Sturgeon mill with Spanish River in 1921. He "remained here until the 1930 shutdown. During shutdown, Ezra worked at Nobel. When our mill re-opened in 1946, he came back to our shipping room. For the past three years he has been one of our watchmen." Isa Landriault, another "real old timer," had started at the mill in 1915: "The interval between 1930 and 1946 when our mill was shut down was a hard time for Isa and his family. He worked in bush, rangers, and anything he could turn his hand to. In 1946 he started work again with Abitibi and was in the woodroom until 1955, when he transferred to watchman duties at the gate." His was a story of resilience, as he sent all seven of his children to high school: "Those of us who are old enough to remember the hardships of the hungry thirties can sincerely admire a family who achieved a fine education for their children during those difficult times."[87]

Many of those with a trade were able to find work in other mills. The 1958 retirement notice for Leo Joanis, senior machine tender, noted:

> Leo is a paper maker from away back. He started in the business in 1906 for the J.R. Booth Paper Company in Ottawa, moving in 1909 to Espanola to work as a boss pulp shipper for Spanish River Paper. In 1912 Leo's itching feet moved him out west for a spell of farming, but he soon decided that the east was more to his liking, and the same year saw him settled in Sturgeon Falls until 1926. Then, with the onset of the depression, when our mill was on short time, Leo moved with his growing family to tend machines at Corner Brook, Newfoundland, where he became, naturally, a boss machine tender and tour foreman … In 1947, when Abitibi started the local mill again, Leo headed back to Sturgeon Falls.[88]

Another skilled worker was Bill Bunting. Born in 1894 in Almonte, Ontario, he moved to Sturgeon Falls as a boy. In 1909 he was "engaged by the old Imperial Paper Company in Sturgeon Falls and became a full-time employee in 1912. Bunting worked at different jobs out of town for a few years but returned in 1919 and worked at Abitibi until it closed during the depression. Toward the end of the depression he became pipefitter foreman at Ste. Anne Paper Company, the Beaupre Division of Abitibi. In 1947, Bill Bunting returned to Sturgeon Falls as assistant master mechanic, a position he has filled ever since."[89]

Frank Sullivan's retirement in 1953 provided an opportunity to reflect on the history of the mill as a whole. He first came to Sturgeon Falls with Imperial Paper Mills as an accountant, and married a local woman before relocating to a paper mill town in Maine. In 1913 he joined the Spanish River mill at Espanola, where he was in charge of the office and townsite before returning to Sturgeon Falls with Abitibi, where he resided for the next thirty-four years: "Beginning with his association with Spanish River in Sturgeon Falls and on through the amalgamation with Abitibi in 1928, through the prosperous twenties and depression ridden thirties, and the reopening and construction of the forties, Sullivan has come to represent in the Community a personal symbol of the fortunes of the local Abitibi Division. He has provided a link between the old and the new and old timers and new comers alike have been vocal in their praise of his co-operation during the changing periods."[90] As office manager Sullivan had been part of the skeleton crew that continued to maintain the closed mill. He remembered the hard times when 60,000 cords of

Sturgeon Falls from the air, 1950s. Below the river are managers' housing and the mill; Nipissing First Nation is the rural area beyond the town at upper right. Ontario – Sturgeon Falls – Abitibi Power & Paper Company, 1951–1966, C30, Northway-Gestalt Corporation Fonds, Archives of Ontario, Toronto.

Table 2.2 Demographic Change, Sturgeon Falls, 1921–61

Demographic Group	1921	1931	1941	1961
	(population)			
English-speaking	1,004	954	833	1,093
French-speaking	2,943	3,114	3,621	4,843
Indigenous	12	41	22	145

Source: René Guénette, "Histoire de Sturgeon Falls (1878–1960)" (master's thesis, Laurentian University, 1966).

wood from the mill yard were loaded onto railway cars bound for Sault Ste Marie: "This, followed by the dismantling and sale of two paper machines spelled doom to the inhabitants of a town who watched their raw material and means of production removed with no hope of return. Perhaps the deeply etched lines that distinguish Frank's lean face are permanent witnesses to such sad scenes."

Also found in the retirement notices in the *Abitibi Magazine* is previously encountered Bob Verdon – sometimes spelled Verdun or Verdin – who stepped aside as foreman of the mechanical crew in October 1950. Born in Quebec, he attended school in Pembroke in the Ottawa Valley, and learned the blacksmith's trade in Schenectady, New York, before returning to Canada to work for Gordon Lumber in Cache Bay and then Imperial Paper/Spanish River. In 1946 he restarted with the construction company refurbishing the old mill. In the end, despite the long layoff, he had put twenty-one years into the mill and was described as a "staunch" member of Local 71 and its president for six years.[91] No mention was made of his political activism for the unemployed during the shutdown. Even so, these retirement notices allow us to see the extent to which the prolonged shutdown ruptured the working lives of this generation of mill working families.

Conclusion

The shutdown of the mill had a similarly lasting impact on the city. Those who could find work elsewhere departed; others streamed in from surrounding rural areas in search of relief. The first to leave were managers and skilled workers who had employment opportunities elsewhere. These families were overwhelmingly English-speaking. By contrast, those moving into the community from adjoining rural areas were mostly French-speaking. The result was a demographic shift in the town's population from English to French (see Table 2.2). One might even say that the mill's extended shutdown from 1930 until 1947 helped make Sturgeon Falls the Franco-Ontarian town that it is today.

Many of those we interviewed understood this connection, as it has long since become part of the town's historical narrative. For example, Ed Fortin, born in 1924, one of the oldest people we spoke to, recalled that many of the town's English-speaking residents "moved away" during the shutdown. By the time the mill reopened, the community had become "very, very French." Despite the hard times, he reassured his listeners that Sturgeon Falls was nonetheless a "comfortable place. Nothing ever really serious ever happened when I lived here." Although the Depression years cast a long shadow over the decades that followed, this rupture also served to extinguish the public memory of the earlier industrial and trade union history. Forced forgetting did not begin with the final 2002 closure. It is an integral part of capitalist development.

SHOP-FLOOR REALITIES

3

WORKING LIVES

When I was going to high school I could see guys who were working there, who were in high school before I finished ... maybe half of the men in the town were working in the mill. They had a big crew in there at that time. I wasn't too keen on keep going to school. I wanted to get out, so I got on at the mill as a labourer.

– Lionel Sarazin[1]

On 1 October 1946 Ontario premier George Drew announced that Abitibi would "rehabilitate" the Sturgeon Falls mill, converting it from newsprint production to corrugated medium. "This is the happiest day of my life," exclaimed Mayor Ray Cockburn: "This is a godsend for the people of Sturgeon Falls, scores of whom were on relief after the tragic shut-down of the mill."[2] In the years that followed the plant continued to expand, with the addition of a hardboard mill in 1951, a plate-wood mill in 1957, and a second hardboard mill in 1962. At its peak the industrial complex employed six hundred people. As Ed Fortin, the mill's long-time personnel director, noted in an interview, the Sturgeon Falls mill was in reality a "group of mills" under one roof. This is an apt description. These new production lines meant additional revenue for area farmers, who could now deliver poplar and other softwood as well as pulpwood to the mill's wood yard.

The immediate post-war period was a time of prosperity for the pulp and paper industry. It was Canada's leading sector in terms of gross and net production, and accounted for one-fifth of total exports. Pulp and paper was also Canada's third-largest employer. In 1948 there were 123 pulp and paper mills operating in Canada,

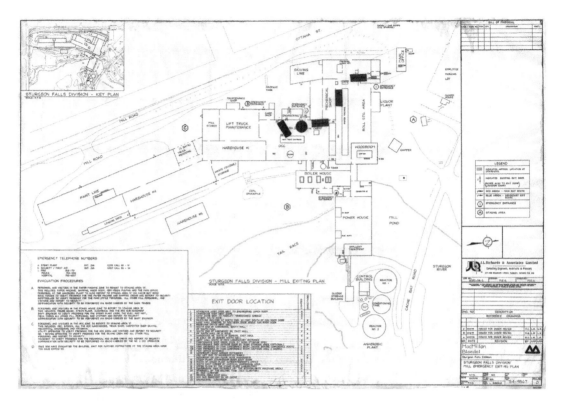

The emergency evacuation floor plan of the mill. This plan was salvaged from the closed plant as it was being dismantled. Courtesy of the author.

including forty-four in Ontario.[3] Almost all of these mills were located in rural areas or small towns. The Depression years had convinced paper companies such as Abitibi to diversify out of newsprint. "I am no longer going to place all my eggs in one basket," reported the company's president at the time.[4] The reopening of the Sturgeon Falls mill and its further diversification reflected this hard-earned knowledge. A construction crew of 230 men refurbished the mill, as its interior had to be gutted and the remaining paper machine restored and converted to corrugated medium.[5] One of the first to be hired was Ken Colquhoun, who recalled using a jackhammer to tear out the old equipment: "Bing, bam, boom. Oh, boy, that was noisy and loud. You come out of there and your ears were still rattling. And the dust! Oh, something terrible." His body still reverberated at the memory.

With this chapter we shift to the everyday working lives of mill workers and their bosses. None of these work-life memories, however, predates Ken Colquhoun's jackhammer, as most of our interviewees were hired during the 1960s and 1970s. By then the mill had already expanded or was on the downward slide as one production line after another fell silent: first platewood (1967), then #1 hardboard (1974–5), #2 hardboard (1991), and finally the corrugated paper machine itself (2002). As a unionized workplace, the "political apparatus of production" at the mill, to return to Bob Russell's idea, was designed to provide a measure of stability to employees and to the company as the occupational structure, hiring, job transfers, bumping rights, and layoff procedures were all regulated by the collective agreement.[6] Workers could move from one department to another depending on their seniority rights and skills accreditation. Work reorganization at the mill was thus a matter of negotiation between the employer and union members, but it was at best a "limited and unstable truce."[7]

The post-war diversification of production, and the subsequent discontinuance of product lines, required substantial physical alterations to the mill. New buildings were added in the 1950s and 1960s, including those at the south end near the highway, and entire sections of the mill later stood empty for years before being repurposed or converted into warehouse space. Superintendent Gerry Stevens recounted how he sometimes walked through the mothballed hardboard mill. "Had a lot of experiences come back to you," he mused. "You remember this, and you remember that." The physical changes to the mill were such that it was sometimes difficult for interviewees to locate their memories without some directional signage. Hence, memories of the paint line, which was tied to hardboard production of wood panelling, were often accompanied by a clarifying statement that it was located where the warehouses were now. We also saw overlapping memories, as areas converted to new uses.

It was nonetheless a relatively stable working-class formation for a half-century, as sons followed their fathers, uncles, and grandfathers into the mill. The resulting social structure and multigenerational intelligibility "gave the workplace a predictability that allowed a certain moral order to emerge and reproduce."[8] This chapter explores the making of a working-class subjectivity. The great British labour historian E.P. Thompson noted that class is a historical phenomenon that binds a group of people who share "the same categories of interest, social experiences, traditions and value systems."[9] Here I delve deeper into the oral accounts that form a collective biography of the mill's everyday operations. I begin with the interviewees' childhood memories of work and the forestry industry, their early entry into the workforce, and first being hired-in at the mill. Hiring stories were a hot topic during the interviews, as everyone had a story. The chapter then follows our interviewees into the mill, as they joined the labour pool, and ends with their finding their place in the mill. The seniority system governed much on the shop floor, including one's ability to bid for or hold onto a specific job. Mill work was not homogenous, but comprised a wide range of occupations and functions. Some workers sought the highest pay, others the most autonomy. As we will see, there was considerable mobility within the plant itself, laterally between departments and vertically up (and down) the employment ladder, sometimes into supervisory roles on the other side of the union-company divide. Above all this chapter reveals the social reproduction of class, as young men and a handful of women entered the mill's workforce and accommodated to its demands.

Work Culture

Class can be understood as a sensibility grounded in "experiences and practices" that reach all the way back into childhood.[10] These "deeply engrained dispositions," says Andrew Sayer, assert themselves in commonly shared values and ethical responsibilities.[11] Young people in Sturgeon Falls and the surrounding area grew up in and around the woods industry. Many farming families sold wood to the mill from their lands, and many smaller communities had a local sawmill. Those living along the Sturgeon River were also witness to the spectacle of thousands of logs being driven downriver each spring. At age sixteen or seventeen, the next generation of mill workers joined their fathers, uncles, or older brothers in the mill as summer students. Naturally this work experience gave them an inside track for permanent employment after high school or college.

The value of hard work was instilled early on. André Cartier's first paying job was the clearing of land with an axe. He was eleven years old and earned fifty cents an hour from his neighbour. "It was hard labour," he recalled. "So I knew what work is, from early age." Other interviewees began work at age fourteen or fifteen. Bruce Colquhoun, for example, used to shovel driveways for cash: "And then one year, the roof caved in at Levesque's [a major store in town]. Big snowstorm, a lot of snow, so we got calls, me and a buddy of mine: 'shovel my roof.' Well, we made a mint that year." In the summer, he cut grass. Though "it's kind of gory," he also dug graves for six years: "Dug graves by hand and got $10 a grave. Take you three, about three to four hours to dig a grave by hand. Ten dollars doesn't sound like much, but that's back in the late sixties, early seventies. So, that's a little less than three dollars an hour, about three bucks an hour. So that was pretty good." Those who grew up on a farm were also no strangers to hard work. In the summer months, Benny Haarsma did the haying, springtime the disking and seeding, and every morning he had to take the manure out.[12]

The woods industry loomed large in childhood memories. Hubert Gervais was born in the village of Field, fifteen miles upriver, in December 1939. His father had come to the area from Quebec on "the CP Rail tracks in a boxcar in the summertime. My grandfather rented a boxcar. Put everything in, horses at one end, and people, and the furniture at the other end of the boxcar."[13] Hubert's own childhood coincided with the end of an era for the "big lumber camps" on Crown-owned lands to the north, towards Temagami. The bush workers would go north in November or December, when the river was starting to freeze over. In the spring the loggers would come out of the woods and settle their accounts in Field. Gervais recalled: "Guys are fighting all over! One day deal and that was it. And then they'd bring the horses down." They would also drive the logs down the Sturgeon River. Gervais has vivid memories of the river drives:

> I remember when I was a kid, Field lumber would bring down 10,000 logs and leave them along Field ... so that they could start the sawmill. And then Gordon's, from Cache Bay, they'd bring down 125,000 logs. And then there was Smith, in Calendar, they'd bring down 125,000 logs. And they'd bring them down here, through the dam ... But Smith used to boom the logs, take a steamboat and take them across the back end of Lake Nipissing, and down Calendar Bay. Because you could see it, if you'd go to my aunt, I can still remember that, you'd see that steamer going across slowly with that bunch of boom logs. And then the Field lumber was the last one, you know. They'd bring some first and then they'd be the last one for the summer. Cut the logs.

When Gervais was fifteen years old, he started to work at Field Lumber, once his village's major employer.

There is a long history of layoff and industrial closure in the woods industry. Mike Lacroix, born in 1956, grew up in the community of Cache Bay, where there had been a big sawmill. Located a few minutes' drive west of Sturgeon Falls, Cache Bay used to be a bustling place with a couple of hotels, barber shops, a clothing store, a restaurant, even two or three food stores. "Now, well, there's nothing," he sighed. The Gordon sawmill shut in 1965, "and it went downhill from there." As there was no more work locally, people had to move away or find work nearby. Some of those displaced from the sawmill, including one of Lacroix's uncles, found work at the Sturgeon Falls mill. His father would work there, as did he. Henri Labelle's father was likewise displaced when the Cache Bay mill closed, as were other fathers and brothers.[14]

There was still a lot of blue-collar employment for young people in the area during the 1960s and 1970s. When Mike Lacroix quit school, his father told him if he was not going to go to school he had to find himself a job: "'You're not gonna lay

Hubert Gervais at the site of the demolished Sturgeon Falls mill, 2005. Photograph by David W. Lewis.

around in bed all day,' and I had a month to get a job, and if I didn't get a job, I was out by a month. He warned me. Today, I know that my mom wouldn't let it happen, but the old man said it, plain as day, 'you go out there and get yourself a job.'" So Lacroix contacted an uncle who had a plumbing and heating business, and he went to work for him, at sixteen years of age. He hated school, so paid work was "a thousand times better than school for me, because I was doing stuff, and he was showing me what to do."[15] Later Lacroix landed a job at Inco in Sudbury, working in the mines for three years until he was laid off. At this point in the interview, he noted that he had been "laid off quite a few times" in his life. He loved working at Inco: "Made a lot of good money, that's how I paid my house. Put all the money on my house, didn't take long to pay my house, I worked at it. Worked long hours and working bonus. It was good. It was a good job. But then we got hit with the layoff. But back then I was young enough, there was no problem. Within a couple of months, I had another job. Not even a couple of months."

Mike Lacroix got the job at the Sturgeon Falls mill because his father worked there: "It's my dad mostly that got me in there, and the old man, back then, the old man he said 'you know, I got you in there you know. You better not screw up or you'll have to deal with me.'" Mike had a lot of respect for his "old man" and for the family, so "you would have been damned if you would have dragged your feet on the job. The old man would have heard about it, he would have called, told us, 'what are you doing? If you don't want to work here, go on, get out, because there's somebody else who wants to work here, they'll come over and work.' The main thing is that you didn't want to make your dad look bad. Cause the old man, he put in a lot of hours."

Working the Land

At first the mill relied on wood cut on Crown lands assigned to it to the north. Abitibi lost this pulpwood concession in the 1930s, however, so when the corrugated paper operation reopened in 1947, it turned to area farmers, jobbers, and sawmill waste (wood chips) from the area.[16] Working as independent contractors during the winter months, farmer-loggers depended on the mill for their livelihood. The opening of the first hardboard mill a few years later was celebrated by area farmers, as the mill could now utilize any kind of wood, including poplar and other softwoods.[17] This meant additional revenue.

We know something about these operations thanks to Claude Lortie, one of our interviewees, who shared with us a box of documents that detailed the mill's relationship to area farmers during the 1940s and 1950s. His neighbour, an "old Irishman," had sold a garage to him on the condition that he empty it out. That is where he found the box of old mill records. Among other things, these salvaged documents provide a comprehensive understanding of where the mill got its wood between 1948 and 1963. The purchasing area covered a fifty-mile radius, and most of the contractors delivered fifteen to sixty cords of wood in a given year.[18] The mill was thus an important revenue source for area farmers. J.E. Gracie succinctly described the woods-purchasing system in a 1959 letter to a landowner who claimed that 150 cords of pulpwood had been cut from her land illegally and delivered to the Sturgeon Falls mill. Gracie replied: "Our company purchases pulpwood on a delivered to mill basis and our contractors supply us with crown clearance papers which show the Township, Concession, and Lot from which the pulpwood was cut."[19]

The recovered box also contained various versions of the mill's *Manual of Purchase Wood Procedure*, which enables us to track changes to the mill's policies governing these transactions. In 1952–3 Oscar Rivet was directed to acquire 15,000 cunits – or 18,750 cords; a cord of wood was measured as four feet high by four feet wide and eight feet long – of truckwood. As the term suggested, the wood would be delivered by truck, and the cost of unloading and switching would be factored into the price offered to suppliers. Accordingly Rivet wrote: "we must insure that there is no discrepancy in the prices paid to contractors who are equal distances from our mill. Nothing would wreck our program more quickly than this." To that end he directed his staff to prepare a list of the distances from Sturgeon Falls to specific towns and villages "in our purchase wood area." Delivery times were strictly controlled due to the limited yard space at the Sturgeon Falls mill.

Claude Lortie, 2005.
Photograph by David W. Lewis.

Not all of the contractors were farmers, however, as some jobbers had permits to cut pulpwood from Crown lands. J.J. Kearns, provincial sanitary inspector, reported on the camps associated with Pierre Aubin, of Field, who supplied the Sturgeon Falls mill. According to Kearns, Aubin hired local labour in groups of three or four, who then had to provide their own facilities:

> Each group of men builds a shack to live in and a barn to keep a horse. These buildings are built side by side with no attention given to ventilation, lighting, etc. Some have no floors or windows. All were in a filthy condition. In some cases, the stables were cleaner than the sleep-shacks. The poor type of buildings gave the men no incentive to keep clean. Manure, garbage and human excreta was evident beside each shack. In some cases, the garbage was in the buildings. Wash water was thrown outside the door. Medical care was nil. The men claim no deductions were made for the Ontario Hospital Commission. There was not first aid equipment. No provision was made for toilet accommodation. The men walk into the bush to eliminate their bowels ... A creek which would appear to be heavily polluted by the stables was the drinking water supply.[20]

The horrendous working conditions in these camps seem like something from an earlier era, not 1959. Kearne also wrote Pierre Aubin the following day, ordering him to provide new sleeping facilities with single-tiered bunks and clean bedding and to separate stables and cabins by at least two hundred feet. The work had to be done in a little over four weeks.

The Sturgeon Falls mill was also an important source of revenue for area saw-mills that sold it their woodchip waste. The wood buyers sought to purchase first from the closest sawmills and then farther afield.[21] One file in the box provided a comprehensive survey of sawmill waste in the area and the distance of each saw-mill from Sturgeon Falls. It noted, for example, that "Charlie French's mill," a small operation sixteen miles distant, got its wood from farmers and small producers. Leo Gervais's mill, twenty-four miles distant, was much larger, and D.J. Cockburn's mill at Emerald Lake was bigger still. Other small sawmills were located in the villages of Bonfield (45 miles away), Mattawa (70 miles), and Temagami (36 miles). In all, thirteen sawmills were listed in the waste survey.

The introduction of the chainsaw in the 1950s enabled farmers to cut more cords of wood faster.[22] This resulted in their writing to ask if they could deliver more wood than contracted. For example, Carl Backstrom from the Verner area apolo-gized for not providing the contracted wood the previous year, but went on to say that he had bought a chainsaw, "so can now 'go you one better' by selling you 150 cords this year." He wanted to cut 50 acres of his land for rough pasture for his 200 cattle and "plow and cultivate" the land the following spring.[23] In the meantime the Reverend W. Bradley of the Paroisse Sainte-Rose-de-Lima in River Valley wrote that, because the parish church had recently burned down, "I think I will have to handle the chain saw just like anybody else. It will do me good."[24] Abitibi refused these requests, however, due to an already full mill yard.

The challenges for farmer-contractors and other small contractors were legion, but a pressing issue was hauling the wood to the road. In April 1957 J.M. Becking of Powassan had intended to use an old army Bren Gun Carrier – a tracked fight-ing vehicle from the Second World War – to bring the pulp wood out. However, he later admitted: "I found that this machine was next to useless in the bush. I decided to stop operations until such time as I am able to purchase a small crawler tractor. With this I would be able to extend the present road into the bush and truck the pulp right out of the bush, instead of loading it on sleighs or wagon."[25] Taken as a whole, the correspondence files reveal the economic importance of the mill for area farmers. Timely delivery was key, as contracts could be revoked or cut back by the company.

Many of the children of these private wood suppliers would later go to work in the mill itself. Marc Côté, who was born in 1942 and rose up the ranks to become one of the few francophone superintendents in the mill, came from Verner, to the west of Sturgeon Falls in the heart of the agricultural area of Nipissing. He noted with pride that his great-grandfather was the "first one in Verner. He came off the train when the railroad went through here. He was working there. And in those days, you could get a farm if you'd farm so many acres, so he had three sons and he bought a farm in Verner and he continued working on the railroad, [and] left his sons here to start cutting the trees and get everything ready."[26] Later he "quit the railroad and came back down here. And the hotel in Verner was owned and operated in the beginning by my grandfather." He noted that the mill had always been a big influence on the area, but its importance grew with improved roads in the 1950s. People in Verner and other outlying villages could now commute to their jobs in the mill itself.

Hiring Stories

Pulp and paper workers occupied a "privileged economic position" in Northern Ontario, as they were among the highest-paid manual workers in the region and usually worked year-round.[27] Ontario's pulp and paper industry was unionized early on, and industry-wide pattern bargaining prevailed in the immediate postwar decades. This worked to the advantage of Sturgeon Falls mill workers, as their wages were pegged to the higher pay scale then prevailing in newsprint production, rather than to the lower wages found in mills producing other wood products. The Sturgeon Falls mill offered the highest wage rates and best working conditions in the area for blue-collar men. Jobs in the mill were finely divided and situated within detailed job ladders, as set out in the collective agreement.[28] Seniority governed much on the shop floor, limiting the arbitrary power of the foreman or superintendent.

Everyone we spoke to had a hiring story to share. There was none of the reticence that sometimes accompanied discussion of shop-floor divisions or linguistic tensions. We got a good overview of the company's hiring practices from our interviews with Ed Fortin, who served as the mill's personnel manager from 1962 until his retirement in 1989, and his assistant, Ruth Thompson. Born in Sturgeon Falls in 1924, Fortin was something of a rarity in management: a locally rooted manager and a francophone. "Nobody could fire a person unless I approved it," he recalled. To get a job at the mill, they first had to submit an application. Ruth Thompson explained the standard procedure: "When it came time to hire, I would bring out the recent applications and I'd put them on Fortin's desk. Mr Fortin, he would look them over and then he'd go pick out the ones that [he] figured that he would like. Then I would call them in and he'd interview them." Sometimes people would stubbornly drop by. Thompson recalled one man who kept "coming back and coming back and we had a little waiting room and he'd sit there and sit there and finally Mr Fortin said one day, 'Hire that moonfaced guy, I'm tired of looking at him!' So, it just goes to show you that if you keep at something, you're going to get someplace."[29]

For many years the mill had a formal policy of hiring the children of mill employees for student summer employment. It was done on the basis of the mill seniority of their father or mother, and the educational level of the student. No distinction was made among the seniority of unionized workers, salaried staff, or the mill manager himself. Ed Fortin originally came up with the idea, he explained, because he "always hated to play God in placement of students." He realized that student hiring was a potentially explosive issue, as "these were all children of employees." So the question became how to decide whom to hire first. Then one day he had an epiphany: "And, you know, it came to mind one time, why don't you use the parent's seniority for the placements? So, I did! It was easy after that, I didn't have to play God. I'd let my secretary do most of the work ... Then there were no hard feelings, no favouritism, nothing. I have children as well. I had a son that worked at the plant. I had one that worked, a number of years ago, in the offices. But I had one in the plant proper. And he had to go on the basis of my seniority. And he wasn't the first one. There were people hired there before me! You see what I mean? And that showed the fairness."

Naturally the student employment policy was wildly popular in the mill itself. It benefited long-service managers such as Gerry Stevens, three of whose children worked in the plant as students. It also benefited the sons and daughters of hourly paid mill workers, who could earn union wages in the summer months – enough to buy a car or go to college or university. As Marc Côté explained: "One nice thing about the mill, in the summer time we used to hire students. And if your kid got a job at the mill, he could just about ... pay his complete year of university or college with what he made in two and a half months. So, when you're living at Dad's house and you don't have any expenses, your dad drives you to the mill, and ... you watch your money, you get paid good wages ... And if it went well you got a job there, depending on your dad's seniority and the department that you worked in ... It worked out; it worked really well. Daughters had jobs too." That said, high school students were required to return to school in September. Ed Fortin recalled one student who did not want to go back afterwards, and so he "told him that he had to go back to school. And, [if not], he couldn't come and ask me for a job, because the rules were there and we applied them strictly and if we allowed him we would have to allow others." Laughing at the memory, Fortin noted that this particular fellow ended up being a high school teacher. The great downside of this policy of course was that the hiring policy effectively shut others out of the mill. Ruth Thompson recalled that "[w]e had a little bit of trouble with the town sometimes, they were mad because we'd only hire sons of employees."

The advantage to mill families did not end there, as student employees had the inside track for permanent employment, too. "I guess we did prefer more or less sons of employees before anybody else," recalled Ruth Thompson. They had work experience and someone to vouch for them. Thompson also noted that they "hired locally rather than someone out of town unless we were hiring trades people. If we were hiring trades people, then we would take them wherever we could get them." Many production workers thus began as summer students and literally graduated to full-time employment at the end of grade 12. Bruce Colquhoun got in at the mill in 1973: "October 22nd, '73." He had already worked there as a summer student because "my dad worked there." He was there ever after. Colquhoun explained how it worked: "[I]f your father, parent, worked there you could work in the summer or weekends as a student. So I worked there for a year and a half, off and on, you know, weekends and in the summer as a student. And then the spring of '73, when I got out of high school, I went to the mill and applied. And they said they weren't hiring. So I looked around. It was getting hard. I was in Toronto at the time. And my mother called when I was at my cousin's place … it was a Friday. She said, 'the mill called, they want you to start Monday.' Okay. So I grabbed a bus and went back home and started from there. Two days after my nineteenth birthday."

For the sons or younger brothers of mill workers, the hiring process was often swift and applications were little more than a formality. Marc Côté, for example, learned his trade of machinist in Sudbury before finding employment at the mill. His father already worked there and, as he explains it, the company "favoured sons and daughters of employees – they would get first crack. So I went in there in 1962." Hired in 1974, Raymond Lortie similarly benefited from the fact that his father, grandfather and two brothers worked there. Much could be forgiven if you had a close relative in the plant. "I had long hair because I was a hippie then," recalled Henri Labelle. He had already lost jobs because of how he looked, relating a story of when he was hired on the phone as a busboy: "I went there and started to fill up all my tables. And then one guy comes to me and says, 'who are you?' I said, 'I'm the busboy.' And I always had this [points to his mustache]. He says, 'you're not a busboy here.' I said, 'I was hired.' He said, 'not with that long hair.'" Shortly after this incident, he heard that the mill was hiring. Three days later he started to work there. Labelle figured he'd been hired-on because his brother had worked there for a decade and never missed a shift. He was a "good, good, good guy," Labelle emphasized with a smile.

Abitibi summer student Archie
Flora (seated), 1954. Courtesy of West
Nipissing Public Library.

Those applying from outside sometimes had a tougher time of it. Many spoke
of family, friends, or neighbours who helped get them in. It was a small town, so
these kinds of connections were commonplace. Merna Nesbitt, for example, used
to babysit for the man across the road who was the purchasing agent at the mill.
After finishing high school, he offered her a job at the mill. "I was very fortunate
to get into the mill," she recalled. She worked there for about three years, but "my
daughter was coming so I quit work." Then, in 1965, she put in an application and
was interviewed and "got the job again." She was there twenty-eight years. There
were few strangers in Sturgeon Falls. Even so, the stories were sometimes quite
humorous. When asked how he got hired-on, André Cartier smiled: "Honestly?"
Yes, honestly, Kristen O'Hare smiled back. "I met and started going out with the
human resource's daughter," he laughed. Ed Fortin later became his father-in-law.
This was a joke, of course, and Cartier got more serious and noted that his father
also worked there. It was reason enough.

Other newcomers to the mill got hired through sheer persistence. John Dillon
had heard the mill was hiring, so he went there every morning for two weeks, "and I
was sitting there when the boss came in. I think he got tired of seeing me and hired
me!" With a smile, he then admitted that the reason he went there every morning
was because his mother "got me up and made me go!"[30] As he explained: "It was
different in those days because you didn't stay at home and live with your parents,
for nothing. You had to get out there and work, and if you weren't going to go to
school then you better get a job." Hubert Gervais likewise called in on the mill one

or two times a week, asking "'any opening yet? Any opening yet?' So, I guess [the manager] was sort of tired of hearing my voice. So, he says, 'would you take office boy for two weeks?' I said, 'sure. Why not?' Gotta start someplace. So I went in, I was office boy." As office boy, he had to deliver mail to some twenty superintendents at eleven o'clock and again at one o'clock and four o'clock. "So, you'd be walking four to five miles, at least, a day." Gervais worked that job for two weeks, and went home: "After the weekend, Eddie Fortin called me. He says, 'you want to work downstairs?' I says, 'where?' He says, 'the coalbin.' Oh, I says, 'you gotta start someplace.' Started in the coalbin. And then, I stayed there for two days. Then he moved me over to … I was in the labour pool, so I moved all over. And the next day, well, I'd come in, he'd say 'oh, Gervais, you go and work over there,' and 'Blo, you go work over there,' and 'Harvey, you go work the other place.' So, that's how I started." One wonders if Hubert Gervais could have been the "moonfaced" job-seeker Ruth Thompson mentioned earlier.

In sharing these stories, interviewees were telling us that nothing was given to them. Mostly, however, incoming mill workers were just plain lucky. The hiring of full-time employees happened in "spurts," remembered Ruth Thompson. Sometimes they hired twenty people in a single day, or just one or two in a month. Marcel Boudreau got the call from the mill the day before his birthday: "they called me in and had a meeting. There was about fourteen of us. We all thought we were going in for interviews. And they gave us all hard hats and they took us for a tour of the mill, and when we were done the tour somebody asked, 'well, how many of us are you hiring?' I mean, there's a whole bunch of us here. And the fella at the time was Ed Fortin, and he said, 'well, you're all hired.' And a couple of the guys started to work right away … And the rest of us started the week after."

Several others also had to start abruptly. Percy Allary was hired on the spot: "And I applied, actually, I filled out my form at noon hour and I could have started work at four o'clock that day. But I was working, at the time, part time for the Brewer's Retail. And I was scheduled to work Friday night, so I couldn't. I said, 'I'll start graveyard.' So I worked graveyard that night. I left the beer store at nine o'clock and I went over there at twelve and worked graveyard. And that's where I started." Work began with a similar flurry for Randy Restoule. When the mill called, he had to rush back to Sturgeon Falls from London, Ontario, an eight-hour drive: "I left on a Friday night, late, around midnight or so, travelled all night, I came into Sturgeon at seven or eight o'clock in the morning and I slept for a couple of hours and my first shift was at three o'clock. [laughs] So that's how easy it was, no interview, I only signed whatever I had to sign the following week." That first shift was "a little scary" but he was young then.

One of the most detailed hiring stories came from Denis MacGregor, who worked for an underwater cement operation repairing the mill dam before being hired on at the mill itself. He noted that the outfit worked at sites across North America, including at the Hoover Dam in Nevada. MacGregor was local to Sturgeon Falls, and was hired on to assist the company's diver, a man named Pete. The story speaks to the value of hard work and MacGegor's attachment to the area. Notice his extensive use of direct speech to tell the story. It can be divided into two parts, with the first focused on his decision to remain in Sturgeon Falls:

So I went to work for them for the summer. And that's how I got in the mill. I never applied to the mill. My boss, he was a seventy-years-old guy … Anyway, at the end of the job, … it was late September, he told me, he says, "we're going to the Hoover Dam." Pete, the diver, great big hunk of a guy, huge – I mean his shoulders were one and a half the size of mine – and 6 foot 4. Anyway, great big guy, with an accent and he told me, he says, "Pete likes you, as a diver tender," and that's what I was doing, I was taking care of him. Suit him up in the morning, and put the bell, it was the great big bell thing there, suit him up and then, and with his accent, we had a two-way radio and at the beginning he'd swear at me because I didn't understand him. And it's like talking into a tin can. The radios were really bad … He told me, he says, "Pete really likes you," he says. "Would you like to follow us?" I says, "Well, what do you need?" "Well," he says, 'you'd become Pete's diver tender, you'd be his tender from now on as long as you want. Wherever Pete goes you go." I said, "well, will I always be with you?" He says, "Oh no, Pete takes contracts with all kinds of companies. But," he says, "mostly he's with us." I said, "Well, where are you going?" He says, "Well, we're going to the Hoover Dam." He says, "What you do there, is you're the diver tender." He says, "Depending on how deep the diver goes, he could work for three hours or four hours. And his eight hours are done. Well," he says, "you get the same hours as he does. So if you work four hours, and he can't anymore, that's what the law prescribes. You get your eight hours as a diver tender, and then you can go on the site for four more hours as a labourer. So," he says, "you can make money coming out of your [unclear]." But every night these guys couldn't finish work. They'd run to the hotel. Take a shower, and head for the hotel. And then I said, "Oh no. That's not for me." Don't get me wrong, I used to have a drink, I used to have a good drink. Used to be fun, you know? But eight hours of work, and then eight hours at the bar? … Anyway, he asked me if I wanted to go with him. Finally I told him, "No, it wasn't for me." He asked then, "Well, what would you rather do?" "Well," I says, "to tell you the truth, I finished my grade 12, I had a half a year of college. Never finished that, because they sort of discouraged us back then. If you don't have 85 you may as well quit …" So he told me, he says, "What would you do?" I says, "Well, with the education I have" – and back then, grade 12, well, holy smokes, you could get any job! – "Well, to tell you the truth" – you know, I was getting a little wiser, I was twenty at the time. Wiser, and older. I said, "You know, I like living here and" – well, I didn't have the house yet. I had a girlfriend. Decided, you know, "to tell you the truth, been talking to the guys at the mill, this and that, and the other thing you know I'd really like to work at the mill." "Oh yeah, well that's fine. Well, if you change your mind let me know."

With this, Denis MacGregor decided that his future rested in Sturgeon Falls. He was clearly valued by both Pete and the underwater cement company. He was a good worker. It is a great story, revealing one of life's forks in the road that make us wonder "what if?" Yet this story is not a lament for the road not taken, but a vote of confidence in his subsequent life as a mill worker. MacGregor could have left Sturgeon Falls and travelled, but he *chose* to stay. In the second part of the same story, we hear how he found himself working at the mill itself:

So, late September, early October came along, and the guys were leaving and we shook hands and I had a good time, "and if ever you're looking for a job, Denis, you know, here's my card …" Okay, fine. So I farted around for a couple of weeks. Next thing you know, Ruth called me from the mill. Ruth Thompson … She says, "Okay, we need you next Saturday, the 11th of November, for a graveyard shift." And I'm going, "Okay, all right." You know? So, that was it … Anyway, I worked a couple weeks before I finally said to somebody, "I need a job here." "Well, I filled out this application and this and that." "I never filled out an application." "What the hell, how'd you get a job?" Well, everybody said go see Ruth, she'll tell you. So finally I said, "Well, I guess I have to go up." I didn't want to sort of rock the boat. Well, I got a job – I mean, if I go up there and she says, "What do you mean you didn't fill out, like, you don't work here anymore!" … I went up and I said, "You know, I know you called me, and I really like what I 'm doing, and I don't want to lose my job" – because, hey, I was making money – and I said, "I never applied here." And she said, "That's fine, I have your application here." So just at the time, Mr Fortin came up. I knew him as Ed, but he was my boss, and it was, you know, business, so I said, "Mr Fortin." "Oh, come on in here." I said, "How'd I get a job here?" "Oh," he says, "your foreman Roddy," he says. "He gave me a glowing report on your work and this and that. He says that he offered you a really good-paying job going to the States and this and that, he said you really didn't want to go, all you wanted to do was work at the mill." … So that's how I got in the mill. A long story, but just telling you that's how I got in the mill.

All of these stories are grounded, to varying degrees, in notions of respectable manhood. Respect was earned through strength, shop-floor knowledge, and sheer persistence.

To a person, mill workers pinpointed the year, month, and day they were officially hired – one of the few dates to surface in the interviews. This speaks to its importance in a unionized environment. Generally, production workers spoke strongly in favour of seniority as the one way to counter the arbitrary decisions of their bosses. For them, the alternative was favouritism. The claim to seniority became less clear, however, when more than one person was hired on the same day. When André Cartier mentioned that he was one of ten people hired on the same day in 1970, interviewer Kristen O'Hare asked where he was placed on the seniority list. "I remember that – number four," he quickly replied. "Good question – you're sharp," he added. Ron Demers was likewise hired with ten or fifteen others on a single day, so, "on the seniority list, we would be very, very close." As he explained, no two people could have the same seniority:

> You fell in place on the sheet. They had to be in order on the sheet. You had to have a number. And if they hired ten people the same day, somebody had to be number one, somebody had to be number ten, depending on what time they hired you. If they gave you the interview first, they said, "you're hired," then they gave me an interview, said, "you're hired" – that would be one, two, three. [pause] We liked to think that it was done that way and that no preferential treatment was given to anybody. [chuckle] But it didn't really matter at that time. When you were hired, you were hired. You were just so happy to get a job. You were just out of high school or college, or university, and you get a job, and a good-paying job, too. Benefits. So you would satisfy yourself with that, knowing that eventually you would become a full-time employee.

Not surprisingly those who ended up at the bottom of that day's list were the most likely to raise this in an interview. There was a lot at stake. Thirty-five years later, Henri Labelle could still name the five others hired with him on 20 August 1971, as they were located just above him on the seniority list. Asked if this came back to haunt him, Bruce Colquhoun replied with a succinct "yep." The others "worked a little more than I did. Not much. The guy right in front of me he worked maybe a few shifts more than I did in a month. But the guy who was the first one of that day worked a lot more." Bruce Colquhoun later regretted being "too slow to get there" that day. "If I'd got there a little faster I wouldn't have been the last one."

I explore the gendered division of labour in the mill in Chapter 5, but it is important to note here that women were largely confined to the mill offices. They did not hire women for jobs in the "plant proper" in the post-war period, noted Ed Fortin. This practice began to change in the mid-1970s, however, as legislation made it illegal to sex-type jobs. In our interview, Fortin recalled the day when the daughter of the local union president came in for a job interview. "I told her that we weren't hiring," as they weren't at the moment. But he could tell that she didn't really want to work there anyway, and that her father had probably "put her up" to it to test the company. "He just wanted to see what my reaction would be," Fortin smiled. A handful of women eventually did find a place on the shop floor. Marcel Boudreau's sister was hired in the 1980s, and worked there for three years before deciding it wasn't for her. She was, he thinks, the third or fourth woman hired in production. "It was fun having my sister in the mill. You know, something different. None of my brothers wanted to work there." Like so many women who entered industrial work-places at the tail end of the post-war boom, this new generation of mill-working women did not have sufficient seniority to survive the layoffs to come.

Pooled Labour

When Mike Lacroix entered the mill, it was a thriving place with a large work-force: "There were a lot of people back then. Three shifts, full pin." His memories of a time when the mill was filled with noise and activity, of course, contrast with what happened later, as the mill was gradually emptied and closed altogether. This knowledge no doubt coloured Lacroix's recollections, as it did those of everyone we interviewed. Unless they were in the skilled trades or the office, everyone started out in the mill's labour pool. As Karen Beaudette explained, the labour pool served as a "holding pot" that "everybody had to go through." These were the ones, she added, "who had to pull the doubles and got called in at the last minute." They were then placed in specific jobs posted internally on the basis of seniority. So the mill never hired someone from outside to be the fifth hand on the paper machine or for other production jobs at the bottom rung of the occupational ladder. Produc-tion fluctuated, particularly in the hardboard and platewood mills, so the labour demand was not the same year-round. The labour pool thus gave management con-siderable flexibility in terms of employment levels and a flexible workforce trained for a variety of jobs. It also gave incoming workers a chance to try out different jobs, giving them a good sense of where they wanted to be over the long term.

Once hired into the labour pool, mill workers were not guaranteed their forty hours a week or even steady work. As Marcel Boudreau explained, they were called up on the basis of seniority: "It was a situation where, if the work was there, you worked, and if there wasn't work, well, you went home until there was work. And

I worked about a month and then was laid off. But, I mean, I still had a job. It's not like I got to go look for another job. It was work a shift or two here and there, and then went on unemployment. So there was always a cheque coming in every two weeks." Individual experiences therefore varied from one interview to the next, depending in large part on when the individual was hired. As the mill's workforce contracted, low-seniority workers were pushed out or took longer to be placed in a department. Boudreau was in the pool for three years, Henri Labelle for ten years. A few people chose to stay in the pool for their entire working lives, as it was one way the mill accommodated people who couldn't work afternoons or couldn't work shifts for medical reasons.

Ron Demers started as a general labourer "like everybody else" and for the first five or six years he was on call. He went "where they put you."[31] According to Demers, "[t]hey could call at three o'clock and say, 'be at work at four.' Or they could call you at five and say 'be here in fifteen minutes' if you were close enough to the mill. So that's how it worked for a very long period of time. If you were lucky enough, you would get into a department. You would have to apply for a job posting within and you would get in, if you had the seniority. And everything was based on seniority." Marc Côté agreed with this assessment. While on relief, "sometimes you wouldn't get a call. Then you'd work a week, solid." He remembered working "on and off" during the winter months, but working three or four days a week steadily in the spring and summer. But it still made financial sense, as "you made more at the mill in two days than you made anywhere else in town for a week."

Asked what departments he worked in over his career, Percy Allary replied quizzically, "What departments? Well, labour pool. I worked in the hardboard process for a number of years. Then I went to the paper machine for a number of years." He ended in the OCC (old corrugated cardboard) recycling plant. He worked "every shift: days, afternoons, nights. And at the end we went to twelve-hour shifts." Almost to a person, mill workers told us they worked "all over the mill." Raymond Marcoux bounced "from one department to another," and never knew where he would be from one week to the next. "You didn't know," he laughed: "Sometimes you're one day here, one day there – you'd go from starting the week on a day shift and finish the week on night shift." It was similar for others. Sometimes Percy Allary got only two shifts per week, "then you'd get lucky and get a full week in. Especially during the hunt season, a lot of guys took their holidays. So we were the low guys on the totem pole, so we had to wait."

In the beginning a lot of manual work was required to run the mill. Over time, automation and mechanization made many of these jobs redundant. Ken Colquhoun's department would cook the wood, starting off with one keg, a tub of coke, and a rotary digester. They ran that for a number of years before management introduced a continuous cooker. "It was fifty feet high," Ken recalled. "Chips come in off the top, mixed with black liquor, go up there and down the top, and they'd fall in down there fifty feet, and go through a defibrator, and the defibrator would break it up into a mash and everything, and then it was washed and everything, basically, turned into pulp." At this point, I asked if there were any chemicals. "Oh, lots of chemicals," he replied:

> Oh, yes, the chemical was there to start with. We used a lot of, basically, soda ash and I forget what the black liquor was, at the time. I worked there so long, I can't remember it. I know I made liquor there for twenty years. I was the guy making it. It was soda ash, and sodium sulphide. That was it. Before we went to the new cooker. I remember, fifteen bags of sodium sulphide and eight bags of soda ash. And you had to make one batch for every digester that you loaded. And we loaded up seven of them a shift. They were all a hundred pounds. The soda ash was bulky, but it was the easiest one to handle. The goddamn sodium sulphide, it was, you know, soft and hard to hold onto, bulky as hell. But we handled it. I can't say that I enjoyed part of it then, because it was hard work.

Given the uncertainty and the daily pressure of being on call, Raymond Marcoux noted that most people didn't want to stay in the labour pool for any longer than they had to. "It was hard to plan anything," he said. Asked about why people were willing to be on call for so long, Ron Demers replied:

> I don't think it's a matter of being willing. It's just a matter of being there. Being hired. And accepting that that's the way it was – that's the way things happened. If you didn't like it – well. A lot of people got in trouble, too, because they weren't available for work. They would go out and get a part-time job someplace else. Or they would go out with their family. And if they called them and they weren't at home, they would be expected to go into the office soon after and be called upon to explain why they weren't. And if they missed too many calls, well, they were reported back to employment insurance, and they would have been terminated.

If they were young, they were not so worried about getting another job. The high wages made it all worthwhile. Besides, the company continued to pay their benefits and health care regardless.

Even so, mill work was sometimes challenging to young workers unaccustomed to shift work or an industrial environment. In the beginning, their bodies ached.

Bruce Colquhoun recalled his first day on the job: "I got called in, me and another guy, both students. We had to show up at the mill at four o'clock." They were directed towards the North Yard, where they piled all the logs. He told us what they had to do that first shift:

> They used to put the logs on this big conveyor and bring it across to the chipper, grind it down to chips. And on the cable that would bring the logs, they had these big buttons like [shows their size with his hands]. They're bolted together on the cable so they could grab the log as it helped pull the logs up. You couldn't just have it bare cable. We had to take all of those buttons off. The millwright took all of those off. He would hand them down to my buddy, Ricky Benoit. Ricky would hand them down to me, [and] we would clean a whole bunch of them. We'd put a pile there, and then Ricky'd jump down, we'd clean all the dirt and stuff off of that. And then Ricky'd get back up and I'd hand them over my head to him, he'd hand them over his head to the millwright. And we worked until two o'clock in the morning. By the end, we're going [grunts], these are solid steel, you know. We were just young, young lads. Seventeen years old. So all that steel, at the end we could hardly lift it up to the next guy. He'd bend down and pick it up and he could hardly bend up and lift it up to the next guy. That was a long night. But we had fun. And then we got called in again the next morning to go work in the yard and clear out some stuff in the yard, down in the conveyor. It's called a yard, but downstairs where they have the shakers and that, and the screens, to screen out all the junk and all that. All the sawdust falls on the floor, we had to clean that out. We worked quite a bit. But, we got along good. And that was one shift I'll never forget … Oh, we were so sore the next morning. We were [chuckle]. When they called us at eight o'clock in the morning, 'come on in and help clean up in the yard,' [we] got out of bed, and it was, "oh, my God."

Industrial work was not for everyone, and many interviewees spoke of brothers and sisters who left the mill because they did not like it. At first, Bruce Colquhoun told himself that he was only going to stay there for a year or two, "until I can find something better." Smiling, he continued: "But twenty-nine years later I was still there. It went fast." Asked what he liked most about working in the mill, he replied, "The money, the people. I had friends working there, and friends I got along with, real good. And the money was good." Gradually he got "used to it, I guess because it was so new, and I'm outside all the time, shovelling driveways, digging graves, whatever, I'm outside. And now, I'm stuck in a factory. It took a while to get used to. But I got the hang of it."

Henri Labelle inside the chipper building as the mill was being dismantled, 2004. Photograph by David W. Lewis.

Some found it more difficult than others to adjust to industrial work discipline. Sometimes this restlessness resulted in conflict on the shop floor as young workers challenged work rules and the authority of their supervisors. The interview with Henri Labelle revealed this generational confrontation. "I got days off because I got insubordinate," he recalled. "I was very cocky then, too." Whereas his brother was "very, very good. Me, I got eleven days off in the first year of work. I was charged with insubordination, not doing my job, reading on the job, sleeping on the job. I was a bad boy." Asked if this was an eleven-day suspension, all at once, Labelle replied that it was not:

The first time I got caught, I think I was in the fabricating. I can't recall if the pulping was first, or that one there. I found it was unfair, because it wasn't even my job.

I was a labourer, not a truck driver. The truck driver was sleeping, but the operator – I think the operator didn't like me. And the lift was ready to take out, he couldn't run the machine anymore. And he knew where I was. So he called the foreman in. And it just happened, if I would have woke up three minutes earlier, he wouldn't have caught me. I was getting up. And then the foreman came in. He says, "You want to go to bed? Go home." I said, "Sure. I don't mind." I was young, and all full of vinegar. So, no, I think then they gave me three days off for that. Then they put me in the fabricating, in the pulping. And I did not get along with the superintendent … We could be mixing twenty bags, then I would have had thirty, forty minutes to spare before I go back at it. And I used to go see the guy in the lab. And the superintendent didn't like that, he said, "You're supposed to stay in your department." But the lab is only six feet away from the department … So, we didn't start on the right foot. When I was doing the cleanup, I still remember … I made all piles. I was sweeping, making a pile, sweeping, make a pile, sweeping. Then I went to see, oh god, the screen maker. And I started to talk. And then there was a *Playboy*. So I looked at the *Playboy*. And then the super came down and he saw all the piles. And, you know, like, this is an eight-hour shift – you can only sweep for so much, you can't sweep for eight. So then now, when he caught me, I'm reading. Then that's when not doing my job came in, when they saw my piles, that's where not doing my work came on. And then we had a rumble, about six o'clock in the morning, I had enough and ba-pa-pa-pa, and I opened my mouth and told him off. So then, if I would have shut my mouth then, nothing would have happened. But then I was talking with an operator, and he says, "Maybe you should go see Ed Fortin and tell him," and if "you don't want to work in this department anymore, because you're going to be losing your job." So, I did. That opened a ball of wax. Mr [his supervisor] would have never said nothing. But now that Ed talked with him, "What's going on with him?" Then all this came out. So I went to court.

Court?

Well, when you do that you have to go in front of Ed Fortin and the superintendent. It's like a grievance, it's an internal thing. We went to court. And then my shop steward didn't say nothing. And I was getting blasted. So, I blasted them back. That's when I was charged. But after that I was clean. After that first year, it was just the learning process. After that I was clean.

Shift work was also a shock to their bodies. Entire families had to adapt. Pierre and Jane Hardy were interviewed together for this project. Pierre noted that he worked all three shifts at the mill: "Eight to four, four to twelve, and twelve to eight. But the last few years we were working twelve-hour shifts. From seven in the morning, seven at night, seven at night 'til seven in the morning. That was hard." They would work two nights, for example, then have two days off. Then work three days, then three days off. "But it was hard. I found the twelve-hour shift harder than the eight-hour shift." Jane concurred, noting that it affected the family most when the children were younger: "Because, you know, when Dad was sleeping, well, you tried to be quiet and sometimes the more you try to be quiet the louder you got. But there always seemed to be some sort of distraction around when he was trying to sleep. Whether it be the dog barking or something going on around. And, you know, he's such a light sleeper that he would be up early. He'd go to bed at 7:30, and … most of the time, he's up before lunch … It really disrupted his sleep patterns." It also made it difficult for her to work outside the home, as his hours kept changing. She therefore started up her own accounting business in the home: "I found that was really convenient with his shifts. And then the kids were growing up … so it kind of worked out well."

Not surprisingly those occupations in the plant that were "steady days" appealed to incoming workers. "I was very happy in the yard because it was days all the time, no shift work," Randy Restoule recalled. Frank Gerbasi, born in North Bay in 1935, noted that he left his previous job because of the shift work. "It didn't agree with me," he recalled. "Some people love shift work. But me, I think if I had stayed there much longer I wouldn't be alive today, because I weighed about 105 pounds when I worked there. And the shift work was just too hard on me … and my system was always trying to catch up."[32] Gerbasi left and went to work in the maintenance department at the Sturgeon Falls mill, on steady days. Soon thereafter his weight bounced back to 135 pounds.

Only a handful of our interviewees actually preferred shift work. The advantage for Harold Stewart was that he could get more work done on his farm than he could on steady days. With the four-to-twelve shift, he'd come home at eleven o'clock at night, sleep until morning and then "work at home." Others liked it when the mill moved to twelve-hour shifts from eight hours. "When we went on twelve-hour shifts," recalled Marcel Boudreau, "it was like I started a new job. The most I was going to work was three days in a row. And it was always a Friday, Saturday, Sunday. And the rest of the time was two days on, two days off. It was terrific." The timing and duration of work were hence an integral part of people's decisions about where to work in the mill, as industrial work schedules varied considerably under the same roof.

The control room in the closed mill. Photograph by David W. Lewis.

Finding One's Place

Mill workers went through most of the departments during their career as they worked their way up the occupational ladder and into positions that most suited them. "There was a lot of migration between departments except for the ones that were specialized," recalled superintendent Gerry Stevens.[33] You needed a special "ticket," or qualification, for example, to work in the steam plant. The skilled trades were also restricted. Otherwise it was a criss-crossing "migration" from one department to another. Like everybody else, Ron Demers moved from one posting to the next on his way up. "You would try to better yourself, not just workwise, but moneywise, and try to move up the ranks." Workers always had the option, however, to stay where they were, "but along with that there was a little less pay, maybe a few less shifts."

Workers could bid on job openings as they came up. Generally it went by seniority. "There was a union," noted Percy Allary, "so you had to go by the union rules." Mill-wide seniority enabled you to get into a department, but once inside there was also departmental seniority. "See," Pierre Hardy told us, "they had a system at the mill they called postings. And the way it worked, they had a posting, [and] they posted the job on the wall there. It usually was for a week. And the senior men would usually get it. The senior man would bid on it, and he would probably end up with it." As Ron Demers explained, this was a "union mill where seniority prevails – or should have prevailed at most times." There were exceptions, according to Demers: "Unless he had a whole pile of black marks against him, then they would deny him the posting. Then the union would get involved and question it and grieve it – the whole process."

The interviews revealed a variety of personal trajectories through the workplace, as workers sought more money or more fulfilling work. If "somebody wanted the money," noted Henri Labelle, the "paper machine was the place to go." There was considerably more downtime in the hardboard mill, as "you don't sell siding in the wintertime." Marcel Boudreau, who had a post on the paper machine, agreed. But it was often stressful tending the machine, so "most guys didn't want to work [there] ... Working on a paper machine wasn't for everyone. Not everybody could do it." Others searched for positions where they had more autonomy, or the freedom to move around the mill during their shift. André Cartier started off on the paint line, where he packaged wood siding panels that had just been painted. "So, what I had to do," he explained, was to work with "boxes" of sixteen-foot siding, stacked eight planks high, and secure them with glue and staples. Decades later he could still make the remembered repetitive hand movements required for that first job, saying: "That was my first job. So, wasn't too hard." After the paint line, Cartier worked in fabrication, loading the siding onto trucks. He liked this job because he could control the pace of his work to a greater degree. A work gang would load the transports together: "Once those three transports were loaded, there is no more loading, we got a little time off and ... one [person] was cooking while the other one worked, then we stopped, had a big meal. We all got along, and that was a good part of the work."

Bruce Colquhoun was another who worked "all over the place": on the paint line, where they painted the hardboard siding, and then in the hardboard plant, where they made the board itself. But in December 1974 they shut down "half the hardboard," so he was laid off for "four hundred and some days. Got rehired, again." The only place he did not work was on the paper machine. "I didn't want to either. It's too fast. The machine runs you, eh? You don't run it, it runs you." He enjoyed moving around, so "you're not stuck in the same place all the time. You get to go different places. And a different job all the time." Eventually, a posting for an oiler came up, so his father said, "Apply for the oiler." "I said, 'Dad, I'm off. I'm on sick leave.' He said, 'Doesn't matter. Apply.' So, I applied and I got it. And I was oiler for the last twenty [years] … I loved that job." As an oiler Bruce Colquhoun oiled and greased all the machinery in the mill. At one time there had been an oiler in the hardboard, another for the paper machine, and a third in the yard. But one department after another closed down. It kept him busy:

> You do your work and then you walk around. You can go anywhere in the building. Nobody can say, "What are you doing here?" because I could go anywhere. And I'd go all over the place and talk to the guys. And that was great. Like I say, you're not stuck in the same place all the time. Oh, there were times when you'd go in at eight o'clock in the morning, you didn't know if you were coming home that night. I've gone home at eight o'clock the next morning, close to twenty times in the twenty years I was oiler. I worked twenty-four-hour shifts. And that screws you up for a few days. You're walking around at five in the morning all [makes hang-dog face], duh, just waiting for that paper machine to start. Because you can't go home until it starts. But, no, I enjoyed it.

Bruce Colquhoun had his own lunch room. There was a big oak table, a microwave oven, fridge, stove, and a deep fryer: "We had fish and chips sometimes, and steak and all that. That's where I had all my breaks." Other guys would drop in to chat, in part because it was in the mill's basement and so it had cooler temperatures. There was even a little air-conditioner, good enough to keep the room a little cooler than it was outside: "And on a hot day a lot of people came in there and talk, read books, and play cards sometimes [smiles]. I don't care if the bosses see that." In Colquhoun's memory, there was always somebody to talk to. He would go from one department to the next one: "There was always somebody throwing a joke, or an insult at you. Yeah, it was great. I got nailed by water hoses a few times. Ha. You know, you're all sweaty and hot there, you're bent down by a gear box checking something, sweats just pouring off you, and some idiot comes and hoses you down. You go 'huuuh!' you jump up, you get mad for a minute, but then you go, 'oh, that feels good,' eh? No, I got along with everybody. No, it was great in there. It was fun. They made it fun. You had to. You work too serious there, the job would really get to you, you know."

Workplace friendships animated many of the interviews, but none more visibly than our joint interview with Ken and Bruce Colquhoun, father and son, respectively. As we already heard, Ken worked on the digester, where they cooked and prepared the wood and made mash to produce pulp stock for the paper machine.

Maintaining the paper machine. Photograph courtesy of André Cartier.

"We mulched it," Ken recalled. Bruce worked with his father for a couple years before moving to another department. In the joint interview he started things off by saying that they "eat well." This recollection sparked a warm exchange of memories between the two men:

> BRUCE: I worked with him one, a couple winters there, eh? Me and Tico and Roy. Oh, geez, I worked hard and I gained ten pounds. I ate like a pig there.
>
> KEN: He liked his spaghetti.
>
> BRUCE: Yeah, well, the whole mill could smell when we were cooking something. They'd all come around like seagulls.
>
> KEN: Mill manager, mill assistant manager, Big Red Stevens, always said, "What the hell he's having for dinner? Get out of here!" Wondered what the hell he's cooking. Tico was a good cook. He always prepared something real good. I was just like the cook-ee when it came to cooking. But he was great. We lost him, quite a while ago. Good man.
>
> BRUCE: Yeah. A lot of fun.
>
> KEN: A lot of fun with him. Oh, my God, we miss him.

Ken and Bruce Colquhoun, father and son mill workers. Photograph by David. W. Lewis.

This was a beloved story shared by a father and son. Later in the interview, they returned to this story of spaghetti and shared meals. Bruce Colquhoun recalled one time being called to lunch by Tico and his father:

> BRUCE: Tico comes out and yells downstairs, "Colquhoun, supper's ready!" Okay, I went and cleaned up a little bit, washed my hands. They're sitting there with this big jug of water, and they're sweating, eating the ice, spaghetti and sauce. I said, "Aw, you bunch of wimps!" So I put spaghetti on my plate start mixing sauce in it, lick the fork, and "huuuuuh!" I grabbed the jug of water [laughter]
>
> RUTH [KEN'S WIFE]: It was too hot!
>
> BRUCE: Tico's laughing, "Who's the wimp now, Colquhoun?" Oh, geez.
>
> KEN: My good friend, Tico, eh?

The resurfacing of this story prompted me to ask if they enjoyed working together. Bruce laughed. "He was my boss for a few winters in a row." As a student, Bruce had to clean up the department:

> BRUCE: And I had these big huge chip bins, eh? And there was a screw down at the bottom to pull the chips up in the chip bin. They had enough chips in them bins to run the machine 'til the next day. And sometimes them chips, in the wintertime, they'd freeze up. So the screw would go by on a little track and pull the chips up and drop it on a conveyor belt and then bring it up, so dad could cook it. And my job was to make sure the chips would fall down. But there were times, eh? Geez, you want to get dynamite and blow them up. 'Cause they're just not budging. The screw would go along there on that track and just make, a nothing. We would clean it out and they're just laying there.
>
> KEN: The track right through it and the rest hanging up there.

BRUCE: Yeah. And we'd be poking with poles, there, big fifteen-foot-long poles. And it's a small area where, just a little catwalk under the chip bins there.

KEN: At least you weren't [?] the logs, eh? I remember that.

BRUCE: I would say. We worked hard. And I gained ten pounds that year.

KEN: Tico's good cooking.

BRUCE: Homemade bread and,

KEN: Ah, can't forget our friend Tico.

RUTH: No.

KEN: Oh, he was the greatest.

BRUCE: Quite the joker, eh?

…

BRUCE: Yeah, we got along good. You and Tico would come in the chip bin and help me sometimes. I was a skinny guy. I mean, I'm like a toothpick back then, trying to get that, poking a long pike pole, get it through the soft chips and get it down to the frozen chips at the bottom there. We'd be poking and poking, we'd take a sledgehammer and hit the end of the bar, the end of that pike pole, and try to ram it through the frozen chips. Get a hole in there, "Hey, we got a hole!" and stick an air hose in there and let it flop around, try to knock it down.

KEN: First thing you know, it would break open a hole though, eh?

BRUCE: Yeah. And everything would start going again.

KEN: Start going again. It was like that every winter. Because snow come in with the chips, eh? And the snow, that was the trouble. The logs, no problem. Goddamn snow there binded everything together with, like shit to a blanket – you couldn't get it apart. Or through.

Once placed in a department, mill workers worked their way up the occupational ladder. When Raymond Lortie was hired in 1974, there were still quite a few older guys who had been hired on when the mill reopened in 1947. In the years that followed, because of a wave of retirements, you could work your way up the ladder relatively quickly. The paper machine department is a good example of this, as several of our interviewees spent their careers there. Others bumped their way onto the paper machine after the hardboard mill closed in 1991. This generated some resentment. Paper making was once a trade, with its own craft union, but this changed over time and the unions merged into one bargaining unit. There was still "a lot of things to learn" for an incoming mill worker such as André Cartier, who started as fifth hand and then worked his way up from there. The rate of someone's progression depended on the retirement of those above you in the hierarchy. Cartier was "stuck" being fifth hand for a couple years while he learned the rules. Fourth hand was a much more complex job, running the winder. There was much to learn about the speed of the motors, about pressure and the winding itself. Then,

André Cartier hams it up for the camera; shop-floor playfulness was a theme running through the interviews. Photograph courtesy of André Cartier.

it took him less than a half-year to go to third hand, where he was again "stuck" for a long time. He was just about ready to move up in 1992, when the hardboard mill closed and he was bumped back down to the bottom by those with higher seniority, and he had to start over again. Like a children's game of snakes and ladders, he worked his way up again.

Interviewees often drew contrasts between departments. Harold Stewart noted that workers in his (pulping) department would get up from their lunches if there was any trouble. Indeed, he recalled, "I know in my department, anyways, you don't sit down and eat until you're out of trouble and everything was running. And sometimes we have a problem with some of the guys that came from the paint line, or another department. They were used to sitting down, eating their lunch. And they didn't care if the mill shut down. But in my department … we didn't look at it that way. The mill had to come first." Many workers spoke with pride about their work, and their productivity as a group. Laughing, Stewart remembered when the powers that be told the men that they couldn't reach a certain point in production. "Well, the men got together and decided 'We'll show them we can.'" They achieved their goal, but all they got for a reward was a chocolate bar. "The men all returned it, and said, 'That's all you can give us? You keep your chocolate bar.'" Management then came up with something better – "I can't recall what it was, but I remember that chocolate bar." He could still taste the sweetness of the memory when he and the other men from the pulping department "turned their back to the superintendent and said, 'Here. Keep your chocolate bar. We're not kids here.'"

A number of interviewees were locally rooted managers who worked their way up from the shop floor. In some departments, the line between union and management was drawn right on the occupational ladder. Benny Haarsma, who worked in the steam plant, "did all jobs from superintendent, shift engineer, operator, helper, and utility man. From shovelling coal to ... " [laughs]. Production workers could also work their way into the skilled trades. For years the mill had an apprenticeship program that allowed them to do precisely this. Henri Labelle, for example, got an apprenticeship as a millwright. At the time of our interview, he was a Class-A millwright. He noted this was "the same thing as a mechanic" except he repaired motors, pumps, and other machinery. Whenever something broke down, they had to "open it up, we inspect it, if we can order a new part ... then we put them all back together and put them back on the line." As a millwright, they'd take care of the whole mill: "One day I could be in the paper machine, the other day I could be in the yard, the other day I could be in the hardboard, the other day I could be in the paint line." The line between different trades used to be hard and fast. As a result, Labelle could not use a torch or even "touch a pipe" because "the millwright was the millwright, pipefitter was the pipefitter, welder was a welder." By the end, after waves of layoffs, skilled tradesmen had become "multitraders." Labelle said he was "never good" with his hands, but he adapted: "You learn fast." Henri Labelle chose to be a millwright primarily because it offered more job security than other production workers enjoyed: "That's it: security. Because they work twelve hours, they work twelve months a year. They do get more money. And I think it was mostly security." Workplace-based learning, in an apprenticeship framework, was once commonplace in Canadian mills and factories. It provided several of our interviewees with a pathway to skilled work. At Sturgeon Falls, Marc Côté noted, "we really tried hard to get 'em going, there are certain costs, the government stopped the grants, and it became a little more expensive."

Conclusion

With the exception of the skilled trades and office staff, production workers at Sturgeon Falls were hired as mill workers, rather than into specific occupations or departments. This practice led to a great deal of mobility in the mill as workers migrated from one department to the next in search of the right position. Some sought "steady days," others the highest wages, still others relative autonomy in what was a highly regimented industrial workplace. The hiring policy ensured that whole families were tied to the mill. The gendered division of labour in the mill was such that, with few exceptions, only men were hired in production. The uncertainty that accompanied the labour pool and shift work made it difficult for the wives of production workers to work full time outside the home, further entrenching the male breadwinner.

Most important, perhaps, the mill-wide labour pool made it difficult for either the company or the union to build barriers to interdepartment transfers. When production of certain products ceased, *internally* displaced high-seniority workers were able to bump lower-seniority workers out of their jobs in those departments that were still operating. The gradual decline of the mill over several decades, and the contraction of the workforce, caused a great deal of uncertainty, and pushed people out of their preferred places. When Marcel Boudreau entered the plant in 1978: "The paint line was running. Fabrication was running. The hardboard was running. Paper machine was running. You had a pulping department that was running. You had the powerhouse that was running. You had a steam plant that was running. And [that] pretty well covers it. And when the mill shut down last year, well, just about a year now, paint line wasn't there, hardboard wasn't there, fabrication wasn't there, and it was just basically a paper mill. A 100 per cent recycled paper mill to boot. Yet it wasn't good enough to keep it open."

ACCIDENT STORIES

Today is the official day of mourning for the workers killed at work. Please take some time to reflect on what this means … At this time, we must think of one of our own who lost his life during 1989. Denis Ladouceur lost his life in the Paint Line while working on the banding machine. Let us reflect on this situation and it will help us make this mill a safer place to work in.

– Marc Coté, *Insider*, 28 April 1998[1]

Nearly every mill worker we interviewed remembers the 21 April 1989, the day Denis Ladouceur was crushed to death on the paint line, where newly pressed exterior siding was painted and bundled together for shipping. "Everybody knew the guy," recalled Raymond Marcoux. "He had worked there for quite a few years. And you knew he had a family, had a baby on the way." Yet few chose to name Ladouceur in the interviews, preferring instead to speak of him indirectly as a "young married man" or as a friend and co-worker. What accounts for this reticence? Was it a desire to protect the dead man's family from further pain and hurt? Did mill workers not feel authorized to name names? Or, unlike workplace disasters, was it an indication of the residual shame or blame that is still directed at workers injured or killed on the job?

This chapter explores how injuries and deaths are remembered in a single workplace, as revealed in our work-life interviews, as well as the visual traces of workplace struggle over health and safety issues. Although the Sturgeon Falls mill was considered safe, at least compared to working underground in the nearby Sudbury nickel mines, accident stories quickly emerged as a major topic of conversation,

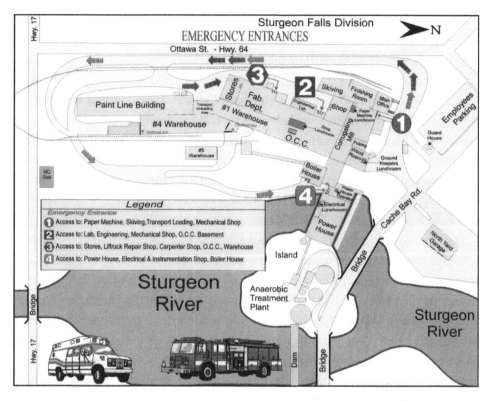

Emergency entrances to the Sturgeon Falls mill for first responders, 1990s. Courtesy of Hubert Gervais.

stories that tell us about industrial work, workplace relations, and working-class masculinity in the second half of the twentieth century. The chapter builds on the research of Robert Storey, Arthur McIvor, and others on the remembered experiences of injured and dying workers. Accident stories have been found to serve an important political function, helping to mobilize public opinion and reinforce solidarity among injured workers themselves – transforming private hurt into public knowledge.[2] But what was the cumulative effect or legacy of industrial accidents in the workplace itself? How did co-workers view these accidents and those injured?

It is important to remember that responses to such questions are not "free-floating experiences," but are profoundly located in class, gender, and racial structures.[3] Historian Arthur McIvor, for example, has written of a "high risk threshold" that predominated in twentieth century Scottish industry, where working-class masculinity led men to tough it out in stoic silence. For McIvor, "[w]orkers were enmeshed within the dual exploitative pressures of a productionist culture and gendered ideologies that exalted the tough, risk-taking, competitive, hard-grafting worker."[4]

Those who sought to protect themselves were thus "pilloried as lesser men, subject to peer pressure to take risks, to compete, to conform, and to maximize earnings."[5]

When planning this chapter, I initially thought to focus on the stoicism of working-class masculinity and how this might have generated a high-tolerance threshold in Sturgeon Falls. Having grown up in Northern Ontario, I was familiar with this. A closer listening to the interviews, however, revealed a somewhat different narrative than the one I anticipated. Although the interviews we conducted in the immediate aftermath of the mill closure indicated little in the way of male bravado – hardly surprising considering the unfolding closure – they did point to the ways in which interviewees understood danger and discursively contained risk. A higher-risk threshold was thus achieved, mainly on this basis.

Our interviewees contained workplace danger in three principal ways. First, they relied on their working knowledge of the mill to identify the "danger spots" where accidents could happen. This localization of risk served to contain the problem, sustaining their belief that, overall, it was a safe working environment. Second, our interviewees emphasized that working conditions improved over time. This narrative line effectively located unsafe working conditions safely in the past, rather than in the present, temporally containing the problem. Finally, workers localized risk to a momentary lapse of judgment by an individual, or to youthful inexperience. If carelessness was raised, it was always cast in the broadest possible terms, and never in relation to a specific co-worker or accident. Having contained the risk of injury, workers were free to say that the mill as a whole was a safe working environment.

The Spatial Containment of "Danger Spots"

The Sturgeon Falls mill was part corrugated paper mill, part wood products mill. The workplace was therefore filled with fast-moving machinery, conveyor belts, saw blades, presses, and other machinery that could cause grievous injury or even death. There were other hazards, too. In some areas the noise was deafening. Chemicals and gas could also prove deadly. Yet, to those who worked there, the mill compared favourably to other more "dirty" or "dangerous" industrial jobs in the region. Before being hired on, for example, Henri Labelle worked at the Copperfield Mine in Temagami, less than an hour's drive north of Sturgeon Falls. It was a dirty job, as "everything stuck to you." After work, his "hands were still black. It was all in the pores." When he washed a second time, "it would come out of the pores again. Ah! That was a dirty job. You needed a mask, but we didn't have any in those days. And you would have the taste in your mouth all the time … But it was a job." In my experience, industrial workers often speak of their early work in these terms. It was "a job" speaks to limited options and the need to start somewhere. Similarly, when asked how mill work compared to his time in the Falconbridge mine in Sudbury, Benny Haarsma insisted that it was a "picnic." At the mill, you sometimes "get black, but when we were working in Falconbridge you were off three days and the black was still coming out of your pores." That was a "different type of work"; in fact, most of our interviewees tended machines.

But mill work had once been more physically demanding, when much of the heavy lifting was still done by hand. When Marc Côté started at the mill, "There was not that much equipment in those days. The equipment that made the paper was a lot of heavy equipment, but the wood came in chips and it came in cars, on railroad cars. And there was no automatic truck dumping, you just opened the doors under the rail car and pick at it with a big pick, and the chips started falling into the bed, and then they build up like the inside of a tent and you had to go in under and pick at it. So they all fell out and some guys really got buried in chips. And that was a day's work … It was interesting, but a lot of hard work. Everything was done by hand." Naturally, some people could not sustain this hard physical labour for their entire working lives. Bodies simply gave out. No doubt prodded by the local unions, the company placed older, sick, and disabled workers into "lighter" jobs in the mill. Retirement announcements in the 1950s, for example, confirm that many workers ended their careers as watchmen or janitorial staff. This practice appears to have continued until the contraction of the mill's workforce in the 1980s and early 1990s.

The work could be dangerous. "You had to be on your toes all the time," recalled Mike Lacroix. Marc Côté, a locally rooted manager responsible for maintenance, spoke of the inherent dangers of "heavy machinery, it'll kill you, and everybody knew that." Raymond Marcoux similarly insisted that "there was always, always a lot of danger and somebody getting hurt." Others were more fatalistic. When asked if it was a safe place to work, André Cartier replied, "Yes and no." He noted that "you can always have an accident," even crossing the street and a car comes. "This is the same thing." Gordon Jackson acknowledged that there were accidents, "but not because the mill wasn't safe." Shrugging his shoulders, he said that "accidents happen, you know."

To varying degrees, risk was normalized as part of the job. When asked if the mill was a safe place to work, mill workers and their managers insisted that it was a safe mill. This particular framing of the issue of risk suggests that some workplace accidents were an unavoidable part of industrial life. For example, Larry Shank explained: "Well if you're working in the mill, as soon as you get in the door, it's an industry. It's dangerous. You might not think these things, but it is. And then there's machinery overhead, and there's trucks and there's carrier lifts and there's rollers and there's paper rolls, and, I mean, you know, there's lots going on. You're not there for fun. You gotta watch what you're doing. But they tried to make it as safe as possible. Try to put a hat on your head, and good shoes and gloves and glasses. But there's moving stuff."

Workers prized their tacit or local knowledge of the mill.[6] John Dillon, an electrician, spoke of the dangers of electrical work and the value of having a thorough working knowledge of the mill: "You had to be very knowledgeable about the mill and how the power was distributed and how the power came in. You had to be very knowledgeable to know what was dangerous and what was not ... That's just knowing the mill. Forty-six-and-a-half years, you know a lot about the mill." Clearly some aspects of the job were more dangerous than others. "We got to know where the dangerous spots are," recalled John Dillon. André Cartier cited one such spot on the paper machine where he had to concentrate extra hard, as he knew the work was dangerous. If it wasn't done right, you could lose an arm: "you were close, but not that close."

During the interviews, workers identified many other unsafe places, while still maintaining that the mill was safe. One of the "dangerous jobs" identified by Ben Lajeunesse involved "changing tanks of chlorine, pure chlorine, that they used to purify water, I guess. I really don't know what it was used for. But every once in a while, we had to go down to the sub-basement and disconnect one tank and put in a new tank. And if you didn't do it right, and you got a whiff of chlorine, you could be awfully sick, it could be deadly. But we were trained by the engineers to do it properly. And we did it properly." Otherwise, Lajeunesse reiterated, his job was not dangerous. To make his point, he spoke of the safety features of the saws in the platewood and hardboard mills: "Oh, yes. Everything was closed in. Even the first saw that I worked on, when you pull that saw across, there was a cover came down over the blade, and as you pulled it across the board to make your cuts, you couldn't put your hand out and get cut, unless you were behind the saw doing something back there. All the other jobs: the double-cut-off saw, you're feeding boards into a saw, but you can't reach them; the trimmer, you really couldn't reach the saw, the only time you got near the saw was if you were changing the size of the boards that you were cutting. Other than that, it was very safe." For his part, Marcel Labbé identified several danger spots, only to end each story with an assertion that the mill was safe. It happened repeatedly. For instance, he recalled one incident where a man cut his finger because the company "never put a guard over the gear and head to work that way with his hands and moving boards. And his hand went under the belt, through the gear. Well, as soon as that happened, they fixed it. Well, it's an oversight from somebody … It wasn't negligence. The guy in charge of the safety never saw the possibility of an accident occurring there. But, in general, it was safe."[7]

Experiential knowledge was thus the bedrock of the mill workers' pride in their work and the source of their confidence that they could avoid injury. Consider this passage drawn from the interview with Marc Côté, a machinist who rose to become the superintendent of the maintenance department: "being a machinist, you worked with moving machinery, you haven't got any choice, and you've got flying chips of steel next to you, and they're red hot. If they touch you they burn you." Shop-floor knowledge was important, Côté continued:

> Being in maintenance they always called us if anything has got a different noise or if a machine is dead … The operators got so good at the end there that you could sit in your office running the machine and you'd get a vibration in the floor and right away you knew that something was wrong somewhere. So guys would get up and go walk next to a machine and say, 'This one here's wrong because it's not shaking right, there's something wrong.' They'd give us a call, we'd go over there and assess the problem. So that was done usually in the afternoon … We had somebody on call, they called names, and there'd be a rotation, so somebody was called in. You had to assess, "We're gonna shut it down, he won't make it 'til tomorrow morning" or, "Yes, there's probably something stuck inside it that's creating the shaking." And we had all kinds of vibration analysis mechanisms, machines that we could go in there and say, just by putting it on there and taking a reading, you'd know if the bearing was about to go or if it would last a couple of days. There's machines like that, and that was nice. No more second-guessing and screwdrivers in your ear. You just put that on there and the metres would tell you if the bearing was going.

Warming to the subject, Côté expanded on the dangers of industrial work:

> If you're working next to a paper machine where the dryers are working at a temperature that will burn you if you touch it or steam pressure – there's a couple hundred pounds of steam in the line – that could burst and give you a real burn, it makes you a lot more conscious of it. We didn't have that many good-sized accidents; we had a good record. But it's heavy machinery, and paper mills are fast-starting machinery. The paper machine was running at 1,400, 1,500 sheets a minute. That's thirteen sheets wide and drums and gears that are five tons, ten tons. So it's dangerous equipment. Big machines. Clark trucks are lifting four tons, five tons, eight tons, and the hardboard and plywood, stuff like that, they're big loads. If you stop too fast, they'll

come off, and they come off just like knives. And if you have twenty boards that are sixteen feet wide on a big leg and you stop and the truck goes like this [holds both arms before him and lurches forward and downward], you dump the load. So we start abandoning it when the truck goes, you can't, if you're too high, then the truck'll tip. It's a combination of safety devices and safety consciousness. It's mostly having people, [pauses] aware of the danger.

Workplace accidents often led to change on the shop floor as new safety guards, training procedures, or signage were added to formalize tacit knowledge. Being "aware" of potential dangers came with experience and training.

The Temporal Containment of Injury

The second way mill workers contained the problem of workplace injury in their oral accounts was to locate risk in the past, not the present. Virtually all the mill workers we interviewed insisted that the mill became safer over time. "When I first started," recalled Harold Stewart, "safety was not the biggest factor that you were worried about. But it got better." As a unionized environment, health and safety was a matter of negotiation, and there were grievance procedures in place.[8] The signage in the Sturgeon Falls mill was visibly part of this new emphasis on workplace safety. Even so, workers continued to be injured on the job right up to the mill's final year of production. A safety report published in the mill's September 2002 newsletter, a month before the mill's closure was announced, indicated that five workers required medical treatment so far that year and another thirteen had received first aid.[9]

Nearly everyone spoke of an increased safety consciousness. Workers recalled that they never wore ear plugs, or safety glasses, in the beginning. Ron Demers noted that people would not always report minor accidents as they did not want to be reprimanded. Raymond Marcoux believed that the company did not promote safety much when he first started working there, recalling: "There were a lot of accidents back then. More than there were towards the [end]." Asked if he ever saw any accidents, Marc Côté paused, looked up, and shrugged his shoulders: "Yes, some. Mostly conveyors … We had some conveyors in the beginning. Chain conveyors, and so – people, I wouldn't say, weren't careful. They were close to it. There were not as many safety rules as now … Production was more important in those days than whatever else." By the end, "everything was safety. Everything was checked."

Brian Laflèche, who worked in the mill in the late 1960s and early 1970s, shared another story about how things used to be. He told us about how they used to bring in eight- or ten-foot logs into the mill on a ramp. Water was poured on them to make them slippery, so they wouldn't stick together. The logs would fall into a trough and then they would float down to the splitter. The logs would be split, then sent down a ramp to their destination in the mill. Sometimes there would be jams, recalled Laflèche: "And you'd be standing there, and you have a long pipe maybe fifteen feet long – you know, a pipe that [had] a kind of hook on one end and straight – and pick the log, grab it. So you'd be picking and you'd try to get one. You knew if you got that one, everything is coming down." Sometimes, he recalled, logs would come down the ramp too quickly and miss the trough: "They'd bounce off of each other and they'd go down ... on the working floor where everyone was working. I can remember, when that would happen, everybody was clearing the deck [laughs] ... In those days, it was funny. Looking back now, yeah, you'd never do that job again."

The documentary evidence, such as it is, supports the oral interviews. For example, the mill rules established by the Spanish River Company in 1923 said little about safety. Employees were simply directed not to wear clothing that "can readily become entangled in machinery." They were also told not to remove machinery safeguards without permission and that all accidents had to be reported immediately. Finally, the mill rules indicated that, "in the interest of safety every new employee shall be instructed exactly how to stop machinery which he is required to work around regularly."[10] In each instance the company's rulebook clearly shifted the responsibility for health and safety to mill workers themselves.

Collective agreements between management and the mill unions provide another opportunity to track changes in mill safety. In the post-war years the mill unions negotiated improved health benefits, disability pay, and special company payments for protective footwear, to cite one example. But protracted health and safety issues appeared unresolved over the life of several collective agreements. Excessive heat and noise in the paper machine room was flagged as an issue of particular concern. In the 1956 negotiations between Abitibi and the Pulp & Sulphite Workers, it was noted that "considerable discussion was devoted to the problems of noise and heat in paper machine rooms and Management reported on the steps taken to date to alleviate and improve these conditions. Assurances were given that this effort will continue."[11] But the problem persisted. In 1961 Abitibi acknowledged the continued concern "with the problems of heat and noise in our mills," and promised to work to improve working conditions.[12] It noted that "extensive ventilation improvements" had recently been completed and that noise reduction was a major goal in new investment in equipment and machinery. Fourteen years later, in 1975, heat and noise remained a matter of concern, and the company and union agreed – yet again – to "jointly strive to eliminate the physical and mental effects of heat and noise by taking precautions, and elimination of the hazards."[13]

On the shop floor, workers struggled to make their workplace safer. Bruce Colquhoun remembers the precise date – 9 June 1999 – when he badly hurt his ankle at work, and was put onto "light duty" for three weeks. He eventually had to get surgery on the ankle. Meanwhile he pushed the company to do something about the dangerous spot where he got hurt:

> When I told them why I got hurt and where I got hurt and something should be done about that, that was June. It was November before they got it fixed. All they had to do was make a little gate so I didn't have to climb over a gate, a handrail, to get to a coupling on a gear box. It took them that long to do it. I kept complaining to my safety guy. He said, 'oh, no, they know about it.' They weren't doing anything. So I wasn't going to grease that part. I said, 'I'm not going there anymore. I got hurt there. Not until you fix it.' Safety with some managers was a big deal, they would do something about it. Safety with others, well: 'yeah, yeah, just don't go there.' Or 'just be careful,' you know. It was a joke to some people. And it was serious to other people. All in all, I guess, it was half-half.

Interviewees often distinguished among individual managers, saying that some were more committed to safety than others. For Bruce Colquhoun, his superintendant Marc Côté was one of the good guys who wanted it fixed: "He was one of the best. And he knew I got hurt. He knew I got hurt bad. And he wanted that thing fixed. And finally, he got it, he got it fixed. He said, 'go check on it. I got it fixed.'" Pierre Hardy generally agreed that "they were very safety conscious [at the mill]. And if it wasn't safe, we didn't do it. Simple as that."

The mill had a big safety board outside the front gate "stating the number of days we had gone without any lost time or any incidents or accidents," recalled Raymond Lortie. There were also visits of "safety auditors" from other plants, and "people from here used to audit other mills." All of this sought to affect an attitudinal change on the shop floor. Mike Lacroix, a former vice-president of the union local and before that a shop steward, noted that the union movement was largely responsible for Canada's health and safety laws. The local union president had asked him to run for office because of his longstanding interest in health and safety issues. To explain his interest, he noted that, soon after being hired at the mill, his supervisor had made him remove asbestos without a mask or other protective gear: "Back then I didn't know any better. I just had a little dust mask, and I removed the whole pile and I started to sneeze and cough, and I said 'man, I can't take this no more.' So he said, 'leave it there for now.' What exactly he did with that, I don't know, with the asbestos I removed. But today this is why I tell the young people: 'Be careful, don't do what they think is [not] right.'"

These early experiences were a motivating force among other unionized members. When asked about the value of the union, Bruce Colquhoun responded with a specific example of how the union protected him when he refused unsafe work. As he explained, the union

> protected me, you know. 'Cause once, I was threatened one time by the guy who did the hiring and firing, and the union stepped in and said, 'No ... what are you doing?' Because I couldn't go on the paper machine because of my knees. It's hard to stop them three-thousand-pound rolls of paper, you know, when you've got a bad knee. And he told me, he says, 'If you can't do the job, we'll find somebody else that can.' I told him, I said, 'Don't threaten me.' And he says, 'Well, Bruce, you're gonna go on the paper machine.' I said, 'Don't threaten me.' I said, 'I know my rights.' I said, 'If you ever say anything like that again, you're gonna see what I do know.' I went and seen the union, I told 'em. They said, 'Don't exaggerate.' I said, 'I'm not exaggerating. He threatened me. He threatened to fire me if I didn't go on the paper machine.' So they went and talked to him and straightened him out.

Other union members took first-aid courses and served as first responders in case of mill accidents. One of these, André Cartier, pointed to this training when he explained his decision to retrain as a nurse after the mill closed down in 2002. He noted that two others had done the same after the mill's hardboard production line was discontinued in the early 1990s. His work on health and safety issues inside the plant thus opened a door for him to the health care sector after the mill closed.

If unionized mill workers emphasized their own working knowledge of the mill and their activism, mill managers naturally placed more emphasis on the positive influence of rules, training, and incentives. Wally Shisko, mill manager during the 1980s and 1990s, noted that Sturgeon Falls was recognized as the "safest mill in Ontario in a number of classes a number of times."[14] He noted that the mill had a full-time person who "did nothing but that [safety training]." Gerry Stevens, a long-time mill superintendent, likewise maintained that safety "was our number one concern within the mill." Stevens suggested that the best way to promote safety was to convince people to take responsibility themselves:

> I mean, you don't have beams falling down and hitting people ... If you decide when you go to work in the morning you're going to work safely, you're going to make it

home safe tonight. The chances are you will. So you have to be conscious of what you're doing. You can't have any lapse of judgment or you're going to be in trouble. That's my philosophy. Now, there's various gimmicks been tried. We tried them all and, yeah, that's what they are: they're gimmicks. I don't believe in setting prizes if you've gone so many days [without an accident] … [What happens then is that] there's a lot of peer pressure on somebody that gets hurt that they not report the accident. I just don't … agree with that particular way of promoting safety.

Certainly, by the 1970s and 1980s, departments held regular safety meetings, and problems were logged. Benny Haarsma recalled that, when he was in charge of the steam plant, "we had a log book, and the shift engineer – every shift reports who's on shift and what happens. And it's always said that if something happens, just put it in the log and then the next morning, when they call the shop, 'Come and fix this.'" But, as Gerry Stevens conceded, "it was a constant job, safety. If you're going to be successful."

As a unionized environment, health and safety was a matter of negotiation, and there were grievance procedures in place. The struggle for workplace safety was evidenced in union demands for new safety guards and other measures. According to André Girard, "Sometimes we had a hard time to convince the company to do it, and they would drag their feet and they wouldn't do it." Bruce Colquhoun told us about the time when an air-operated hose came off a piece of machinery and was whipping all over the place: "So the guy I was working with was looking at that, 'Geez, where's the shut off for that?' And the boss comes up, says, 'What are you guys doing?' Well 'we're trying to look for the shutoff, to shut that air hose off.' 'Never mind that, just pull the door open.' 'No. That hose is whipping all over the place, you're gonna get that in the head or somewhere.' 'Never mind that!' Yeah. So, like I said, it depended on the supervisor."

To resolve differences, a health and safety committee was formed by the local union and mill management in 1980. André Girard, who served on it for "years and years," noted that the 1980s and early 1990s was a period when Ontario legislation "gave more power to the union and to the workers for protection." He noted that the company at first resisted this shifting balance of power: "It was quite the battle at times." He should know. Girard qualified as a union health instructor after taking a two-week training course in Thunder Bay and later served as a director of the Ontario Pulp and Paper Makers Safety Association: "So I was fortunate by being active in the union and active in health and safety and stuff like that, to get a lot of education." The documentary evidence that we were able to access reveals union efforts to keep the workplace safe. In April 1980, for example, local union president

Cautionary signage was posted
or hung throughout the mill.
Photograph by Kristen O'Hare.

Andy Cull wrote the national president of the Canadian Paperworkers Union asking him to look into a label from a chemical being used on the paint line in Sturgeon
Falls: "We would like a check on this as some of our people are complaining of
itchiness and rash when working there as opposed to being away from the place."[15]
In his interview Girard noted that "we [the union] exaggerated safety, but then you
have to exaggerate to make sure that people don't get hurt." One of the chief ways of
doing this was cautionary signage.

The pervasiveness of safety signage in the industrial workplace was apparent
during two semi-clandestine tours of the closed mill as the machinery was being
dismantled. We did not gain entry via the departing company, but rather with the
support of the municipality, which had just purchased the mill's hydroelectric plant.
One of our interviewees, Ray Lortie, managed the facility, and offered to have us
taken through the rest of the plant – an offer we gladly accepted. We walked through
the mill taking photographs, except in the steam house and the former paint line, as
both areas were sealed off. Black and yellow tape emblazoned with the word "asbestos" barred the way – a very effective deterrent.

For the purpose of this chapter, I re-examined these photos for traces of the
"danger spots" and the safety regime of which the interviewees spoke. Cautionary
signage tells us something about the kinds of dangers that existed in the workplace
and where these dangers were located. Here the risks ranged from moving equipment, fast-moving machinery, tipping forklifts, chemical spray, gas, noise, burning,
electrocution, noise, asbestos, even radiation. The proliferation of cautionary signs,

Safety signs in the OCC facility. Photograph by Kristen O'Hare.

often in close proximity to one another, speaks to the fact that these dangers or risks were recognized over many years, rather than all at once.[16] The sheer number of safety-related signs inside the mill – there were hundreds – also speaks to the multiple and varied risks of working in an industrial environment.

Cautionary signage was not the only visible evidence of dangerous conditions. We also encountered several emergency eye-washing stations, a cabinet for gas masks, posted labour inspection certificates, and emergency evacuation maps. Most notably, large accident charts were displayed prominently throughout the plant, identifying the number of accidents, their severity, and the number of days lost. One of these charts recorded the "Safety Record of Lost Time Accidents" since 1999, but nobody bothered to update the chart during the mill's final two months of operation. Instead management offered soon-to-be unemployed mill workers a $5,000 bonus if they maintained production levels and kept the accident rate at current levels. Several workers spoke bitterly of how this last condition provided co-workers with a powerful incentive not to report minor accidents.

The visible presence of prescriptive industrial signage in abandoned industrial buildings has lent itself to ironic readings in the writings of urban explorers and scholars such as Tim Edensor. In his influential book, *Industrial Ruins*, Edensor revels in the "disordering" of once highly regulated industrial spaces. Pointing specifically to leftover cautionary signage, he notes: "Ruined factories are replete with the traces of this redundant power."[17] For Edensor these notices were produced

Emergency eye wash station and signage, paper machine room. Photograph by Kristen O'Hare.

by management to notify workers of "correct procedures." Somewhat gleefully, he remarks: "There is something comical about these remaining signatures of hierarchy and authority. Like the strident orders barked out by a solitary sergeant major in the middle of a deserted space, no one is there to listen and obey. The trivial warnings and commands to follow procedures seem ridiculous outbursts of petty authority."[18] But, as we have seen, other readings of this prescriptive signage acknowledge the agency of industrial workers. The Sturgeon Falls interviews make clear that many of these precautionary measures originated in protracted shop-floor struggle and negotiation. Rather than "trivial warnings," these words of caution were erected because people were being injured or killed on the job. Workers knew from decades of experience where the "danger spots" were located, and sought to inscribe this knowledge on the interior and exterior walls of the mill itself.

Momentary Lapses and Inexperience

If mill workers believed their knowledge of the working environment helped keep them safe, how then did they explain recent workplace accidents or the need for formal signage? To explain this apparent contradiction, our interviewees frequently spoke of momentary mental lapses and the youthful inexperience of those injured or the inexplicability of what happened. Others spoke of being "bumped" into unfamiliar parts of the plant as the workforce contracted during the 1980s and 1990s. The long decline of the mill over a thirty-year period saw one production line after another discontinued, resulting in considerable internal dislocation as well as outright layoffs. Even production managers faced some of the same challenges. One, for example, spoke to us about a near-tragedy in the 1990s when the mill's hydroelectric dam opened its floodgates and three children "got swamped" downriver. They had been playing below the dam and could have drowned. Two of the boys were sent to hospital. The accident took a personal toll on the superintendent, who had recently been given responsibility for the hydro plant as well as his home department. Soon thereafter, he took early retirement. "I've had enough of this," he sighed. "I had no training whatsoever." So, "[t]hat's enough … that's it. Goodbye Joe."[19]

Not surprisingly, perhaps, any mention of carelessness was restricted to general comments, and never tied to individual cases or specific co-workers. Marcel Labbé noted that you always "had to take precautions" to avoid injuring yourself or others: "You just couldn't go fly by night. You had to think before you acted. As someone told me, 'never run. Walk.' So, that was it." Some injuries were caused by nothing more than "tripping over something" or "just being careless," observed Ben Lajeunesse. "I mean, it wasn't because there was a hazard. Just being careless." Gordon Jackson believed that "you couldn't really blame the company" for these accidents: "You're working in an environment, with the amount of time that you forget safety sometimes. As you work along, you say nothing can happen to me. But it does happen." We all make mistakes." Wally Shisko, the mill manager, recalled that, "usually accidents happen because people aren't paying attention. I am not saying that people are the sole cause of accidents, but basically, in most cases, by far it's people [who] stop paying attention." Of course this emphasis on individual lapses in judgment prevents wider questioning of the dangers built into capitalist industrial production.[20]

Everybody agreed that accidents happened. "Oh, there was tons of missing fingers, sore backs," noted Hubert Gervais. "There were always a few guys [who] lost some fingers in the saws," added Percy Allary. It was an "old mill" with a lot of "nooks and crannies," explained Mike Lacroix, which resulted in "cuts, scrapes, bumps, bruises, broken bones ... you know, bang your head on the beam." Asked what kinds of accidents occurred, Marcoux replied: "A guy lost his fingers, one guy got killed, one guy got killed there at the mill – his head got crushed. What else? Well one guy, that was before I started there, cut his limb off – well, crushed so bad they had to amputate it. Ah, a few fingers, broken legs, a broken leg, broken arms, ... One fellow fell on his shoulder so he had a bad shoulder after that. One guy got his arm twisted, so it was more or less arms and legs."

Interviewees also mentioned cases where co-workers suffered more serious injuries. Percy Allary noted that one man lost a leg in a wood splitter, another had his leg crushed in a strapping machine, and yet another had both legs broken. He recalled that most were not surprised when the man lost his leg in the splitter, as "there were no guards or anything where he worked." Gordon Jackson also recalled the accident: "It's a big splitter," he noted, and the area was "always wet. The floors are all wet. And bark and stuff like that." Speaking of the same incident, Marc Côté went into more detail:

> Yeah, I did see some accidents ... Severe ones, some. But I wasn't there on the spot when it happened. We've had one gentleman cut a leg off ... In those days we used to have axes, there was a cylinder – an air cylinder – that was approximately sixteen inches in diameter and a shaft of four inches. There was an axe on a trolley about this high [holds hand about 16 inches off table] and it would come out and split a four-foot log because it wouldn't fit in the machine, okay? And in order to activate the log cutter you had to throw an arm in and the guy – the log was sideways on the splitter – and he went with his foot to push it [makes pushing motion with hand], he missed and slipped, and his leg went in front of the log and when he fell it pulled the arm so [smacks fist to palm] it cut the leg. But he has a prosthesis now, and he's walking right below the knee. Clean cut. But, ah, who's to blame? It's too bad that it happened. Everybody learned from something like this. The machinery wasn't safe, the man wasn't safe, so we fixed the machinery and everybody's got these small courses that they have to go on now. But you always learn too late with a lot of stuff.

Repeatedly, workers spoke of the bloody consequences. Another serious accident surfaced in our interview with Hubert Gervais, who described what happened: "There were two guys one night ... I don't know how they did it, but they got burnt with hot water ... Anyway they went to Sudbury right away, and they were treated properly and they come back. They were all peeled. But they were lucky, very lucky. One of them got a bit in the face, because they went like this [puts arm in front of his face] and they were protected. Apart from that? Oh, the ambulance would come in for some guy that couldn't breathe because he had inhaled something that was left in the can someplace."

Relatively few interviewees admitted to being hurt on the job. Frank Gerbasi, for example, had a couple of toes broken when a bar of steel fell on his foot – falling just above the safety toe. "But nothing too serious," he assured us. For his part, Mike Lacroix once got his arm cut, showing us where. He noted that it happened in the summertime, after he got "a little bit of sun" that "you can actually see the burn." He used this story to emphasize, again, the dangers of working inside the mill: "So you had to be on your toes. It was dangerous. You had to watch, and you had to watch the other guy, you had to work as a team." Not surprisingly safety became a major concern of Lacroix's, and he served for many years on the plant's health and safety committee.

Workplace bravery also surfaced in a story shared with us by Bruce and Ken Colquhoun, relating to their grandfather/father during the 1920s – the oldest accident story we recorded. Bruce prompted the story during our interview with his father: "Hey, Dad, tell Steve about when grandpa saved somebody's life at the mill and he got an award for that." With this, Ken retold a story that had clearly become familiar in the Colquhoun household. "Anyways," he began. Someone "got caught somewhere" and there were live electrical wires. "My dad jumped in and threw him off the belt and saved his life. And he was awarded quite an award for it from the Spanish River Power and Paper Company. I remember that award. My brother, Howard, has it." With this Bruce reminded me that he included a photocopy of the award certificate in the giant mill history binder that is the focus of Chapter 11. Bruce noted that his grandfather "got burned a little bit." At this point Ken added: "Yeah. He saved the guy's life. And the guy he saved was Jack Fraser. And they're around. His son's around." The Colquhoun family is rightly proud of their grandfather and father's bravery, reinforcing the family's intergenerational connection to the now-demolished mill.

When asked about workplace accidents, mill workers repeatedly told us that there was "only" the one fatality: that of Denis Ladouceur on the Paint Line in 1989. Only the most senior employees interviewed suggested that there were other workplace deaths in the mill's early days. Interviewees who had spoken matter-of-factly about severed limbs became squeamish when asked about Ladouceur's death. They had all known the dead man, and it was a particularly violent death. According to Percy Allary, "he never had a chance." Frank Gerbasi noted that Ladouceur "didn't shut the machine down, and he slid underneath the machinery to adjust something, and maybe his foot or something like that, hit the eye, there's an electric eye in it, and

STURGEON FALLS DIVISION			
SAFETY RECORD OF LOST TIME ACCIDENTS			
01	02	1999	2000
JANUARY	0	0	0	0
FEBRUARY	0	0	210	0
MARCH	0		0	0
APRIL	0	0	0	0
MAY	0	0		0
JUNE	0	0	0	0
JULY	1	0	0	0
AUGUST	0	0	0	
SEPTEMBER	0	0	0	0
OCTOBER	0		0	0
NOVEMBER	0		0	0
DECEMBER			0	0
TOTALS ↓		0	0	1

Wall-mounted safety chart in the closed mill. Photograph by Kristen O'Hare.

it came down and he was killed." Denis MacGregor similarly noted that Ladouceur had gone into the machine to "get a scrap that was stuck. It had happened how many times before – you know, a thousand times before. And he had seen older guys, often, bend over and grab and pull it off … Well, he got in there and he couldn't get it, so his shoulder went in – he only needed that [indicating 3 inches between his fingers] – and when he did that he just went right in there. Now, is it the company's fault? … Was it the kid's fault? Everybody else did it. So who do you blame?"

Wally Shisko, the mill manager at the time of the accident, explained to us the functioning of the automatic strapping machine for the sixteen-foot sheets of siding, admitting that "[n]ow every once in a while, it would hang up." This was a recurring problem. This time, however, Ladouceur had gone "into the machine to look up [at the hang up], and boom!" It was an "awful day," agreed Ed Hatton. He remembered the ambulance arriving and the incomprehension on the shop floor. Marcel Boudreau, who worked with Ladouceur at the time, noted that the accident affected some people hard: "Especially the guys, there was probably two or three guys that saw him, saw him die. And those guys took it pretty hard." In fact, whispered Raymond Marcoux, the mill worker who ran over to shut off the machine that day is "still shaken up about that."

The April 1989 death of Denis Ladouceur came at a critical moment, as three other Northern Ontario paper workers had died in a two-month stretch at the mills in Red Rock, Dryden, and Smooth Rock Falls. Two others died later that year. These fatalities sparked an Ontario Ministry of Labour investigation that did not reveal much.[21] Marc Côté noted that there had been a "great big government investigation, and we were all cleared." Once again, he walked us through what he thinks happened:

> We still can't understand why, what happened. The gentleman was working on a great big bundle wrapper: it's a machine about five and a half feet wide and the mouth opens about four feet and a bundle slides through automatically. When it hits an automatic switch, it stops and the arm goes down and squeezes the bundle tight and then it puts a band on it and then raises it back up. For some reason one of the bands got stuck in there. The employee reached on top and between the arm and the bundle, [and] went in to try and free the band. His head was underneath the, everything, his whole body was underneath this big ramp, but when he put his arm up he hit the right switch and it activated the machine, and when it came back up he got caught on the side of the head. Somebody ran over and stopped it, but it was too late. He was pronounced dead. So we [pause], we put in all kinds of safety devices after that, but how far can you go? Can you tie a man down or a person down to a machine, I don't know.

Ruth Thompson, the mill manager's personal assistant, also remembered the accident. The Ontario Ministry of Labour came as soon as it happened and "interviewed everybody, checked things over" with a "fine tooth comb." They concluded it was the employee's mistake. The death of the "young fellow," whom many were close to, was a "sad thing" and "scared a lot of people." Afterward a "kind of calmness goes over the mill and quietness. People are thinking of how easy it could have been them that made the mistake. It's so easy to make a mistake. We can't judge." The accident made everyone more careful, and the company started "writing more rules."

Asked if there was an investigation afterwards, Wally Shisko replied that the government "came in, looked at the equipment, went through our guidelines, our training procedures and everything." The dead man had been trained. "So, naturally, we were found not guilty of what happened." As "nobody could understand why he did it," Shisko didn't think mill workers blamed local management or the company for what happened. Yet there is a strong sense in the interviews with unionized workers that they thought the company indirectly blamed Ladouceur for his own death. To a person, workers sought to protect the memory of their friend and co-worker. Yet nobody blamed the company either. It was "one of those things that happens." Denis MacGregor observed that, like "every other company," there was "big talk" about safety: "Not much else. If you did something wrong and there was an accident, 'We told you, we told you, we told you.'" Anger at the company focused instead on management's decision to continue to operate the rest of the mill on the day of the accident. According to Dan Demers, "the hardboard was still operational, the paper machine, the shop, [but] … nobody's mind was on their work [that day] … So maybe, in retrospect, perhaps they should have shut it down in order to get the guys to think about it a little bit more."

This issue surfaced again, far more forcefully, a decade later, when interviewees recalled the company's response to the death of another co-worker on the job. The paper machine "wasn't for everybody," recalled Marcel Boudreau. "It was hard work. Not everybody could do it." Asked to explain, he noted that it was "physically hard work and very, very stressful." Although not a workplace accident per se, as the man died of a heart attack in the paper machine room, interviewees bitterly recalled how the company continued to operate the entire mill and they were forced to work around the stricken man. More egregious still, the man's brother-in-law worked in the same department. According to Percy Allary: "He lay there on the floor. They called the ambulance. His brother-in-law was there. You know, they didn't even lose five minutes of production. They should have stopped. Everything should have been stopped right there. I don't know why. The guys were in shock … Everybody was running around just trying to do their job and keep that off their mind. But that was the odd thing. He was in and out and gone. And his own brother-in-law was right there and had to phone the family to tell them that he passed away. Meanwhile, he was the operator. And everything kept going."

Marcel Boudreau and Denis MacGregor were similarly repulsed by the company's decision to continue production that day. MacGregor provided the most detailed recollection of what happened:

Now, on the paper machine, we had a guy take a heart attack. So once again, something that had never happened, everybody sort of went [makes a shocked, gaping expression]. Now Gabby, which is this guy's brother-in-law, gets off shift, it's a graveyard shift, Gabby's machine tending, he's in charge of the machine. When the super's not there, the machine tender is like the foreman – well, he's the foreman anyway, but he's in charge because the super's not there. They never even stopped the machine. It was like, well, if we stop the machine what's it gonna help? I mean the guy didn't even put his hands out in front of him to stop himself. He was dead standing. His heart just … he went down and broke his nose. That's how dead he was. Bang, that was it. And Gabby came down from the other end and gave him CPR and everything else, but he was dead. He was dead, his heart had exploded. That was something that happened that nobody saw coming. There was nothing written about what to do. Or who to call. Or whatever.

Continuing, MacGregor noted how management compounded the initial mistake to continue production:

The shift came in to relieve them. They went home. And they were on a short change, which means they left about four o'clock in the morning, and they worked at four o'clock in the afternoon. Nobody phoned anybody to tell them, "hey guys, we'll fix it. You stay home, get some rest, because we know you're not going to sleep much from eight in the morning." And Gabby looked like a zombie when he come in. We were there, graveyard. We were coming in graveyard the day after the accident, so we were relieving people again. And Gabby had not slept, he had not eaten, he was white, he was pale, he was, you know. And that's what angered everybody. They came in, they were told, and they only came in the next morning. When they did come in, they didn't do much about it. They did finally get some counselors in on the … Tuesday. So I think most of the guys were over the shock by then. Except for maybe Gabby because he was like, "He's my brother-in-law and I tried to save him and I couldn't save him, and it's my fault." Out of that came, "If this happens … " [knocks hand on table in a row, making a line of items as in a list]. That's great. That was great [shrugs]. But people were pissed off, not really at MacMillan Bloedel, I guess, as much as the people that were in charge at our mill. It was like, you could have done more, you could have done [it] sooner, you could have done it way quicker. So the relationship between union and the company regressed by five years.

For Boudreau, at least, it revealed the company's degrading attitude towards its employees: "And he dropped dead right in the lunch room. And the mill being what it was, they never missed a beat, they just kept going. The rolls kept coming out, they didn't worry about it. All the boss wanted to know was if there was somebody else coming in to take his place. You're just a number. That's all you were. That's all you were, just a number."

5

UPSTAIRS, DOWNSTAIRS

People like Marc [Côté] moved up from the shop floor, pushing a broom, and worked his way up [to mechanical superintendent]. But in the last ten years they brought in a lot from outside, engineers, with school, but they come in with big ideas but they had no clue … I think that caused some friction, a bit, nothing serious. They come and say "I am the boss."

– Wayne Pigeau[1]

Hierarchical social values are often inscribed in bricks-and-mortar, and the Sturgeon Falls mill was no different: the offices were physically located upstairs from the shop floor.[2] Decisions therefore came from "upstairs," or from "above." Language and education heightened the social distance between the two groups, as most managers were English speaking, university educated, and from out of town. Production workers, by contrast, were mainly French speaking, high school educated, and from the immediate vicinity. The two groups were therefore demographically different, although they cohabitated the same small town and knew one another. Shop-floor managers, who had worked their way up, were most likely to reveal a shared masculine identity in the interviews. This familiarity led managers and production workers to resist wholesale generalizations, acknowledging competent and less competent individuals on the other side of the labour-management divide. The social location of unionized office workers, many of whom were women, was far less certain in the interviews. They might have been "upstairs," but they weren't management and had their own union. The verticality of the mill's physical and social structure thus surfaced throughout the interviews as relational signposts, signalling where people located themselves in the mill hierarchy and with whom they identified or opposed.[3]

Not a particularly militant mill, Sturgeon Falls nevertheless experienced two wildcat strikes, in 1967 and 1985, as well as a bitter industry-wide seven-month strike in 1975–6, shortly after Canadian paper workers split away from their US-based International Union. As with everything else, how these events were remembered and narrated in oral history interviews was informed by people's subsequent experiences of job loss. Mike Lacroix, a former vice-president of the local union, for example, was one whose ambivalence towards the national union led him to question his past involvement. When asked if he was active in the union, he sighed, smiled sadly, and looked down. He then admitted that "that's one place I shouldn't have went, but I did." Mill and factory closings also tend to collapse old workplace hierarchies as locally rooted managers, foremen, skilled tradesmen, office workers, and production works are *all* displaced in the process. Only a lucky few are invited to transfer to other company plants. Otherwise, they share the same fate. The oral accounts of the Sturgeon Falls workers therefore should be understood in the frame of this changing socio-economic and cultural context.

For the most part, locally rooted mill superintendents and office workers sounded a lot like unionized production workers. There are several reasons why this was the case. Most important, perhaps, with only four exceptions, our interviews were conducted with those still living in the Sturgeon Falls area. Accordingly nearly everyone came from the area or married into it. Also, locally rooted managers had worked their way up from the shop floor. Had we tracked down more out-of-town managers, who were clustered at the top of the mill's hierarchy, we would have found more social distance between the two groups. It is also important to recognize change over time, as the social divide between management and unionized workers narrowed as more local men worked their way up. Language and religion became less of a barrier to advancement, as we will see in the next chapter.

Shop-Floor Relations

In a town as small as Sturgeon Falls, managers and workers knew one another personally – leading most to locate workplace problems in individual troublemakers or tyrants, rather than in the wider social structure of the mill itself. Asked if he got along with management, André Girard laughed and said that he "had to deal with them all my life."[4] He did not get along with them all the time, but "we managed to settle our differences." He also learned to "keep going, so you've got to forgive I guess and forget a little bit." André Cartier likewise "never had any problem with

Ken Colquhoun, 2005.
Photograph by David W. Lewis.

management," but he did have a problem with the paper machine superintendent: "small words, things like that." Raymond Marcoux also distinguished between individual managers: "some staff were a pain in the neck. But some were good ... Some were fair and some were not fair." Bruce Colquhoun agreed, recalling that some managers "really wanted you to know that they were boss, and they rubbed it in your face. Often enough they'd make these stupid decisions and you'd tell them 'No, it's easier to do it this way.' 'Look, I'm the boss here. You do it my way.'" Shrugging at the memory, Colquhoun added that "it didn't happen often, but sometimes you wanted to strangle the crap out of some bosses." But, "for the most part, it was pretty good."

When asked if there were tensions between management and the unions, Ken Colquhoun replied that "we had bad days with some of them. We had some real assholes there as managers. And we had some good ones. Not real good ones, but better ones [chuckles]. But some of them were real snotty. That's the word for them." They used to call one manager "Big Red." He had come from the east coast, which triggered a memory of some old shop-floor trash talk: "A guy said, 'What'd he do?' And he was there [the manager]. I said, 'He had the job of closing the eyes on the sardines before they put the lid on the can.' And he was just roaring mad at me when I said that [laughter]. [Shakes head] Son of a bitch, you know. That's what I said in front of a few guys ... He wasn't much of a guy to take a joke."

We heard the same kind of precision from former managers, but they avoided naming individuals. Mill superintendent Gerry Stevens never had a problem working with the union, "because I knew them all very well and we could talk. Now [pauses for dramatic effect], some were easier to work with than others." For his part Ed Fortin admitted that, "for many years we had one … very difficult person to deal with." It "was a case of having to live with him. I never found dealing with the unions a difficult thing … Once you have a collective agreement, the only activity that you should have is the interpretation of [it]. And that was my job." Marc Côté, the superintendent of the machinists, suggested that shop-floor tensions peaked during contract negotiations. But "after everything was settled, everybody went back to working together." The degree of contact that interviewees had with those on the "other side" varied greatly, and was largely dependent on the mobility of their job and where they were located in the mill hierarchy.

Earlier in his work life, Pierre Hardy had little direct contact with management. If he had a problem, he approached his shop steward, who took it from there. That said, he did not think there was a huge chasm between labour and management: "There wasn't that type of thing: 'well, he's management and we're union,' you know?" In fact, "everybody talked to each other and joked together." Later on Hardy worked as the custodian, or janitor, and so had the "whole mill to take care of." As a result he "had a relationship between the superintendents and the guys on the floor, even though I was union." He knew management and they knew him. But there was a line, adding that "I didn't talk about mill stuff. I'd talk about general stuff, you know?" The same caveat could be heard elsewhere as employees signalled that they knew their place. As a non-union "company girl" and an assistant to the personnel director, Ruth Thompson had to be discrete: "When I went to talk to the union people on the floor … I just talked about general things … I never talked about what went on in a meeting or what I knew. If they were to hear it, they would hear it from the proper channels, like the manager."

Nobody was mentioned more in the interviews than Ed Fortin, the mill's long-time personnel director. He surfaced in most of their hiring stories as well as in other aspects of their work-life interviews. Starting in the accounting department, Fortin "[m]oved through the ranks and ended up as [human resources] manager." Having grown up in Sturgeon Falls, Fortin knew "practically everybody in the community." As he said, "I knew their wife's first name and I knew many of their kids." He was widely respected. "Maybe I shouldn't say this," Harold Stewart began, "but Ed Fortin ran the mill … Ed was the authority. Ed was a very smart man. Very smart."

Claude Lortie noted that most of the managers were engineers. They tended to work up from the mill's laboratory, moving from one department to the next. Near the end, Weyerhaeuser's policy was that all superintendents had to be engineers. MacMillan Bloedel had also required that they be engineers, recalled Lortie, "but for relief super, they didn't ask for that." Typically, a relief superintendent was in place for a few weeks or a month or two, not three years as he was: "They never did that before." Placed in charge of the new recycling plant, which was having teething problems, Lortie's authority as a relief superintendent came from his years on the shop floor and his natural ingenuity with machines and an ability to fix things: "You know, there's fifty different answers for it, but once you've got a lot of experience around machinery, a lot of that stuff is not too hard to figure out. You jam it two, three times, and say, no, no, no, that's not working. I tried this. No, that's not working. I'll try something else. And then it's a process of elimination."

Several other interviewees who had worked their way up from the shop floor spoke of their initial reluctance to cross over into management. Born in 1929, John Dillon went to work in the mill in February 1948 as a paper tester. When the paper rolls came off at the end, he took specific parts of the paper and tested its strength. If it wasn't "up to snuff, you culled it, and everybody got mad at you, and the next day a guy would come in and he'd take more parts off, and he would send it out. It was a waste of time, basically." Soon thereafter he was approached by the superintendent of the electrical department to see if he was interested in changing jobs: "And I never left the electrical department. I was there forever. I worked as a helper, I worked as an electrician, and then I worked as a foreman and then I became superintendent ... In those days, you could work your way up." Dillon said he refused the superintendent's job four times before finally agreeing:

> I didn't want to take it. I didn't want to take it because, as foreman, I had the best job in town, I could come and go as I pleased. I worked for figure-skating clubs in North Bay and Sturgeon Falls for fourteen years, and I built all the props, and done all these things that were down on the ice. I could go into the carpentry shop. I never had any problems with management. I used the carpentry shop, I used the materials, I did everything, and I did that for fourteen years. So I'd say to the boys, 'Now, I'll be gone for two or three of hours, I'll be in such-and-such a place if you need me.' But they wouldn't do that – they wouldn't bother me unless it was really critical ... And when I wasn't available, they wouldn't call me, they'd see me later and say, 'I did this, I did that.' So it was quite easy. I didn't want the superintendent's job because it was too [much] every day. But I took it because the guys in the shop, they said 'take it.' They didn't like the guys they were hiring as superintendent. Some were doozies.

Albeit a reluctant manager, Dillon liked the challenge. He enjoyed figuring out how things worked when new equipment arrived so it could be repaired later on: "I had to do a lot of studying and getting up to snuff because you could get a call in the middle of the night. You get a call at five o'clock in the morning, you had to make sure the guys knew how to repair it. So it was always a challenge to me."

Upward mobility sometimes came at a price for locally rooted managers. Marc Côté acknowledged the resulting social separation: "There was always a break between staff and production people, for some reason. Well, I still had friends that were on production, or people I used to work with, but we didn't socialize that much with the crews because we found it difficult … You might be a good friend, but come daytime, eight o'clock in the morning, somebody had to be the boss. And whether I'm your friend or not we still have production to meet, we still have a mill to run. I can still be your friend, but we both have jobs. And that was always a little bit difficult." Dealing with people was the most difficult part of the job. Even though Côté was responsible for maintenance, machines proved to be far less troublesome:

> When you have to make decisions that involves people, it's always difficult. Some guys sometimes are put in a very difficult situation and you have to decide what's going to happen to this man. Now, he might have done something very wrong, but you have to take into account that he also has a family at home, he also has a job, so you have to make a decision that is going to solve the problem and not create too much tension at the same time … I always found [that] … with management, it was more stressful problems, because machinery you can always deal with – you can fix, replace, repair, oil, build up, you can do whatever you want, you're not hurting anybody. But with people, it's quite different. That's what I found very different. Dealing in instances where feelings are hurt because some decisions have to be made, the mill has to run. People have to get along. If they can't get along, well …

Côté learned a lot about people during his eleven and a half years as a superinten-dent: "I knew a lot about machinery, and so what you learn as a superintendent is about people. And companies." As managing workers in a unionized environment is highly regulated, Côté was thankful that he did not have to deal with grievances or compensation issues himself: "You have your job to do and you do your job and keep your nose clean."

It could be a tough life, as managers were on call at all times. Marc Côté had been there thirty-eight years when he retired: "I was starting to feel the stress. I was in the job the longest or close to the longest of anybody that's been in the company. It's not a job that people usually stay in a long time. So eleven and a half years is just about a record for somebody [in] a job like that. It's very, very stressful, being that it's twenty-four hours a day. You wouldn't believe the calls you get at two in the morning, three in the morning … I could've stayed on another two or three years, but I'd done my share."

He was not alone. Larry Shank took early retirement in 1997, at age sixty-one: "You go up the ladder. At that time, I was shift electrician, the best-paying job in the mill. And then I was foreman, and then I was super when my boss was gone. I had these three jobs. All good-paying jobs. And then I'd go on to one, and I'd go on another, and then go on the other … And then my boss would say, he'd even call me, 'Hey, Larry, I have to go to Montreal for two weeks.' Okay, I was the superintendent … So, at one time, I was always there. I mean, when you've got the seniority, you're always there. I was close to the mill. They'd call me, I'd be there. Enough was enough."

By comparison, our questions about the local union did not elicit long or detailed responses from production workers. Most downplayed their involvement or muted their support. "A lot of us didn't bother," Marcel Labbé recalled. Asked if he was active in the union, Pierre Hardy's first impulse was also to minimize it, saying he went to union meetings. His wife Jane then prompted him to say more: "You sat on the union executive as a trustee and whatnot." To this Pierre added: "Yeah, once. But then, well, president and so on and so forth. It was, more or less, my first early years."

The 2002 closure clearly haunted our interviewees' recollections of their working lives before then. When asked if the union did a good job negotiating contracts with the various companies that owned the mill, Marcel Boudreau drew a distinction between the local and national union: "I have no complaints about our local executive. But I do have issues with our national." Invited to expand on this, Boudreau volunteered that the national union had "strung us along" after the mill's closing. "In June they told us that, by the end of June, this would have been all settled here. And then July rolled along. Then August rolled along. And for three months, basically, nothing happened. They were just telling us a lot of bullshit – and that's what it was. And they strung us along, and now, who knows where they are, you know? I don't talk to them." As a result, Boudreau insisted he "was never really too gung-ho working with the union."

During Pierre Hardy's first decade in the mill, the union was very militant. He noted that "the guys just liked it that way. They knew that the company couldn't push anything towards us because these guys were so militant." Jane added: "It was a strong membership, and they looked out for the men." Without naming names, Harold Stewart spoke glowingly of one local union president whom he worked with in the mill's pulping department: "He was smart. They didn't put anything over on him. No." It might have been a strong local union, agreed superintendent Gerry

Stevens, but it wasn't "in the same category as somewhere like Hamilton," which was a hotbed of union militancy. Randy Restoule noted that some union leaders were more militant than others: Their "heads butted" with management "now and again." At times Restoule thought that the union was "too militant," as he "always thought that we could have worked better together."

Asked what it was like working in a unionized environment, Raymond Marcoux replied that he could not imagine "not having a union there – [It] would've been real bad." The union curbed managerial favouritism in terms of who was assigned what shifts, what jobs, or what holiday time. With the union, "you got to earn your stripes to move up." As Marcoux explained, the "union kept it fair." After noting that she worked precisely thirty-seven and a quarter hours per week, Karen Beaudette laughed: "I'd never been in a union before. It was really … a different environment." She observed that, in a unionized environment, you "had to take the breaks." Or, if you worked "five minutes overtime" and somebody with higher seniority did not, there was a problem: "You had to really watch it."

Most of our interviewees regularly attended union meetings. John Dillon recalled that, when the mill still employed more than five hundred, the meetings were held downtown in a hall or the town's cinema. Asked what they were like, he laughed: "Well, they were ridiculous. The old guy's up in the back couldn't hear, and you'd discuss a certain subject for twenty minutes to half an hour, and then all of a sudden, his hand would go up [raises right hand], and he'd say 'what about …' the thing you were talking about" [laughs again]. The meetings were "pretty hectic at times," recalled Gordon Jackson. "It would get hot."[5] Bruce Colquhoun also attended them, serving as an "inside guard" for many years. "I used to make sure it was nice and quiet," he smiled. "Anybody got unruly there, settle him down. I never had to throw anybody out. And I'm glad, because everybody else was bigger than me."

Day-to-day trade unionism was not exactly glamorous. Harold Stewart, a union shop steward in the platewood division in the 1960s, recalled that it was the "most thankless job in the world" because he couldn't "satisfy everybody." There was always someone who said "you're no damn good and all this." Shrugging his shoulders, he sighed: "You do the best you can. You know, you can only do so much. You can't order the company to do this or that. You have to suggest or ask. Request." Machinist Henri Labelle, another shop steward, similarly recalled that it was "not a gratifying job." As he explained it: "If you help one, you hurt a few more. So you can't please everybody. I've seen guys that we worked hard for … and we succeeded. Then he'd go back in trouble, and then we couldn't succeed. He would forget what we did before."

There were a lot of grievances. Union activist André Girard, who started working at the mill on 8 October 1959, and stayed for the next forty-two years and eight

Marcel Labbé, who worked in the powerhouse. Photograph by David W. Lewis.

months, was involved with them "for most of my life." Some were hard to resolve, others easy, "but it is an ongoing thing, never stops." According to Raymond Marcoux, most grievances occurred when management tried "to pull a fast one and see how far they [got]." This might involve a job posting, or the assignment of better shifts, or asking people to do something that was not in their job description. People would be warned by their line supervisor. Asked about the kinds of grievances that arose, Ed Fortin told us that "there are always requests. You can never dry up the list. So, if there were ten requests on the list and you didn't want ten more, you didn't give in on the first ten. You see what I mean? So it's a living approach." If things got "really bad," noted Ruth Thompson, they would be "brought up to Mr Fortin's office." They would have their union representative with them. Some years employee relations were good, other years less so. Thompson credited "different union presidents with different natures and different personalities." Mostly they managed to "work out" their problems. But some issues festered.

Ruth Thompson used to type all of the letters for Ed Fortin "about the different grievances that [were] put in. There were a lot of different grievances." All in all, "Mr Fortin had his hand on things. He was very, very good at his job. He knew how to handle the men and the superintendents, the union presidents." Fortin also backed her up when needed. One time they had put out a job posting that directed people to apply by nine o'clock in the morning:

> Well, this employee came up and he said he had put his application in and he was
> accusing me. He said, "Mrs Thompson never put my application in, she didn't like

me and she didn't put my application in … So he went to the union president and the union president come up and talked to me. And I said, 'No, he didn't have his application in.' So then Andy [the local union president] went down and hit the young fella up, and he said, 'Well, yeah, it was in my lunch bag. I forgot to put it in' and everything. And Andy said: 'Don't ever, ever accuse Ruth again.' Because he knew that I was honest. He really reprimanded his own employee. He was mad. Over the years, I never had too much trouble with the union.

Generally speaking, contract negotiations were tough. At contract time the company always warned that the mill would shut, so mill workers just took it with a grain of salt. Mill manager Cam Barrington told us that, at contract time, he pleaded with his bosses: "Don't send me into the game with an unloaded gun."[6] He wanted to be able to say that the mill would close if the union stuck to its own guns. Tensions therefore mounted at contract time. According to Percy Allary, "Well, then, management was management and you were union. So they had one story and you had the other story. But … we didn't avoid each other in the mill or say, 'here comes the manager,' stop talking, or turn your head the other way. We still talked to them and they talked to us. But union was union, management was management. You had two different outlooks. That's why you ended up with strikes sometimes. Nobody wanted to give in." But there were wider issues. Ron Demers noted that the Sturgeon Falls mill was "a small mill in comparison to others," so "we were not the ones setting the pattern whenever you had a collective agreement negotiated. We would follow, we would get the pattern, or we'd try to get the pattern."

Our interviewees' subsequent experience of job loss infused their interpretation of past bargaining. Many, like Harold Stewart, thought the union's benefits plan "could've been a lot better." He was critical of fellow trade unionists for not thinking longer term when they had the chance. "They weren't looking down the road," he lamented. Pierre Hardy shared this frustration, adding the issue of job security to the mix: at contract time, the "guys are after benefits and money. They don't think about places closing down." Hardy "always said" to the local union leadership that they needed to "get security put in contracts. 'We don't know what's going to happen in ten, fifteen years.' 'No! Don't need that.'" Even pensions were not a priority until the final decade of the mill's existence. Before that, "they were peanuts." When workers are twenty-five or thirty years old, pensions are not a priority:

JANE: You're not thinking thirty years down the road.
PETE: You don't think about that.

JANE: You just want what you can get for today, kind of thing, you know?

PETE: So, then, when they did announce it, well, the guys, some guys said, "Well, gee, I guess you were right. We should have asked for this." And the company would have gave it to us ... You know? And maybe that would have made a difference ... You make it so hard for them to shut down, they would have thought twice before shutting the place down.

The circumstances of our interviewees, now that the plant had closed, coloured their past recollections and infused their analysis of what did and did not happen.

The Gendered Division of Labour

The interviews also revealed a great deal about the gendered division of labour. Merna Nesbitt told us that, in the early years, "there were jobs that were classified as women's jobs and jobs that were men's jobs. You didn't cross the line, you know? These were girl's jobs. And usually they were secretaries, typists at that time." Given this reality, Nesbitt frequently spoke of "down in the mill" as a place apart from where she worked upstairs in the offices. But this line was not always a stable one. In the old days some women worked downstairs in satellite offices on the shop floor. But as the mill declined after the 1960s, office work became centralized until "we were all upstairs." Even upstairs, however, the sex labelling of office jobs prevailed into the 1970s. Men once did many of the jobs later done by women: "Towards the end, the girls started to take over what had – years ago – been called a male's job," Nesbitt said. Earlier, she noted, "it was impossible for a female to do a male's job or vice versa." Ruth Thompson and Merna Nesbitt were the two "company girls," as they worked directly for upper management. There were also unionized workers such as Hubert Gervais, Ben Lajeunesse, and Karen Beaudette. At one point in her interview, Beaudette insisted that she was not treated any differently because she was a woman working in an industrial environment. "Not me, no," she insisted. "I never acted like a woman." Perhaps realizing the implications of what she had said, Beaudette quickly corrected herself: "I shouldn't say that. I wasn't one to beat around the bush."

Everybody had a defined job. But office work was changing. At first Merna Nesbitt worked in the mill's storehouse area on the shop floor. Her job was classified as a female position, and so was the lowest-paid position in the section. "That's the way it was," she recalled. She left the mill when she became pregnant, but returned to work years later in payroll, upstairs. By then things were

The mill's women's baseball team, 1 July 1919. The mill began to employ women on the shop floor earlier in the twentieth century to make "hanging" paper (or wallpaper). Courtesy of West Nipissing Public Library.

Spanish River Pulp and Paper Company office staff, 1920s: (from left to right) Edmon Roy (laboratory technician), Alice Bourgault (stenographer), Jean Ratchford (stenographer), Margaret Sullivan (stenographer), unknown, Mr Ewing (chief of department), Mr Brawn (graphic designer). Courtesy of West Nipissing Public Library.

"beginning to change a bit." Women began to move into positions that previously had been occupied by men. But there were no computers or photocopiers yet. Nesbitt told us about the "big old tall Underwoods" [manual typewriters] and Gestetner copier she worked with. She asked the student interviewer, Kristen O'Hare: "Have you heard of it?" When O'Hare shook her head, Nesbitt explained how it worked. First she would type on the stencil, and then "it went onto a roll on the machine and you turned it. The first one we had, we turned the roll, and it caught. The paper was sent in and the person had it copied. You had to turn the handle," she repeated.

When Merna Nesbitt first worked at the mill, there was no staff union; only the "men in the mill" had a union. When she returned in 1965 after raising her children, however, there was an office union as well: Local 282 of the Office and Professional Employees International Union (OPEIU), which had been formed in 1950 as part of a wider organizing drive among white collar workers at Abitibi's Canadian pulp and paper mills. At first there were separate seniority lists for men and women working in occupations covered by the office union's collective agreement, until it became illegal to sex-type jobs this way.[7] Nesbitt noted that she was the first woman to join the pension plan: "Some of the women never joined the pension plan until MacMillan Bloedel took over in 1979, and there was no choice then." With the continued downsizing of the mill and the abolition of the gendered division of labour in the collective agreements, post-layoff bumping further blurred old boundaries. One anonymous interviewee recalled how one man had no choice but to take the traditionally female position of switchboard operator or face layoff, but soon quit because he could not type.

Except in the office areas, the Sturgeon mill was a masculinized workplace. When asked about women working the plant, many said that women *only* worked in the offices. "Women don't belong in the mills in West Nipissing [the municipality of which, after amalgamation, Sturgeon Falls is now a part]," noted local historian Wayne LeBelle. "That was the very standard thinking at the time and it is still." This is not to say, however, that women never worked in production. Marc Côté noted that "women always worked at the mill." Indeed, "even at the beginning," he said, women made "wallpaper for houses" on one of the paper machines: "They did the designs, all the girls, they were all women in there." A handful of women were also hired in to production jobs in the 1970s and 1980s, only to be laid off shortly thereafter when the hardboard mill closed and the workforce was halved.

Interviewees drew a clear distinction between the "offices" upstairs and the "mill" downstairs. There is a particularly strong sense of the verticality of the plant in Karen Beaudette's interview: "There was a downstairs and an upstairs, and then, when we left, we were all upstairs. So everybody's in one office." John Dillon similarly recalled how Wally Shisko, the mill manager in the 1990s, "would come into the mill and come down." Office workers drew the same discursive line. Merna Nesbitt, for example, noted that the old purchasing office had been "down in the mill, it wasn't in the main office." Later, she noted that her husband "worked down in the mill." For his part, Hubert Gervais liked working "upstairs" as it "wasn't" monotonous." Otherwise, he added, "most of the jobs were monotonous." In his job, it was "different every day. You never knew what you got on your desk the morning you come in. But in the mill, it was monotonous. You're a truck driver, you're a truck driver. Brrrrmm, get the load of OCC [recycled cardboard], go and put it on the belt. Brrrm, brrrm, all day, eight hours. I couldn't stand that."

Asked how she became vice-president of OPEIU Local 282, the office workers union, Karen Beaudette laughed and said it was "my turn." She was always pro-union, citing her grandfather and uncle in Scotland, who worked in a coal mine, "and they were big for unions. I remember them coming home from work and black, black, and you could only see their eyes. And their teeth when they opened their mouth." People were "disposable" back in the 1920s and 1930s, she added. "Not so much now, but back then." It was interesting to hear her locate the need for unions in the past, rather than in the present, and to locate this need in male proletarian production, particularly since she had just gone through a devastating plant closing herself.

Unionized office workers functioned in an in-between space between unionized production workers down on the factory floor and mill managers in the offices above. OPEIU was what one anonymous office union member called a "polite union" compared to the rough-and-tumble of shop-floor struggles inside the mill. The "big union downstairs had the big sledgehammer," recalled Hubert Gervais: "What they got, we had to negotiate the same thing. But the company told us, at one time, 'what they got, you're gonna get. No more.' They tried to give us less, but we said, 'Hey, you give it to the people downstairs, why not us?' So it was easy negotiation at times. Because we could tell as soon as they settled that we had to go through the rigmarole of going through negotiation." Karen Beaudette agreed, laughing "We would just wait until after the big union negotiated and then just say, well, you know, 'We just want what you want.' What are they going to say – 'No'? And why not? They're bigger, they have more money. Why not let them do the grunt work, you know? Ah, that's right, we used them." As a result the unionized office workers never walked a picket line of their own, but were expected to respect the picket lines of production workers whenever they walked off the job.

Abitibi mill workers, 1970. Courtesy of Hubert Gervais.

A Wildcat Strike and Its Repercussions

Post-war compromise had seen unions win a measure of workplace predictability with the closed shop, mandatory dues checkoff, and routinized collective bargaining instituted in exchange for workplace discipline (no striking during a contract) and the recognition of managerial prerogatives.[8] As historian Peter McInnis concludes, "unions were drawn into the existing capitalist structures."[9] This consensus began to fray in the late 1960s and then unravel in the 1970s with trade liberalization, the onset of mass layoffs, stagflation, and the rise of neoliberalism. Societal conflict and protest also spilled into the industrial workplace, where younger workers in particular chaffed at the monotony of some labour and sought to reform unions that had grown complacent, bureaucratic, or corrupt. Shop-floor resistance took many forms, but most spectacularly in the proliferation of illegal "wildcat" strikes, typically involving local issues such as promotion or dismissal, the disciplining of a union member, or changes to the status quo. From 1971 to 1973, for example, half of British Columbia's strikes were illegal, with 702 in forestry alone.[10]

A wildcat strike erupted in Sturgeon Falls in May 1967 when more than four hundred members of Local 71 of the Pulp & Sulphite Workers walked off the job to protest the promotion of a pipefitter – and union member – as a local foreman.[11] It erupted after the company changed the process in the pulping plant, reducing the number on a work crew. At that time mill workers belonged to two different unions. "Then there was a big question as to who would be responsible, who would have jurisdiction over those jobs," recalled Ed Fortin, They had to do some preparatory work, so a new crew was set up from the mill's maintenance workforce and the chemical superintendent was put in charge. He took some of his regular people with him, including a "very unpopular guy, a pipefitter, who was responsible for the piping and also some welders." The welders, however, would not work for him, "so they went on a wildcat strike," Fortin explained. "They pulled out. And that's illegal. And they were [out] a week. We negotiated with them and talked to them." At one point the strikers "decided to develop what was called a 'book of sins,' on this individual, and they set themselves up in a motel room in town, and they interviewed people who had been subject to this individual, and they wrote everything down for each person that attended. They wrote up their complaint." By the time they presented it to the company, the book seemed two inches thick. The wildcat strike ended only after a compromise was reached.[12]

During this time, members of the office workers were put in a difficult position. Should they cross the picket line, as demanded by management, or respect it? Hubert Gervais was one of those who crossed, and he deeply regretted his decision. Gervais recalled that they were bused into the plant that week: "And that aggravated the men in the mill, and that stayed for about ten years. You know, like, 'you crossed a picket line, you son of a … !' and 'you were a union man, you crossed a picket line.' But, the management had called each of us, and told [us], 'you come into that bus or you're gone tomorrow.' So, after fifteen years, you said, 'what?' I get on the bus."

At the time of the walkout, Ken Colquhoun was working in the tool crib, where he sharpened saws. He recalled that the millwrights came down to him from up top and said, "Hey, Ken, get ready, we're leaving in about half an hour. We're walking out!' So we all walked out. That strike lasted … I think, it was a week long." Everyone went out, causing "a lot of stink." Colquhoun then related that the superintendent of the machine shop had told the "machine shop people" about his decision on the promotion: "The guys said, 'No goddamn way! We are not going to go with that.' They said they wouldn't work in there under him. They wouldn't work with him because nobody liked him to start with. So they said, 'Sorry, that's the way it's gotta be.'" Other interviewees confirmed this chain of events. Several suggested that the new foreman was "a pretty tough cookie," telling the men that when he got "to be boss, some of the guys here are going to get fired." When the members of this department walked out en masse, the rest of the mill followed suit.

Looking back years later, national union leader James M. Buchanan concluded that the wildcat strike had been "costly to all concerned."[13] The would-be foreman brought Abitibi and thirty-three individuals, including three union staff members, to court. As personnel director, Ed Fortin, along with the mill manager Herb Evans, had to go to Toronto to appear before various lawyers. "We were asked a lot of questions," he recalled. It was a long process. The strike occurred in 1967 but it did not go to trial for several years. First they had to go into discovery, where Fortin had to answer some five hundred questions. The union leadership and the named members stayed as a single group of defendants. At the trial, under Justice Keith of the Ontario Supreme Court, Fortin spent a day and a half on the stand being questioned by lawyers for the union, the company, and the individuals. As Fortin explained, after a week, "the union saw themselves going down the drain. And, they broke up for the weekend, came to Sturgeon, had a general meeting – in the basement of the church, I believe, and they decided to offer a settlement. And we got back to Toronto on the Monday for another court day, restart. And there was discussion between the lawyers. They asked the company to kick in $5,000. I said no, that we hadn't done anything. And they phoned … my superintendent vice-president in Toronto, and he said, 'Well, what did Ed say?' They said, 'No.' So it was no. So I was supported." The court awarded the plaintiff $40,000 as well as legal costs amounting to $27,000. The local union had to take out a loan to cover its share of the settlement, paid out in 171 monthly instalments of $350, most of which went towards the interest, rather than the principal.[14] As it was the inflationary 1970s, the financial burden on the local union was immense. Fortin said the president of the local told him that "if any one of us failed to meet our obligations, they can zero in on one person." There was real concern.

In 1975 Andrew Cull, the local union president, with two other union officers – including André Girard, second vice-president – requested that the national union pay the balance "owed by us on the labour dispute," as it was "creating an immense burden to the membership in a very serious manner financially wise."[15] Many mill workers were now on layoff. It was not until 1984, however – fifteen years after the walkout – that the national union assumed the remaining payments. Explaining the decision, Buchanan wrote that the executive board had "taken into consideration that your local has continued to make the payments on a regular basis for eleven years, without default."[16] After the incident several local managers, including the machine shop superintendent and the mill manager, were transferred elsewhere. Personally, Marcel Labbé didn't think the mill manager "had anything to do with it, but he could have stepped in. So they were shipped out. Got new management. Haven't had any problems since."

Given the lawsuit, interviewees were understandably reluctant to say much about the wildcat strike. When queried, Gerry Stevens sighed, began to answer, paused,

Sturgeon Falls mill from the air, 1970. Courtesy of Hubert Gervais, Library Archives Canada.

and continued, but kept things safely vague. Asked if it was resolved satisfactorily, he agreed: "It was resolved. It should have never happened. If I'd been manager of the place it wouldn't have. But … I don't want to talk about that." For his part Bruce Colquhoun didn't want to say anything on tape, only that he knew the pipefitter in question, who was a nice guy. Other interviewees put distance between themselves and the decision to walk out. It was not a strike anyone was proud of. As for the man at the centre of the storm, he never returned to the mill.

National Sovereignty and the Paper Workers

For much of the twentieth century, workers downstairs in the mill were represented by two unions. The largest of these was Local 71 of the International Brotherhood of Pulp and Sulphite Workers; the other, representing those who worked on the paper machine or the pulp digester, was Local 135 of the International Brotherhood of Paper Makers. Both unions were affiliated with the American Federation of Labor in the United States. The merging of the two great labour federations in the United States to form the AFL-CIO in 1957 eventually provided the opportunity for the two unions to merge in 1972 to form the United Paperworkers International Union (UPIU). As a result, Locals 71 and 135 in Sturgeon Falls formed Local 7135.[17]

At the same time as unions were merging into ever-larger units, rising nationalism in Canada was pushing trade unionists to demand greater autonomy and even outright independence from US-dominated International Unions. Things came to a head soon after the UPIU was formed when the Canadian region left to form the Canadian Paperworkers Union (CPU) in 1974. But the fight for more Canadian autonomy had begun long before. Leo H. Lorrain, from Gatineau, Quebec, was first elected to the Pulp & Sulphite's international executive board in 1955, becoming first vice-president and its Canadian director in 1965. The union's constitution was then amended so that the Canadian director was selected by the Canadian caucus, rather than by the entire convention. The Canadian director was now clearly responsible for collective bargaining as well as organizing, research, education, lobbying, and public relations in Canada.[18] A March 1967 conference of Canadian Pulp & Sulphite locals, meeting in Ottawa during Canada's centennial year, debated Canadian national identity and agreed to form a committee as well as a series of recommendations to further increase Canadian representation in the International Union.[19] The committee's report was adopted the following year.[20]

Canadian demands for more autonomy in Pulp & Sulphite, and later the UPIU, were aided by widespread dissatisfaction with the union's leadership. A rank-and-file

Workers leaving the mill (no date). Courtesy of West Nipissing Public Library.

insurgency demanding democratic reforms emerged on both sides of the Canada-United States border, starting in the late 1950s. In March 1961 dissidents met in Denver to establish the Rank and File Movement for Democratic Action. I have not found any evidence that Sturgeon Falls joined the insurgency. The defeat of reform motions at Pulp & Sulphite's 1962 convention led several British Columbia locals to withdraw and form the Pulp and Paper Workers of Canada. A little later a number of US locals in the Pacific Northwest also left the union. Then-president Joseph P. Tonelli's son and nephew were named by US officials as being partially responsible for the disappearance of nearly $1 million from the UPIU pension fund, of which he was trustee. In 1978 Tonelli himself was convicted of embezzlement.[21] But by then the Canadians were already gone.

The final straw was Tonelli's decision to interfere in industry-wide bargaining with Canada's Abitibi Paper. Preparations for pattern bargaining had been undertaken by union locals from across the country since February 1973, including which company to target first to set the pattern. The union's overall strategy was to "run them close together and then apply for conciliation, with the ultimate aim to have as many as possible in an identical strike position should it be necessary."[22] In all there were forty-four local unions representing 15,250 members facing sixteen major companies.[23] An agreement was reached first with Kimberly-Clark (at Terrace Bay, Ontario) that summer, breaking the employers' united front. Abitibi then requested a resumption of negotiations in late August, prompting the union to start with that company.

The negotiations with Abitibi are well documented in the Canadian Paperworkers Union Fond at Library and Archives Canada. When James H. Buchanan, who was heading the negotiations, arrived at Toronto's Royal York Hotel on 29 August 1973, he discovered that Leo Lorrain had been trying to reach him:[24] uninvited, President Tonelli had travelled to Toronto to meet with Buchanan about the negotiations. The next day Abitibi presented a three-year offer, but without any provision for a cost of living allowance, which was unacceptable to the union in the inflationary seventies. Two days later Tonelli indicated that he would like to be updated on the negotiations. Then, on 4 September, Lorrain advised Buchanan that Tonelli "was on his way" to the conference room where Abitibi and the Canadian leadership were negotiating. According to Buchanan, "Half-way through, there was an interruption at the door, and entry onto the scene was made by President Tonelli and one of his assistants. He had just got settled down and the presentation resumed, when it was again interrupted by the entry of Mr Tom Bell, the president of Abitibi Company." Clearly, unknown to the union's negotiating team, Tonelli had already been in direct contact with the company. The Canadians were stunned by this turn of events.

Faced with this interference, the Canadian region decided to increase its pressure on Abitibi, directing the Iroquois Falls local to strike on the morning of 7 September. It was a symbolic choice, as the company had originated at this Northeastern Ontario mill: "The wheels were now in motion. The basic plan was one mill down at a time, every eight to twelve hours and maybe try to rotate in sequence, provided the Company did not take it out of our hands and take them down."[25] Although an eleventh-hour agreement with Abitibi was reached, Tonelli's interference was keenly felt.[26] In the days that followed, the International Union issued a press release declaring that President Tonelli had "guided the negotiations to a successful conclusion in Toronto."[27] The union's newsletter likewise credited Tonelli for the Abitibi deal. Disgusted, Buchanan felt that the article "seemed to overlook completely the bull work done by the delegates and staff and therefore detracted from the credit that was theirs."[28] This lack of respect for Canadian autonomy prompted Buchanan to send a strongly worded letter to Tonelli, and on 5 October "All Hell Broke Loose."

That December Tonelli met with the Canadian regional leadership and told them that he was "disenchanted at the cold reception he had received from the staff and delegates at the Abitibi negotiations." He then revealed that many members of the union's international executive board were also dissatisfied with the "never-ending demands from the Canadian members for special considerations; of his own feelings of frustration from the continual harassment in the form of veiled threats of Nationalism if this or that weren't done. He suggested it could not continue, that if Canada could not be realigned financially and otherwise, that perhaps the time had come to be on their own."[29] More specifically, Tonelli spoke of the steep financial cost of maintaining the Canadian region's office and newspaper.

At its meeting in Puerto Rico in January 1974, the international executive board voted in favour of a resolution put forward by the Canadian officers of the International Union calling for an independence referendum: "Since the turn of the century, the United Paperworkers International Union and its predecessor unions served the needs of United States and Canadian workers in the paper and related industries. In the formative years, assistance was generously provided by the Internationals to help organize, maintain, and promote the interests of the members of both the United States and Canada." The resolution went on to say that this task was not easy, as the union faced employer resistance as well as "prolonged and bitter struggles." However, the "Canadian membership, moving with the tide of national sentiment, demanded a greater degree of autonomy and additional considerations in many fields – its own Canadian Conference, its own bilingual newspaper, its own Research and Education Department, and the right of the Canadian Director to grant strike sanction and approve contracts for Canadian local unions." In consequence, "the Canadian membership in recent years has conducted its own affairs autonomously, with a few exceptions, as a parallel organization to its United States counterparts."[30] Although the international executive board agreed to a Canada-wide referendum on independence, Tonelli could not resist complaining again of the "continual harassment from the Locals and individuals threatening Nationalism and it had become almost intolerable." He even shared one letter that warned that the local union "would go National if certain things weren't done."[31] The Americans had had enough.

Armed with this decision, the Canadian leadership convened a special meeting of local union presidents in Montreal on 19 February 1974, who voted overwhelmingly in favour of proceeding with a referendum. The *Canadian Paperworkers Journal*, the official organ of the Canadian region, heralded the moment: "A thunderous roar of 'yeas' rocked the convention hall … in response to a special resolution introduced by the Canadian Executive Officers."[32] By contrast, it said that only three or four "nays" could be heard in the convention hall. The proceedings, however, tell a somewhat different story, as 31 of the 215 local unions voted against the motion.[33] Dozens of trade unionists participated in the debate, but Andy

Cull and Sam Jackson, representing Sturgeon Falls, do not appear to have done so. Still, the howling nationalist winds of the time were very much in evidence, with Buchanan declaring that "there was a strong movement abroad in the nation calling for Canadian independence and that our reluctance to recognize these forces at this time could result in major difficulties in the not too distant future."[34] Lorrain also appealed to the hearts of those present and to the prevailing nationalist mood, calling on them to become "masters of our fate." Writing in the *Toronto Star* about the unfolding story, journalist Richard Gwyn observed that a "nationalist fervour" was sweeping Canada's union movement.[35]

As expected, the referendum result overwhelmingly favoured Canadian independence. Fully 87 per cent of Canadian paper workers opted to form their own national union.[36] The vote in Sturgeon Falls was even more lopsided: as yet unmerged, the mill's Local 71 voted 235 to 2 for independence, while another 209 either didn't vote or spoiled their ballots; in Local 135, members voted 27 to 1 in favour of independence, with only 6 spoiled or unused ballots. Elsewhere only a handful of local unions voted to remain with the UPIU.[37] It was a "Vote for Canada," declared the Montreal *Gazette*.[38] With Andy Cull and André Girard among the 450 delegates in attendance, the new Canadian Paperworkers Union was founded on 3 June in Toronto, becoming Canada's largest independent union.

But divorces are often messy. Despite the international executive board's initial approval, the US leadership took a hard line on the division of assets, going so far as to threaten to take possession of all union-owned automobiles, furniture, and fixtures unless the Canadian locals paid their per capita dues to the international office.[39] The International Union also refused to transfer Canada's share of the strike fund, leaving the CPU vulnerable. To make matters worse, Tonelli decided that the UPIU should remain in Canada and represent the ten local unions that had voted not to join the CPU.[40]

Today these national struggles seem far removed from the post-closure lives of our interviewees. It was another time, a different world. As a result, the only person to speak of these events was André Girard. When they "became a Canadian union," he recalled, "we were proud to do that even though it was hard on us because all the money the Americans were supposed to give us didn't pay us and this and that. I was involved in all of that, too. So that was rough and tough, too." By 1987 the CPU had 57,000 members organized into 274 union locals across Canada, including 78 in Ontario. In 1992, battered by mill closures, the CPU merged with two other national unions to form the Communications, Energy and Paperworkers Union of Canada (CEP).[41]

The Abitibi Strike of 1975–6

Canadianization proved to be financially costly, as the new union was left without a strike fund. The forestry companies therefore sought to break the new union in the 1975 round of negotiations.[42] By all accounts it was a "desperate struggle to entrench company-wide bargaining rights for the new union."[43] Clearly the CPU had something to prove, calling for a $2 an hour increase in eastern Canada to achieve parity with the more highly paid paper workers of British Columbia.[44] This bargaining position represented a whopping 41 per cent increase from the current base wage of $4.71, a testament to the rapidly rising cost of living in the inflationary 1970s.[45]

The negotiating team was headed by the national vice-president of the CPU, with local delegates being named from each mill. Sturgeon Falls was represented by Andy Cull, M. Gosson, and André Girard.[46] In his interview Girard noted that, in those days, all of the Abitibi mills negotiated as one: "We'd all meet in Toronto and then there would be like the three mills from Thunder Bay, Sault Ste Marie, and Iroquois Falls, Beaupré in Quebec, ourselves in Sturgeon – a big group negotiating together. And we had more power that way in a roundabout way because if we were weak a little bit in one year, well, the others would carry us." Contract talks broke down almost immediately, however, "when the parties were unable to agree on which of nine Abitibi mills would be represented at the master contract talks."[47] The company wanted to separate its three Ontario paper product mills (including Sturgeon Falls) from the more highly profitable newsprint mills, thereby breaking the pattern.

Sturgeon Falls mill workers legally walked off the job on the morning of 15 July 1975.[48] When they first went out, Percy Allary recalled, most "everybody said 'ah, maybe six weeks, two months.' But then it kept going through Christmas." And yet the company "never really offered anything. They just kept us out." For the first ten weeks, strikers received no strike pay whatsoever and only $22 a week thereafter.[49] To survive, striking paper workers had to take temporary jobs elsewhere.[50] Raymond Marcoux had just got married that year, and was on his honeymoon when he heard on the radio that they were on strike. Fortunately his new father-in-law was a building contractor, so he worked for him during those long months. Nor was the strike "the end of the world" for Harold Stewart, who owned a farm and so had plenty of other work to do: "I guess, for the guys in town who had nothing else to do, the time must have been long. And the pay wasn't too good. But myself, I didn't suffer because of the strike." According to Pierre Hardy, for "the families involved, for the married people, it must have been hard. I mean, eight months without work? Nothing coming in. Couldn't even collect unemployment insurance or anything. It must have been pretty rough for those guys." This was certainly true for Lionel Sarazin, whose daughter was born in late 1975 while he was on strike, and who was in the middle of building a house. His family had to "tighten up" its finances considerably. For his part, Bruce Colquhoun had been laid off from the mill in December 1974, and so missed the big strike. It was a good thing he was on unemployment benefits at the time, Colquhoun recalled, as he could help out his father Ken, who was on strike.

The fifteen members of OPEIU Local 282 were in a difficult position during the strike, as they refused to cross the picket line. Luckily, a week into the strike, management did them a kindness by laying them off so that they would be eligible for unemployment insurance benefits. "Otherwise, we had nothing," recalled Ben Lajeunesse. "We couldn't go to work, and we weren't on strike. We didn't get strike pay, we would have had absolutely nothing. So they agreed to lay us off, and we could draw unemployment all the time the strike was on." Salaried personnel were not so lucky, as they were expected to cross the picket line every day. Merna Nesbitt laughed when asked, as she had to cross the line manned by her husband. But people understood. She recalled that another striker had asked her husband if this caused any problems at home, but he said, "'No, Merna works and pays the bills.' He was very proud of the fact that we didn't have to go into our savings during the strike. And that was more than six months." Visibly sighing, she recalled it was a

long time to cross the picket line. But there was never any trouble except one morning. It was getting cold, and … they had to start up the steam plant to stop pipes and things from freezing. And they brought some people from out of town – in fact, quite a few of them, I think, from out of province – and they came and were going to be taken into the mill. The men on strike became quite militant that morning, and there were a lot of them around. Mr Barrington called me in the morning and he said, "When you come to the mill, when you get to the gate, if anybody approaches at all, just turn around. Don't say anything, just turn around and leave." There were three women, we were all non-union employees, so we went together, and when we got to the gate they slowed down to go in. And people, the men, knew who we were, of course, and they approached us. So … we just drove slowly on and went around and went back home. I think we were home about two days, three at the most. And then they got an injunction, something like that, and then we were allowed to go back to work. And there was no other problems.

Nesbitt's account of the hardening of the picket line likely occurred in November 1975, when the local union leadership decided to blockade the closed mill, preventing supervisory staff from entering. The strike was in its eighteenth week, and the life savings of those on strike had dwindled. Not surprisingly frustration boiled over. This was a risky strategy, as it was early winter and pipes could freeze unless heating and water pressure were maintained. By barring management's access to the mill, according to mill manager Cam Barrington, the union had effectively withdrawn "essential services" needed to operate the steam plant and heat the mill. When mass picketing at the plant prevented their entry, Barrington arranged for them to use a helicopter until a court injunction and a threatened lawsuit reopened the main gate. "It was a long haul, that one," recalled John Dillon. For his part, Gerry Stevens remembered moments of camaraderie on the picket line: "I used to go down and sit in the shack and talk with them." It was a long strike, so, "to keep our sanity, we did various jobs within the mill. I did, anyway. I had to schedule everybody. That was my job. I even worked in the powerhouse on Christmas Eve. So that's what we'd have to do. But everybody pitched in and did whatever you asked them to do. And we did quite a few jobs within the mill."

After seven months, workers accepted a contract proposal that gave them only modest raises.[51] The federal government's wage-and-price controls had kicked in mid-strike, meaning they were forced to return to work for little more than they had been offered in the first place. It was a far cry from the $2 an hour the union initially demanded. But a 24 cents an hour cost of living allowance was achieved, and the union won its case to keep the three paper products plants in the pattern. Even so, the tentative deal was so weak that the union's negotiating committee made no recommendation one way or another, letting the membership decide: fully 82.9 per cent voted in favour.[52]

And yet Joseph Tonelli still found a way to interfere in the negotiations. First, the ten remaining UPIU locals in Canada had signed an interim contract with employers during the long strike that undercut the CPU,[53] which Leo Lorrain called "nothing short of a sellout."[54] Writing to Tonelli, he said that, "[i]f someone had set out to deliberately torpedo negotiations in the pulp and paper industry of Canada on behalf of working people of this country he couldn't have done a better job." To make matters worse, Lorrain believed that the strike could have been avoided in the first place had the local union president in Terrace Bay not circulated the "most disgusting letter" to CPU locals in December 1974 that "probably contributed to a rejection by our joint memberships of the not totally unreasonable offer which had been made by the Abitibi Paper Co."[55] Years of anger and frustration concerning Tonelli and the UPIU finally exploded at the 1976 convention of the Canadian Labour Congress, when the AFL-CIO president sent Tonelli to give its traditional fraternal greetings. He was met with a "chorus of boos and jeers and a protest parade in front of the stage by 65 delegates of the Canadian Paperworkers Union."[56] More than half the convention then exited the hall, leaving Tonelli to give his speech to those remaining.[57]

The 1975 strike might have retained the industry-wide pattern negotiations, but it came at a steep price. Four years later Abitibi sold the Sturgeon Falls mill to Mac-Millan Bloedel, and the pattern was broken for good in 1984–5. Henceforth "[i]t was a little harder when you negotiated because we were negotiating alone, not as a group," recalled André Girard. Raymond Marcoux agreed: "Negotiations were shorter, and better," when Sturgeon was part of Abitibi, "because the company had more to lose there. When we just had one mill, that was the difference." He believed that the local union had "one good negotiation" with MacMillan Bloedel, then "we fell behind in wages." Almost to a person, mill workers in Sturgeon Falls saw the 1975 strike as a defeat – it "hurt us," insisted Percy Allary – even though the CPU's official history hailed it as a moral victory because the union had "won a raise and an indexing formula. More importantly, the union showed it could stand firm."[58] Afterwards the union did not have much power, and the men had no choice but to accept what was offered. According Gordon Jackson, "three years of nothing. Zero-zero-zero for three years, because management would come over and say, 'we got nothing. You go out, you're only hurting yourself. We got nothing.' Of course, they had us there for a while." "Yeah," Raymond Marcoux laughed, "we lost out on that one."

Removed from industry-wide pattern bargaining, the local union now had to negotiate directly with local management.[59] The timing was not opportune, as it was a "volatile period" in the forestry industry, as companies such as MacMillan Bloedel aggressively sought increased flexibility.[60] In January 1985 the local union's leadership addressed an open letter to its membership about "our problems with the Company." Members were told that mill management had "taken a ruthless and uncompassionate posture with all of us."[61] Indeed the company had "used a big hammer" of the possible closure of the hardboard mill to force the union to accept an "inferior contract as compared to all our brothers in the Primary Mills in Eastern Canada." The letter also lamented the fact that, of the twenty-eight grievances filed in 1984, only a few had yet been resolved. The company was dragging its feet. In response the local union leadership asked members to "stand up for their rights at all times and bring every problem and grievance to the shop stewards and the executive officers." Indeed, "we may have taken a beating in this Local, but we are not going to roll over and play dead."[62] It was nothing short of a call to arms for the years of trench warfare to come.

The local union's dissatisfaction with management led it to go over the head of mill manager Cam Barrington and appeal to the company's central office. In May 1985 Andy Cull, the local union president, wrote Don McLauchlin, executive vice-president of MacMillan Bloedel, and attached a brief on the panelboard mill operations, admitting that it "is not common for a local Union to write a brief on the operations of a Mill. However, we feel at this time we must make someone aware that the Union has absolutely no confidence in the senior management at Sturgeon Falls. We suggest that the Machiavellian management skills that are practiced here are not conducive to continued operations. We further suggest that in our opinion these skills could border on incompetence and mismanagement."[63] The seven-page brief outlined the union's concerns in four key areas: supervision, repair and maintenance, training, and viable and realistic operating procedures. Poor planning and inadequate communication between various departments was also flagged, particularly as it related to quality control.[64] The document was very specific in locating the problems in production, deploying the shop-floor knowledge of union members to highlight perceived managerial incompetence.

Tensions continued to rise in the mill. Andy Cull wrote again to McLauchlin later that September to say that repair and maintenance at the plant was insufficient: "The feeling of our people is that we run on a wing and [a] prayer or run until it breaks and then repair it." He then cited a variety of specific examples of poor management where "things have been let go." He noted that "dozens of grievances" had been filed in the "last year alone," and yet "the personnel department and top management continue to rub our face in the dirt." Due to the lack of repairs to the mill, "We feel as if we are on a rudderless ship with no captain, going from crisis to crisis with problems and grievances started by supervision and compounded by personnel and management. How long can it go on? We feel we have taken enough." The national union was kept informed, with Cull warning that "the operation of the Mill is in jeopardy and Labor Relations are in a shambles caused by personnel and management here in the Mill." He even claimed that local management was "trying to kill the Union."[65]

Given the war of words, it is not surprising that a one-day wildcat strike broke out on 29 October 1985 after Andy Cull was ejected (or briefly fired) from the mill the day before. Everyone walked out at noon, returning to work at eight o'clock the following morning after their president was reinstated. The national union was not amused: on the morning of the walkout it sent an urgent telegram to the local union, copied to the company, stating: "Unauthorized work stoppage by your local union members has been reported to this office. STOP. If this is correct, you are hereby directed to instruct all members to return to work immediately. STOP. You are further instructed to read this telegram to a special meeting of the local union and publicize its contents if necessary. Failure to return to work promptly is a violation of the national constitution and by-laws. Request you report promptly on steps taken to carry out these instructions."[66]

Nonetheless, alone among the post-1945 strikes, many of our interviewees recalled this job action with pride. There was none of the reticence that accompanied the 1967 wildcat strike. Smiling, Gordon Jackson told us that Andy Cull "was kind of tough. He didn't take 'no' for an answer. He didn't really like the company," he laughed. "He'd go for it. So one day they fired him." Union members had to "back him up because he's our president." Jackson added that "He's the president, so we closed the mill down." Bruce Colquhoun also told this story with enthusiasm, saying Cull had gone into the personnel director's office, where "he told him off, swearing at him. In retaliation the manager said, "'that's it, get out, pack your bags, ten minutes,' or whatever, 'to leave the premises or we're calling the police, you're fired.' So he left. Then we all left." Harold Steward worked with Cull in the pulping department, and remembered the incident well. Apparently the mill's long-time personnel director Ed Fortin was in Toronto at the time and another manager was filling in:

> [T]hey fired Andy. And the union gave them an ultimatum: if he wasn't rehired by noon the next day, we're shutting the mill down. And I told my superintendent that. I said, "You know, you gotta get up there and get this thing settled, 'cause the mill's going to go down." "Oh!" he says, "you can't shut the mill down." I said, "Oh yes we can" [smiles], "and we will." At noon the next day it still wasn't settled, they pulled the thing, and the paper machine went down. My chum and I … we didn't want to leave things in a mess, so we didn't get out of there until one-thirty or two o'clock. So they flew Ed Fortin home that night. And by the next day we were going back to work. But Andy was rehired.

Stewart was amused by the stupidity of management's action. "I mean," he laughed, "that's unheard of. It's not a very popular thing to do." Ultimately, concluded André Cartier, because of "our actions, we won."

Conclusion

The union might have won Cull's reinstatement, but the war with local management was just getting started. In 1987 James Buchanan, now CPU president, reported that "the ongoing battle" between Local 7135 and the company was still being fought. During this time Madeleine Martel, the local union's recording secretary and one

Looking westward towards the mill; Trans-Canada Highway is on the left.
Ontario – Sturgeon Falls – Abitibi Power & Paper Company 1951–1966, C30,
Northway-Gestalt Corporation Fonds, Archives of Ontario, Toronto.

of a handful of women hired into production during the 1980s, wrote regularly to the national union expressing the anger and defiance of the local. Apparently local management wanted to change the mill's vacation policy "and screw up one of the few remaining important & sacred policies which have been in existence for many, many years." Martel went on to say that "there are few things" in the past few years that local management had "not done to us." The sense of grievance was palpable: "The ramming down our throats of a poor contract, a pension plan not up to par compared to others ... the forcing of the Local to go to arbitration on many grievances, not resolving grievances or complaints and not even resolving minor problems, and [the] crossing of trade lines."[67] The local union had sacrificed wages "to help the company" in the last round of negotiations, which "we feel saved the panelboard [production line] in 1985 and yet local management continues to hammer us in every way." Martel then blasted management as a whole, saying that they "don't give a damn about us and even the operation of the mill. I guess they are making so much money that they can screw up and it doesn't show. The entire mill is operating better than ever and with record profits, with less employees in the mill itself and yet the staff is getting bigger."[68] In April 1987 Martel informed the national leadership that the local wished to "go on record that we will settle for nothing less than the pattern settlement in Eastern Canada including catch up and the resolving of our grievances, contract languages and local issues." Martel also expressed the "very deep concern" of local members that local management had failed to provide the necessary leadership to modernize the mill.

THE RAISED FIST

And in '71 there was a revolution …

– Denis MacGregor, mill worker

Language and faith represented a fundamental social divide in Sturgeon Falls for much of the twentieth century. Sturgeon Falls Secondary School, the town's only high school until the 1970s, with English as the language of instruction, had a very special relationship to the mill. One might even call it a pillar of mill colonialism, as it prepared young people to enter the mill in more ways than one. Among other things, Ben Lajeunesse recalled, it "acclimatized" French-speaking children to the predominant language of work. It was therefore fitting that Abitibi Power & Paper commissioned Frank Casey, the school's principal, to design a mosaic of the mill for one of the school's corridors. It was 1967, Canada's centennial, and the mill was at its peak employment. The resulting ten-by-fourteen-foot mosaic, made up of 15,036 one-inch square tiles, remains in the school, but it is now largely forgotten.[1] When we tried to track it down one day, nobody in the principal's office knew what we were talking about. Eventually someone made the connection: the building is now Franco-Cité, a French-language high school.

This chapter explores the school crisis that rocked the town and the province in 1970 and 1971.[2] What began as a local outcry for a French-language high school became a *cause célèbre* in an election year, forcing the Ontario government to name a commission of inquiry.[3] Eventually Sturgeon Falls got its French-language high school and the province got a report that favoured sweeping changes. The mill, and the social structure it produced locally, was very much at the epicentre of this political crisis.

To date, published research on this event has examined the Sturgeon Falls school crisis in provincial or national perspective. We therefore learn of its contribution to the making of Ontario's existing French-language school system and its resulting place in Franco-Ontarian history. What we do not get is a sense of what it meant in Sturgeon Falls itself. Yes, the victory resulted in the creation of Franco-Cité, but what else changed? And what did any of this have to do with the local paper mill?

The Sturgeon Falls school crisis became something more when Cam Barrington, the Abitibi Power & Paper mill manager, stood up at a public meeting in opposition to demands for another high school and warned that the mill might close as a result. All hell broke loose. It was as if decades of pent-up fury over Anglo capital were suddenly released all at once. In a mythic moment, hundreds of Franco-Ontarian protesters marched on the mill, through the gates, and into the mill yard itself. As the marchers peacefully streamed onto mill property, Ed Fortin, one of only a handful of Franco-Ontarians in mill management, turned to Barrington and said, with a smile, "they've come to get you." Things would never be the same again. Henceforth, said local historian Wayne LeBelle, the "English [had] lost their power," as "the [francophones] were no longer afraid of them."[4] The school crisis, and the decolonization movement that drove it, is therefore bound up in the history of the mill.

From Mill Town to Franco-Ontarian Community

Sturgeon Falls was not always a Franco-Ontarian town, but underwent considerable demographic and political change over the course of the twentieth century. The census tells part of the story: in 1901 the town was evenly divided between anglophones and francophones, then hard times in the 1910s and again in the 1930s and 1940s, caused by the protracted closure of the mill, saw an exodus of English-speaking families, tilting the balance. Today Franco-Ontarians make up more than 80 per cent of the population of Sturgeon Falls. This shifting demographic reality has profoundly influenced how earlier linguistic tensions are now remembered.

Yet the political power of the town's English-speaking residents never depended on demographics alone. "Having less of them did not change very much," noted Wayne LeBelle dryly. Very few francophones got positions of power in the mill, and only near the end of the mill's existence. As the town's major employer and its largest source of municipal and school taxes, the mill ensured that anglophones remained the major social and political force in the community. In this context the mill and its

Local officials with scale model of proposed Sturgeon Falls High School. Courtesy of West Nipissing Public Library.

English-speaking managers came to symbolize the persistence of Anglo power and privilege for some of our interviewees, most notably LeBelle. The similarities with the inequalities that prevailed in Quebec before the Quiet Revolution are striking, and made manifest in our interview with Gerry Stevens, an electrical engineer at the Sturgeon Falls mill who formerly worked at Shawinigan Paper until Quebec's transformation made his job there untenable. He was not comfortable speaking French – it was a "major *chez nous* thing," he said. So in 1963 Stevens moved to Sturgeon Falls, where he found an environment that was much more familiar to him. Things, however, soon began to change there as well.

Although the class divide in the mill elicited considerable comment in the interviews, we were surprised to hear little commentary about how language politics played out inside the mill or in the wider community. Our archival and newspaper research had revealed a long history of linguistic tension in the area, but a policy of "live and let live" seems to prevail in the community today.[5] When asked, most interviewees shrugged and insisted that people got along. "We were a mix," observed Percy Allary. Some, like André Cartier, suggested that it was largely restricted to sporting rivalries. Asked if there was any animosity between French and English in the mill itself, he firmly answered, "absolutely not." Asked this again, he insisted: "I never seen anything of the sort. Zero!" He then waited for the interviewer to move to the next topic. For his part, Larry Shank indicated that people often mixed English and French "into a distinctive slang." Those who did acknowledge past linguistic tension usually located the problem in a few hotheads, linguistic elites, or in neighbouring communities. Raymond Marcoux, for example, noted that most children were raised bilingual in Sturgeon Falls. Asked if there was any linguistic tension at work, he replied that "there was a little bit, but not too, too much," as the town was overwhelmingly French speaking. Generally there was "no conflict," just "a few English people didn't like the French and vice-versa."

Older interviewees, however, were most likely to recall deeper divisions. There was "much more conflict" in the town's early days, admitted Raymond Brouillette.[6] Others agreed. Lionel Sarazin, for example, conceded that "there might have been frictions before, years before, between French and English." Sarazin remembered hearing workplace stories of earlier friction with bosses under the influence of the Orange Lodge, trying to keep the province English. Another interviewee told me that, long go, English- and French-speaking mill workers in his department once ate their lunch separately, but this practice had long since vanished. Day-to-day, around the coffee table, people spoke both languages, switching back and forth. Only the persistent linguistic divide between managers and workers was freely acknowledged.

Linguistic accommodation and confrontation in Sturgeon Falls have been on display at various times in its history. Much has been written about the long struggle for French-language schooling in Ontario. The prohibition of French in the province's schools in 1913 met with determined resistance. This struggle was, according to Gaétan Gervais, a "foundational act" of the Franco-Ontarian community.[7] School taxes were also an issue, involving the mill directly. Ontario law required that individual and corporate ratepayers direct their school taxes to either the public or the separate (Catholic) school board. Although this system worked reasonably well for individual ratepayers, much more was at stake when large businesses declared their support for one or the other. The issue was further complicated when these same companies approached municipalities for financial assistance.

Just such an issue erupted in Sturgeon Falls on 1 April 1904, when the Toronto *Globe* ran a front-page story provocatively titled "A Question of Ethics," in which the editors reported that the paper mill in Sturgeon Falls had been awarded a bonus in 1898, but separate school supporters were now insisting that the school taxes be evenly divided between the public and Catholic boards. A local subscriber to the *Globe*, an English-speaking merchant and supporter of the public board, was quoted as saying that the "French had a majority on the Town Council," and that it had forced the public school board to sign over half of the taxes to the Catholic school. When questions were raised about the legality of such a move, the Ontario legislature unanimously agreed to the passage of a bill requiring the public school board in Sturgeon Falls to carry out the signed agreement, thus side-stepping the underlying issue.[8]

When the *Globe* asked its readers what they thought of this situation, it received a flood of responses, a number of which were printed in the days that followed. On 6 April a letter from H.E. McKee, the solicitor for the public school board, published on the front page, sought to clarify various points made in the original article. In it he suggested that francophone councillors had "blackmailed" the school board by threatening not to ratify the municipal bonus, thereby putting the mill's continued existence into question. He noted that the mill's owner was never party to the so-called agreement, and that it had chosen to direct its school taxes to the public board alone, as was its right.[9] For his part, the Reverend R. Mann, also of Sturgeon Falls, explained that the bonus had been passed back in 1896, when another company had sought to develop the mill: "They never went on with operations, and in 1898 a company of English capitalists bought the property" and inherited the bonus, although it still had to be ratified by the town council. Because the Sturgeon Falls Pulp Company refused to split the taxes between the two boards, the solicitor of the separate school board approached the public board to say that the bonus would be prevented from being made available unless the public board agreed to hand over half of the taxes.[10] The controversy raged on over the coming days.

On 8 April the *Globe* declared it would not publish any more letters on the issue, "as all phases of the question seem to have been presented."[11] The newspaper's editor lamented the "general disposition" of many letter writers to blame the separate school supporters. For example, the Reverend J.W. Ruddell of Sturgeon Falls heatedly wrote that the "so-called agreement is better termed a diabolical conspiracy against the liberty and rights of the pulp company." He went on to argue that, according to law, ratepayers had the freedom of choice as to where to direct their school taxes. The bill, Ruddell continued, thus represented a "gross injustice," as it was both "unconstitutional and morally indefensible, and ought to be disallowed."[12]

The school tax issue stoked the fires of sectional conflict across the province. The Toronto Board of Education, meeting to discuss the "Sturgeon Falls school question," voted 4 to 3 to voice its disapproval of the bill. The rancorous debate bitterly divided those in the room.[13] That same day the Orange Lodge in Orange County held a special meeting to consider the "Sturgeon Falls schools case" and to hear the solicitor from the Sturgeon Falls public school board. It then passed a "very strong resolution" against the act adopted by the Ontario legislature. Later in June the Grand Orange Lodge of British America met in Picton, where delegates from across Canada heard the grand master strongly condemn the Ontario legislature.[14] There the matter stood until 1909, when both school boards were called to appear before Judge Joseph Valin with respect to the "celebrated Sturgeon Falls Case." Indeed, "so much excitement resulted at the time that nothing has been done up to the present to enforce payment but now, with a favourable Town Council and other things, propitious, a move is made, but it is expected to meet with strong opposition in principle."[15] In the end, the judge sided with the separate school trustees, finding that the separate school was entitled to one-half of the school taxes paid by the pulp mill from 1899 to 1903. As the pulp mill had gone into receivership in 1904, no taxes had been paid in the five years since.[16]

The court-ordered transfer of monies from the town's public schools caused a great deal of hardship. These were tough times in the town, as the mill was closed. Here is the *Globe*'s description of the situation:

> Since the plant of the Imperial Paper Mills went into liquidation about two years ago business has been seriously affected in the town, as the plant was the principal and only industry of any size in the community and employed a large number of hands the mill being practically closed down during the receivership. On account of a dispute over the amount of taxes due from the mills and the liquidation proceedings a large sum in public school taxes has been tied up, and the town owes the public school $9,000 on the levies of 1907-08, besides this year's levy. The teachers have received only thirty dollars each since the midsummer vacation and to-day they resolved to quit in a body as there seems no immediate prospect of receiving any money on their salaries and the prospect of living without means does not appeal to them after subsisting three months on ten dollars per month.[17]

In December 1909 public school teachers in Sturgeon Falls went on strike to protest the non-payment of wages. Local public school ratepayers were incensed by the town council's decision to authorize payment of $1,500 of public school monies to the separate school in response to Judge Valin's award. The issue was not resolved until mid-January 1910, when salaries were paid and the public schools reopened.[18] In the years that followed, language and faith continued to divide the town's citizens.

In our interviews the most devastating critique of the mill's subordination of Franco-Ontarians came from Wayne LeBelle, long-time journalist and, as noted earlier, author of a book commemorating the town's centennial in 1995. Centennial books are by their nature "happy books," providing community members with a unifying tale. In writing *Sturgeon Falls, 1895–1995*, LeBelle had a "hard road to walk" because he did not want to "piss off the English," but there was "a lot of pain" in the fierce competition between French and English. Yet under the circumstances he could raise certain issues only indirectly. Some of the statistics he included showed, for example, how French Canadians moved into the "big houses" built by the town's pioneer families after they left during the hard times that accompanied the mill closures from 1907–11 and 1930–47. According to LeBelle, this handover was a "slap in the face for anyone who was English or Scottish." It "flipped" the culture around: "You are not a poor little French Canadian anymore." He contrasted his book to others he had read that began with a statement from the mill manager: "They are deified, they are Gods in their communities."

Throughout our multi-session interview, LeBelle and I returned to the idea that the mill town was a colonial space. Two things happened, he explained. First, Indigenous lands were occupied by white settlers. Then, the mainly French-speaking settlers were put to work by Anglo capital to work in the mill. We agreed that it was a double colonialism. For LeBelle there was a "colonial attitude that's reflected by the way the English treated people in India, by the way that they treated people in North America." He searched for the right word to describe the relationship: "There is that kind of colonial, magisterial, not caste … it was like a feudal system." None of these quite fit though. He settled on "class": "The class system was part of the colonialism that was happening in Sturgeon Falls. They were still acting in the sixties, seventies, eighties, and nineties like colonial lords … They would walk uptown. You would see them walking on the street. 'Oh,' you would say, 'oh' [whisper], 'there is the mill manager.' [shout] 'Hello!' They would be yelling. They were emperors." LeBelle then broadened his analysis:

> Colonialism – that is a really good way [to look at it]. But it has to be kept in perspective. If you look at the communities in Northern Ontario – if you go right to Hearst, to Kap[uskasing], to Smooth Rock Falls, to Cochrane, to Timmins – you go all the way down the corridor. In each of the communities, they were colonized by the mill coming in and all of that. But the point of the mill was not to colonize. The point of the mill was to make money. It was part of the capitalist system. And the capitalist system,

certainly, has a diminutive power on its principals, on the people, on the worker bees, but that is just how our society works. We are not egalitarian in any sense of the word. Nor should we even think that we ever were.

The Sturgeon Falls mill was tied up in Wayne LeBelle's mind with the subordination of the Franco-Ontarian community. It profoundly structured his understanding of Sturgeon Falls and its history. His analysis is penetrating and well worth exploring here. The mill "created a very big dynamic tension within the community," according to Lebelle. "There we were, with four or five English, Scottish, or Irish people running the whole town, including the mill. The mill managers always had people on council or they were on council, so they ran the council. They ran the municipality. They ran the stores. The Masonic Lodge is a stone's throw from the corner of the mill." The Masonic Club looms large in LeBelle's narrative. If you went through the list of its members, he told me, you would find everyone with any kind of position in the mill: "They were all Masons." For him the mill controlled the town "completely."

Yvon Marleau, a city councillor at the time we interviewed him, noted that English- and French-speaking residents generally gravitated towards different "social circles."[19] One of the main reasons for this, he explained, was that "a lot of the English-speaking citizens in town were people that were brought in by the [company]. So they weren't local people in the sense [that] they weren't from the area. They had their own circle of friends. And a lot of them didn't stay around too long because they were working for a multinational company. So that was sort of a separate circle."

Although the forestry company never controlled the Sturgeon Falls townsite itself, it did provide housing to some of its employees; however, much of this company-owned housing appears to have been reserved for senior managers and other salaried staff members. The mill's English-speaking managers and their families thus lived in a cluster of homes, referred to as "the compound" by Wayne LeBelle, next to the mill's North Yard. "They had their little road," he added with a smile. Clearly it was a place set apart. Pietro Carello, son of a mill engineer, told us what it was like growing up in these houses during the 1970s and 1980s: "We were the mill rats. When I grew up on Simcoe Street, it was all mill houses. There were about ten of them. The whole lane was just mill houses. So that was where my early friends were made."[20] In the post-war period, the only other company-owned house was that of the mill manager, located across the river in the most prestigious part of town. Carello described it as an "absolutely gorgeous house." When his family renovated the kitchen after purchasing the house from the company, they peeled off the linoleum floor and found hardwood, and "right in the middle was a big Star of

David." Otherwise, with the exception of the neighbouring Nipissing reserve, there did not appear to be significant residential segregation in Sturgeon Falls: French and English generally lived side-by-side.

Like its predecessors, Abitibi continued to refuse to direct its school taxes to the separate Catholic school board. According to *Le Droit*, Abitibi paid $124,458.80 in municipal taxes in 1962, representing more than a quarter of all municipal taxes paid in Sturgeon Falls, yet "[n]ot one cent of tax from this powerful company went to the separate schools."[21] For Wayne LeBelle, "that mill did not give any funding at all to any of the separate schools and they were 95 per cent of the population of the area. They controlled the language that was used in the mill. It was almost in the same way as Aboriginal people were treated. Get rid of their culture, get rid of their language." "They hated the French Canadians," he insisted.

Structuring LeBelle's narrative of place is the notion of ethnic class. Sturgeon Falls was a town of English kings and queens, who expected to be treated royally, and their "little French-Canadian" subjects: "Everyone was on bended knees in front of this God. The God at this time was Abitibi." Cam Barrington seemed to personify this social order. "Cam is royal," LeBelle said. "He was aristocracy." LeBelle cited another former manager from the 1950s who would "almost pop a vein," he hated Franco-Ontarians so much. Anglo capital demanded subservience: "they acted like they were the kings and queens of everything."

For a small town such as Sturgeon Falls, the mill was "a goose that lays golden eggs." Accordingly, "you don't kill it." It was a "one-horse town, a one-industry town." But dependence on the mill came at a steep social price. As LeBelle noted, "The mill, while it created lots of jobs, had a very crushing force on the French-Canadian population here ... The mill became their mother, their father, their accountant, their priest, their banker, their mortgager ... It became their whole life. And many people never left town. maybe never became the people ... they could have been. There could have been more doctors, more lawyers ... but a lot of people just chose to go to the mill with their lunch pail. It really was very hurtful." Throughout the interview, LeBelle referred to the "little French Canadians" when he wanted to communicate management's condescending attitude. The "little French Canadians working in the mill" got their big pay cheques, their "$50,000, $60,000, $70,000 trucks," but lost their independence. "Before the mill shut down, you would drive down this street ... and there [was] truck after truck after truck ... It was great. I was happy for them." This ambivalent attitude towards the mill workers was shared by others we interviewed who did not have a direct connection to the mill.

Despite the town's progress, local people had little choice but to work at the mill, and area farmers had few other options but to sell their wood to Abitibi. Most of

Gathering to mark 26 years of "Devotion to Sturgeon High"; the coat of arms includes a tree and pair of hockey sticks. Courtesy of West Nipissing Public Library.

the mill workers we interviewed got hired on at the mill directly out of high school, so there was a certain economic logic to an English-only high school. It prepared working-class Franco-Ontarians to work in English. Several interviewees made this connection. Lionel Sarazin, for example, grew up in the neighbouring Franco-Ontarian community of Lavigne. When he first entered Sturgeon Falls Secondary School, he spoke little English. It took him months to understand what was being said around him. "The first year in high school was a little hard," he recalled. But it got better. By the time he entered the mill, he was quite fluent in English and encountered no more problems.

"They've come to get you"

Surging public demand for a French-language high school in Sturgeon Falls in 1970–1 therefore struck a blow against one of the underpinnings of mill colonialism itself. The first public meeting was organized in February 1970 in the neighbouring village of Verner, resulting in the creation of the Association d'éducation de l'Ouest Nipissing (AEON), headed by Marc Cazabon, the principal of the local French elementary school. The group included teachers, school administrators, priests, business people, and others drawn from the ascendant Franco-Ontarian middle class. It seems likely that the "real thrust" for the school came from Verner and other Franco-Ontarian villages in West Nipissing, not from Sturgeon Falls itself.[22] Fully 60 per cent of the students at the high school were from outside the mill town. To make matters worse, the school was badly overcrowded, forcing some classes into a nearby convent.

On 8 March 1970, a petition signed by 2,277 parents favouring a francophone high school was submitted to the Nipissing Board of Education.[23] Bill 141, passed by the Ontario legislature in July 1968, had provided that "[a] board may establish and maintain secondary schools or classes in secondary schools for the purpose of providing for the use of the French language in instruction" when there are sufficient numbers of pupils, calculated at twenty or more per program.[24] The law did not, however, compel the creation of a separate school – the decision was left up to local school boards to determine when and if this was feasible. The "locality" in this instance was Nipissing district, which encompassed the mainly francophone West Nipissing and the mainly anglophone city of North Bay.[25] On 24 March 1970 five hundred francophone high school students refused to register for school.

The school issue became a full-fledged crisis on 6 April when seven hundred people crowded into a meeting of the Board of Education in North Bay, where a motion to create the new high school was soundly defeated twelve to two with two abstentions. Nor did the AEON's idea of applying the "shift system" receive support. "They walked in calmly, but left with 'war' in mind," reported Wayne LeBelle in the next day's *North Bay Nugget*.[26] The massive crowd became incensed at the board members sitting on the stage. What began with jeers quickly escalated to the throwing of placards. The spark that ignited the crowd was probably provided by mill manager Cam Barrington, who had stood up at a packed public meeting the week before to say that, should residents go ahead with plans to build another high school, Abitibi might close the mill. Although higher taxes were cited as the reason, few in the crowd likely believed this to be the real issue. Certainly Ed Fortin, the mill's personnel manager and one of the few Franco-Ontarians in management, believed that Barrington was convinced to intervene in the affair by one of his superintendents who was very "pro-British." Years of resentment erupted in fury, now directed as much against the mill's Anglo management and Barrington himself as against the anglophone majority on the school board. Barrington's intervention invited a wider social and political critique of what was at stake in the Sturgeon Falls school crisis.

Cam Barrington, 2005; he donated the painting of the mill behind him to the local museum. Photograph by David W. Lewis.

The response was immediate. The next morning seven hundred students jammed into the gymnasium of Sturgeon Falls Secondary School and answered a "resounding 'no'" to a request to return to classes.[27] Hundreds then "marched up and down town streets and at one point through the grounds at the Abitibi panel products division mill."[28] Former personnel director Ed Fortin recalled the first incursion onto mill property like a scene in a Hollywood movie: "There was a parade of the pro-French that came from the far bridge to the gate ... Barrington and I are standing side-by-side there, and I said 'they've come to get you'" [laughs]. Wayne LeBelle was at the meeting when Barrington threatened to close the mill down. "Cam [Barrington] made those statements," he told me. "He did not want a French school." There were some repercussions within the mill itself, according to Marc Côté: "A little bit of trouble between the French and English started with the high school kids [and led to a] few skirmishes in the mill ... Some guys used to put some French on the board and some of the management got really excited. And everybody got together and said, 'hey, this is the way it's going to be here. We want to talk both languages, and if a guy wants to speak French in the shop or around the mill that's the way it's going to be.' And they kind of settled down after a little while there. But the official language in the mill was still English." As Wayne LeBelle explained to readers of the *North Bay Nugget*, "The reason for the march through Abitibi grounds was that mill Manager B.C. Barrington said last week that his plant was opposed to more taxation that was inevitable with the building of another school."[29] For the next two days, hundreds of students and their supporters marched on the mill daily. Mill management did not turn them back, but let them walk through part of the yard.[30] AEON president Marc Cazaban condemned the intimidation tactics of the mill manager.[31]

Faced with the Nipissing school board's refusal to consider the building of another high school, the AEON and the local student association organized mass protests and a student strike. "*On veux notre école*," they shouted in the streets, and burned a local trustee in effigy. In a memorandum, the school's principal directed the teaching staff to come to work regardless: "Do not take any position. Do not compromise yourselves. Don't take any unnecessary chances. Teach your classes as usual."

One teacher at the school was Yvon Marleau, at the start of his career. On his "first day of school," he was on the picket line: French-speaking students and parents "were all in the streets" and had "blocked the school." Marleau thought they had good reason to protest. He recalled that one teacher was teaching history in French, since every single student in the classroom was French speaking, when an Ontario school inspector "happened to be in the building that day" and "walked by the classroom and heard him talking French. He walked in and he chastised him and he told him you cannot do this – teach in French in the classroom. The only time that you can speak French is when you're teaching French conversation or French literature." The incident, and others like it, "started brewing the pot," said Marleau, until it finally exploded. It quickly got "very rough, extremely rough." There were threats of violence, some shoving, and a lot of angry words. Students would come back for a day or two and go out again. Marleau recalled: "It was off and on. You never knew what to expect. One morning we got to school and all the doors were blocked." When students got wind that the school board president was visiting the school, "rather than picket outside the school, they just swamped inside. They went down [on the floor of] the hallway, all over the school. So Mr Monkland and the school principal had to walk over the bodies to visit the school. We thought it was kind of funny." The boycott extended to the francophone primary schools in the area, where a a number of teachers failed to show up to work, reporting "indigestion."[32]

Almost overnight other Franco-Ontarian organizations entered the fray.[33] The striking students received telegrams of support from across Ontario, and the

Sudbury Star reported that there was a "wildcat walkout" of fifty students at Macdonald-Cartier High School in Sudbury in solidarity with Sturgeon Falls.[34] Dozens travelled to Sturgeon Falls to join the protest marches, and for a time there were fears that the student strike would spread to other communities.[35]

Not surprisingly the school board offices in North Bay were the target of several protests, including a march on 9 April by two thousand students. Walking in pairs, the "silent march" stretched for four blocks, making it the city's "biggest protest march in memory."[36] The first phase of the Sturgeon Falls school crisis ended abruptly on 13 April when the board revisited its decision. More than a thousand people filled the high school auditorium: "Onlookers stood in the aisles, sat on the floor, spilled out of the doors of the auditorium, and stood in the halls, waiting."[37] Fifteen minutes later it was over, with the board voting unanimously in favour of a compromise resolution that split the existing school into two sections, one English and one French.[38] Each section would have its own vice-principal but a common bilingual principal. The decision was met with "resounding applause," but the issue did not go away. A second, more radical wave of protest erupted a year later, led by teenagers who adopted the raised fist, or *poing fermé*, as its emblem.

La cause

The compromise agreement that created two schools under one roof served only to heighten tensions in the building. In all, 1, 247 students registered for the French section and 554 – including 140 francophones – for the English (bilingual) one.[39] The president of the English student council, Michael Sullivan, lamented the separate dances, yearbooks, and sports teams: "Former students of our school functioned well and happily without this type of segregation," he protested.[40] Like other Sturgeon Falls anglophones, Sullivan blamed outsiders for the conflict: "The present trouble all seems to have begun about three years ago when the grade 9 and 10 groups were brought in from the outlying communities." By contrast, Jean St-Louis, president of the Conseil d'étudiants, section française, called the results of the compromise inadequate, as there were mounting conflicts between teachers and students as well as conflicting student activities: "These conflicts led to mounting friction within the two student bodies." He told the Nipissing board that francophone students were "fed up" with its failure to create two separate schools: "We ask for our school. We will settle for nothing less."[41] The compromise failed, with anglophone students "dressed in their colours, francophones in their colours, and adversaries in their colours."[42] A lack of space exacerbated matters, with a journalist concluding: "At the heart of the controversy is a lack of space in the school which has resulted in French-speaking students travelling to a convent several streets away to take some courses."[43]

In response a group of students formed the Comité d'action étudiante, under the leadership of Jean St-Louis, and began to prepare a second strike. Wayne LeBelle, who interviewed St-Louis at the time, generously sharing his yellowed paper notes with me as well as a draft article that was never published. In the moment, LeBelle wrote that St-Louis, the eldest of five children, had just turned sixteen when he emerged as the leader of "*la cause*," as they called the movement at the time. The students' nerve centre, also nicknamed "La Cause" after the newsletter they published, was a small building on Highway 17 just west of town,[44] and the "striking students were waiting on the doorstep the first day of school."[45]

Tensions continued to rise. In June 1971 the Nipissing board refused to vote again on the issue, but agreed to the creation of an ad hoc committee to consider the matter. Reporting back on 12 August, the committee recommended in favour of a French-language high school, but a slight majority of school board members refused to reopen the issue.[46] Sturgeon Falls was a "powder keg," screamed a front-page headline of the *Sudbury Star* two days later. Dr Roger Gervais, one of only three francophones on the board, said that Franco-Ontarians were "tired of taking orders from Anglophones."[47]

Sturgeon Falls was once again on the front lines of minority educational rights in Canada. Major Franco-Ontarian organizations supported *la cause*. La Société Saint-Jean-Baptiste du Québec even waded into the controversy when its president general, André Roy, declared (in French of course): "French-Canadians of Sturgeon Falls, we support you in your efforts. We are 100 per cent with you!"[48] In August the Association canadienne-française de l'Ontario (ACFO) told the school board: "It needs to be said that the conflict has surpassed a regional issue, it has drawn the interest of Ontarians and there is a national dimension to it."[49] In its eyes, "compulsory school co-habitation" was now tantamount to assimilation. The compromise agreement was no longer tenable. In fact, the ACFO now believed, the system of school co-habitation was "equivalent to a cultural genocide."

Not all Sturgeon Falls residents supported the campaign. Some francophones opposed the separation of local students; others sought to maximize the employment opportunities of their children in a predominantly English-speaking province. Likewise, some local anglophones supported the two-school solution for other reasons. A petition in favour of a second school that circulated among teachers is indicative: although fifty-three of sixty-two francophone teachers signed the petition, twenty-one of forty-four anglophone teachers did as well.[50] Mayor John Valiquette, who supported the compromise agreement, defended his position forcefully.

The demands for a unilingual French high school smacked of segregation, he said. "I was opposed to something and it is the incomprehensible position that the French and English-speaking students of our town cannot walk together in the same halls, eat in the same cafeteria, and take their athletic training in the same gymnasium, while receiving their secondary education in the language of their choice."[51] It was contrary to everything he was brought up to believe. For their part the anglophone parents at Our Lady of Sorrows Elementary School opposed the new school out of fear that their children would be left with second-rate facilities. This possibility was not far-fetched, as their children had already been asked to leave their former primary school after it became French-only. "We were given run down facilities," they reported.[52] For them, the only group that benefited from the separation of students was "the group of teachers who are agitating for this separation."

Other voices raised in opposition similarly equated *la cause* to segregation in the United States. One such voice was that of Ruth Couchie, representing the Education Committee of the Nipissing First Nation. Twenty-five Anishnabe students were registered in the anglophone section of the school. "We value the present school," she wrote, and worried that the anglophone minority would be left with inadequate school facilities should a new school be built: "Now we are faced with a division that confuses us and makes us wonder whether we have made a drastic mistake by choosing to be mingled with an integrated society. Maybe we should have refused the educational opportunities offered to us and preferred a separate kind of education on the reservation as so many Indian groups are now advocating. We should all try to realize that we are obliged to foster and protect the needs of the minority as well as the needs of the majority."[53] These attestations complicate our understanding of minority education rights. Francophones were a linguistic minority in Ontario and in the Nipissing school board, but represented a strong majority of students in Sturgeon Falls. As a result, the fight for unilingual primary and secondary schools often meant expelling anglophone students from their existing schools.

These opposition voices were largely ignored by the ACFO, which focused instead on the continued opposition of mill management. Abitibi Panel Products, the town's major employer, supported many anglophone ratepayers in opposition to the proposed unilingual French secondary school. In Abitibi's 25 June 1971 letter to the Nipissing board, Cam Barrington wrote: "Since Abitibi is the single largest taxpayer in the area I would like this committee to hear our petition." He noted that, "Last year I made a statement which was directed to the Board indicating at that time that Abitibi Panel Products could ill afford to have any increased taxation burden. Since that time, the events have shown that the situation has become even more critical." Barrington was, of course, alluding to the layoffs at the mill. He then noted that Abitibi had contributed $219,297 in general municipal taxes and $111,570 in school taxes in 1970.[54]

The general secretary of the ACFO visited Sturgeon Falls in mid-August 1971 and summarized the "Abitibi problem" as follows: "It seems more and more, revealed by a flurry of events, that Abitibi opposes the principal of a French-only school. Evidently, Abitibi will not let itself say this. Is this the policy of the company? Hard to say, but according to the people of Sturgeon Falls, the managers had the bad habit *de s'immiscer* in the school questions and to oppose it, more often than before according to francophones."[55] He also noted that, earlier, when the Ontario Ministry of Education approved the teaching of history, geography, and Latin in French, "[t]he manager at the time, Mr. Evans, who was also a member of the School Board, opposed this recommendation for Sturgeon Falls. Mr. Wylde, a superintendent, was also there. The same Mr. Wylde, is today Assistant Manager who permitted, in the absence of the manager, Mr. Barrington, a petition to circulate in the Mill against the proposal for a French High School. He even signed this petition." Abitibi's claim that its opposition was based on the mill's dire financial position resonated, however, due to recent layoffs and a precarious situation in forestry overall: "The Sturgeon Falls Mill has not been profitable for three years. For several months, they had to close part of the mill and lay off 85 men. The economic situation of pulp and paper mills is precarious across Canada."[56]

To counter Abitibi's position, the ACFO was determined to demonstrate to the public that a second school would not cost Abitibi significantly more than the proposed expansion of the existing school. It also considered pressuring local management to cease and desist by approaching the company's head office: "It seems that the objections of Abitibi come from the local level and not the head office. There might be an opportunity to meet with the president of the company to inform him of the proposal and to ask him to direct the managers of the mill to cease their opposition. Abitibi might be convinced even to support the principle of a French-only school."[57]

The school crisis came to a head in September 1971, when more than four hundred students boycotted registration and several hundred blockaded the school itself. A school occupation followed, with those who had registered having to force their way through the crowd.[58] Jacques Deschênes, of the province-wide organization Direction Jeunesse, praised the students who were boycotting classes, saying "they paraded in the streets of Sturgeon Falls to reclaim their school for themselves."[59] The ACFO also supported the student blockade, disbursing almost $6,000 for the printing of the student newspapers *La cause* and *Coup d'oeil*, the rental of buses, and food for those occupying the school itself.[60]

The clenched fist quickly became the official symbol of the student activists in Sturgeon Falls.[61] Sudbury's *Le Voyageur* supported the campaign, but blasted this newly discovered sign of radicalism and revolution: "The usage of the raised fist as an emblem came out of the affair of the high school, and this could have grave consequences in several areas."[62] Student leader Jean St-Louis replied that the raised fist "is not a symbol of violence but of power."[63] *Le Voyageur's* editors disagreed: "The 'raised fist' is a revolutionary symbol of political character. It is a rallying sign for ALL the communist parties and Marxists around the world, including the Communist Party of Canada. It is also the rallying symbol of 'nihilists,' 'anarchists,' 'Trotskyites,' and the Marxist Revolution in Russia. It is the sign of mobilization of communists under Castro and of Mao. It is the collective symbol of the Black Panther group in the United States, who wish to establish a political state for Black Americans."[64] For good measure, *Le Voyageur* retorted that all groups that use the raised fist are opposed to distinctions based on religion, race, and language: "In utilizing this symbol, the Comité d'action étudiante therefore joins those they are struggling against – and who wish to assimilate them."[65] In the language of revolution, words such as violence and power were synonymous: "It is therefore extremely regrettable that these young students in Sturgeon Falls have been influenced to this point."

In media interviews, Jean St-Louis, then seventeen, frequently cited the influence of Pierre Vallières on his thinking. Wayne LeBelle, for example, visited a half-dozen students making picket signs, many of whose slogans were taken from Vallières' book, *White Niggers of America*.[66] According to LeBelle, the "book is [a] bible of French Canadians who fight the 'English establishment' and for many years was banned in Canada. The English edition has recently been published."[67] St-Louis explained that Vallières' book "changed his mind about a lot of things."

The spectre of violence climaxed a week later when envelopes allegedly containing dynamite powder were mailed to the Nipissing board office and at least one of its members.[68] In one case, the note was signed "FLO Cellule Ontario." It had been only a year since the federal government invoked the War Measures Act to crush the Front de libération du Québec after it kidnapped British diplomat James Cross and murdered Quebec Minister of Labour Pierre Laporte. One would therefore be hard pressed to think of a more provocative act at this point in Canadian history. Faced with a local situation that seemed to be spiralling out of control, the Progressive Conservative government of Ontario invited St-Louis and the older leaders of the AEON to Toronto to meet with Robert Welch, the minister of education. Subsequent negotiations resulted in an agreement that saw the students return to classes. In return the Ontario government named Dr Thomas Symons, president of Trent

University, to review the administration of Bill 141 as well as the specific case of Sturgeon Falls.[69] The sense of political urgency was such that Symonds was tracked down and stopped on the highway by the Ontario Provincial Police as he travelled from Peterborough to Ottawa. He was asked to get into the police car, where he then had a telephone conversation with Welch and accepted a three-month assignment as commissioner.[70]

Some Franco-Ontarian student leaders were openly critical of the compromise. In a substantial two-page article entitled "Sturgeon Falls Blues," published in the University of Ottawa student journal *La Rotonde*, Paul-André Rochon and Gilbert Belisle complained that Franco-Ontarians had now been twice betrayed: first, the AEON – dismissed as an "élite" composed of "priests, store owners, teachers, and other 'important' people" – had agreed to the compromise of 1970, and now, a year later, St-Louis had betrayed the students by agreeing to the pause.[71] These complaints were short-lived, however, as Symonds sided with Franco-Ontarian demands. The crisis ended in December 1971 when the Nipissing school board, after meeting with Symonds, agreed to the two-school option. Henceforth there would be two schools in Sturgeon Falls: one French-only and the other bilingual.[72]

Conclusion

How, then, do our interviewees remember this political struggle years later? Bruce Colquhoun, who attended the high school at the time, recalled that the atmosphere was "very tense" and that there were some "scary moments." Before sharing more, he asked us if we wanted to hear more about this. Encouraged to continue, he told us:

> It was a rough time for a lot of people. It was scary. I lost a lot of friends because I was English. But I was standing out there. I stood out there picketing with the French, you know, to get their school, 'cause a lot of friends of mine, they had a hard time with the English. Some were thinking of dropping out because they couldn't under-stand the class because it was English. So I was out there with them, picketing with them. And the next day, I got beat up pretty bad.
>
> KRISTEN O'HARE: By English kids?
>
> BRUCE COLQUHOUN: No. Three French people. Real bad. And my dad, when I got home, I had a couple cracked ribs, and black eyes. I was small in high school, I was one of the smallest people in high school. When I got home I had two cracked ribs, and black nose, black eyes. I mean, my nose wasn't broke, but it was close, and bruised all over the place. He said, "What the heck happened to you?" And I told him. Then I missed school for about a week. And he drove me to school when I was ready to go. I was all taped up

because of the ribs. And he got out of the car, and they were protesting out front. He got out of the car, and he yelled out, "Whoever touches my son again, they're gonna deal with me. I don't care how old you are, you're gonna deal with me." Nobody touched me after that. It was just, everybody got caught up in the swing of things, eh? And it got crazy sometimes. I'm glad they got their own school. They deserve it. Gotta keep your culture alive. It was scary, at times. But for the most part, it added excitement to go to school, too. You had something to look forward to a little bit. School was pretty dull. But I got through it. And then I graduated before they could build the new school. So, I never got to go the new Northern High School.

There is considerable ambiguity in this story, as there is in other accounts from anglophone interviewees. Why would striking francophone students beat him if Colquhoun was picketing with them? Denis MacGregor, for his part, first recalled the school crisis as being initiated by "English-speaking people that wanted their school, so that's why Northern came to be." He later corrected himself, noting that it was the town's francophones who wanted their own school. This momentary misremembering is quite natural, since the old school became the new Franco-Cité high school. English-speaking students eventually got a new school after an extended period in portable classrooms.

There were many other changes. Looking back thirty-five years later, Wayne LeBelle concluded that Franco-Ontarians had never "flexed their muscles" before that time. It was as if the region's francophones finally stood up en masse and said "Listen, you fuckin' *anglais*, we've had it here." There would be no more exaggerated deference to mill management. Indeed, in LeBelle's mind, "the fight, the pride, the feeling about being French-Canadians" left people forever changed. The "little French-Canadians" had grown tall. To some degree Bruce Colquhoun agreed with this assessment, noting: "I think we're a better community for it. Because now the French can preserve their culture, they've got their own schools. That's what they wanted. And they got it. And it's good. And [it's] something to be proud of, you know? They fought for something that went wrong and made it right." Never again would the mill manager have the same political influence. The next mill manager opted instead to live in the English-speaking community of North Bay.

The school crisis was finally over, but nothing would be the same again. Jean St-Louis told Wayne LeBelle a few years later that he had received death threats during this period. In hindsight he realized that it was "plain stupid to pour acid on the mayor's car, it never helped us."[73] He also noted that they did get a lot of visitors from Quebec during the student strike, "but they were turned off when we didn't want to get into violence." The whole experience had pushed St-Louis to his limits.

After it was over, he said that "I was able to put my feet on the principal's desk and say, 'I want this … and I got it.'" But he was tired of it all, and quit school early, saying, "the only time the teachers talk to me is when they need me to do something for them." Thereafter he was never again "an ordinary student. They, the students, used me, I never belonged to a group after that. I was in-between the students and the teachers after that." He ended the interview with Wayne LeBelle by reflecting on how much the conflict had taken out of him. It had consequences for his health, but he was proud that "[w]e were the catalyst for changes to the law."[74]

In victory the anger dissipated, and interviewees were reticent to speak of these old linguistic divisions. The intense heat generated by the school crisis had cooled. Henri Labelle, who participated in the protest as a student in grade 12 and subsequently worked in the mill, recalled playing a lot of pool "when we went on strike." With a shrug of his shoulders, he cast it as simply politics: "For me, I didn't care." André Girard, born in 1939, didn't know what caused the "big controversy." At the time he was busy working in the mill, but "could see the friction" downtown. While "some of the French people had signs," he says that he stayed neutral, noting that his wife was English. For his part Wayne Pigeau – an anglophone – referred to it as the "Plains of Abraham" but in reverse. He, too, then shifted the conversation to his family: his in-laws speak to him in French and his children were educated in French. One interviewee after another responded in kind. Today Sturgeon Falls is a solidly Franco-Ontarian community. The language issue has been largely resolved, leaving little interest in reopening old wounds.

DECLINE AND FINAL CLOSURE

MANAGING DECLINE

We were all prepared; we had statements we had written out ahead of time that we were going
to read because you don't want to make a mistake, because you're not there to hurt people.
You're there to - it's a reality that we're living right now. It could happen any day that fifteen
hundred people are going to lose their jobs. So how was it told? The timing is never right,
people have families, they have debts, some people lost their cars, some people lost their houses
and their marriages went belly-up. [leans back] So, to put it shortly, it's about the only task that
I really detested. I mean, there is no nice way of saying it, there was no nice way of doing it.
Shutdowns are ugly. People get hurt.

— Marc Côté, superintendent of the mechanical department

The closure of the #2 hardboard mill in December 1991 was a gut-wrenching experience for everyone we interviewed, managers included. Those laid off entered an
unforgiving job market, with the country deep in recession. Other parts of the plant
had closed earlier, but earlier layoffs had been mitigated by the relatively large size
of the mill's workforce. This time, however, workers with as much as eighteen years'
seniority were let go.

The mill's slow decline began when it was announced in October 1968 that the
platewood mill – which made furniture core for veneering, countertops, tabletops,
flooring, and roof decking – would close in January 1969, displacing 82 employees.
Then #1 hardboard mill – which made a variety of products, including interior
door panels, auto interiors, TV cabinets, signage, shelving, and the once-popular
indoor panelling for basement "rec rooms" – closed in 1975, displacing another
160 workers. The closure of #2 hardboard mill, which made exterior panelling,

in 1991 halved the remaining workforce, leaving 160 still on the job making one product: corrugated medium. As each production line fell silent, the associated costs climbed for the production lines that remained, which now had to carry the entire operating costs of the production facility. If the post-war diversification of the mill had provided a measure of stability for the mill and those who depended on it, this chain of events made the entire plant more vulnerable to final closure, and everyone knew it.

The successive closure of the mill's product lines wreaked havoc on its internal labour market as workers in the closing department bumped lower-seniority workers out of their jobs in other parts of the plant. The chain reaction affected all but the most senior employees, undermining morale. It was tough to be "bumped" by a friend or co-worker, and unpleasant to be the one doing the bumping. Given the extended nature of the mill's decline, bumping was a major topic of conversation in the interviews. Internally displaced workers suddenly found themselves working in unfamiliar, and perhaps undesirable, parts of the mill. They needed to be retrained, and the new jobs were not always a good match with their own aptitudes or skill sets. The decline of the mill also severed the intergenerational connection to the mill, as young workers were laid off and students were no longer hired on during the summer months. With a long list of workers on layoff, nobody new was being hired. These were anxious years.

This extended period of contraction happened to coincide with the tenure of Cam Barrington as mill manager. Promoted in the wake of the 1967 walkout, he remained in the position until he retired in 1987.[1] Barrington came from a well-heeled Toronto family, and took chemical engineering at Queen's University before joining the pulp and paper industry in 1948. At the time the sector was just starting to hire highly trained chemical engineers. It offered the best wages and a good chance for advancement. Engineers were assigned supervisory roles in Abitibi's paper mills, but there was an understudy system in place and a promotional ladder to climb. Barrington saw himself as a company man. "As time went on," Barrington noted, "old school" managers were being replaced by "technical people" such as himself. Technological changes were sweeping the industry. More than once during the interview, he insisted that paper making was "no longer an art" but "a science." Where it once took five men to cook the chips, a continuous digester required only two men to operate. "The world changed around the men's heads," Barrington concluded.

After the Second World War, Abitibi sought to diversify into other paper and wood products. For a time, the company liked to use the Sturgeon Falls mill "as a case history to demonstrate the practical benefits of industrial research."[2] The mill

North Yard, Sturgeon Falls mill. Ontario – Sturgeon Falls – Abitibi Power & Paper Company 1951–1966, C30, Northway-Gestalt Corporation Fonds, Archives of Ontario, Toronto.

was thus converted from newsprint to corrugated medium, and the first hardboard mill was added soon thereafter, modelled on a mill in Oregon. To a certain extent, Barrington had to learn on the job: "I didn't know a damn thing about pneumatic controls, but I happened to have the manual." Barrington helped get the two hardboard mills going, as well as the new platewood mill. It was a time of growth and optimism as new production lines started up. With the particle board mill, Abitibi would pay the price of being one of the first such mills in operation: newer mills were faster, had larger presses, and avoided the early technological kinks in the manufacturing process. As superintendent, Barrington had to manage growth. Then, as plant manager, he had to manage decline. As he explained decades later, "you had to manage change."

The Closure of the Platewood and #1 Hardboard Mills

It is relatively rare to get an inside look at what leads a company to close a plant or terminate a product line. Few corporations maintain their own archives or send their historic records to a public archive. Corporate press releases usually justify any decision based on a drop-down list of external factors or on the local union. Sometimes, however, private records make it into the public realm or into someone's basement, providing an opportunity to see things from the inside. The January 1969 closure of the platewood mill was one such occasion, as I gained access to internal Abitibi Paper correspondence from an anonymous source in Sturgeon Falls.

The documents in question consist of a series of internal memoranda between Abitibi Paper's head office in Toronto and the Sturgeon Falls mill. On 15 March 1968, J.I. McGibbon, vice-president of Abitibi Board Products, made clear that the platewood mill would close sometime between "now and October 1968." He informed Barrington earlier that day, noting that everyone "concerned appreciate the importance of keeping our plans confidential for the moment."[3] Internal correspondence points to problems with the quality of the particle board being produced, no doubt contributing to the faltering bottom line.[4] The platewood mill lost money every year – except for a brief period from 1959 to 1962 – it was in operation.

Preparations for the January 1969 closure were already at an advanced stage in September 1968. Ed Fortin proceeded to draw up a list of the eighty-two employees, including eight salaried staff, to be laid off. Merna Nesbitt then spent a long weekend typing letters at home for those to be laid off. She found this difficult: "These were people I had worked with for a long time. Not a nice thing to do. Because people in an office seem to have a sense that something different is happening, something is going on, and [hesitating] it was not nice." Once mill seniority was factored in, the distribution of job losses was distributed widely.[5] At the time, 350 people were employed at the two hardboard mills, 150 at the corrugated paper mill, and 100 at the platewood mill.

Barrington received a memorandum, dated 26 September 1968, indicating that one of Abitibi's public relations consultants had previously worked for Ford Canada in the 1950s, "when they moved the bulk of their operations from Windsor to Oakville and, therefore, has some firsthand experience on a similar problem which he can draw on to guide us on the Platewood Mill Situation."[6] What I found surprising here, and elsewhere in these documents, is the degree to which the platewood mill closing was understood as something new, even unprecedented, for Abitibi. There was no established procedure on how to handle mass terminations, and so the company had acquired none of the routine that would characterize downsizing in subsequent decades. In 1968 it stood at the end of a period of rapid economic expansion – what historian Jefferson Cowie has called the "great exception" in the history of capitalism – and so fretted about how best to break the bad news.[7] J.I. McGibbon even visited Sturgeon Falls in mid-September to go over the closure announcement with Barrington in person. Nothing was being left to chance.

On 1 October Abitibi's public relations department further advised Barrington on how to approach the announcement: "I think the best way to approach the whole thing is this: You are Mr. Abitibi. You are front stage centre. In the wing is Ian McGibbon and back stage making sure the show goes on is the Public Relations Department. We are at your service. We believe this is the way to do it. You are bound to have some thoughts and ideas, so be free with your comments."[8] We also have access to an eight-page company appraisal of the expected local impact of the closure. The company understood that Sturgeon Falls was "inseparable from the Abitibi plant and its employees, because Sturgeon Falls is virtually a company town."[9] The primary objective was thus to "make this announcement in such a way that the information is simultaneously released to each group; leaving no time nor margin for rumors, speculations, misunderstandings, or repercussions. And, of course, to do the job in a thoughtful *but business-like way*" [emphasis in original].

The uncovered documents also include a script, prepared in Toronto, about how the announcement itself would play out. At eight o'clock on the morning of 21 October 1968, employees were asked to assemble in the stock-storage area of the mill, where they would hear from Cam Barrington. After assembling, "Mr. Barrington would deliver the announcement of the company's intentions and read the formal press release being simultaneously issued. His remarks, which would be developed in cooperation with public relations counsel, would be designed to be sympathetic, frank and factual in tone and would anticipate most of the questions which might conceivably be in the minds of the employees."[10] Key supervisory employees in the mill would be notified just beforehand, "according to the company's assessment of these men's individual trust-worthiness to keep the matter confidential." And, while the meeting was under way, the company's press release would be posted on bulletin boards inside the mill to reach workers on other shifts. After informing employees, the company would then meet the local press and inform the wider community.

Although it is difficult to know if the meeting went according to script, we do have Cam Barrington's speech to the workers. With a handwritten reminder in the margins to "read slowly," Barrington sought to reassure workers that the mill's corrugated paper operations were on a firm footing. However, the two hardboard mills were only "touch and go," and the platewood mill was closing. His written statement is worth quoting at length:

> Gentlemen, I'm quite sure that the calling of a meeting with you has aroused curiosity and concern. I wish I could say the news is good but it *isn't*. We have to talk about a matter that involves all of us ... Some of you know that our industry has been having economic problems for some time ... While our corrugating medium mill here has been successful, the hardboard operations have been touch-and-go for some time. But our particle board production, which has been operating at increasing losses since 1963, now presents us with losses that we can no longer ignore. I am sorry to tell you that Abitibi can no longer justify the manufacture of particle board and has decided to go out of business in this product. This means that we will phase out of particle board production at Sturgeon Falls. We will operate the Platewood Mill here for approximately three more months ... Your main interest is to know who is going to be affected and *how* this will affect you. Early this spring we alerted the unions here that the Platewood Mill might shut down. They expressed some thoughts to us as to how we should relocate people in such an event ... The more senior men displaced by the Platewood Mill shutdown will be allowed to bump in bottom jobs of some other departments. The men bumped by these senior people, together with the more junior men displaced by the Platewood Mill shutdown, will revert to the labour pool and the most junior men in the labour pool will be laid off. We have prepared several lists which we have with us. These lists will be available to you at the conclusion of my talk [emphasis in original].

Barrington went on to say that management was "very actively searching for a profitable manufacturing operation that could be located in the platewood mill building, and that would provide employment for some of the men to be released by the phasing out of the platewood mill. One possibility that we are looking at is the manufacture of primed and prefinished siding." He then listed the reasons for the closure. Sturgeon Falls was the first particle board plant opened in Canada, but it "paid price of being first."[11] What is interesting here is that all but one of the other reasons correspond with those listed in private correspondence and in the press release issued by Abitibi's main office. Only in his spoken remarks do we see an emphasis placed on high wages, suggesting that Sturgeon Falls was uncompetitive as a result. This seems to have been an effort, on Barrington's part, to discipline the remaining workforce.[12]

Despite all the attention to detail, the closure announcement sparked public controversy, as Abitibi had recently received a $395,000 grant from the federal government to expand its production in Sturgeon Falls and create new jobs. Abitibi maintained that the grant was for its core corrugated paper operations, not the platewood mill.[13] Although the federal government seems to have accepted the company's explanation that Sturgeon Falls was in fact "three mills, within a mill," a critical article published in the *North Bay Nugget* on 29 October ignited a public relations brush fire that had to be stamped out quickly before it spread. Cam Barrington responded to it by distributing a strongly worded letter to employees calling the article "misleading and not in accordance with the facts."

Decades later, mill workers still insisted that the platewood mill should never have been closed. Several suggested that it quickly proved a costly mistake, as the price for particle board shot upward immediately thereafter. "They knew it after," insisted Claude Lortie. All the company had to do was invest a few million dollars in new equipment, as the mill's four by eight presses were too small, but Abitibi did not want to. Marcel Labbé thought they could still be in operation today, pointing to other producers in the region: "So that's why I say it was lack of planning. I think we had a very lax manager at one time, not to mention any names. When it went wrong, the solution was to shut it down. They should have gone to the planning board, they should have gone to the head office and [said], 'Hey, there's a demand for this product, all we need is a couple of million dollars,' and change the machinery … It hurts to see other mills produce what we were producing and make a fortune. We had it here. Well, so much water under that bridge since that day."[14] Interviewees did not express the same conviction, however, about the closure of the #1 hardboard mill: the production line was temporarily halted in November 1974 and closed permanently on 1 March 1975.[15]

Unfortunately we do not have a comparable set of internal company documents related to this closure. What we do have, thanks to the generosity of Wayne LeBelle, is the final report of the adjustment committee formed to find new jobs for the seventy-six workers laid off on 1 March 1975. None of those displaced, including a number of our interviewees who retained their recall rights, had more than two years' seniority at the time. In Canada, labour-management adjustment committees had become a standard feature since the formation of Consultative Manpower Services in 1963. This particular committee was chaired by LeBelle, and included representatives from local management and the unions. Once formed the committee developed a skills inventory of those displaced and a contact list of possible employers.

As unemployment in the area passed 20 per cent, the committee expanded its geographic focus beyond the usual fifty-mile radius. The most promising lead was the Weldwood sawmill in Longlac, several hundred miles northwest, and a committee member was dispatched there to investigate and report back. Jacques Daoust, a union representative, reported that Longlac was a nicer community than he had been told. Weldwood was a unionized flakeboard and plywood mill employing 320, but Daoust expressed some surprise that 34 per cent of the mill's workforce were women. In Sturgeon Falls, he said, "sometimes a girl will take on a more difficult job (woman's lib) and tough it for a while, but will eventually return to an easier one." In the end nobody wished to relocate to Longlac, preferring to wait to be recalled at the Sturgeon Falls mill. A few, such as Brian Laflèche, who had already been laid off once when the platewood mill closed, went on to do other things. In our interview, he told us that he had had enough: "I'm going to take a little different trade, so then I veered off into sales." In his final report Wayne LeBelle expressed his frustration with the immobility of the town's workforce due to "the hold that the company has on the community and area, particularly on its labour force. It is both a good and a bad 'hold.'"

Some believed that local management could have done more to secure the mill's future. Claude Lortie claimed that local management made a number of mistakes that contributed to the mill's long-term decline. When Abitibi added a second hardboard mill in 1962–3, for example, they made the presses exactly the same size as the first one. Everywhere else, Lortie observed, they were moving to larger, twenty-four by sixteen presses. As a result Sturgeon Falls was unable to make certain things. Shaking his head, he repeated: "I could never understand why they built it the same size." The failure to modernize the old paper machine probably sealed the fate of the entire facility in his estimation. It eventually "got too small, too soon." Sturgeon Falls seemed to be a step or two behind the mill's competitors during these years. Lortie, like others we spoke to, emphasized the importance of proactive local management: "Because all big companies, if you don't have a good manager that's after them all the time for money for this, money for that. 'I want to improve this, I want to improve [that] …' What happens is, you don't get anything. So, first thing you know, everything starts to be obsolete. You're way behind everybody else." Asked if the two closed mills could have survived over the long term, Raymond Marcoux replied, "not unless they wanted to spend a lot of money." Abitibi could have done so, but the lack of investment was partly due to "bad [local] management."

Some held Cam Barrington personally responsible, saying that he seemed to pay more attention to the landscaping outside the plant than the modernization of the machinery within. According to André Girard, Barrington was "not interested in resolving anything, all he was worried about was the lawn outside." This appears to be a common complaint among production workers at the time. Denis MacGregor told us that Barrington liked to "cut the grass, it looks good, add the flowers, oh, those are nice flowers. Now I only have four years to retire so everybody be nice, let's not make any rash decisions." Meanwhile, inside the mill, "No rash decisions, no decisions at all. So Sturgeon just stayed on an even keel, which I know today was a bad thing." As far as MacGregor was concerned, Barrington "more or less coast[ed], went with the flow … [He] should've looked into the future, which they didn't do."

Yet one wonders if it is fair to blame local managers for the failure to modernize. They could envision, promote, even champion, but the decisions ultimately were made elsewhere. Managers also inherited a cost structure that was unlike other mills, as Sturgeon Falls was part paper mill and part manufacturing site for other wood products. Ed Fortin explained that, as a corrugated paper mill, when it first started up it was grouped with the newsprint mills in industry-wide pattern bargaining that established wage rates and benefits. Newsprint mills were the highest paid in the industry, paying considerably more than other sectors. This proved to be problematic, as the hardboard and platewood mills were not as profitable as the corrugated paper machine. Had the wage rates in these parts of the mill been $2 less per hour, Fortin believed they might not have closed when they did. However, the integrated nature of the mill and the labour pool made it difficult to implement or enforce such a wage differential. Fortin cited the example of a millwright who fixed machines throughout the plant: he could not be paid two different wage rates depending on where the machine was located. "That was the history of that mill. We were faced with wages, and I'm not being critical of them it's just the mix. We were faced with wages much too high for the return being earned out in [the] marketplace by those inferior plants. And that's where the bulk of our people were working." Fortin concluded that, "if there's a lesson to be learned: never build a plant with several plants within one common surface. Because, you know, no matter what you do, any contract should be based on your ability to pay."

Closure of the #2 Hardboard Mill

Chemical engineer Walter (Wally) Shisko first came to work at Sturgeon Falls in 1956 as a control engineer on the new platewood mill. Cam Barrington was his direct supervisor. He stayed for four years before moving on to other paper mills. When the hardboard mill was having trouble in the 1980s, Barrington called Shisko up and offered him a job. When Barrington retired, Shisko became the mill's new manager, a position he filled from 1987 until 1996. Each morning he would meet his number two, Gerry Stevens, at seven o'clock for a coffee and spend the next hour going over everything and doing some long-term planning. The rest of the day was taken up with operational issues. Shisko and Barrington had very different styles, according to Frank Gerbasi:

> Cam Barrington – I don't mean this in the wrong way, but Cam Barrington looked like the manager. He dressed like the manager. But anytime I wanted to talk to him, if I went up to his office ... he always had time to talk to me. Wally Shishko, on the other hand, was a different type. He didn't dress like a manager. He'd have a little jacket on, and he spent a lot more time out of the office than Cam. And he would go through the shop and go through all the departments and [was] more hands-on as far as seeing, going everywhere through the shop or through the mill. But Cam was a manager. He was different. Two different styles. But both nice people.

Shisko, however, also had the unpleasant task of closing down a product line. This time the announcement was handled locally. "Shutting down an operation, any operation, is probably the worst job you can have," he recalled. "And there's nothing that you can say that is going to make people feel better."

Management "dropped the bomb on us," recalled Bruce Colquhoun. "We all knew it was coming. But then, when it hits you, you know, it hits you." The closure announcement came at a time of enormous economic upheaval in Canada, as trade barriers were coming down and technological changes were sweeping through the pulp and paper industry. New pulping technologies were being introduced and older, less efficient (and smaller) paper machines retired.[16] For example, paper machines introduced in the 1960s operated at 915 metres per minute, while those started up in the 1990s could go 1,350 metres per minute.[17] Although it had been refurbished, the Sturgeon Falls mill's solitary paper machine dated from the 1920s. There were other factors. Protectionist feeling in the United States led to "voluntary" countervailing duties being imposed on Canadian softwood lumber exports to that country. The United States argued that Canada's Crown-owned lands represented a state subsidy of the industry, as companies only had to pay a stumpage fee, rather then purchase private lands. Under financial pressure, Mac-Millan Bloedel moved out of some products, including plywood, shingles and shakes, and paperboard.[18] It also led to a tough round of negotiations with the local union in Sturgeon Falls, resulting in a three-year contract in April 1991 that members accepted only by a lukewarm 150 to 94 vote in favour.[19] A strike was narrowly averted. The October 1991 closure of #2 hardboard mill was thus part of wider changes in the industry.

During these years of decline, mill workers were constantly told by management in Sturgeon Falls that "we're going to close." It was "always like that," recalled Larry Shank. Bruce Colquhoun told us that, come contract time, management would threaten them with "if you don't do this, we're gonna shut the hardboard down." Once a new collective agreement had been signed, however, management's message would change, and workers were now told that the hardboard mill was getting by. "I think that's why it ran so long," suggested Shank. Changing consumer tastes were also a factor, said Percy Allary. He blamed the hardboard mill's closing on the fact that "the market was drying up in the hardboard. Vinyl siding took over, and our product wasn't good enough to compete with vinyl siding so we lost that market." Sales tanked.

"We tried, we really tried hard to save the hardboard mill," recalled mechanical superintendent Marc Côté. The company started to make new products, such as garage door panels. They "really cranked it out, and it was too much for the market. But we spent three, four million dollars to put that on the market, and it didn't work." When asked if people in the mill expected the closure of the hardboard mill and the resulting layoffs, Côté replied: "Partly and not partly." Nobody knew for sure, or how deep the layoffs would be: "Nobody knew how high [up the seniority list] it was going to go. But when the mill did go down and the cuts did come, they went deep and the crews were cut – some 50 per cent, 60 per cent. That was difficult."

Others blamed the closure on poor quality control in the mill. Bruce Colquhoun noted that inferior exterior panelling was being shipped out despite workers' protests. Siding was "supposed to be smooth," he said, but sometimes it felt "like coarse sandpaper. And they were counting that as top grade." Colquhoun shared a story with us to illustrate the perceived mismanagement:

I was on grader one night. The boards come down a conveyor, they hit a switch, and then four of 'em lift up, cut boards, and you take a look at it, flip it over, put it on the line, and it goes down and gets packaged. Anyway, [rubs table] whoo! I mark number two on it, put it on another pile. Whoo! I keep marking them, and they're all going there. The foreman come out and says, "What's going on?" And I said, "Look at that!" He says, "That's number one, let it go." I said, "Come on! Would you put that on your house?" He says, "Put it number one." I said, "No." He went and he got the superintendent. Superintendent comes out and he says, "Bruce, what's the matter?" I said, [rubs table] "Feel that." He said, "What's the matter with that?" "Come on, Terry!

That's coarse sandpaper!" I mean, you've got to have no feeling in your hands not to feel that. And everybody else was going, "Yeah. Look at that." I'd send a few boards down, they'd all come over and look at it, and they were really bad boards. And he said, "Do your job or go home." I said, "What?" He said, "Do your job or go home." I said, "I am doing my job. And if I don't do my job, we're all going home." He said, "I mean it. Do your job. Or go home. That's number one board." Fine. I didn't care what the board looked like, I didn't care if there was a chunk taken out of it. "That's number one, my super says that's number one, I'm going to put it as number one." And I did. Everything that went through. So I went and talked to my dad the next day and I told him what was going on. He said, "Oh yeah? So, we gotta call somebody upstairs." And they went and they rechecked all that. They downgraded it to scrap, or number two, or secondary hardboard siding. And the super got a pile of crap for that. There was no reason to send that out like that.

For Colquhoun, local management was interested only in quantity. They didn't care if there were problems in the time spent pressing the hardboard, leaving the panels "soft" or "very brittle."

The inferior quality of the siding resulted in customer complaints. Many of our interviewees spoke to this. Ben Lajeunesse, who worked in the offices, noted that the company received "a lot of complaints on their exterior siding that they had to make good by replacing it, and paying somebody to go down and put it on the house, take the old stuff off, put the new stuff on. That's what was costing them the money. I think we were still making money with the production end of it, but covering the complaints was devastating." These persistent problems made the hardboard mill closure inevitable in their minds. "We all knew it was going to happen eventually," concluded Colquhoun.[20]

I sought to access corporate archives to gain a sense of the company's own reasoning for closing the second hardboard mill. This was easier said than done. Abitibi sold the Sturgeon Falls mill to Vancouver-based MacMillan Bloedel in 1979, only to have the Canadian company acquired by Weyerhaeuser twenty years later. It was Weyerhaeuser that closed the plant altogether in 2002. I therefore wrote to both Abitibi and Weyerhaeuser to inquire about any corporate records that I might access related to the Sturgeon Falls mill. From its corporate headquarters in Federal Way, Washington, Weyerhaeuser provided a series of press releases, including a MacMillan Bloedel release dated 9 October 1991 entitled "Decade of Losses: Finally Closes MB Hardboard Siding Plant." In it Wally Shisko is quoted as saying, "Competition from vinyl siding has been killing us slowly for more than 10 years and this announcement comes as no surprise to our employees or he community."[21] The company also maintained that the closure followed losses amounting to $20 million over the past decade. To make matters worse, the hardboard mill had operated only at one-third capacity in recent years.

In all, 162 jobs were lost, cutting the mill's workforce in half. Those laid off included workers originally hired in 1972, with nineteen years' service. Managers were informed of the impending news four or five days ahead of time. Keeping it a secret was extremely difficult for local managers such as Marc Côté:

> And you couldn't even show it in your eyes that you knew, you know, because it was something that had to be planned. We spent nights at the mill planning how we are going do it. And you'd have to justify – when the shutdown comes down, if you're a superintendent with the department, you have to justify everybody you keep. It's not who [you] let go, it's who you keep. So you say, "Well, I can't run this mill, the rest of the mill, without two or three machinists, I need at least two welders, I need so many riveters." And you had to go out and justify and fight to save these jobs because they would just say, "Well, if you don't need them, they're gone. We're shutting down here." … It's a very difficult task. It needs a lot of planning. It needs a lot of heart.

Not surprisingly, in a small town rumours of an impending layoff began to circulate. The day before the announcement, the Sturgeon Falls *Tribune* spoke of the heightened anxiety: "There is something big happening at the mill as of press time today. It's been kept very secret, very mum, but the situation has been described by one mill worker as 'very touchy.' As of press time it wasn't clear what is going on, and no-one wants to go on record. Some millworkers have phoned the *Tribune* fearing the worst, loss of jobs. Given the situation across the country, it's a real concern for everyone in Sturgeon."[22] The journalist went on to note: "It's not an exaggeration to say that the phone has been ringing off the wall with people wanting to know what has happened, what is going to happen. I've even received phone calls at home."[23] She hoped that the news was "not so bad … I know in our office we're keeping our fingers crossed."

The news, when it finally came, was done differently than in the past, when Mac-Millan Bloedel had sent in "somebody from outside," recalled Marc Côté. This time, the company delegated the unpleasant task to individual superintendents in the plant. Côté told us there were meetings to prepare supervisory staff on how best to do this. But "there is no proper way of telling a person they're losing their job. There is no nice way." Although layoffs in a union shop go by seniority, this was not so easy in Côté's mechanical shop, as there were different trades: "You have machinists, millwrights, tinsmiths, welders, pipefitters. So, how many machinists? How many pipefitters? You have to assess the needs of the mill. The company [is] telling you, you need to cut the crew by 20 per cent; well, then, who's the 20 per cent? Who's it gonna be? And that to me was traumatic. I was a machinist with them and so were a lot of other superintendents. You know, we worked together."

Despite the rumour mill, the news was met with disbelief. Benny Haarsma explained that they had heard this story so often they thought it was just another bluff. It came as a "total shock" to André Cartier: "As far as I know, every single person that I knew and talked to, it was a total surprise, a total shock. Nobody knew. It was kept extremely secretive and it was a big move. So the only thing that we knew [was] that there was something going on, because for the last month before we heard the news, in the beginning of December 1991 … the management staff were staying late … until nine o'clock at night, ten o'clock at night, later … There was a lot of things going on, but we didn't know why." Cartier noted that management timed the announcement to coincide with the shift change at seven o'clock in the morning. They were told to shut down the paper machine, as there was "going to be a little meeting." Continuing, he said: "That's when they told us, exactly like that. And verbally, we went in the lunch room, 'everybody come in, meet in the lunch room,' and each superintendent of each department announced it at eight o'clock." It was all timed, as the superintendent looked at his watch, saying: "Okay, it's five to eight, now let's [tell] everybody to shut down and meet in the lunch room." At that meeting they were not told who was staying and who was being let go.

Confusion reigned for some time about who was actually being laid off. It was unclear how the "bumping process" would work and how the three seniority lists (mill, departmental, and trade) would be reconciled. Even a week later, it remained unclear. Not surprisingly the company's handling of the layoffs upset the union: "We haven't even met with the company yet! We've asked the company if they have a package for us, but we're going to be doing the work for them."[24] In the end pension eligibility was set at seventy-five, service plus age, with a bridge to retirement available for those who were sixty or older. We have a sense of the union's talks with management thanks to the handwritten notes shared by André Girard. The inevitable training costs associated with seniority-based bumping in the mill were discussed, while management pushed for increased "flexibility" on the shop floor.[25] The union issued a press release on 18 November 1991 condemning the "lack of compassion" with which the company implemented the announced layoffs. It did not appreciate management's request to open up the existing collective agreement to provide more flexibility with the trades, casting this as a demand for concessions.[26]

The Sturgeon Falls *Tribune* grappled with the significance of the layoffs for the local community: "It's devastating news, not only the shock, but the sheer weight

Percy Allary, 2005.
Photograph by David. W. Lewis.

of numbers in a town of this size. I would hazard a guess that there won't be a single family unaffected by this news."[27] One businessman was quoted as being so incensed by the company that he wished it would "just shut the whole damn thing down and sell it to the people who work there! Get rid of the management, and run it like Tembec." The community newspaper took a somewhat different position, saying, "[w]hatever happens, one thing is clear – the Town of Sturgeon Falls can no longer depend on the mill."[28] In response the community formed an adjustment committee to mitigate the impact of the layoffs.[29] According to André Cartier, the layoffs were "all that people were talking about for weeks on end." But, as Gerry Stevens reminded us, Sturgeon Falls "has a history of going through these things." Pointing specifically to the seventeen-year closure of the mill, Stevens added: "So, they've had hard times. And people remember." In her interview Merna Nesbitt agreed, saying, "people in Sturgeon are survivors. Because they survived a lot, you know. The mill closed in '29 and they managed to survive until it started up again, and then the platewood closed and still people managed to [survive]. There's a lot of changing of jobs … when a portion of the mill closes."

Depending on their seniority, some knew they were safe and others understood they would soon be out of a job. "In my case," recalled André Cartier, "I was borderline, I didn't know." In the end he kept his job, but it was "very close." Those without seniority did not stay, but some had a skill or certification that was needed. The final determination resulted in considerable acrimony and ill-feeling.

This meant that some high-seniority workers in the hardboard mill might become a lowly paid labourer in another part of the mill. Or they might opt for a higher-paying job on the paper machine – a part of the mill in which they had never worked before. Denis MacGregor, who worked on the paper machine, spoke at length about the problems that arose. "As far as the union goes," he said: "if you're the last one [in], you're the first one out. But … somebody's got to take your spot there. Nobody's trained." But, with seniority, the incoming person "bypasses … sixth hand, fifth hand, fourth hand, and falls third hand." Normally it took someone a year to climb from sixth hand to fifth hand and so on, learning as he climbed the employment ladder in the department. But here was someone – with no relevant experience – who leapt up to third hand literally overnight. MacGregor explained what happened next:

> By the time you get to third hand, you have learned a little bit about machine tending because you've been there for four years and you've seen the machine-tender work, you've seen stuff that he does to fix problems and this and that. But when you go from the hardboard to us, and you move up four jobs right after that, that is hard. That's hard for a young man. But this guy is fifty-five, fifty-six, okay? It's harder. Now, I applaud this guy, and I'll applaud quite a few of the other guys that really worked hard at it to move up, you know? … But some of them didn't really try … I think it disrupted the mill a lot. It made it really, really hard for the guys on the paper machine that were still there.

Initially, MacGregor was one of those who would lose their job. He was to be "eighth man out," which meant that he needed eight of those left to quit or retire before getting recalled. Luckily for him, twelve men accepted early retirement packages offered by the company. His almost immediate return to work, however, caused friction:

> Guys got pissed off at me because I went back to my position, which was back tender at the time. But the company had said, "Listen, this guy is a trained back tender, there's no way we're putting him in sixth hand, and putting somebody who doesn't know what the hell he's doing as a back tender. So he's in the middle, he keeps his spot.

You still have your job, you're gonna be the sixth hand." And that's all they ever gave them, was a job. They said, "We're not going to guarantee you a $22, or $24, or $18 an hour job. We're gonna keep you, we'll pay you for forty hours, you shut up." Was it fair, was it not fair? I guess it made sense. To be fair I guess if I'd been one of the guys who went from $22 an hour down to $18 an hour, and I'd been there longer than me, I would have been pissed off too. But … as far as I was concerned, it only made sense the way they did it. But that was me.

The layoffs also undermined the trades, leading to "trade swapping" and a lot of "griping, and growling, and grumbling" among those left, recalled John Dillon. Asked if the company handled the layoff well, André Cartier replied with an emphatic "absolutely not." There were "mixed emotions," as he had been bumped down the ladder. He felt like pointing an accusing finger: "You're bumping my job? *My* job! I trained you! Trained you to bump me!"

Others were pressured to retire early. Merna Nesbitt opted to retire to prevent another woman (Ruth Thompson) from being laid off. Ben Lajeunesse, who worked in accounting, was told that, if he stayed on and bumped somebody more junior, but couldn't do the job after two days training, "I was gone. And then I'd wait 'til sixty-five to get my pension. It was a bit of a threat." Once the early retirement package was offered, however, and he realized he would receive 70 per cent of his salary for staying at home, he gladly took it, "because I was going to retire anyway. And everybody knew it, that I was retiring, at fifty-eight, which was a year and a half away."

Those remaining felt some relief. According to Larry Shank, "Well, you were just happy to have a job – not to have to start looking. And, well, younger people … it didn't bother them. If you're young … you go. But .. once you're old enough, and you bought a house or you got this and you got that, and the kids are at school, well, you don't want to get up and leave … You want to stay." But there were some hard feelings. Afterward the mood in the mill was "ugly," admitted Karen Beaudette. She was personally "very hurt" by the layoffs, noting that there was a "big controversy over your seniority based on department, based on seniority and qualifications. They also, at the same time, started cross trades. In the mechanical shop, they started to eliminate a lot of electrical positions … I think a lot of guys started feuds at that time … I know [in the] mechanical department there were a couple of guys that just don't get along today because of that." Mike Lacroix, who was one of those laid off, remained bitter about how the layoffs were implemented by management and the union. In our interview, he said that a "bunch of us" were "screwed over" in the process. Asked what went wrong, Lacroix shook his head and replied "Well,

I better not get into that." Afterwards, Harold Stewart recalled people saying, "this damn mill this and this damn mill that," or "we shouldn't have to work under these conditions." Stewart didn't share these feelings. For his part, Raymond Marcoux sighed when asked about the hardboard mill's closure. His decision to transfer to the paper machine proved to be providential: "I knew I was one of the people they needed to run the paper machine."

Conclusion

The Sturgeon Falls mill's long decline mirrored that of industrial North America, which also began its long descent in the late 1960s. A new sense of job insecurity began to take hold. "For a long time it hurt," recalled Marc Côté. A lot of questions were asked: "How long is this going to last?" "They just shut one down, when are they going to shut the next one down?" "Do they really care?" "Are they going to spend money?" Marc Côté and others did not have any answers. Nobody knew if the paper machine was going to continue to run. Côté observed that the "atmosphere in the town was gloomy, for a long time." As a manager and someone who had to break the news to his department, Côté recalled the personal price to be paid as a locally rooted manager: "You walked down the streets, you weren't the most popular person around, I can tell you that now. And I'd been born and raised here, you know? I lived in Verner, and I lived in Sturgeon for thirty-eight years. Went fishing with all these guys."

The 1991 layoffs had far-reaching ramifications inside the mill itself. One of the consequences was the decline of the employee credit union at the mill. After his interview, André Girard shared with us his files, which detail the rich history of mutual aid in the mill. It is an interesting story. The Abitibi-Price Power and Paper Employees Credit Union was started in 1965 by mill workers when mill employment was at its height. Over its thirty-year existence, the credit union directed over $4 million in small loans, of up to $7,000 each, to mill workers, active and retired, as well as family members. André Girard was its driving force, serving as president for twelve years. In the early days the credit union hired a mill worker who would meet people in the mill's laboratory at noon hour. A group of mill workers met monthly to determine the interest rate: "We would go higher or lower and this and that, and how much we'd give on the investments and everything." By the 1990s, however, the era of small, workplace credit unions was coming to a close. The growing complexity of the financial sector and an increasing tangle of government regulation had become too onerous, forcing most to dissolve or merge into larger formations.

Workplace credit unions like the one in Sturgeon Falls were also vulnerable to layoffs and mill or factory closures. Good loans could turn bad at the push of a button. The files reveal that the credit union went into the red after the layoffs in 1993 and 1994, as its membership dwindled from 233 in 1990 to 172 in 1994. The number of new loans was also in sharp decline, dropping from 117 to 33 over the four years.[30] In his annual report to the board of directors in March 1994, André Girard reported: "Your Credit Union has felt the partial shut down of the mill in October, 1991. As a result of this shut down this will be the first year the Credit Union has had to deal with a deficit. Due to the deficit we will not be able to pay a dividend this year."[31] The credit union closed in 1996, and everything was moved over to the local Caisse populaire. It was an uncertain time, but prospects at the mill were looking up.

RECYCLED DREAMS

You got to remember, Sturgeon Falls was a very old mill … Now, naturally, we maintained it, upgraded it bit by bit over the years, but it was still an extremely old mill. And … we started studying it, and we came up with recyclable. We went to recycled [cardboard] 100 per cent. Our anaerobic system could handle that and the cost of that would be somewhere between 12 and 15 million. So I went through [MacMillan Bloedel] and told them, here is an option to do this … but they had no money … So then I said, "If I can find ways and means to get that, will you allow us to put it in?" "Go ahead."

– Walter (Wally) Shisko

The emergence of the environmental movement in the 1970s and rising public awareness of the effects of air and water pollution compelled governments to strengthen the regulatory regime governing industry. As one of the biggest industrial polluters, the pulp and paper industry faced immediate pressure to curb its air and water pollution. Paper mills consumed vast amounts of water, pumping 95 per cent of it back into rivers and streams. In 1959, for example, the US industry discharged a staggering 1.6 trillion gallons of wastewater.[1] These massive discharges of suspended solids and organic materials used up much of the oxygen in the water, killing or poisoning fish downriver. Meanwhile the sulphur "rotten egg" smell that most paper mills exuded was an unmistakable sign of air pollution. Forestry companies, therefore, were forced to adopt new technologies, modify old ones, and change their logging practices. One of the biggest issues facing the pulp and paper industry as a whole was the dioxin that was a by-product of the use of elemental chlorine in the pulping and bleaching process.[2] Dioxin, publicly associated with the defoliant "Agent Orange," was first linked to pulp and paper in 1985 by the US Environmental Protection Agency when a study was leaked to the public by Greenpeace. The industry was under political pressure to curb pollution. Indeed, according to David Sonnefeld, "no industry has been affected by environmental social movements to such an extent, in so short a time, and in such a wide geographical scale, as pulp and paper manufacturing."[3]

In Canada the first effluent-abatement rules for the industry came into effect in 1971, with new federal regulations under the Fisheries Act to control the total levels of suspended solids, biochemical oxygen demand (BOD), and acute toxicity to fish.[4] The pulp and paper industry was the first such regulated sector in Canada, but the new rules were compulsory only for new mills or those undergoing expansion; existing mills were not required to meet the regulations. Accordingly, in the years that followed, the risk was greatest downriver from older mills in places such as Sturgeon Falls, where companies proved unwilling to make major new investments.

The earliest water-pollution survey of the Sturgeon River I could find was one undertaken by the Ontario Ministry of Environment in 1965, which estimated that the mill dumped ten million gallons of waste effluent into the river daily. At the time there was no treatment whatsoever, save a mesh screening device to stop wood chips exiting the mill. As a result the mill's discharge was found to exceed Ontario's "maximum objective" for BOD. The report also indicated that down-river tourist operators were complaining about the "unsightly conditions of their launches and docks due to the accumulation of raw sewage [from the town, which was also untreated] and wooden chips. The operators have reported a decrease in business on account of this condition."[5] Another survey, conducted in 1977, similarly reported that water quality was "poor" below the mill, with bacterial levels that "approached and in some cases exceeded the Recreational Criteria for total body contact."[6] The authors of the 1977 report recommended the introduction of a new environmental cleanup program at the mill.

Various pollution-abatement systems were proposed and implemented, but they were not "up to par," according to Marc Côté. The new system, inaugurated in 1990, used anaerobic bacteria to digest the mill's waste, with the methane gas produced as a result burned off. Not only did it produce "noxious odors,"[7] it did not meet the new environmental regulations being implemented by the federal government. These regulations introduced enforceable effluent-quality standards for all paper mills in the country, requiring major upgrades to manufacturing processes and effluent-treatment systems at existing mills. "With the new legislation, it wasn't enough," recalled Wally Shisko of the mill's new pollution-abatement system.

Amid this uncertainty, the Ontario Ministry of Environment again tested the fish in the Sturgeon River in June 1991 after anglers complained of "foul odor and

An industrialized river: logs were driven down the Sturgeon River to the mill or past it to Cache Bay and Callander; booms directed the logs down a giant chute (centre right) to bypass the dam. Ontario – Sturgeon Falls – Abitibi Power & Paper Company 1951-1966, C30, Northway-Gestalt Corporation Fonds, Archives of Ontario, Toronto.

taste in some fish which were caught."[8] Speaking to the *Tribune*, Frank Nault told readers how his father-in-law was fishing below the dam for silver bass: "When we ate it, covered in sauce, two people in the family had diarrhea for two days. I'm really concerned because the silver bass are in the lake all year, and they've been in the river only one week, and they're gone bad. It's very offensive, an oily taste."[9] A Ministry of Natural Resources spokesperson initially noted that "off flavours" in fish were common "below pulp mills," but this had never happened with this mill. Also, the flavour typically was a "sulfide taste," whereas these fish had a "phenol taste" to them. As the paper was not bleached, dioxin was not considered a factor here. It was then noted that water quality had improved since the company put its new pollution-abatement system in place. Even so, the mill still tainted fish downriver.[10]

With stricter government regulations coming into effect, the mill would find itself shut down unless it could reduce its pollution levels dramatically. The cooking of wood chips required a lot of caustic acid, explained Percy Allary, and "[t]his stuff was being dumped in the river." According to one report, the pulping process consisted of converting the logs to chips and cooking them "in the presence of sodium sulphite cooking solution. This resulted in a discharge to the Sturgeon River of some 40 tonnes/day of … BOD. Some $10 million was spent in 1988 to treat the effluent for BOD removal, but there still remained the problem of fish toxicity in the effluent."[11] Impending regulations required the company to invest another $15–20 million in pollution controls, which would increase the cost of annual operations by a further $3 million. MacMillan Bloedel made it clear, however, that it was not going to make any new large-scale investments in the mill's pollution controls. So, concluded Marc Côté, "it was either shut the mill down or go to something else."

This was the unambiguous message delivered to the union after the shutdown of #2 hardboard mill. Unless a solution could be found, and funded, "we are dead," wrote André Girard during one of these meetings.[12] The local union president told the newspaper that the future of the entire mill was "just about zero! The way it looks now, if the government does not come up with some money, it's just not there. The office in Vancouver is not putting in a damn penny!"[13] Then the idea emerged, championed by mill manager Wally Shisko, to convert the mill to recycled pulp and thereby sidestep much of the pollution problem. The proposed old corrugated cardboard (OCC) repulping facility would be significantly cheaper to build and operate, as it was "merely" a cleaning process "to remove the contaminants, i.e. tape, staples, etc., [as] opposed to a washing and cooking process when producing pulp from virgin chips."[14] The OCC conversion required an initial $13–15 million investment, however, and MacMillan-Bloedel still refused to invest anything fur-ther in Sturgeon Falls.

The new environmental regulations were being implemented at a time of deep global recession and massive job losses in forestry and other sectors of the economy. "Has the forest industry hit rock bottom yet?" asked one journalist in November 1991.[15] A few months later, another wrote that "good news has been a rare commod-ity for Northern Ontario's pulp and paper-making."[16] It was a region-wide problem, as Algoma Steel in Sault Ste Marie, the country's third-largest steel producer, threat-ened to close, as did other paper mills in Thunder Bay, Kapuskasing, and Sault Ste Marie. A 1994 report prepared by Price Waterhouse estimated that one in five jobs in Canadian pulp and paper mills could disappear by 2000, with the oldest mills in Ontario, Quebec, and Atlantic Canada taking the brunt.[17] How, then, to pay for the proposed conversion?

If the economic timing for the OCC proposal could not have been worse, the political timing proved fortuitous. The Ontario New Democratic Party (NDP), a social democratic party with strong roots in the region, elected for the first time in 1990, sought ways to save these closing mills and with them the region's industrial base. As a result, the government facilitated the 1992 employee buyout of Algoma Steel in Sault Ste Marie, which saw union control of the mill, with contract conces-sions used to purchase company shares. But no two rescues were the same. For example, the 1991 effort to save the Kapuskasing paper mill was the result of a year-long negotiation that involved employee and management groups, the pro-vincial government, local protest (a road was blocked) to maintain pressure on the departing company and the government, and a private partner in Tembec. The resulting company, Spruce Falls, incorporated in December 1991, was initially 52 per cent employee owned, 41 per cent owned by Tembec, and 7 per cent owned by Kapuskasing residents. But Tembec managed the mill as though it owned it, and early efforts to create a more cooperative workplace with employee-management committees were said to have tapered off after the first year.[18] The struggles to save Provincial Paper (Thunder Bay), Saint Mary's Paper (Sault Ste Marie), and MacMil-lan Bloedel's corrugated paper mill (Sturgeon Falls) were similarly hybrid private-public partnerships.[19]

None of these mills was nationalized, as had been the case with Canada's aero-nautics industry in the 1970s or with steel mills in Quebec and Nova Scotia in the 1960s.[20] In those instances, troubled industries were run as provincially or federally owned Crown corporations. By the 1990s the political winds had shifted. Govern-ments of all political stripes were privatizing the Crown corporations of the past, not creating new ones. The Ontario NDP sought to open up a third way between

state ownership and the open market by facilitating employee and community ownership or other public-private partnerships, and to put a stop to the hemorrhaging
of jobs. All of these buyouts occurred under the gun of a mill or factory closure, so
time was of the essence. The departing company needed to be convinced to sell the
mill as a going concern, a business plan had to be developed, financing obtained,
and new concessionary collective agreements signed.[21] This often required the presence of strong local managers willing to take a leadership role during the transition.

If the government saw itself as a facilitator or catalyst, rather than as an owner, it
likely found inspiration in the Employee Stock Ownership Plans (ESOPs) that were
being used to "save" a few large-scale mills in the United States. Weirton Steel (in
West Virginia) and McLouth Steel (in Michigan) were two of the highest-profile
industrial ESOPs.[22] One inspiring example in the region was the successful effort
in 1972 to save the paper mill in Temiscaming, Quebec, just a ninety-minute drive
east of Sturgeon Falls. There, the departing company had initially refused to sell the
mill, but a five-week blockade of the Ottawa River by a flotilla of fishing boats effectively halted the company's efforts to drive its wood downriver past the shuttered
mill.[23] The result was the formation of Tembec, which emerged as a major forestry
company in Canada and continues to produce paper in Temiscaming.

Sociologist Jack Quarter notes that unions became part of a growing number of
buyouts of struggling or closing plants in Canada. He counted thirty-nine worker
buyouts where employees owned a majority of the company, with a number of others (such as Tembec) where workers controlled only a minority of company stock.
He notes that these initiatives often came from the wider community, "with the
union taking a more passive role."[24] There was a great deal of reluctance within the
trade union movement about their potential to save jobs and to maintain superior
wages. The Canadian Region of the United Auto Workers, for example, indicated
that it was "less than enthusiastic" about employee ownership in its 1985 brief to
the Royal Commission on the Economic Union and Development Prospects for
Canada. Buyouts tended not to endure.

The union was right. The record of ESOPs in the United States and the varied
employee or community buyouts in Canada is not a particularly promising one.
Historian Jeremy Brecher, for example, conducted a book-length study of the various efforts to save plants in the Naugatuck ("Brass") Valley in Connecticut, all of
which ultimately failed.[25] The ESOPs at Weirton and McLouth Steel likewise failed.
A similar story unfolded in Northern Ontario: three of the four paper mills in the
region "saved" in the early 1990s subsequently closed. But their failure was due, in
part, to their initial success, as workers and their unions willingly sold back their
shares for a tidy profit, only to lose their jobs a few years later to decisions made

in far-off corporate headquarters. This perverse cycle happened again and again. Although the mills in Kapuskasing and Temiscaming are still running, workers at both plants sold their shares to Tembec for ten and twenty times the price they initially paid, respectively.[26] Otherwise, there had been "no resurrection" in deindustrializing regions such as Northern Ontario, but these efforts did help in the short term, and gave people hope in bleak times.[27]

It is within this charged environmental, economic, and political context that the effort to save the Sturgeon Falls corrugated mill from closing unfolded. As we will see, due to the herculean efforts of mill manager Wally Shisko, with the energetic support of the local community as well as the provincial government, the mill was saved, and a formal company-community partnership was formed to run the new OCC recycled pulp facility. For a time, Sturgeon Falls became a national success story, and this new lease on life contributed to a renewed sense of solidarity and possibility on the shop floor. The mill as a whole, however, remained firmly part of MacMillan Bloedel, and the underlying problem of a company unwilling to invest in the mill's future also remained. Sturgeon Falls "dodges kiss of death," declared the *Globe and Mail*, but, as we now know, the mill's struggle for survival was only beginning.[28]

Saving the Mill

When MacMillan Bloedel announced the closure of the #2 hardboard mill on 1 October 1991, plans to shift to recycled paper from virgin wood were already well advanced. Working with Gerry Stevens and other local managers, Wally Shisko came up with a bold plan to sidestep the pollution problem: old corrugated boxes would be shipped to Sturgeon Falls in bales, repulped, and fed into the mill's paper machine to make corrugated medium for new cardboard boxes. Curbside recycling was just beginning in Canada, and recycled products were relatively new things.[29] Sturgeon Falls would be the first 100 per cent recycled paper mill in Canada. As MacMillan Bloedel was unable or unwilling to invest more in pollution control, unless the new OCC facility became a reality the Sturgeon Falls mill would close in 1993, when the new federal regulations would come into force. As Shisko later explained, "We went through the federal regulations coming in for 1993–94 to meet toxicity tests. This test calls for rainbow trout to be able to live for forty-eight hours in pure effluent. We couldn't pass it."[30] Accordingly he understood that, "As soon as the toxicity requirements came in, it's closed." The proposed OCC repulping facility also promised significant operational savings. "It was based on economics," recalled Gerry Stevens. "First of all, the cost of fibre was a lot lower. And it was harder and harder to get wood all the time. It was a good fit for us because most of our product, 90 per cent of it, went to Southern Ontario. That's where secondary fibre is generated. It was paper down, waste back; paper down, waste back. And it made a beautiful fit, in that respect."

Hoping to convince MacMillan Bloedel to invest, Wally Shisko submitted a formal proposal to his superiors at the company's head office in Vancouver.[31] It, too, was turned down, however, and Shisko was told that the mill was not part of the company's core business. At this moment, things might have looked bleak, but there was a glimmer of hope. In the face of MacMillan Bloedel's insistence that it had "no money," Shisko continued to push, asking his superiors "If I can find ways and means to get that, will you allow us to put it in?" The company agreed to let Shisko find another partner willing to foot the bill. "Try whatever you like – just don't show up on our balance sheet," was their message.[32] But where was Shisko going to find $13–15 million?

Earlier in the year, he had toyed with the idea of selling the mill's hydroelectric dam to pay for the proposed OCC facility.[33] This idea was probably quashed by the company, as the sale would have greatly increased the operating costs of the mill. Shisko then went to the federal and provincial governments, to the banks, and others to pitch the OCC proposal. He needed partners. J.P. Charles, the reeve of Springer Township, which adjoins Sturgeon Falls, recalled that, after the hardboard mill closure and the public's realization that the rest of the mill would close in two years' time unless something was done, he and the other mayors of West Nipissing's five municipalities decided to act. As chairperson of the West Nipissing Municipal Association, Charles called a meeting and told those gathered that "We're going to try to beat this thing." He took pride in the fact that "We did. Everybody chipped in. All the five mayors, we worked really good together. We sat together. Then we met with Wally Shisko, the manager of the mill at the time here." Shisko informed them about the OCC proposal: "We've been talking about a recycling mill here for years. But nothing has happened about it." He had no way of doing it, as the "company will not put the money up." So, after further discussion, it was agreed that they should proceed on their own. This convergence of interests is a good example of what Ray Hudson and David Saddler call a "territorial based alliance."[34]

The mobilizing power of a shared community identity was strong locally, but would anyone anywhere else listen? The timing was propitious, as the Ontario NDP government wanted to respond energetically to the unfolding crisis in Northern Ontario. Jim Thiebert, a senior official in the Ministry of Northern Development and Mines, was quoted in the newspaper as saying, "Frankly, I didn't care if Sturgeon Falls was making cardboard or bowling balls … My job was to look after the well-being of this area. If that meant pushing and pushing, so be it."[35] Ontario sought only to avoid a direct subsidy to the company, as MacMillan Bloedel was not insolvent and had refused to put any of its own money into the project. At first, Shisko attempted to forge a partnership directly with the town of Sturgeon Falls, but this got "strangled by red tape" as municipalities were forbidden to "enter joint ventures with private corporations."[36] According to the *Globe and Mail*, the town clerk in Sturgeon Falls, Guy Savage, "broke the log jam" at a pivotal point in a meeting with the various parties: "Mr. Savage pulled his large frame out of his chair and roared at the group, 'I've had it!' Pounding his fist on the table, Mr. Savage told them: 'I've sat here for three hours and all I've heard is what we can't do. Let's talk about what we can do.' At that point, Mr. Shisko recalls with a smile, 'it was as if a dam broke.' By the end of the day, the group had come up with a plan."[37] The plan involved the formation of the West Nipissing Economic Development Committee (WNEDC),[38] which would serve as MacMillan Bloedel's legal partner in the proposed OCC repulping facility. The WNEDC also had the advantage of representing a wider geographic area than Sturgeon Falls, thus bridging the five area municipalities.

OCC financing came primarily from the Ontario government's Ministry of Environment (a grant of $4 million), the Northern Ontario Heritage Fund (a loan of just over $4 million), and the Northern Ontario Development Corporation (NODC, a loan of $500,000). Neither loan required interest payments in the first five years.[39] Two commercial loans from the Royal Bank of Canada were also secured, one (for $500,000) guaranteed by the NODC and the other (for $2,605,000) secured by the assets of the partnership itself. In all, $14 million in financing was secured. Everybody chipped in except the company. Not only did MacMillan Bloedel refuse to contribute money to the project; it did not even guarantee the commercial loans.

There was one final problem. In Ontario, economic development committees did not have the legal authority to do what was being proposed. So a private member's bill was quickly drawn up and passed in the provincial legislature giving the WNEDC the power to create and promote industrial and commercial development.[40] More specifically, it gave the committee the ability to form a partnership with MacMillan Bloedel in Sturgeon Falls Repulping, a holding company that would be responsible for paying off the loans. For its part, MacMillan Bloedel agreed to lease the equipment for $19 per tonne, or about $1.4 million per year. As the *Globe and Mail* confirmed, "When all debts are settled, the two partners in the holding company will split the yearly lease income."[41] There was little risk that the loans would not be repaid, as the mill had a guaranteed customer for its entire output of corrugated medium. The so-called evergreen contract, first signed in July 1983, would be in effect for as long as MacMillan Bloedel remained co-owner (with Stone Consolidated) of MacMillan Bathurst "and for five years thereafter unless terminated earlier by mutual agreement."[42] Everything was now in place.

Naturally, most of the people we interviewed credited Wally Shisko for saving the mill. Denis Gauthier, who served as the main staff member of the WNEDC, insisted that "Wally was the one who made the whole thing happen. He was a visionary, and really was brought back out of retirement to come back to Sturgeon Falls. He had some ideas … the guy was quite knowledgeable."[43] Karen Beaudette agreed, telling us that Shisko "was very concerned about the mill. And he made it his job to try and do something." Bruce Colquhoun concurred, saying, "We owe a lot to Wally." He added: "Oh, sometimes it was haywire, but he knew what he was doing. Yeah, he did a lot for the mill. If it wasn't for him, I don't think we'd have that recycling plant. He had vision. He saw that … they were going to shut the whole thing down. But Wally convinced them to go 100 per cent recycling."

Those outside the mill usually highlighted the community's role in the effort. Alan Korell, the town's engineer, for example, said it was "essentially a community effort."[44] The "community" was likewise the central protagonist in the account of Raymond Brouillette: "They were going to close the mill. Some people, in particular from Sturgeon and Springer, got involved and they said 'No, we're not going to close the mill.' That's what they said to MacMillan Bloedel. Because they could very well see what the effect would be of closing the mill. They decided to campaign for some money, and they managed to raise $1 million. And they formed a partnership with MacMillan Bloedel and they started the recycling process. It was something that was never done in Ontario before." What Brouillette was referring to here is the community campaign to pledge $1 million to the OCC facility. Almost as an afterthought, when the financing was already in place, the Ontario government insisted that the local community contribute to the partnership. As a show of its commitment to the recycling facility, the community was now required to raise $1 million, which would be placed in interest-bearing deposits with recognized financial institutions. The interest earned from these accounts would then be used to pay the interest charges on the partnership's debt for five years, at which point people's pledged money was to be returned to them.[45] Denis Gauthier recalled that the million-dollar requirement was "kind of imposed on us at the last second … [The Ontario government said], 'You got to show community involvement, you guys better put up a trust fund with a million, we'll take the interest on that and that will help keep the cash flow as far as the nineteen dollars that we had to generate from the mill to pay off the loan,'" but Gauthier felt that was unnecessary. Although this might have been the case, the community campaign proved symbolically important to residents who came to see themselves as part-owners of the recycling facility. It also obscured the role of the province, which had put up the lion's share of the financing.

After a faltering start, J.P. Charles became the public face of the community campaign. There was much at stake.[46] Sturgeon Falls mayor Mike DeCaen, a powerful voice in favour of saving the mill, told residents: "This being a one-industry town, we have to make sure we keep our one industry going strong."[47] Then the campaign sputtered again.

By mid-January 1993 the funding thermometer had risen only to $250,000. Mill workers had committed $150,000 in payroll deductions, an amount that would grow further in the weeks to come. One organizer admitted that people were not "running after him on the street, but he does get the occasional pleasant surprise."[48] With perseverance, the fund reached the half-way mark in March thanks to a $100,000 pledge from the reserve fund of the Town of Sturgeon Falls. Elected leaders such as DeCaen continued to insist publicly that this effort was do-or-die, saying this was "our only chance for economic survival."[49] Speaking to the local Chamber of Commerce, Rod Blais invoked the memory of the Great Depression in his appeal: "I remember 1930 … when three hundred people were working at the mill, and this town was the best municipality in northern Ontario … In a very short while it was the worst … No one was working, homes worth thousands of dollars were going for hundreds, and there were men who spent years without a dollar in their pocket. I don't think we're immune to that. It's practically sure the mill would have closed in 1993. We would have faced the same circumstances as in 1930. I'm sure you, all your friends, and co-citizens, will benefit by this."[50] Others pointed to the successful effort to save the paper mill in Kapuskasing, or suggested that the OCC facility would put Sturgeon Falls "on the map" in terms of recycling.[51]

The campaign undertook a variety of events to raise money from the community. A spaghetti supper in neighbouring Cache Bay drew three hundred people, while the children at Lady of Sorrows school raised a thousand dollars over an active month-long campaign. The Scouts and various service clubs also donated, as did Nipissing First Nation chief John Beaucage, who pledged $5,000. J.P. Charles was constantly being called at work, as a barber, to pick up a cheque: "I just finished my haircut, and then asked my customer, 'I'll be gone for fifteen minutes, I'll come back.' And most of them understood, they were still waiting here." Lists of contributors began to appear in the local paper, a none-too-subtle attempt to shame others. Much of the money came in large amounts. In the final push in the campaign, for example, the local branches of the Royal Bank and the National Bank gave $80,000 and $75,000, respectively.[52] As the banks held their own capital, they had only to turn over the interest on their contributions each month. On 4 May 1993 organizers celebrated the end of the campaign. In all, 602 local people, organizations, and businesses pledged $1,123,924.23 to the campaign, which ultimately contributed $37,725.08 in interest payments to the partnership.[53]

If the community campaign elided the Ontario government's central role, it also revealed some of the underlying fault lines between the "community" and mill workers. There was a fair amount of grumbling that some mill workers had refused to donate to the campaign. Denis Gauthier expressed the frustration of some community leaders:

> The only guys that I found that had most to gain from it were the employees of the mill. And most of those guys … I mean we'd call a meeting and two guys showed up. They just didn't want to be part of it … [Y]ou know, to this day, I think they felt like closing the mill was a joke: "You're playing a bluff on us." I think most of them even seeing it torn down today feel that, the mill's still going to be active … So getting in the OCC [facility] was always a challenge, but participation of guys, that was alarming. They thought, "Hey, close the mill [shrugs shoulders]. You're not going to close it on us and we're not going to put money into it." They weren't the largest participants. That was very obvious. And the guys that did come out didn't want their names to be published, didn't want anybody to know that they were even close to the table as far as doing anything to save the mill [was concerned]. But they were the first ones to cry the blues, to go to the municipality, the government, [and say] "give us more handouts."

Interviews with workers confirmed that the community campaign proved divisive within the mill. Harold Stewart and Randy Restoule contributed funds, as did many others. "It was a continuation of our job," Restoule explained. That said, the prevailing feeling on the shop floor was that the company should be the one investing in the mill, not its hourly workforce. It did not instil confidence. Others saw it simply as corporate greed. Percy Allary noted that those workers who refused to donate to the campaign, said: "'I'm not buying my job.' So the ones that put in, I guess they felt good because they were helping to keep their job. And I guess the others were more or less saying, 'Look, there's no way I should have to. I'm not going to. I'm not putting anything in.' So who gains?" The phrase "I'm not buying my job" surfaced repeatedly in our interviews. Asked if these differing viewpoints caused friction at work, Randy Restoule replied: "Yeah, there was friction." Those who did contribute "kind of stayed away from those people," and "if there was a comment made, you just kept quiet rather than stir it up." Bruce Colquhoun insisted, however, that "It wasn't serious friction. Guys get mad when you talk about it, you know, 'I'm not giving for this reason,' or 'I'm not giving for that.' But they raised the money." Given this divide, many people simply kept their views to themselves. "It really was nobody's business," Colquhoun concluded.

Although I was unable to determine the proportion of workers who agreed to payroll deductions, the interviews made clear that many did not. André Girard, local union president at the time, recalled that the membership was "split on this." Karen Beaudette, who worked in the mill's offices and had access to reports, noted that "very few of us actually donated from our pay cheque … [People would say], 'Why bother? They're just going to take the money anyway.'" She estimated that only one in four mill workers contributed via payroll deductions. I could not confirm this, but I did uncover a report that, in the end, this method of contributing to the community campaign totalled $282,110,[54] representing nearly one-third of total pledges, a substantial financial commitment from the remaining 150 employees. It was all the more impressive considering how much of the remainder was pledged by area municipalities, banks, and businesses, rather than individuals.

Another point of contention, particularly for residents of the townships and villages outside Sturgeon Falls, related to the economic impact of going to 100 per cent recycled pulp. The shift to old cardboard sidestepped the pollution problem, but it had a devastating economic impact on area farmers, jobbers, and sixteen area sawmills that supplied sawmill waste to the paper mill. Although the paper mill was saved, Guy Ethier observed that it "still meant that they weren't using any more virgin fibre. So all the little sawmills that were in existence had no place to send their wood chips and sawdust and bark, so that had a major impact."[55] Some sawmills probably closed as a result. One estimate suggested that 125 jobs "in the bush" were at stake, and some believed that "not enough consideration has been given to [these] jobs."[56] Ultimately this led a lot of young people to leave rural areas and villages, eventually resulting in school closures and the acceleration of rural decline. The shift to old cardboard thus isolated the mill politically as its economic importance to the surrounding area continued to shrink. This would have devastating consequences in the early 2000s, as we will see in the next chapter.

Despite these points of tension and the limited financial value of the interest from the $1 million pledged, area residents and their leaders heralded the campaign as a grassroots effort that saved the mill. Once this moral claim took hold locally, it shaped how people understood this crucial moment in the mill's history. Our interviews with area political and economic leaders were unanimous. For Ken Landry, "the community came together, pulled every resource they could find … and it worked. These were the people trying to help the community."[57] Gary O'Connor, who had the misfortune of being the town's mayor during the final closure of 2002, went even further: "It was a massive effort, with a clear cause, and people understood the writing on the wall. And they were ready to make a collective effort ... To be honest, the municipality and the municipal council saved the mill."[58]

The new OCC recycled pulping facility was celebrated twice: first, at the onset of construction, and then when it went into operation. In April 1992 various dignitaries such as Shelley Martel, the Ontario minister of northern development and mines, and Bob Findlay, the president of MacMillan Bloedel, came together to celebrate the new partnership and the beginning of construction. "We think this community has given its heart and soul to put this corporation together," said Martel.[59] Findlay expressed his pleasure in the partnership, and Sturgeon Falls mayor Mike DeCaen heralded the end of the uncertainty: "It's a sigh of relief. We always asked the question, is it a go, isn't it a go? But today, that is all behind us."[60] At the operational start of the OCC facility on 4 June 1993, two hundred "neatly dressed executives and politicians as well as hard-hat workers" came together. By then, people were openly touting Sturgeon Falls as a model for one-industry towns facing the loss of their mill.[61] "It's an astounding story, how everyone pulled together," proclaimed the *Tribune*. "During the last few months many communities throughout Canada have been watching us. We're a success story!"[62] Expressing the euphoria of the moment, J.P. Charles declared that the people of West Nipissing "don't wait for good things to happen here. We make them happen."[63]

The OCC Repulping Partnership

The old corrugated cardboard pulping facility was owned by the Sturgeon Falls Limited Partnership, an agreement between MacMillan Bloedel and the WNEDC dated 17 March 1992. If the primary objective of the limited partnership, which entered into a twenty-year lease on equipment, was the continued operation of the mill, it also indicated a shared desire to develop new business opportunities and increased employment in the MacMillan Bloedel–owned mill.[64] But the most pressing concern was to pay off outstanding loans, of which, as of December 1993, the partnership owed $3,563,500, and another $500,000 in debentures.[65]

In the years that followed, the partnership set the rental fee to be charged MacMillan Bloedel. During the first three years, the rental was set at $19 per tonne of pulp delivered to the company, as agreed to in the commercial loan arrangement with the Royal Bank of Canada. Once this particular loan had been paid off – a clear priority for MacMillan Bloedel – the partnership set a lower rental rate of $2 per tonne. The minutes of these meetings make clear that the WNEDC's representatives accepted the assurances of mill management that this was a necessary but temporary reduction, given the instability in the price and supply of old cardboard. The bulk of the mill's supply came from Southern Ontario, but also from as far away as Winnipeg. Later the lower rental was justified on the basis of the mill's need to fund new capital expenditures on equipment, as MacMillan Bloedel remained unwilling to invest in Sturgeon Falls.

At the time the OCC facility was cutting-edge technology. It was so good, in fact, that MacMillan Bloedel copied its design and built a much larger repulping facility at its plant in Henderson, Kentucky. According to Wally Shisko, they "copied our design, it was so good, it was the best." The main piece of OCC equipment was a large beater: "Bales of used corrugated boxes are delivered to the beater by a conveyor belt system. The beater breaks down the cardboard into a fibre pulp, which is then screened. The clean pulp is then stored until needed.[66] Cardboard was fed into the "great big beater" and water was added, explained Harold Stewart. Inevitably there was a "lot of junk in those bales. It went through a process to be cleaned and then went to the paper machine. Same as the other [virgin wood fibre] stock. Just a different way of doing things." Cleaning proved to be the biggest challenge. Old beer cases sometimes had "a half dozen broken bottles in there. That glass had to come out." Sometimes there were even two-by-fours in the bails and the repulper had to be stopped, drained, and the "heavy stuff," which could be heard pounding in the "big tub." Stewart, shaking his head, recalled that, one time, a propane cylinder found its way in. Pulp production suffered in the early days because of this. In his interview, Marc Côté confirmed as much: "The first little while, we jammed everything up, there was paper stock on the floor a foot and a half deep. We'd have to hose it down and back into the tubs … They were having an awful lot of problems, so they took me out of the mechanic department and made me superintendent of that department until it started running. And I lived there for a month … Well, it was a task and a half."

In initially designing the OCC facility, Greg Corello travelled to other mills picking out the best equipment. Claude Lortie explained: "The engineers here, they designed it. And they figured that was supposed to be the Cadillac. Well, the Cadillac had a few failures. We ended up making it work anyway." For example, Lortie recalled an argument he had with the resident engineer, who wanted to make a certain change to fix a recurring problem, but Lortie knew it would not work. Every time they shut down the green water chest, six or seven feet of stock would be left, and it would take six men twelve or fifteen hours to clean it out properly: "So I went in there three times, and I got after the resident engineer. I said, 'Your intake is too big'" – there was too much stock coming in for the water to dilute it. "The opening was too big, so the pump wouldn't pump it … I finally convinced them, and we put a ring in there to shrink it down." Initially the engineer did not think it would work: "He said, 'Oh, how do you know that?' I said, 'I don't have a slide rule and all the shit that you guys use. I figured that out in my head.' So Wally [Shisko] … said, 'Try it.' So we tried it … After that, they had no problem." Lortie's knowledge was experiential, based on his decades working with machinery on the shop floor. Lortie, like others we interviewed, reminded me of US labour historian David Montgomery's old essay, "The Manager's Brains under the Workman's Cap."[67]

Claude Lortie had always been good with machines, figuring out the underlying reasons they were not working right. Lortie saw himself as a problem solver: "In the beginning, why is the screen always plugging up? Or, you know, is it we're feeding it too much? Or not enough water? Or you've got the wrong screen in there? You know, there's fifty different answers for it, but once you've got a lot of experience around machinery, a lot of that stuff is not too hard to figure out. You jam it two, three times, and say, 'No, no, no. That's not working. I tried this. No, that's not working. I'll try something else.' And then it's a process of elimination." The entire OCC facility could be operated with just three men, but the company tried to do with only two: an operator and a trucker to feed the line. Lortie had tried to tell his boss that two people were insufficient, but he wouldn't listen: "'Oh,' he said, 'we'll run two guys, two guys to blah, blah, blah.' 'Yeah,' I said, 'but nothing's adjusted. And you never start a mill by pushing a button and everything moves.' I said, 'You're making a mistake. Put an extra guy to start, and then take him off.' 'Oh, no.'" Six months later they added the extra person.

In recognition of his mechanical ability, Claude Lortie was named the acting superintendent of the OCC facility for three years, relieving his boss Greg Carello, who was sent to Henderson, Kentucky, to design the new OCC mill being built there based on the Sturgeon Falls specifications. The men working in the facility had to shift from the old "charts and a whole bunch of buttons" to a "fully computerized" environment with touch-screen computers. Lortie recalled that some found it hard "in the beginning to learn it, because it was day and night." What made it hard was that many of the guys placed in the OCC facility were older: "They had never worked with stuff like that before. And the training program when we started was not a very good training program. They said, 'Well, read the books and walk around and look at the machinery.' … I know I made a lot of friggin' overtime in the beginning, trying to train some of the other operators." Mechanical superintendent Marc Côté agreed with Lortie's assessment, recalling:

These guys went from manual to completely modern computerized systems. And I mean, when you're looking at a TV, you have machinery next to you working, and on the TV there's a picture of that machine and you just touch the board and the writing comes on the bottom … And you touch the motor again and another screen comes up that tells you how fast it's going. You want it to go any faster, and you just punch in the "yes, I'd like 500 more RPM." Touch go, and you'd hear the motor speed up. The guys could run the whole plant without even going out there. So it required a lot of training, and so when it started we had a one-year learning curve.

Some took to it right away, enjoying the challenge. Harold Stewart delayed his retirement for a couple years to work on the new project. The company sent Stewart and two others to inspect the OCC plants at several other mills. These visits were "really interesting" for him, "because it was something new." As for Lortie himself, he "didn't find it *too* hard." Like everyone else, he had rudimentary training: "My training? 'You open three doors. This is in there, and that's in there, and that's in there.'" At this point in the interview, I asked Lortie why he was chosen to become acting superintendent of the OCC facility. Normally, the highest-seniority person would be selected to be a relief supervisor, but there were men with more seniority than him. Nor was he the best educated: "I only got grade 10." But he could do it.

And run it he did. Typically, when someone relieved a manager, it was only for a week or two, so "you don't have to make big decisions." When Lortie started to relieve Carello, he got sixty cents more an hour. After three weeks of this, he approached Gerry Stevens and said, "'Look! At that rate, you get somebody else. I'll train them. I want back my job.' 'Why?' he said. I said, 'I got to work both day and night just to make the same money! No, no, no, I don't need that.' 'No, no, no, no,' he said. 'We'll pay you.' So the personnel manager … offered me $2.40. I said, 'No.' So I said, 'I want three bucks.' He said, 'No problem.'"

When it was finished, Lortie got to go down to see the new recycling mill built in Kentucky: "That's a real nice mill. That mill was built to last 150 years. They even had the columns in there. Real nice." It was "much bigger than ours." Its paper machine had double the capacity of the one in Sturgeon Falls. And their recycling plant was "much, much bigger than ours. They had forward cleaners, reverse cleaners. We only had forward cleaners." MacMillan Bloedel clearly benefited from the publicly funded innovations under way in Sturgeon Falls, but chose to make its capital investments in the United States.

Thanks to the generosity of our interviewees, especially Raymond Brouillette, we have access to the minutes of the regular meetings of the partnership's board as well as other operational documents. The membership of the board included the mill manager and his assistant (Shisko and Stevens), as well as representatives of the WNEDC. There was no union representation due to the shop-floor resistance to "buying" their own jobs. At these meetings, mill management regularly reported on production, notifying their partner of upcoming downtimes, plans to buy new equipment, the mill's profitability, and how much of the partnership's debt had been retired. Problems in production were a key talking point, as managers met the challenges of being at the technological forefront. We also learn about the volatile price of old cardboard. In 1995, for example, Stevens noted that the cost of old cardboard had gone from $60 per tonne to $300 per tonne, only to settle back down to $75 per tonne. Fully 82 per cent of the old cardboard was brought in from Southern Ontario, with only 8 per cent coming from the North. There were also reports on the expansion of recycling in the area and other aspects of the mill's relationship with the local community.[68] J.P. Charles, for his part, provided annual updates on how much interest had been directed that year to the partnership from the community investment fund. The minutes make clear that there was a lot of energy and optimism in the room, as well as a clear commitment to making the partnership work.

Despite the challenges, the various loans were being paid down aggressively, and soon community representatives began to turn their minds to what should happen next. In November 1996 a community representative was quoted as saying, "After all loans have been paid off, the WNEDC will benefit of a 50 per cent profit that will be shared within the West Nipissing Area to improve economic growth." Nobody in attendance objected, not even the vice-president of MacMillan Bloedel, Jim Emerson, who was visiting from his base in Alabama. The issue of profit sharing emerged as a point of sustained discussion, as the WNEDC wanted to use its share to fund its own operations.[69] A special meeting was held on 17 December 1996 to consider a motion to start distributing profit of $1 per tonne to each partner (estimated at $89,400 each), which was accepted.[70] Then, in December 1997, the partnership organized an appreciation ceremony at the local hospital to thank publicly all those who had contributed to the community investment fund, as they were getting their pledged contributions back.

As Denis Gauthier observed, the OCC partnership had five good years. Once the debt was retired and community investors got their money back, there seemed to be some confusion about whether or not the partnership remained in place. Gauthier explained:

[The] only discussion we'd have once a year was transferring and paying off and taking action on certain loans and managing the two or three million dollars that was given to us yearly with the $19 a ton. In the fifth year, that's when there was a shift in managers, and Wally retired and Shisko went away and this new guy came in. So it took a while to adjust … Also, very few people understood all the clauses and how serious the OCC was as far as a partnership [was concerned] and what it really meant. And the issue was the initial intent beyond repaying the loans, in principle, when they were negotiating all this, the ownership of that, that the OCC machine would be a source of income for incoming development during and afterwards. But in those last final drafts, those exact words, "beyond the repayment of the loans" got omitted. So it was basically the manager of the day and the committees that knew and understood that, "Hey, the principle of all this is that we're going to have money beyond to reinvest and to use as economic development." So the sunset clause got kind of diluted."

Gauthier recalled fighting "until my last day there" to convince the new manager, Scott Mosher, who took over in July 1996 with Shisko's retirement, that the partnership would continue beyond the repayment of the loans and that there would be a measure of profit sharing with the WNEDC.

Greening the Mill

The rise of environmental awareness brought with it political confrontation over industrial pollution and logging practices. Canada's forestry industry bore the brunt of these public campaigns against clear-cutting and dioxin and other pollutants. In Northern Ontario the late 1980s saw a standoff on Red Squirrel Road near Temagami, less than an hour's drive north of Sturgeon Falls, between environmentalists and Indigenous people protesting the logging of their traditional lands, and loggers themselves. It was a politically explosive brew. The mill was implicated in the conflict, as wood in the area was being machine chipped and trucked to Sturgeon Falls.[71] The town's mayor was also vocal in his opposition to new restrictions on forestry in the disputed area. On the other hand, it has been suggested that these new "green" sensibilities also "anesthetized the middle-class to industrial decline."[72] Once stained by their association with environmental pollution and degradation – or mill colonialism, in the Canadian context – smokestack industries became unsightly, and their elimination could be construed by the socially distant to be a public good.

Given this shifting political and cultural context in the 1990s, it was only natural that MacMillan Bloedel and the local community were eager to wrap themselves in an environmental cloak. After all, the new OCC facility made Sturgeon Falls the biggest producer of 100 per cent recycled paper in the country. The limited partnership promoted Sturgeon Falls as a national leader in recycling and, for good measure, a large cardboard recycling bin was placed in a prominent location at the plant's front gate. The public's embrace of cardboard recycling was such that the bin soon had to be emptied daily, prompting the company to issue a press release thanking residents for their support.[73]

There was evident interest in recycling on the shop floor as well, with a number of mill workers asking management to provide recycling boxes in the workplace. Copies of the mill's newsletter, the *Insider*, saved from the shredder by Hubert Gervais and an unnamed staff member in 2002, provide a unique window through which to peer inside the mill. During this period it published anonymous "suggestions" submitted by employees. In May 1995, for example, someone asked: "Is everyone serious about recycling in the mill? So much recyclable ends up in the garbage cans, that one would think that nobody cares about recycling paper and boxes. Every day you look in the garbage cans and you see lots of recyclable paper. More information is needed in every department to clarify what is good for recycling."[74] Another employee asked why the mill was hauling loose cardboard to the city dump, adding, "This makes no sense at all and makes us look like idiots."[75] Mill management reviewed the feasibility of shop-floor recycling, agreeing that "we should promote recycling of material in the mill. In addition to paper, we will locate bins around the mill for cans only … The town has also agreed to come to the mill to pick up the cans."[76] A steady stream of suggestions of this nature was submitted. One person noted that his ten-year-old daughter's grade 5 class was learning about recycling, and her teacher "wants to know what has to be done in order to get her class to come for a tour through our facility. All the kids are anxious to see how recycling works."[77] In reply, the editors of the *Insider* noted that tours were arranged with security.

Indeed, interest in the new OCC plant, and in recycling more generally, was such that the mill found itself giving tours once or twice per week. Most of the tour groups were school children from the area, but also from towns two or three hours' distant. This was something new. Generally the tours were organized to let visitors follow the paper trail, starting with the storage warehouse, where bales of old cardboard arrived, then to the ultra-modern OCC repulping facility, and finally to the paper machine and skiving line, where paper rolls were glued together for greater width. Visitors had to wear hard hats and safety glasses, and no heels or sandals were not allowed. A handout was also developed, and recent retirees such as Ben Lajeunesse were conscripted to guide them. Lajeunesse recalled: "There was two spots on the tour where we stopped. One was a lunch room in the OCC where it was quiet and we could talk for a few minutes before we went into the computer room to see the computers that ran the OCC plant." The mill was too noisy for guides to be heard elsewhere.

The greening of the mill extended to the town itself, as the municipality quickly instituted a recycling system. Denis Gauthier believed this would help the community to be "seen as a recycling community in Ontario."[78] The town's recycling program was inaugurated in October 1995 with the arrival of the first twelve "blue bins" located strategically around town.[79] Soon thereafter the WNEDC sponsored a full-day recycling workshop with discussions and exercises to identify local waste-management problems and opportunities.[80] A great deal of public educational activities were also under way. The pamphlet, "The Inside Story of Recycling at Sturgeon Falls," designed by Wayne LeBelle, provided a brief history of the mill and touted the "unique partnership" with the community.[81] In April 1996 the mill began to receive paper and OCC from the town's new recycling facility, and area recycling was extended to the nearby municipality of Verner.[82]

In the years that followed there was a remarkable period of renewal, community engagement, and heightened pride within the plant itself. One might even call it a shop-floor renaissance. The *Insider*, which began during this period as a daily newsletter before being rolled back to three times a week and then twice weekly, showcased production statistics, tracked lost time and the mill's safety record, and provided a platform to share stories of the mill's history. In May 1995, for example, Hubert Gervais offered readers an article entitled "Our Mill – Way Back Then."[83] No doubt the mill history binder (discussed in Chapter 11) grew out of these beginnings. Karen Beaudette, who worked on the newsletter team, fondly recalled that "the guys, if they didn't get it by a certain time, they were panicking: 'Where's the paper?' So I thought it was pretty good. Every department got [it]." Beaudette noted that the *Insider* was a "newsy little thing," but "we always had a safety article, the production stats, and then, like any club, things going on. Yeah, it was interesting."

The transformation of the mill's relationship with the wider community was also evidenced by the inauguration of a special mill section of the weekly newspaper, the *Tribune*, in March 1993. In this way, the newspaper declared, MacMillan Bloedel "can keep everyone in the area communities abreast of what is happening at the mill."[84] A column called "MB Corner" was filled with updates on the community campaign as well as notices of retirement, forty-year-service-pin ceremonies, the annual curling bonspiel, and even employees' first-aid training. "MB Corner" reminded me a great deal of the old mill reports in the *Abitibi News* of the 1940s and 1950s. There were also front-page stories highlighting the cost of old cardboard materials, the mill's improving "bottom line," and when it was declared the safest mill in Canada.[85] Readers also learned that the company and union were meeting to develop a common vision for the division.

During this period, mill managers sought to increase its community presence, entering a float in the Sturgeon Falls centennial parade in 1995 and reviving the old practice of sounding the mill's whistle for shift changes three times daily. It continued to do so even after the centennial festivities were over. According to the *Insider*, "there appears to be many that have an interest in us continuing to do so," as there was an "element of tradition associated with blowing the whistle."[86] The community campaign mobilized residents to an impressive degree, giving the mill community new visibility and renewed confidence.

The mill was clearly in the public spotlight. As a result, many of the suggestions published in the *Insider* sought to spruce up the mill's public face. One worker thought it would be nice to see some flowers in the flower beds in front of the mill's main office building. Another asked, "Why don't we display in the front office some products that use our 'Corrugated Medium'?"[87] A few weeks later, someone else built on this idea, suggesting that a "small display case can be fit into the lobby area."[88] Hubert Gervais, another interviewee, later asked that some framed pictures of "Area Scenes" be mounted. Still another asked to have a sign erected on the Trans-Canada Highway, which passed behind the mill, that proudly declared "We produce through 100% recycled wastepaper."[89] Others simply wanted the company to "improve the overall appearance of our Mill." They noted the bent railing in front of the mill's main office, which also needed a new coat of paint, rotten guard rails, and so on. As one person wrote, "Town people, visitors, and especially employees should have pride in their Mill. First impressions are lasting impressions."[90] Something had clearly changed.

Mill workers writing to the *Insider* also expressed support of local management's efforts to "close the gap between employer and employee. It was long coming."[91] Many shared their ideas about how this might be achieved. One suggested a free pizza day, where workers would be asked to eat lunch in a different department than their own, "communicating with people they don't normally talk to. This way a transfer of knowledge, ideas, and problems could be casually exchanged and possibly lead to solutions. Staff people that are going to be here for that day would have their names drawn at random for each department."[92] The same person also suggested that informal relationship building was needed between "floor employees" and "office employees," which "might be a catalyst for real change!" Other suggestions included a golf tournament, fishing derby, and a family barbecue with a dunk tank where "Wally, Gerry, etc." could be dunked for three balls for a buck. "Whatever you decide to do, remember that actions speak louder than words and time spent enjoying one another goes a long way to mutual understanding."[93]

Of course, there were more critical voices. Someone, for example, asked why they all had to "go in and out [of] the mill by the punch-clock entrance? We are not little children, don't treat us that way. As long as we pass in front of the guard house as we go in and out of the mill, what is the problem?"[94] Another testy exchange involved the mill's blowing the whistle to mark shift changes, complaining that he worked 12 p.m. to 8 a.m. "and [went] to bed after the kids have gone to school, only to have the mill whistle wake you up at noon. Who is behind this stupid pet project? I don't think it's anyone who has to work nights. What about noise pollution?"[95] Other suggestions were more pragmatic, ranging from filling potholes in the parking lot to inviting all retirees to an annual reunion.[96] These submissions flagged the inevitable disconnect between soaring rhetoric and shop-floor realities.

Among the materials André Girard shared with me were documents related to the mill's "Vision Committee" from 1993 to 1994. In a memorandum to employees dated 3 December 1993, Wally Shisko noted: "As you know, we have just come through a difficult but necessary transition related to our fibre supply. This will help to establish our long-term future."[97] But, he added, everybody still needed to work together to make the mill more competitive. Sixteen people, representing union and management, met for three days. An office memorandum to all employees dated 30 May 1994, from Reg Hawkins, the mill's financial manager, indicated that one focus of the process was to generate ideas to further improve the mill's efficiency.[98] In December 1994, Shisko met with all employees to outline the results: "We needed to develop a sense of direction within a process, so that all employees have a fundamental knowledge of where and what we want to be."[99] The consensus of opinion was that the OCC facility resolved one problem, but the mill needed a new paper machine to be viable over the medium or long term.[100] It was a very narrow machine, according to Marc Côté, "so that was another reason why the mill went down. If we would have been a little bit wider it would have survived."

The price of OCC was also higher than expected, reducing the expected price differential between it and virgin wood. When Sturgeon Falls moved into cardboard recycling, it was a relatively new thing. A few years later it became big business, and the mill had to compete for old cardboard with other producers not only in Canada, but as far away as China. "They would come here and import all they could buy," recalled Ron Beauchamp. They therefore wanted to reintroduce virgin wood pulp into the mix, as the old pulping facilities were just sitting there. There was also mounting evidence that a mix was necessary in order to retain the strength of the cardboard material.[101] Claude Lortie still believed that the blend of recycled and virgin fibre would have made "one of the best corrugated sheets in the world." Every time wood fibre is recycled, it gets shorter and shorter, and 100 per cent

Roll of corrugated medium. Photograph courtesy of André Cartier.

recycled boxes "feel kind of mushy," whereas boxes made with virgin fibre are "rigid and stiff." The plan, therefore, was to get a larger paper machine and renovate the old pulp mill, starting it up again.

In October 1995 local management submitted a formal proposal to senior company officials for future expansion of the mill. It would be a two-phase program, as "the required capital may not be available in one shot."[102] First, the old pulping facility and wood yard would be reactivated, with "some minor improvements" to the old pulping machinery as well as the mill's water treatment plant. The second phase would consist of "installing a new paper machine and boiler," which would represent a sizable new investment. Once again, however, MacMillan Bloedel declined to invest in the mill. In December 1995, Wally Shisko informed employees that "it has been decided not to proceed with the new [paper] machine at Sturgeon Falls at this time."[103] Instead the company made only small improvements to keep the plant operating.[104] None of these modest investments tackled the underlying problem.

"What happens to us now?" asked one worker. Local management acknowledged the "shortage of capital funds" and the "downturn in the demand of our product," but asked employees not to "lose sight of the new machine for some future date." With this, and Wally Shisko's retirement in July 1996, we see a return to anxiety about the future of the mill. Claude Lortie said the final closure of the mill was "just a matter of time" after Shisko tried, and failed, to get a new paper machine. Not surprisingly, our interviewees considered Shisko one of the "best managers" the mill ever had. But, as Lortie lamented, "he got here too late" to make a difference over the long term. In the end, the OCC plant bought the mill only a decade.

Conclusion

For a time, Sturgeon Falls stood as a success story. This small mill, on the brink of closing, was saved by a unique partnership between local management and the community. Unfortunately the collaborative atmosphere evident in Sturgeon Falls during these years could not resolve the underlying issues of technological obsolescence and corporate unwillingness to invest. Capitalism is spatially uneven, as we see how the modernization of one mill and deindustrialization of another were interrelated. The irony of the name of the mill's newsletter, the *Insider*, is that nobody locally was truly an insider where it counted. As Wally Shisko once said, "This mill is meaningless in the corporate structure. We have been told directly that we are not a core business. Whether we exist or not is of no concern."[105] The company's decision not to invest in a new paper machine came as a crushing blow.

With a new boss, Scott Mosher, a young and energetic manager originally from Northwestern Ontario, the focus shifted towards the development of a new product line in the mill.[106] The plan now was, once again, to refurbish the paper machine, rather than replace it. Ron Beauchamp, a councillor in Springer Township who sat on the board of the OCC partnership during this period, was impressed by Mosher: "He really wanted to do something for the mill."[107] Mosher's hopes for the mill lay in the "Sturgeon 2000" planning process, partly funded by a new grant from the Northern Ontario Heritage Fund.[108] It included another round of brainstorming meetings and five active subcommittees to pursue strategies. A consultant was also hired, who noted that the mill's chief strengths were its local wood supply, community support, motivated team, experienced labour pool, and the OCC limited partnership. The points of weakness, however, were significant: an old and narrow paper machine and rising prices for OCC.[109] The proposed new product line, high-quality cardboard used in cereal boxes and fast-food containers, would have enabled the mill once again to tap area hardwood and create jobs in rural areas.

Unfortunately Scott Mosher did not have a chance. By 1997 the situation was grim. Mosher noted that the mill was a small, high-cost producer and its labour, salary, and administrative costs were 128 per cent higher than those of the company's Pine Hill, Alabama, mill.[110] MacMillan Bloedel was losing money, and there was talk of plant closures and job losses. The company's new CEO, Tom Stephens, previously president of Manville Corporation in Denver, was brought in to restructure the company to enhance its value for shareholders. According to Stephens, "Our first order of business is to aggressively cut costs throughout the system, to focus on our key businesses."[111] On 28 January 1998 Stephens announced the layoff of 2,700 of the company's 13,000 employees. That day, there was a conference call with all the newsletter editors from the company's North American mills. After Stephens spoke, the editors were invited to ask questions. The first questioner asked if people could "relax a little bit" after the ninety-day assessment period was finally over, as, "we've got people on the edge of their seats wondering what's coming." Stephens responded with a succinct "No." To this the questioner haltingly said, "No. Okay, I'll let them know." Stephens then elaborated: "In today's world, if you relax you're dead. We live in a fast-changing world, so relaxing is not the word that I would use. You can have confidence that we have gone through the cuts that we need to make … The bad guys are not on the twenty-third floor in Vancouver, the bad guys are the other mills around the world that want to take our customers away from us. We're the high-cost producer in the world and we're the target they go after first.[112] It was a far cry from Abitibi's hesitant approach to the relatively minor closure of the platewood mill in 1969. These were different times. During a radio talk show later that day, Stephens insisted: "The only jobs that are secure are those that are won in the marketplace through productivity, quality, and … there is no free lunch."[113]

It was at this critical juncture that Tom Stephens threw the dice, gambling away the Sturgeon Falls mill's future. The five-year evergreen contract with MacMillan Bathurst amounted to a guaranteed market for all of the mill's corrugated paper. Once Stephens triggered the compulsory buy-sell option on 24 July 1998 with partner Stone Consolidated in order to purchase outright MacMillan Bathurst's twelve corrugated container plants in Canada, it would go one of two ways: either Stone Container would sell all its shares to MacMillan Bloedel or MacMillan Bloedel would be forced to do the same.[114] If MacMillan Bloedel succeeded, it "would make investment in Sturgeon Falls more likely. This would probably mean a greater need for corrugated medium and liner. This could mean a growth opportunity for us."[115] If not, Sturgeon Falls would lose its only customer on 3 September 2003. Unfortunately, this is precisely what happened. Stone Consolidated purchased the remaining interest for $185 million, opting not to buy the Sturgeon Falls mill with it.[116] Stephens had "pulled the trigger," and Sturgeon Falls paid the ultimate price.[117] Soon thereafter came news that MacMillan Bloedel had been purchased by Weyerhaeuser, a US-based company with 35,000 employees.[118] Tom Stephens left with the merger; he had been with MacMillan Bloedel for only one and a half years.

9

BETRAYAL

It was pretty hard. My wife, I told her the day before "they're going to close the mill, and I'm sure that's what's going on." I told her that day, but, you know, it's hard for you to know where to put that. It actually took her about two days to really realize that they are going to do this. It's really happening [pause]. More or less everybody was walking in circles. Even at work, people were walking in circles. That was very dangerous, at the mill. For safety. People weren't paying attention – too much on their mind. "What am I going to do? Where am I going to go? What am I going to do now?"

– Raymond Marcoux

At ten o'clock in the morning of 8 October 2002, Weyerhaeuser announced the mill's closure at a meeting of employees held at the Cache Bay Community Centre. It "had to go out of town to do that," one person recalled bitterly.[1] Management had handed out fliers to employees the day before: everybody had to be there. Because the company was shutting down production for the day, which was unprecedented, they all knew it was going to be something big. Could it be a major new customer to replace the evergreen contract that was coming to an end in September 2003? Might it be a major new investment? Was the mill being sold off? Or was it trouble? Most thought it was going to be trouble. André Cartier came to this conclusion the night before, "when they had all the gates locked … no trucks could come in, no trucks could leave. One of my buddies lives around the mill, and I went to pick him up [to] go for coffee. We came back and one of the truckers is about my age and I knew him personally … I spoke with him, and he says, 'Since 6 o'clock, everything is out, they've got security personnel installed in there just in case something happens.' And I said, 'They're closing the mill.' It has to be, it has to be something like that.'"

Employees who were off work the day before the big meeting got a phone call. Pierre Hardy was reached at home during the day, as he was machine tender on the night shift and in charge of the paper machine: "'Pete,' he says, 'at three o'clock this morning … I want you to shut the machine down.' I says, 'What? We never shut the machine down.' He says, 'Yeah.' He says, 'There's a big meeting in Cache Bay, there at the Hall, and the machines [have] got to go down.' He said, 'I'll be in around 3:30.' I said, 'okay.'" At this, Jane Hardy piped in, saying "everyone was expected to attend," even office staff. "Yeah," Pierre continued, "you know, we started to wonder what the hell was going on." It wasn't a regular monthly maintenance shutdown. "So, anyways," Pierre sighed, "I did what he told me. And, I mean, there's a lot of rumours going around: 'Why the hell are they doing this?' And, 'locking that?' So I did what he told me. And that was it. Then we went to Cache Bay, and he told us they were shutting the place down in eight weeks." Even the union did not know about it, Pierre insisted. "Nobody knew." The mill was slated to close on 6 December 2002.

The timing of the announcement came right in the middle of hunting season, a period when many mill workers took some of their holiday time to go into the bush. One interviewee, who had retired from the mill a few years before, recalled that he heard about the mill's closing while moose hunting with someone who still worked there. His friend received a call on his cell phone to come back to town for the Cache Bay meeting. Others told a similar story of a hunt cut short. For her part, Karen Beaudette was home sick with the 'flu when she got the call. "Is this the big one?" she asked, to which her supervisor replied, "I can't really discuss it right now." Her husband, Jean-Guy, was out moose hunting at the time. She, too, thought the timing of the announcement was disrespectful: "And that's another thing – to do it during moose hunting? That was awful, awful. They ruined a lot of guys' hunt that year." Earlier she had seen signs that something bad was coming: "I think [that] working in the office … you get more of an idea of what's going on. There have been lots of people busy and closed-door meetings. And you're going, 'Ah, yeah, something's happening.' And everybody's speculating."

Everyone spoke of the Cache Bay meeting in vivid detail. The atmosphere in the room was sombre, with a palpable sense of dread as people streamed in and waited for the meeting to start. As soon as Percy Allary came through the door, he noticed two or three tables to his right with envelopes neatly lined up on them. "Something's happening," he told himself when he noticed that an employee's name was written on each envelope. Once everyone was there, they got the bad news right away. Weyerhaeuser staff from out of town sat at the head table, Allary told us: "And everybody was sitting there, and this guy came right to the point, the head guy, he says, 'you're here. And I'm to notify you that your plant is closed.'"

Many also commented on the visible presence of out-of-town security in the hall. "They were expecting a riot or something," André Cartier protested. "A lot of people found that ridiculous." "They had some goons in the audience," recalled another person.[2] One of the most detailed observations of their presence came from Percy Allary:

> I remember along the back wall they had all these guys that were there. I said, "What the hell?" We didn't know them. Now, I figured out, it was security. They had brought these guys in for security. I guess they figured we were going to go on a rampage or something. And they were there to protect the management. I think the majority of the guys were just stunned. And they were walking out of there and their heads were spinning. Before you went out, you went to a table, by the alphabet and there's your package. It had everything right up to date. Figured right up to when you were going to leave eight weeks from now. It was all figured out. So they didn't just do this all of a sudden. It was prepared for quite a few months, and then they set a date, said, "Okay, we're going now."

People were stunned and a few got "angry, like really angry," remembered Karen Beaudette. Mill manager Naraine Shivgulam, who closed the plant but had also worked there for the past twenty-five years, took "a lot of abuse at the meeting." Having to be the one to close the mill "broke his heart," Beaudette said. She remembered how Shivgulam told those gathered: "'Okay, if you want to yell at anybody, just yell at me,' and tried to answer. He was a very intelligent man." Shivgulam did his best under trying circumstances, as the company was using him as a local buffer. Also present were company officials from out of town, whose "specialty was mill closings." They were there to discuss pensions, Beaudette said, "which was great, [but] people don't want to discuss that stuff that day. They want to go and yell and scream. They don't want to go and sit and discuss." From all accounts, people were too stunned to ask questions. Their future was going up in flames. In his interview, Denis MacGregor explained that, after thirty years of service, "everything sort of falls apart. And then, you're like, I'm lost." For all these reasons, then, the Cache Bay meeting was a difficult one. Ron Demers felt "the confusion, the fear and the worry of my fellow workers."[3]

This chapter explores how workers, their union, and the local community responded to the closure announcement. The provincial and federal governments are almost wholly absent, as their responses were minimal to nonexistent. As we

Workers gather to mark the last bale of OCC, 30 November 2002. Photograph by Bruce Colquhoun.

will see, these were different times. Wally Shisko had retired, and his dynamic young replacement, Scott Mosher, had been transferred to another mill. Naraine Shivgulam was very much a caretaker manager, there for one purpose: to close the mill. Weyerhaueser's 1999 purchase of MacMillan Bloedel meant that company headquarters were now in Federal Way, Washington. Generally, US forestry companies were more ideologically hardline than Canadian ones.[4] The new company was not even open to selling the mill as a going concern, as it was trying to reduce production levels to stabilize or drive up prices. As well, the Ontario Progressive Conservative government – in power since the failed NDP government had been brusquely voted out of office in 1995, thus delegitimating state intervention in the economy – was committed to reducing government expenditures and taxes.

Locally, too, there were sweeping changes. The hard memories of the Great Depression were fast fading, as was the knowledge acquired in saving the mill in the early 1990s. With municipal amalgamation in 1999, a new generation of local leaders had taken office. The main players from the community campaign to save the mill were now on the sidelines. "You have to keep in mind," said Raymond Lortie, "[that these were] different folks than what you have now. The mayor wasn't the same. [And] so on and so forth." As employment levels at the mill itself were only a fraction of what they had been, the facility no longer occupied the same place in the local economy, politics, or imagination. In fact it was no longer a stretch to imagine Sturgeon Falls, now part of a wider municipality called West Nipissing, as something other than a mill town. For all these reasons, then, the political response to the mill closure was muted.

The Closure

Workers exited the Cache Bay Community Centre clutching their envelopes detailing their severance pay and pensions. André Cartier remarked that "everything was done, calculated to the tip." Weyerhaeuser gave production workers one week's severance per year of service, as set out in the collective agreement. "They went by the contract," sighed Pierre Hardy. Not one penny more. Salaried personnel, however, got considerably more: four weeks' pay per year of service. This was a huge difference for workers facing so much uncertainty. I asked Pierre and Jane Hardy if the severance packages were fair. Both quickly said no. It was noted that management "got a lot more than we did," and Jane explained that other Weyerhaeuser divisions had received better severance packages, "like three times the severance that these guys got." Weyerhaeuser also strictly interpreted the years counted. If "you were four months short of a year," declared Percy Allary, "it was four months short of a year. They didn't throw in and say we'll pay it up for the year or something. They paid you exactly what you had." Workers such as André Cartier thought it would have been easy for a company as big as Weyerhaeuser to offer everyone three or four weeks' severance pay per year of service. They felt short changed and disrespected.

Nor did the company offer to bridge workers ages fifty to fifty-five to early retirement, as the Canadian National Railway had done for my own father at age fifty-one. The average age of mill workers at the time of closing was forty-seven, with twenty years of service.[5] Local union officials later opined that this refusal put forty men who were potentially eligible for bridging into the unenviable task of making do until they were eligible to retire. Under the contract, mill workers were eligible for a full pension at age fifty-eight and a reduced pension at age fifty-five. Up to ten workers were in this three-year zone. The company could have softened the blow by enabling them to go on a full pension immediately, but Weyerhaeuser refused, following the contract to the letter. Not a penny more. "That hurt," said one worker.

But this was not just about the economic hit. Displaced workers also recalled the difficulty they had going home that October morning to tell their families the crushing news. Ron Demers said it wasn't easy to go home to his children and tell them that "daddy lost his job."[6] I asked Pierre and Jane Hardy how they felt after the meeting:

PETE: Well.

JANE: You're in shock.

PETE, WELL, IN SHOCK, CAME HOME.

JANE: You know, you've been working there for twenty-seven years and "oh, well," within two months, "gee whiz," you aren't going to be working anymore, period.

With her husband out hunting, Karen Beaudette came home and painted the porch. "I remember, for the next few days you'd go into work ... and everybody just wanted to sit and talk about it. What's the point of talking about it? It's just, you know ... [trailing off]."

Many found it difficult to return to work the next day or the days that followed. Denis MacGregor saw this two-month period as the company's making them "pay for our own severance." Percy Allary understood this period in similar terms, saying Weyerhaeuser "worked us for another ... eight weeks before they closed the mill." Allary used this evocative phrase – "worked us" – repeatedly at this point in the interview, which spoke to the changed relationship with his employer. Here we gain a very different picture of "advance notice" than the one current in labour studies. Compulsory advance notification of mass layoffs was a major victory for Ontario's labour movement, as companies were prone to lock workers out of their jobs at the time of the closure announcement. This was viewed as an unnecessarily violent act that failed to give workers time to adjust, both emotionally and in terms of finding new work or lining up retraining. Since 1970 Ontario has required that companies either give advance notice or pay in lieu of that notice.[7] In the moment, many Sturgeon Falls workers wished they had received the money instead.

To ensure that mill workers continued to work efficiently and safely, Weyerhaeuser offered each employee a $5,000 bonus. Shaking his head, Raymond Marcoux told us that the company "seemed to be afraid of sabotage." The idea was ludicrous to him – it was something "we do not do. Maybe in the States, but it doesn't happen in a small town like that. Sabotage like what? What damage could we do to the mill or machinery or do something that threatened to lose production?" Nonetheless whenever something broke down during those two months, the superintendent would immediately get in their face: "'What happened there? How come that broke? What happened?'" Well, things break, Marcoux shrugged, "but now [when] it breaks, it was 'sabotage.'" If anything the inclusion of safety to receive the bonus was even more controversial. Had more than three people got hurt during that time, Mike Lacroix told us, "the money was gone." Predictably this led workers not to report minor injuries. Lacroix knew several people who got hurt during this period and did not report it. When one man hurt his shoulder, Lacroix told him to report it, but he was told: "'Oh, no, the guys, they told me they're gonna be upset at me if I do, they're gonna lose half the [bonus].'" The $5,000 bonus was also a way for the company to prevent workers from responding politically to the closure while the mill was still in operation, when they had some leverage. There would be no worker occupation of the Sturgeon Falls mill, as there had been in Canada during a previous wave of closings in the 1980s. To do so would be to forfeit their bonuses. Nobody could afford that.

The prolonged misery of those eight weeks was apparent in the interviews. "Guys were like zombies for two months," one person said.[8] A union official expressed surprise that there were no "big accidents" during this period, given the stressful situation.[9] The atmosphere was not the same. "And some guys didn't care what the bosses thought anymore," Bruce Colquhoun recalled. "They told them off. And the bosses took it. They knew the guys didn't mean it. It was just all the tension." André Cartier told us that it was a "*way* different environment to go in to work – like, totally, totally, totally, totally different. It was, like, people didn't care as much if we wasted paper. 'So what [shrugs] if we have to slow down?' It was [a] totally different environment." Workers counted down the weeks until the mill closed.

The mill closed on 5 December 2002, a day earlier than planned, probably to avoid planned protests or out of fear of an impromptu plant occupation. "We were kicked out after lunch," said Dean Pigeau. "Guys began filing out after they were told to leave."[10] Memories of the final shift were sometimes painful, sometimes wistful. Percy Allary recalled that everybody brought in something for a "big feast." People brought in moose and deer meat from their freezers, fish, and much more. After lunch, Allary recalled, some "guys were still walking around, still couldn't accept that the place was being closed. You know, they were kind of in a daze there. It was quiet." He did a final walk through himself to get one last look at the place. When he got back to his department, his manager told him that he could go home. They were supposed to work until three o'clock, but they were released at twelve-thirty. "Everybody grabbed their stuff and walked out," he remembered. "That was it." The noon-hour whistle sounded for the last time as the paper machine fell silent. "Our lives and our children's lives have been ripped away," declared Mike Lacroix.[11] Dean Pigeau was interviewed by the *Nugget* as he left work for the last time. He said it was particularly hard "for the guys who had been here for 30 years. They had tears in their eyes taking the machine down. They've seen a lot of paper come off those machines."[12]

The last roll, on the winder. Photograph by Bruce Colquhoun.

Marcel Boudreau's final twelve-hour shift had occurred a week earlier, as he had had some vacation time coming. It was a "good shift." When his relief arrived, he went down, took his shower, and emptied his three lockers. "I walked out of the mill at 7:30. I got to the end of the driveway, at the end of the mill property. I turned around and took a look. Steam was coming out of the stacks as it always did. Turned around and that was it. I haven't been back in the mill ever since." He was glad he did not have to be inside the mill on its final day: "I went to see what it looked like with the stack. And that was on a Thursday. And Sunday afternoon the stacks went down. The steam stopped coming out of the stacks. And there hasn't been any steam coming out of the stacks ever since. And I know guys that worked when that last roll of paper came out, and they had tears in their eyes. Guys I was hired with. They had tears in their eyes. Very, very emotional for them. And I know, myself, I was glad I wasn't there either. Because I don't know what I would have done."

For his part, Pierre Hardy dreaded being the one to shut the paper machine down: "There was no way I was going to do it. Get some other guys to do it … I am not going to shut the machine down. Get someone else to do your dirty work." But as luck would have it, Hardy's final shift, like Boudreau's, was not the mill's last. It became somebody else's task to shut down the paper machine, "thank God." Even so, he did go back to see the last roll come off the machine and take some pictures. Hardy cut off a sheet of the paper, and wrote "last shift" on it. And he wrote a note on his old locker. Laughing, he told me that he wrote: "'I'll be back,' just like Arnold [Schwarzenegger]."

Photographs taken by mill workers in these final days, reproduced here, show men gathered around the last bale of OCC to be repulped and the last roll of paper produced by the century-old mill. We also see their signatures on the last roll, and the roll being moved away. Two of these photographs were taken by Bruce Colquhoun, who told us what it was like being there:

> We all stood around it, we wrapped it, we stamped it, and all that. I brought my digital camera in. And the guys got all in front of the roll [and] I took a picture of them. And I got a picture of them signing the roll. Right up to that moment it was very hard. Guys would be crying sometimes. You know, they can't believe it. What are they going to do? Forty or forty-five years old? Who's going to hire them? All they did was make paper … No, it was the toughest thing. I never want to do that again. That's why I'll never go in another factory. I don't care what they put up in Sturgeon, if they put anything, I'm not going in another factory and have that done to me again.

Colquhoun considered this to be the longest day of his life: "As much as I wanted out of there, I didn't want out of there that way. I wanted out on my terms. I wanted to retire. To have that happen, I was nervous. I thought I was going to crack up there, saying goodbye to the guys. Yeah, very hard. Some guys still haven't gotten over it. It's something else. You got to live through it to understand it." There was "a lot of anger from October the eighth to December the sixth. A lot of anger … Like I say, I never want to do that again. I got a job where that won't happen. I'll leave on my terms."

Working in the office, Karen Beaudette's last day came almost six weeks later, on 16 January 2003. She therefore saw first hand the closing of one department after another: "As they closed certain departments, they would have coffee and dough-nuts. You know, get together and have coffee and doughnuts, and everybody's try-ing so hard to be like 'oh, well, have a stiff upper lip' and stuff, but it was pretty grue-some. And that's kind of like torture." Then it was the turn of the office workers to

The last shift, paper machine room, December 2002. Photograph by Bruce Colquhoun.

close up. "And they brought coffee and doughnuts for us," she laughed. "And it was sad." During that final week, they had to "clean out all the file cabinets, all the desks, shred stuff. Well, not shred it, but set it aside to get it sorted out. And there was this woman that came from Weyerhaeuser [who] was not a nice person, she was a … a bitch. And she came in and, 'Oh, do this, do this,' and we're sluggin' our guts out there and we're black when we go home at night and it was degrading. She was not nice, and her job, sure, was not pleasant. But she didn't have to be nasty about it." On the last day Beaudette decided that "I'm not working. I'm coming in, and I'm going to have my coffee and doughnuts and I'm leaving." Laughing, she added: "I'm not doing anything else. And that last day the woman was like, 'Oh, you should do this, should do this … '" Still laughing, Beaudette told her, either aloud or perhaps to herself, "Not doin' it! Sorry, see ya!"

It was a gut-wrenching experience for everyone we spoke to. There was considerable anger directed at the company, but also surprising compassion for plant manager Naraine Shivgulam. Many felt he had been put in an untenable position by the departing company. Karen Beaudette spoke for many when she said, "I think he was wonderful. I think he tried to talk to everybody personally. I think he got really hurt by all this. He was in the middle. He had to perform a job function, and a lot of guys are probably resenting him because he's doing it. He's just doing his job. I mean, sucks to be him. Yeah, I felt bad for him." Mike Lacroix said much the same thing. It was too bad that Shivgulam was "there when it shut down. Because Naraine is an awesome guy. He was one of the best people that I've ever known. You know, he's from South America, Guyana. He worked his way through university, and he worked hard to get what he got. And it's too bad that he ended up where he ended because he's too good a man to put up with that mess. He was mill manager when it shut down there, and it's sad that he was stuck in that jackpot. He's too good a man for that." Not surprisingly, after the mill closed, Shivgulam moved his family to Southern Ontario.

With the mill now closed, those unable to retire had to look for a new job. Having been hired on straight out of high school, most had never been in this position before. Indeed, many had never put together a CV or even gone to a formal hiring interview. Labour adjustment is a growing industry in North America, with hundreds of firms offering their services. Initially, Weyerhaeuser hired a US-based company to help mill workers find new jobs. One of our interviewees shared with me a letter from this company, which modestly called itself the "world's leading career transition and organizational consulting firm." It was contracted to provide orientation sessions and financial planning workshops during the eight-week notification period. One of these workshops, "Coping with Job Loss," for example, aimed to help workers deal with the emotional ramification of lost jobs. There were also "employee transition" workshops and more practical ones. Interviewee after interviewee called it a disaster from the very beginning. The company was disorganized, and the out-of-town consultants missed scheduled appointments. Even the mill newsletter, the *Insider*, admitted that "very few employees and families had signed up" for the workshops[13] – they were not worth the bother. Nor did it help that the adjustment process was associated with the departing company. Things got so bad, so fast that Weyerhaeuser changed tack a month later and agreed to a union-run Action Centre.

This kind of adjustment effort provides support to those who criticize privately delivered worker training that often serves as "an ideological legitimation device."[14] A standard feature of these retraining programs is to help displaced workers identify and market the skills they possess and to present themselves effectively to potential employers.[15] But in doing so, such programs also individualize the "private troubles of unemployed workers and [ignore] the structural causes of unemployment."[16] As anthropologist Tom Dunk asks: "Training for what?"[17] As we will see in the next chapter, displaced mill workers who took college courses to become oil and gas technicians or nurses were building new skills, but that was not the case for those who went through private adjustment firms. The emphasis on retraining places the onus on the individual to succeed; failure is the individual's fault, not that of the wider system or economic environment. This corporatized approach atomizes and depoliticizes.

Out of the ruins left by the "world's leading career transition and organizational consulting firm" emerged the Action Centre. Established by Local 7135 of the Communications, Energy and Paperworkers Union of Canada (CEP), thanks to funding from the Ontario Ministry of Training, Colleges and Universities, the Action Centre provided a place to meet where people could vent or just catch up. Everyone who worked there was a former mill worker. Marcel Boudreau, one of the trustees of the Action Centre, praised them for doing "a wonderful job, doing what it was that they had to do." It rented the space from the union, "but it wasn't just the union thing, because management staff were able to access that, too. They didn't have to feel uncomfortable going to union." During its opening hours, the space was an Action Centre; otherwise it was union. Boudreau went there a lot, "even if just to go there [to] have a coffee." There were workshops and individual counselling. Denis MacGregor, who worked there as a counsellor, heard some horrible stories over the next twelve months.

Everyone we interviewed valued this safe space, although Pierre Hardy, asked if the Action Centre was useful, initially replied, "Not especially." He said he went there "once in a while just to talk to the guys. But I [didn't] intend them to really find a job for me." He quickly added, however, that the Action Centre "was good for a lot of people." His wife Jane then interjected: "Well, I don't know, Pete. I think it helped you a lot, in the sense that it's a meeting place." Pierre agreed, "Yeah, meet the guys. That's what I said." Jane expanded on her point: "You have a common – no, I mean, you're all in the same boat there. And you can go cry on each other's shoulder. Or get pissed off. And just vent somewhere. Whereas, you know, talking to other people, they don't know what your situation is, the people that have nothing to do with the mill ... You're all in the same kind of boat. And you have mutual problems. You're unemployed or whatever. You're all looking for work."

Behind the scenes, the CEP attempted to negotiate a plant-closing agreement with Weyerhaeuser that would have provided additional severance and retirement bridging for its members. For example, Local 7135 asked the company to extend early retirement to all those with thirty years' seniority regardless of their age, but was rebuffed. "Not a red penny was put toward the pension," Mike Lacroix exclaimed furiously. "They didn't care about the workers at all. Gave you your severance pay, one week per year, that's it. Nothing was done for the people." Percy Allary was one of the lucky ones, as he was eligible to retire and got his pension immediately. But Allary recognized that other "guys were at thirty years, just like me, but they were younger, and they ... got nothing. They ran their severance out.

Pierre Hardy, who worked on the paper
machine after the 1991 layoffs.
Photograph by David. W. Lewis.

They ran their unemployment out. They're fifty-two, fifty-three, and where are you
going to get a job with a grade 10 education, a grade 12 education? And they've got
kids that [were] going to college." Even though the CEP union representative was
there with the local union leadership, the company would not budge. Their "hands
were tied from the get-go. We had no leverage."[18] Many now regretted not prioritiz-
ing these things in collective bargaining while they had the chance.

But what provoked mill workers the most was the timing of the announcement
and the company's subsequent refusal to sell the mill as a going concern. Larry
Shank noted that people were "really mad" that the plant was going to close in
December even though there was a contract to sell all of the mill's product until the
following September: "We still had a contract, and we were still making money. If
Weyerhaeuser [had] been smart, they would have run out the contract." But they
did not: "Now, why did they do that?" Marc Côté also felt that Weyerhaeuser could
have been "a little bit more [pause] compassionate … make it a little longer. They
had contracts still running with the box plants that they could have continued selling for a while." Instead they "shut down before the end. Well, that caught all of the
guys by surprise." It was incomprehensible. Again and again we heard that the mill
was making money. For Shank, "the mill always made money. Hard times, good
times; good times [they] made a lot of money, hard times, less money. That's the
way that worked." There was a great deal of ambivalence in Percy Allary's voice
when he spoke of Weyerhaeuser. It was "their company, their business," he said, so
they could do what they wanted: "They don't care if they hurt your feelings. Or if

you got to sell your house. So you got to just accept it. I was only bitter at the way they did it. Because the place was making money, they had a contract." So why did the company close the mill?

The wider economic and corporate context for these recollections can be found in copies of the *Weyerhaeuser Bulletin* salvaged from the closing plant. In 2002 it was filled with stories of acquisitions and corporate restructuring. The company had acquired MacMillan Bloedel in 1999 and Oregon-based Willamette Industries in March 2002 as part of its strategy of growth through acquisition, and had become the world's largest producer of softwood market pulp and the second-largest producer of containerboard packaging.[19] In March the *Bulletin* reported that the company was closing its packaging plants in Nashville, Tennessee, and Richmond, Virginia. The stated goal of these closures was "to strengthen Weyerhaeuser's competitive position by using excess capacity in other plants in the same geographic areas."[20] A month later the company's CEO, Steve Rogel, was quoted as saying that "we're building a brand-new company." It then closed a particle board plant in Oregon. Another month later Rogel confidently told shareholders: "It's a brand-new day at Weyer-haueser."[21] He again warned that the industry was experiencing overcapacity. Other plant closures in Louisiana and Oklahoma were announced in August and September.[22] Weyerhaeuser then issued an earnings alert in September, leading its stock price to fall 12 per cent on the New York Stock Exchange.[23] Sturgeon Falls joined the burgeoning list of announced closures in the *Weyerhaeuser Bulletin* a month later.[24]

Displaced workers such as Harold Stewart understood that "we were nothing, A little mill like this is, to Weyerhaeuser, peanuts." The company had newer and bigger mills in the United States that were no longer running at capacity. To some degree, it was logical to workers that the company wanted to save money by consolidating production in fewer plants. But many of those we interviewed also felt that it was significant that Weyerhaeuser was a US-based company. "Why Weyerhaeuser did what they did is beyond my comprehension," sighed Ben Lajeunesse. "Just a Yankee company coming in, taking the money off the top. That's what it looked like. But were they just getting rid of competition? Because we had a contract that ran for almost another year, you know, that was making a million dollars a month." Another interviewee said, "Let's face it, they don't care about us Canucks, whether we worked or not." For former superintendent Marc Côté, Weyerhaeuser was a good company: "Very efficient, but you're far away from the head [office]. And what's your future when you're point five of a per cent of a company's worth?" Production workers, office staff, and even local managers raised this issue. There was also anger. In her interview, Karen Beaudette insisted that they were "Americanized to death. I mean, that's all they wanted were our natural resources. Bloodsuckers."

We found "Yankee Go Home" written in the dust in the paper machine room when we toured the plant as it was being dismantled, 2004. Photograph by Kristen O'Hare.

While walking through the closed plant, I noticed that someone had written "Yankees Go Home" with their finger in the dust on the wall in the paper machine room – one of many small protests.

Finally, the company's refusal to consider selling the mill as a going concern – and thus save the town's major employer – raised the ire of workers. "Why not sell it?" asked one former mill worker.[25] Many of those present in Cache Bay wanted to know if Weyerhaeuser would sell the mill. Raymond Marcoux recalled: "We tried, saying, well, ask them if they'd sell the mill, if they'd do anything. They said, 'No, the mill is not for sale.' They're gonna shut it down, they're going to decommission it. That's what we were told." Karen Beaudette remarked that the company never gave them a straight answer that morning in Cache Bay. What they did say was: "'Not at this time.' Or, 'it's not in the works.' They never said 'No' and they never said 'Yes.' … You know how they talk. It's all gobbledegook."

The Lawsuit and the Dam

When Weyerhaeuser announced the closure of the Sturgeon Falls mill, it failed to notify its community partner in the recycled pulp facility. Despite established procedures for such an eventuality, no written notice was given to the partnership until mid-November, more than a month after the Cache Bay meeting and the issue of a press release. This, and the premature termination of the evergreen contract, made it vulnerable to a lawsuit. This section turns to the effort of the West Nipissing Economic Development Committee and the Town of West Nipissing to get an injunction to stop the company from closing the mill. We know a great deal about what happened thanks to the legal documentation shared by our interviewees as well as interviews conducted with elected officials and key members of the WNEDC.

Although they failed to win an injunction, Ontario Superior Court justice Norman Karam ruled that the plaintiff had a strong case for damages. It gave the municipality leverage at a critical moment, which it used to acquire the mill's hydro dam, rather than trying to compel Weyerhaeuser to sell the mill as a going concern. The unfolding events fractured the community, pitting mill workers against their municipal leadership. Had they "kept on pushing on that," lamented Raymond Marcoux, "maybe Weyerhaeuser could've sold the mill, maybe the mill would be producing today." It is impossible to know for certain, but the unfolding events remind us that the interests of a community are often contested: some are backed by local power brokers, others not. Who speaks on behalf of a local community is, of course, a political question, reminding us that the "community versus capital" paradigm in deindustrialization studies fails to capture the local complexity of the post-industrial transformation.

The amalgamation of five area municipalities in 1999 into the Town of West Nipissing created a new locality. The municipality now had fourteen thousand residents, about half of whom lived within the boundaries of what was formerly Sturgeon Falls. These shifting borders served to decentre the mill and its history further. With amalgamation there was also considerable confusion surrounding the WNEDC and the community's joint venture with Weyerhaeuser, which acquired MacMillan Bloedel the same year. Did the WNEDC continue to exist, or was the municipality its successor? At the time everybody seemed to think that the WNEDC was now dormant.[26] The confusion around the WNEDC stemmed from the fact that, with amalgamation, all previously existing library boards, hydro commissions, local roads boards, and local service boards in the area ceased to exist and their responsibilities and assets were transferred to the new town. There was no explicit mention, however, of the WNEDC.[27]

A month after municipal elections, Scott Mosher and the outgoing WNEDC representatives – Ron Beauchamp, Daniel Olivier, and Denis Lafrèniere – urged the town to send an observer to ensure a smooth transition.[28] In recalling this time, Daniel Olivier was scathing in his comments, saying, "the request fell on deaf ears."[29] Elected officials were preoccupied with other matters. The partnership's annual

OCC facility being dismantled, as seen from the basement.

OCC facility after it had been stripped. Photographs by David W. Lewis.

general meeting was held in June 1999, but none of the newly appointed municipal councillors showed up, to the dismay of those present. Neither did the union.
According to Olivier, those there waited for forty-five minutes before deciding to
retire to a bar for drinks. The mill manager, he said, felt insulted that nobody from
the municipality cared to show. It would be the last meeting the three longstanding
representatives of the WNEDC attended. Six months later the "partnership started
to deteriorate."[30]

Daniel Olivier believed that the partnership fell through the cracks of amalgamation. But it was also a result of the dissonance between the rural and urban parts of
the new municipality: with amalgamation the urban areas were thinking one way
and the rural parts another. It was a merger of "two solitudes" that did not understand each other, Olivier explained. There was also some bad blood between an
older generation of rural politicians, which included the WNEDC representatives,
and a new generation of urban ones. Olivier surmised: "We were rural. The ones
that replaced us were urban. That's basically it." Before the election there had been
a "little tug of war, and they won," so there was no communication. He was con-
temptuous of the new municipal leadership, saying they were not business people:
"They didn't have a clue what was going on. And worse, they didn't care." Whatever
the reason, Olivier believed this exposed a chink in the community's armour that
Weyerhaeuser would exploit ruthlessly in the years to come.

When the municipality's representatives – which included Mayor Gary O'Connor
and city engineer Alan Korell – finally arrived, they came with little understanding
of what had happened previously. The company's side of the table also turned over
with the transfer of Scott Mosher. As we will see, the resulting break in institutional
memory proved disastrous for Sturgeon Falls. At their third meeting, in December
2001, after agreeing to the company's proposal to pay off the final OCC loan, the
community representatives were told by Naraine Shivgulam "that the purpose of
the OCC partnership has been served and that there is no need to continue this
partnership."[31] Not knowing otherwise, the municipal representatives agreed, and
it was determined that a company representative would review the original partnership agreement to ensure that the closure was done properly. On 29 January
2002 Weyerhaeuser offered to purchase the municipality's rights and interests in
the Sturgeon Falls Limited Partnership for a dollar.[32] And, stupidly, on 6 February
the town council agreed. The motion recorded in the minutes seemed innocuous
enough: "Be it resolved that the Mayor and Clerk be authorized to sign the letter of
agreement received from Weyerhaeuser Company Limited." In hindsight it is easy
to read this development as a necessary first step in the company's plan to close the

mill. It needed to disentangle itself from its community partner and to extinguish the community's legal stake in the mill.

The fireside sale was stopped only when the town's lawyer told the mayor that the new municipality had not in fact assumed the legal responsibilities of the WNEDC upon amalgamation. To formalize the transfer, the municipality set out to get the signatures of Daniel Olivier and Ron Beauchamp, former directors of the WNEDC. Albeit horrified by the municipality's actions, Olivier reluctantly signed in March 2002. But as he was in the process of doing so, Beauchamp "questioned whether we should sign."[33] As Olivier told it, Beauchamp "was so persistent that by the time I was done signing the document, I was fit to be tied." In the end Beauchamp refused to sign, preventing the transaction from proceeding. None of this was known publicly until after the closure, when Weyerhaeuser raised it in court and in the media, to devastating effect.

The closure announcement of 8 October took the community by surprise. Mayor Gary O'Connor had heard "ongoing rumblings" throughout the year that there was a problem at the mill, but did not know for sure until word got out after the Cache Bay meeting. Early the next morning, O'Connor met with company representatives from the United States at Gervais's Restaurant. Asked why he met them at this popular local restaurant, O'Connor replied that Weyerhaeuser wanted to meet him "privately," and did not want to meet at the town hall, where they might encounter the media. During the meeting, they were quite calm, even "congenial," but adamant that there "was nothing that we could do or say to stop it." They tried to tell O'Connor that the mill was losing money, which made him chuckle, as everyone in Sturgeon Falls knew otherwise: "We practically begged them for reconsideration. And they simply smiled." They then paid for breakfast.

Afterwards Mayor O'Connor returned to the town hall and held a press conference, telling the media that the closure announcement was a "rude awakening," advising residents to focus on other things, such as the expansion of the Statistics Canada office in town, the development of a major new grocery outlet, and the continued strength of farming in the area.[34] The mayor's low-key public reaction to the mill closure immediately rubbed some workers the wrong way. Ron Demers, a thirty-two-year man, was quoted in the *Tribune* as saying that O'Connor's public remarks merely eulogized the mill. He hoped that the municipality would look at the situation before "throwing in the towel."[35] In "our minds and hearts," he said, "we would all like to see ourselves retire from the mill."

The idea of going to court to prevent Weyerhaeuser from closing the mill originated with the former directors of the WNEDC. Daniel Olivier learned about the closure when the local newspaper called him to ask what he thought about it.

He told the journalist, "They can't do that." Weyerhaeuser was contractually obligated to provide advance notice, and the partnership agreement also contained a provision allowing the community to buy out the company's share. "Then, they [the municipal council] changed their tune," he recalled.

It was quickly determined that the WNEDC needed to be reactivated if the lawsuit had any chance of success. On 24 October 2002, two weeks after the Cache Bay meeting, the newly reconstituted WNEDC met and named a new board of directors: J.P. Charles (president), Mayor Gary O'Connor (vice-president), Ron Beauchamp (past president), and Denis Gauthier (secretary-treasurer). All of these men were interviewed for this book. The new WNEDC representatives on the board of the Sturgeon Falls Limited Partnership also relied on experience, as it included Olivier, Beauchamp, and Lafrèniere. In his interview, Charles said that he agreed to serve because "something had to be done," and they needed someone who had some history with the partnership and knew what was going on.

In the resulting news coverage, journalist Dean Lisk thought that the partnership agreement seemed to make a transfer of ownership possible. When asked, Weyerhaeuser's spokesperson said that the agreement related only to the recycling equipment, not to the land, buildings, or other equipment.[36] Three days later, on 15 October, the *Tribune* reported that a number of local councillors were expressing concern about not being informed of the impending closure. Brian Laflèche took aim at Mayor O'Connor, saying, "Any other mayor, or administrator, or administration would have made sure every member of council was notified."[37] Fellow councillor Paul Finley complained that he had heard of the closure from another councillor, "followed by his wife and hearing it on the radio." Soon thereafter a meeting of local, provincial, and federal representatives, along with the union, met to discuss the mill. CEP Ontario vice-president Cec Makowski told the group that "there's only a thin thread here we can hang on to."[38]

We can track the initial preparation of the lawsuit in the step-by-step accounting provided by Robert J. Arcand, a Toronto lawyer, originally from the area, who was directed to develop a "strategy to try and keep the Mill open." On 18 October he received information on the Limited Partnership and the closing announcement from Denis Lafrèniere. Three days later, Arcand spoke to Jean-Pierre Barbeau, chief administrative officer and clerk of the Municipality of West Nipissing, in order to prepare a draft letter of opinion that set out the recommended steps. On 23 October there was another conference call with Barbeau and Mayor O'Connor, who recommended they move forward with the legal proceedings. Town council was unanimously in favour. The legal team in Toronto then reviewed statutes, background materials, and case law. A draft statement of claim was developed, and on

Paper machine room as it was being dismantled. Photograph by David W. Lewis.

8 November the WNEDC announced it had commenced a statement of claim seeking an injunction and damages of $75 million plus punitive damages of $25 million.[39] As J.P. Charles explained to us, "You have to ask big if you want to get something."

During this process the union found its attempts to work with the municipality and the WNEDC rebuffed at every step. The WNEDC received "many requests" from the CEP to be part of the lawsuit. The minutes of their meetings make clear, however, that the "consensus at this time" was that the WNEDC "will represent the community's interest in this matter and will involve other organizations as the need arises."[40] When interviewed, many WNEDC leaders were critical of the union and the mill workers. "They had no idea," Daniel Olivier said. He thought that the union should have taken an interest in the partnership before the closure announcement. But they did not. For his part, Denis Gauthier said the mill workers were never part of the partnership, which was "basically a municipality-owned and -driven initiative. And the guys never wanted to be at the table. The only time they came crying the blues was [when Weyerhaeuser put] the locks on the gate."

Meanwhile the WNEDC attempted to convene an urgent meeting of the partnership on 8 November. Four days earlier, a notice had been sent to the company about the commencement of legal proceedings and proposing to do so in the name of the partnership. One can only assume that the intention was to see if Weyerhaeuser's local management would defy their superiors or perhaps just drop the ball, allowing the partnership itself to pick up the sizable legal tab for the lawsuit. This was not to be, as Naraine Shivgulam forwarded the notice to his superiors. Soon thereafter WNEDC received a strongly worded letter from Anne Giardini, assistant general counsel of Weyerhaeuser, stating: "We were very surprised to receive your letter of November 5, 2002. We would have expected, in view of the long history of this company and its predecessors in this community, and our history of working cooperatively, that you would have raised with Weyerhaeuser any concerns of a legal or other nature in advance of a bald statement of intention to sue this company on the grounds that you do not care to specify." Of course, the company's response was rich, given that it had not bothered to inform the municipality (or the WNEDC) of its decision to close the mill in the first place. Giardini then asked for a meeting: "Without the consent of the Weyerhaeuser-appointed directors, Repulping is not authorized to incur legal expenses of any kind or nature. Weyerhaeuser will hold West Nipissing solely liable for any costs or expenses incurred by Repulping at the instance of West Nipissing."[41] The message was clear: the municipality would have to foot the legal bill.

The statement of claim against Weyerhaeuser submitted to the Ontario Superior Court of Justice called for "an interim and interlocutory mandatory injunction restraining the defendant from closing the Sturgeon Falls corrugated cardboard recycling facility … and requiring the defendant to continue operating the mill until trial." The grounds for the motion, as laid out, were that the "defendant is bound to continue to operate the Mill by virtue of its contractual and fiduciary duties to the plaintiff and the community of West Nipissing."[42] The factum submitted by the WNEDC indicated that 50 per cent of the profits were to be distributed to the limited partners equally and that any change in the nature of the partnership required a vote, to insure advance notice of significant shutdowns, layoffs, or final closure. As the decision to close the plant came without notice and without the authorization of the Sturgeon Falls Limited Partnership, it represented a breach of Article 7.4 of the limited partnership agreement, "which bars a partner from making a change in the nature of the business of the partnership without the authorization of the management board."[43] Also, it was argued, the agreement indicated that, if the company were to close the mill, it must first to offer to sell its share of the partnership for a dollar, something it now refused to do so. In addition to accessing nearly $9 million in government funding, the WNEDC had financially assisted the mill by agreeing to a reduction in rent from $19 per tonne to just $2 per tonne, thereby "foregoing distributions of partnership income so profits could be used to pay down debt and upgrade equipment."[44] All of these agreements were binding on Weyerhaeuser, it argued, and so the closure represented a "fundamental breach of the Agreements," as the mill was "productive, efficient, and profitable, and the product it supplies is of high quality."[45]

The accompanying affidavit of Denis Gauthier, secretary-treasurer of the WNEDC, who served as the economic development officer from 1991 until 1998, provided the historical evidence backing their case. Gauthier maintained that the WNEDC had lined up the government funding and sought "an ongoing interest in the proposed mill in order to ensure that local residents would have a say in its operations." The provincial government also "felt the community should have an ownership stake in the plant." Profits and losses were to be distributed equally. Gauthier insisted that the community allowed local management to redirect rental fees (by lowering the rate) to pay for needed capital improvements. He tried to explain away the confusion surrounding amalgamation, claiming that "WNEDC has remained a validly incorporated entity since its inception"; accordingly, the municipal representatives on the board of the partnership were appointed improperly.[46]

Naturally the lawsuit garnered a lot of media attention. Writing in the *North Bay Nugget*, Gord Young presented it as a story of David and Goliath: "A small town, determined to save its only industry, faced off in court Wednesday against a corporate giant."[47] The public gallery in the North Bay courthouse was packed with mill workers, union officials, municipal politicians, and residents who had driven down the highway from Sturgeon Falls. Newspaper coverage emphasized the community's position that the company's "conduct has been high-handed, manipulative, secretive, harsh and unconscionable." J.P. Charles was quoted as saying, "Rest assured, we are acting in the best interest of the community and the mill employees."[48] Ever hopeful, Charles went on to say that, in 1991, "we faced a similar situation and we pulled our resources together and worked to save the mill."[49]

In response to the legal arguments advanced by the plaintiff in the case, Valerie Edwards, representing Weyerhaeuser, argued that the partnership was "nothing more than an alleged breach of an equipment rental agreement." Weyerhaeuser denied that the WNEDC was its "business partner in the operation of either the Sturgeon Falls Plant or even in the operation of the old corrugated cardboard repulping facility." Weyerhaeuser also took the position that it was "fully within its right to close down its Sturgeon Falls Plant and to terminate the Mill Operating Agreement pursuant to which it rents the OCC repulping equipment." It referred to the injunction as "inappropriate, impractical, and overreaching in the extreme."[50] Edwards repeatedly sought to minimize the scope of the partnership, alleging that the WNEDC's role had simply been to raise funds, little more. Accordingly the purpose of the rent charged was to pay off the debts and maintain the equipment, nothing more: "It is respectfully submitted that [the] WNEDC has mischaracterized its role in the Limited Partnership, by attempting to describe itself as, in essence, a business partner in the operation of the OCC and even Weyerhaeuser's entire Sturgeon Falls Division." As the government loans were now paid off, there was no reason to continue the partnership. Besides, the WNEDC had "spent the last two years trying to decide whether it exists" after amalgamation.[51] Edwards then shared her bombshell revelation that the municipality nearly sold its share for just $1, so the lawsuit lacked merit.[52]

To support its position, Weyerhaeuser submitted two affidavits. The first, from Paul Whyatt, a corporate executive, spoke from a company-wide perspective about market forces and the old age of the Sturgeon Falls plant. Demand for cardboard boxes was already in decline in North America,[53] so there was overcapacity in the industry. Whyatt observed that twenty-two corrugated medium machines had shut in recent years, including three Weyerhaeuser mills in the United States. He then suggested that these closed machines "were more productive than the Sturgeon Falls Plant. Sturgeon Falls employs 140 people to produce 90,000 tonnes of medium annually. The Plymouth and Hawesville medium facilities employed almost the same number of people and were able to produce double the volume."[54] Its paper machine was the oldest of all of the company's corrugated medium facilities. He likewise noted that Sturgeon Falls produced rolls of paper that were far narrower (140 inches wide) than most medium machines (180–278 inches, the newest 300 inches). Even Sturgeon's OCC facility was considerably smaller than comparable facilities elsewhere – neglecting to mention that other repulping plants were modelled on this publicly funded facility. With the mill's evergreen contract set to expire on 3 September 2003, the Sturgeon mill had no future.[55]

The second affidavit, from local manager Naraine Shivgulam, attempted to demolish the OCC partnership and diminish the community's contribution. Contrary to the WNEDC, "it is my belief that profit making was never a primary goal of the Limited Partnership." Shivgulam also countered Gauthier's assertion that decisions were to be made jointly, saying, "At no time since I became involved directly with the Limited Partnership has it functioned in this manner." He failed to say, however, that he was not involved in the partnership until December 2000. "By 2001," he continued, "it appeared to me that there was no reason left to maintain the Limited Partnership." Shivgulam also downplayed the role of the WNEDC in getting grants, and effectively diminished the OCC facility itself as simply a "series of machines." He also stated that, when he and other company representatives met with Mayor O'Connor at Gervais's Restaurant on 9 October 2002, the mayor didn't question the legality of the closure. Shivgulam therefore expressed his dismay that the reborn WNEDC was going to court "without having received advance warning."[56] Weyerhaeuser was clearly using their local manager and his twenty-five years of service in the mill to hit back at the WNEDC, and the confusion surrounding amalgamation to justify the company's unilateral actions. What was remarkable here, however, was what Whyatt and Shivgulam did not say. Neither affidavit claimed that the mill was actually losing money.

The audience in the courtroom was horrified when Weyerhaeuser's lawyer Valerie Edwards related how the municipality passed a resolution to sell its share in the Limited Partnership for a dollar.[57] One interviewee, who wished to remain anonymous, could not hide his anger: "Fucker, for a buck." Clearly exasperated, Mike Lacroix also lashed out: "One lousy dollar. They sold all our jobs for one dollar. One buck. They destroyed a whole bunch of families and half a community. That's not right." Nor could Marcel Boudreau understand why the town council had agreed to sell its interest. Everyone was dumbfounded. Local reporter Dean Lisk feared that the attempted sale "could jeopardize efforts to stop the mill closure."

Meanwhile, Cecil Makowski, Ontario vice-president of the CEP, sought to insert himself in the lawsuit, filing for intervenor status.[58] The CEP's factum emphasized the devastating impact that the closure would have on workers and the wider

Digester during the mill's dismantling; Ken Colquhoun worked on this machine. Photograph by David W. Lewis.

community. Makowski's own affidavit cited a conversation with Ron Corneil, vice-president of marketing and business Development for Weyerhaeuser, just after the closure announcement, who told him that the company had no interest in selling the mill to anyone "which would manufacture product in competition with Weyerhaeuser." The CEP made no legal argument to speak of – an indication of the limits of Canadian law when it comes to the managerial prerogative to close plants and to lay off workers at will. The union was on the outside looking in. But this was about politics: Makowski and the CEP wanted to be seen fighting for their members.

In his verdict, delivered on 29 November 2002, Justice Norman Karam ruled against an injunction, determining it to be too onerous on the company and difficult to serve or enforce: "After considering all of the factors discussed above, I must dismiss the plaintiff's application. I do so primarily because, aside from the impracticality of ordering the defendant to operate without a market, and then attempting to oversee that operation; the defendant would certainly have been within its legal rights to cease operations anyway by September 3, 2003. We are therefore dealing with a relatively short period of time. There is no purpose in requiring the defendant to continue its operations until that date, when the plaintiff can adequately be compensated in damages at trial."[59] But it was not a total failure. The judge went on to question why the company terminated the evergreen contract on 18 November 2002 when it would run until September 2003. He concluded that Weyerhaeuser breached its fiduciary duty to the limited partnership, as set out in the mill operating agreement, by failing to provide reasonable notice. The WNEDC was therefore well positioned to go to trial for damages. Marcel Boudreau had gone down to the courthouse for the ruling: "Yeah, we went to check that out. I mean, right from the judge's mouth he told us: we have grounds to sue for damages." The *Toronto Star* seemed to think so, too: Weyerhaeuser "had engineered the timing of the closing by agreeing to terminate a contract with a purchaser nine months earlier than scheduled."[60] Sturgeon Falls now had the kind of leverage that other former mill towns could only dream of. What would it do with it?

That evening there was a special meeting of the WNEDC to discuss the ruling.[61] Various options were considered. The municipality was shaken, however, by the resulting legal bill of $105,273.80. It soon became apparent that the municipality did not have the stomach (or sufficiently deep pockets) for a long, drawn-out legal battle with a major multinational corporation and its lawyers.[62] How could Sturgeon Falls compete financially with Weyerhaeuser? The risk of losing in the courtroom was just too great, so they chose not to proceed. According to Yvon Marleau, "We were just gonna let it go to the courts as long as it had to … But … very soon it became obvious that we weren't going to win." Weyerhaeuser was obstinate – it did not want to sell the mill as it did not want the competition. "So that was going nowhere," insisted Marleau.

The paper machine as it was being prepared for dismantling. Photograph by David W. Lewis.

Growing impatient, and perhaps sensing the lack of municipal resolve, the national union became increasingly belligerent. On 3 December a Toronto lawyer representing the CEP wrote the town's lawyer to say that the union wished to "assert its right to intervene" at the next stage of legal proceedings. "Simply put," he wrote, "we believe this matter should not and cannot be resolved without our agreement and consent."[63] Local 7135 president Denis Senecal also wrote to request a meeting to discuss how the union might gain access to the mill for its market study consultant and to find ways to convince Weyerhaeuser to sell the mill as a going concern. He wanted a member of the union executive to be part of future discussions between the WNEDC and the town council.[64] Senecal hoped they could work together, moving forward. But this was not to be. When the union's lawyers asked that the CEP be invited to attend future meetings of the partnership, both the company and the WNEDC agreed that these "internal partnership meetings" were a "private matter."[65]

The partnership meeting, held in the main conference room in the closed plant on 7 January 2003, saw Barbara Crowell, one of two new board members from corporate headquarters, review the company's actions and plans apart from the assets of the OCC facility: "Weyerhaeuser is proceeding with plans to take down and remove certain pieces of equipment in an orderly and timely manner. Certain Weyerhaeuser items have value to other Weyerhaeuser facilities ... Contractors will come on site to provide bids on removing tanks and other items that need to be properly disposed of. The first buildings will likely start to be demolished in the spring of 2004."[66] Crowell noted that, once asbestos had been removed, the boilers and furnaces would no longer be functional. The meeting then discussed the preservation and liquidation of jointly held property. A representative of the WNEDC indicated it was their intention "to continue to explore ideas about further use." To this Shivgulam replied that there was a very limited period of time left to explore options. He added that any "potential parties" would have to "follow a formal process, including a formal offer and appropriate confidentiality provisions." Weyerhaeuser also noted that its monthly rental payments had "come to an end because Weyerhaeuser has returned the property to the Limited Partnership." There was also the matter of the outstanding $2,334,000 loan owed to Weyerhaeuser, as it had paid off the commercial loan. The company was playing hardball, suggesting it had incurred "substantial costs in respect of matters in dispute with the WNEDC and noted that Weyerhaeuser would be looking at how to recover these costs, in addition to amounts owed by WNEDC." It was not a pleasant meeting.

On 11 February 2003, Jean-Pierre (Jay) Barbeau wrote to Anne Giardini to follow up on the items discussed at the meeting. He asked for Weyerhaeuser's cooperation in allowing the Community Adjustment and Recovery Committee (CARC), responsible for mitigating the wider impact of the closure, time to explore opportunities to maximize the use of the Weyerhaeuser site.[67] Barbeau went on to say that it was the town's understanding that Weyerhaeuser intended to sell the hydro plant and take bids, adding, "On behalf of the Limited Partnership, we would hope that you would consider the community's bid, which is critical to the success of the site and possible alternative uses. We therefore request to be given the right of first refusal on the hydro plant, since this asset is critical to the value of the partnership's other assets on the site."[68] Barbeau acknowledged that the matter of the lawsuit was "briefly mentioned" at the meeting, and suggested a "sidebar meeting to discuss our relative positions regarding this matter in a separate venue."[69] Here we see the town and the WNEDC pivot from stopping the closure and saving the mill to acquiring the mill's hydro dam. At the time, the facility produced 7.4 megawatts of electricity a year. Barbeau ended his letter with: "I would hope that we could continue the positive dialogue started on January 7th, 2003, in order that all issues may be resolved to our mutual benefit." The letter struck a conciliatory tone; something had clearly changed.

The negotiations with Weyerhaeuser for the power dam were tough. Several people credit Royale Poulin, the newly appointed chairperson of the CARC, for the final agreement. Politically connected, Poulin not only got Weyerhaeuser to sell the power dam; he also convinced the province to pick up the tab. The public announcement of the agreement was made on 9 July 2003 and it was heralded as a "huge economic development tool" in the *Tribune*. For his part, Mayor O'Connor trumpeted its "real and lasting benefits to the community."[70] At a news conference, Poulin told the media that the municipality would gain a "competitive advantage" with the acquisition – helping the town to attract new industry. In exchange the $100 million lawsuit was dropped and the $2.3 million Weyerhaeuser loan to the partnership forgiven, and Weyerhaeuser got $3.8 million in cash from the province.[71]

"And they accepted," Yvon Marleau told us, "as a goodwill gesture and a sort of compensation for our loss. So, you know, they weren't that bad." But the agreement came with conditions. In reality, Weyerhaeuser was telling the municipality that "We're going to work with you to sell you this power plant at that price. On the other hand, you are going to cease and desist any efforts to try and get us to keep this mill open. You're going to stay out of this. We don't want to hear any inflammatory comments with regards to Weyerhaeuser from the local politicians, and we don't want to see any efforts. So we were stuck between a rock and a hard place." Local politicians felt they couldn't take on the company. According to Guy Ethier, "When you have a bevy of lawyers … and when you're a small-town councilman or CA or mayor, you're out of your league, basically." Ethier felt that, in the end, the lawsuit served a purpose: it got the municipality the dam. He credited Jay Barbeau, the town clerk, who worked

The closed mechanical shop, 2004. Photograph by David W. Lewis.

around the clock to make this happen: "A lot of people don't appreciate how much effort went into that. Not to save the mill as much as what can we get to minimize the damage, maintain some jobs, and maybe get some things for the municipality." In many ways the dam bought the silence of the municipality, much as the prospect of $5,000 bonuses silenced workers for the final two months of production.

Virtually every elected politician and WNEDC official we spoke to viewed the sale of the dam as a significant victory for the community. "We all know how power generates money," Ken Landry told us. The dam would generate money for the municipality, providing a way to entice new employers to locate in the town. It would therefore help fill the tax hole left by the departing company. Ron Beauchamp likewise thought that the town's acquisition of the hydro dam was "very positive" for West Nipissing. He believed Royale Poulin had "got us a very good deal on that." Ultimately, "when the dust settles … maybe fifteen years from now, people are going to realize that this is the best thing that could have happened to us." Brian Laflèche agreed, saying, "[They] came out at least with a fairly good deal. You lost jobs and you can't replace that. That's not the point. The point is we did get the power plant and we did get all that land that at some point in time in the future the Municipality of Sturgeon Falls and West Nipissing will benefit from this deal. It's a negative now, but it will be positive later." Raymond Brouillette also expressed pride in the acquisition: "That's a big one. That was really good. And we have to thank Royale Poulin, in particular, in this case – he was the chair of the CARC committee. He did a lot of work … And that's how we ended up getting such a … good deal on the power dam. Because I think it was assessed at over $7 million, and we ended up buying it for 3.5 or something like this." Asked why they got such a good deal, Brouillette explained:

When Weyerhaeuser was being sued, they said to the town, "If you drop the suit, we'll give you a good deal," which made a lot of sense. So instead of paying $7 or $8 million for the power dam, they paid $3½ million. And it's the province that put up the money. I think we actually got $4.8 million altogether: 3.5 for the dam and the balance is to revamp the dam somehow. And that's a sweet deal because they are going to generate about $700,000 a year on that dam, and that's without expansion. And eventually they might expand on the dam to end up making maybe $1 million a year. So that was a big deal. And it worked out well, because they could have spent all that money fighting it out in court, and nobody really getting anything out of it in the end. But this way, at least, we end up with the power dam, which means a lot. It means a lot for two reasons, not just the $700,000 it's going to generate on a yearly basis, [but also] it makes it very attractive for business people to come in. Where you can supply power, maybe at a subsidized cost, you can use it as an incentive. It's there.

The power dam after the mill's demolition, 2005. Photograph by David . Lewis.

In the end the municipality was more than satisfied with acquiring the power dam as a revenue generator. In June 2004 the *Tribune* covered an open house at the hydro dam to celebrate its acquisition by the town. Those gathered heard Royale Poulin and others speak.[72] Council even received a letter from Weyerhaeuser congratulating West Nipissing on the purchase. But there was no mention of the mill workers in the newspaper article; their interest had been subsumed by the common good as determined by the municipality.

It is no surprise, then, that mill workers felt abandoned by local politicians. Marcel Boudreau, for one, lamented the fact that Weyerhaeuser walked away with millions of taxpayer dollars, saying, "Weyerhaeuser come out of here smelling like a rose. When you're a hundred-million-dollar corporation, I guess you could do things like that, eh? My understanding of the situation is they [the municipality] couldn't afford to go to court. I think that's a crock of bullshit because they should've gone to court … They could have got something for it." Mike Lacroix believed that the municipal administration had a "hidden agenda" all along, but he agreed that a small town did not have the money to take on a big corporation: "Weyerhaeuser could come here and buy North Bay and Sudbury and Sturgeon. That's how big they are."

There is some evidence to suggest that the town was eyeing the power dam from the beginning. Alan Korell, the town's engineer was a personal friend of Naraine

Shivgulam, a fellow engineer. Korell told us that, after the closure announcement, the town started to look at the dam the "next day." But then the council "sort of lashed out, and they started this lawsuit thing with Weyerhaeuser." He never agreed with the lawsuit: "That was just a political thing." Instead Korell favoured working with Weyerhaeuser, and continued to talk to Shivgulam during the lawsuit and tried "to work on the dam stuff through the back door and then, eventually, when the lawsuit went away, then it became more formal." By then, Weyerhaeuser "wanted to do something for the community because they looked like the bad guy."

In turn the dam offered the town a stable revenue source: "You're still making money from the old plant," Korell said. Besides, the power dam also provided employment for six or seven mill workers who continue to work there. Henri Labelle was one of the lucky ones who retained his job, as he had seniority among the trades. As people later retired, mill workers were called back one by one.

Yet, as Daniel Olivier wrote in the *Tribune*, the "blame and shame [were] not exclusive to Weyerhaeuser." It was unfortunate that "the newly appointed councillors did not understand the significance of the agreement."[73] He believed that "the mill closure in December 2002 could have been prevented or delayed had this clause [in the partnership agreement] been understood and used by municipal officials who, at the time, refused to speak with former members of the partnership who knew the agreement inside and out, including myself."[74] Olivier again paid tribute to Ron Beauchamp's decision not to sign at this critical moment: "The community was given the chance to buy the power dam and get some compensation for its loss. So, when you see Ron Beauchamp, I encourage you to stop and thank him for his dedication to our community." His courage made the subsequent lawsuit and dam acquisition possible.

Pickets and Press Releases

Trade unions have struggled to respond effectively to mill and factory closures. Many unions have simply wound up their newly "defunct" local unions, quietly liquidating their assets and closing their halls. The relative strength of labour law in the United States compared to Canada meant that employers there were compelled to negotiate plant-closing agreements with their unionized employees. These agreements served to depoliticize plant closings, as workers agreed not to disrupt the closing in exchange for a six-month extension of health benefits or other modest incentives. For many of those displaced, this orderly approach felt like a second closure: just when the union was needed the most, it quietly departed. In an earlier project, I uncovered reports from union organizers for the United Auto Workers that those most resistant to signing union cards in the 1980s were former members

The mill under demolition, 2004. The top image is the view from the Trans-Canada Highway. Photographs by David W. Lewis.

who had gone through a plant closing. They felt betrayed by their union and had not seen the benefits.

Historically, this has played out somewhat differently in Canada. As I showed in *Industrial Sunset: The Making of North America's Rust Belt*, the post-war compromise in Canada did not extend to plant-closing agreements;[75] employers were therefore under no legal obligation to negotiate one in good faith. Conversely this left unions free to respond politically, as they had nothing to lose. Wrapping themselves in the maple leaf flag, Canadian workers staged protests and occupied factories during the 1970s and 1980s, forcing politicians to legislate advance notification, severance pay, pension reinsurance, and preferential hiring rights – matters that were only won in collective bargaining in the United States. Even Canada's system of socialized medicine favoured workers, as they did not lose their entire medical coverage when a mill or factory shut. The trade union movement's nationalist rhetoric resonated at a time of public anxiety about Canadian sovereignty. It was therefore easier for Canadian unions to adopt tough no-concessions policies. In fact the Canadianization of large swathes of the union movement in the 1970s and 1980s was triggered by these growing national differences in outlook and context. For newly independent Canadian unions such as the CPU/CEP, a militant and uncompromising stance with employers was part of their DNA.[76]

In many respects the closure of the Weyerhaeuser mill in Sturgeon Falls was no different. The national union made a show of its defiance in the face of the 2002 closure, but it could not deliver on its promises to local workers. The national press ignored the unfolding story, and no white knight from the private sector came forward to buy the plant. The union's press releases failed to compel Weyerhaeuser to open its books – a necessary first step if the mill was to be sold as a going concern. The union also failed to bridge the chasm between solidarities based on class and community.[77] As we will see, the national union's rhetorically militant but ultimately ineffectual response to the Sturgeon Falls mill closing left local workers disillusioned and feeling betrayed. Nor did the national CEP seriously consider the employee ownership option.[78] It was only when the local membership had turned away from their national union, many in disgust, to form an "employee group" that a proposal to buy the mill emerged at the eleventh hour, a month before demolition was scheduled to begin in June 2004. By then, it was too little, too late.

Had the union pushed this idea from the beginning, it might have closed the distance with community leaders. There was considerable public support for doing so: for example, when the *North Bay Nugget* asked readers in October 2002 if they believed employees could purchase and successfully operate the Weyerhaeuser mill, fully 92 per cent of the 1,235 who responded said yes.[79] This was an emphatic response, though hardly scientific. Employee ownership became a matter of public discussion in the weeks that followed. The *Sudbury Star* observed: "There have been several examples of employee-led purchases of major industry, including Tembec Inc. and Algoma Steel in Sault Ste. Marie. Tembec's legacy began with the purchase of the Kipawa Mill in Temiscaming in 1973. Employees and townsfolk, determined to not see their livelihoods die, gathered their resources and, with help from government, sank $2.4 million into reviving the mill."[80] Mill workers such as Pierre Hardy were convinced that Weyerhaeuser was "afraid of another Tembec – a David and Goliath type of thing. We knew we could do it." Interviews also revealed that WNEDC leaders such as Daniel Olivier and Ron Beauchamp were sympathetic. Olivier recalled that, when the mill encountered severe turbulence in 1998 and, for a moment, appeared to be in trouble, he had discussed with Beauchamp the option in the limited partnership agreement to buy the plant. Perhaps, they thought, Tembec could be enticed to partly finance the effort, as it had earlier in Kapuskasing. What is interesting about Olivier's recollections is that the two men wanted direct ownership this time, not the ambiguous partnership they now had. And they wanted employees to contribute directly: "The idea was to have the employees directly related, not indirectly like it was in the past." But in 1998 the mill got a reprieve, and the plan was shelved. Olivier believed that, by the time the possibility was seriously raised this time, it was too late: "You have to be proactive in those matters. You can't be reactive in business. We tried. But it became clear it wasn't feasible." By then, that ship had sailed.

What the national CEP did do was try to mobilize its local unions at Weyerhaeuser plants across the country to shame the company into selling the Sturgeon Falls mill. On the day of the closure announcement, it asked its local unions to "protest strongly to the highest local company officials the heavy handed and secretive approach to this 'announced closure.' Make it clear that CEP will aggressively approach the unilateral decision."[81] The union also issued a press release under the headline "Weyerhaeuser abandons Sturgeon Falls."[82] The $5,000 bonus limited local activism in the first two months, and the WNEDC's decision to keep the national union at arm's length during and after the lawsuit meant that there was little immediate action. This changed with the failure of the injunction, and the last shift. The day after Justice Karam's ruling, the CEP prepared a draft plan for a national day of protest to demand that Weyerhaeuser "fully cooperate and put no barriers on a potential sale of the Sturgeon Falls Mill."[83] Informational pickets were to be organized at Weyerhaeuser plants across the country on 6 December 2002. The union declared itself "more determined than ever" to prevent the mill from closing: "This is a long way from being over," said Joel Carr, the CEP's Ontario vice-president.[84]

In these press releases, the voices of the union's regional leadership were privileged over those of the local leadership in Sturgeon Falls itself.

In Sturgeon Falls the 6 December protest began at the municipal offices, then demonstrators made their way to the mill's front gate.[85] A pickup truck was used as a makeshift stage. Wayne Samuelson, president of the Ontario Federation of Labour, spoke, as did several area politicians from the opposition parties. People chanted "free the mill, free the mill" and "Weyerhaeuser go home."[86] CEP banners and placards were scattered throughout the crowd. The banners read "Weyerhaeuser, free Sturgeon Falls," "Weyerhaeuser, no value, no commitment, no vision," and "Libéré notre communauté."[87] But there were only a hundred people in attendance, an early sign of the trouble to come.

For the informational pickets at other Weyerhaeuser mills, Sturgeon mill workers were dispatched to Miramichi, New Brunswick (Pierre Hardy); Kamloops, British Columbia (Louis Benoit); Prince Albert, Saskatchewan (Rénald Robert); Edson, Alberta (René Lebel); and to Dryden and Ear Falls in Northwestern Ontario (Marcel Boudreau). We later interviewed two of these men, with Pierre Hardy sharing the text of his speech in Miramichi: "For those of you that are not aware, this mill will close on December 6th, 2002. Our is a very unique situation." He then proceeded to speak to the 1991 closure of the hardboard siding mill and the building of the OCC facility with public funds. The community was therefore a partner in the mill. Even so, nobody got advance notice of the closure decision, and so they went to court. "Believe me when I tell you that there are no golden handshakes. The packages are bare bones and by the book. One week pay for every year of service and *no* early retirement incentives. And our extended health benefits were set to expire December 6th, the very last day of our employment but they have since extended these benefits for a generous three months."[88] Hardy concluded by saying, "I am here to give the Sturgeon Falls mill a face and a voice and ask for your support. This is an organization that has *no* values, *no* vision, and *no* commitment to the people or the environment – just the opposite of [what] they preach. For those of you that work for Weyerhaeuser, don't be fooled ... you may be next."[89]

Marcel Boudreau also provided a vivid account of his trip to Dryden, where some local union representatives joined him for a "plant gate," during the morning shift change.[90] They handed out pamphlets and explained what was happening in Sturgeon Falls. Boudreau admitted that it was an old mill, but a profitable one. A paper maker through and through, he proudly told them of the quality of paper they produced: "They didn't want paper from anywhere else. If they could've gotten all their paper from us, they would have. But we just couldn't produce enough." The reception there was mixed, but some people cared. Generally, however, the reaction was: "'You know, shit happens, that's just the way it is.' And I told them, 'It could happen to you guys somewhere down the road.'" Indeed, "Dryden was a very strange situation because there, their shift change started at four o'clock in the morning. So … at three-thirty in the morning I was standing outside waiting for people to start coming in to work. And as I was handing out pamphlets, some people just looked at the pamphlets, just threw them away. Okay. Some people didn't even want to talk to me. And I had, probably, a few people that were almost in tears when I told them what they were doing to us. And at the time, you couldn't get anybody to say anything bad about Weyerhaeuser."

Predictably the *CEP Journal* celebrated these modest efforts to mobilize public opinion in favour of the Sturgeon Falls workers: "The message from CEP members was that large American corporations should not be allowed to exploit the resources of a small Canadian town out of sheer greed and then pull up stakes, not even allowing them to help themselves."[91] But, again, it was the national union's efforts that were spotlighted, not those of local workers. It was an institutionalized message, aimed primarily at members, rather than at the general public.

The most sustained union resistance to the plant closure began in early 2003, when local trade unionists started to picket the mill's main gate in Sturgeon Falls. The immediate goal was to ensure that the company did not strip the mill, rendering the national union's efforts to find a buyer mute. "There was one guy who sat there every day," recalled Bruce Colquhoun: "Sunshine, rain, storm, no matter what, winter storm, snow, blizzard, he was out there. His name is Marcel Boudreau. Out there every day. He inspired a lot of people, you know, to go out there. … I'd go out there, 'Marcel, you want a coffee?' I'd go to Tim Hortons and get him a coffee." Boudreau got there every morning at seven o'clock: "Just like I was going to work, Monday to Friday," he said. Boudreau would stay there until about eleven o'clock and then go home. "We're fighting for our mill," he told the media.[92] In our interview with him, he took from his wallet a newspaper clipping of the North Bay *Nugget* where he was quoted. He was proud that they were going down with a fight, at the very least.

Bruce Colquhoun also enjoyed the camaraderie of the picket line. "We'd talk," he said, "we talked about lots of stuff out there. How it was our mill, and we're not going to let them Americans [smirks], whatever, shut us down. We're a good bunch of guys. We can do this. We can buy the mill. Or get somebody else to buy the mill. But we'll all be back to work soon. Everybody was believing. And that kind of held everybody together for a while." Pierre Hardy was another regular on the picket line. He would start the barrel fire and stay until noon, when another crew took over. They had considered occupying the plant, but they would have lost the

$5,000 bonus. Guys also worried about getting a criminal record just when they had to re-enter the labour market. Hardy was the one who made the big "Free Sturgeon Falls" banner, featuring an image of broken handcuffs, which was tied to the chain-link fence next to the main gate until it vanished one night.

The picket line was also a space of confrontation as the mill workers delayed or blocked vehicles from entering the front gate. While walking the picket line, Marcel Boudreau "had a purpose … I had a reason for getting up … I wanted them to see my face." Specifically he wanted the person whom he derisively called the "mill babysitter" to see him "walking that picket line." For Boudreau this person was the embodiment of the elusive, faceless corporation. Pierre Hardy also took some pleasure in thinking that the Weyerhaeuser managers hated the picket line with a passion. Mike Lacroix told us that there were several incidents on the picket line, with vehicles trying to force their way through. He recounted one such incident in a letter he wrote to the *Tribune*: "About an hour after we began our non-violent blockade at 6 a.m. a company supervisor started moving his truck through the picket line a few inches at a time. He had the legal right to come into the plant and it was our intention to allow him in after a suitable amount of time. Suddenly he lost his temper and assaulted a picketer from behind by striking him with his bumper."[93] For Lacroix, who signed the letter "In solidarity and non-violence," the man used his truck "to bully our line." He pointed to three other incidents of this nature during "our six-month vigil."[94] In retrospect, however, Hardy wished the picket line had been stationed on the other side of the mill, facing the Trans-Canada Highway, not at the mill's main gate, which faced the town itself. The other location would have allowed the protesters to be seen by thousands of passing motorists and, in the process, to transmit their message beyond the locality. That nobody considered blocking the highway itself speaks to the changing political environment since fishing boats blockaded the Ottawa River in the early 1970s or even the direct action undertaken in Kapuskasing in the early 1990s. Few now believed that the provincial or federal governments would intervene. Still, the picket line irritated the company.

In late February 2003 the picket line managed to turn back a hired mobile document-shredding van trying to enter the plant. The CEP then issued a news release saying, "Every mill document destroyed by Weyerhaeuser stabs the heart of Sturgeon Falls. CEP refuses to allow Weyerhaeuser to further denigrate and degrade the community of Sturgeon Falls."[95] Local union leader Denis Senecal told the local newspaper that he was worried about the plant's records: "They have all the files and plans … everything … in boxes, ready to be shredded."[96] Nonetheless, the van returned, and the documents were eventually destroyed.

Most of our interviewees wanted nothing more than to return to work. Their reactions, however, depended very much on when the interviews took place, with their hopes that the mill would reopen rising and falling based on the latest news. Our 5 December 2003 interview with Pierre and Jane Hardy revealed that many were still hopeful: "The hope is always there that the mill will reopen," said Jane. "I mean, we haven't lost hope, yet. Not entirely. I mean, you get kind of down in the dumps sometimes, you know? You think, 'oh, well, here we go again.'" They looked for signs: why was this person entering the mill, or why was this piece of equipment moved? Some did their research on the Internet; Jane Hardy told us that she kept a file on what she and Pierre found there. She noted that there had been "closures upon closures, and layoffs, and downtime. And they're selling off assets, like all their timberlands, just to keep afloat. And you wonder, how long can this go on?" And "that's only the ones we know of," added Pierre. They surmised that Weyerhaeuser wanted out of Canada. In fact, they were right – Weyerhaeuser sold its remaining Canadian pulp and paper assets in 2007, only eight years after acquiring MacMillan Bloedel.[97]

The picket line was up from February until September 2003, and a core group of ten or fifteen people showed up there every day throughout the cold winter months and long summer days. Mill workers who were eligible to retire when the mill closed also joined them from time to time. Percy Allary visited the picket line, but stayed away from the larger protests – he did not feel comfortable, as he had a pension and others had nothing. He felt for them. Ben Lajeunesse would also "stop and talk to the pickets. I knew them all. Stopped and see what the news was. Was there anything going on? Any interested buyers?" Marcel Boudreau noted that the picketers got a lot of support from area business people, especially early on, "and we had people stopping, wanting to know what was going on."

That said, there were also opponents. Marcel Boudreau remarked: "I had a comment made to me that it's about time that mill shut down. You guys will see the real world now." Moreover, most of the mill workers never joined in. The activists on the picket line explained their absence in several ways. Some found work in the mines in Sudbury or elsewhere. Others were in school, becoming oil and gas technicians or nurses. "Sometimes me and Marcel," said Bruce Colquhoun, were "marching alone for a while, then more guys would come. Yeah, I was there for as long as I could, then go do my job. Then it got to a point where nobody went. Guys started getting sweet little jobs, and couldn't go." As the days turned to weeks, then months, their numbers gradually dwindled. According to Marcel Boudreau, "After a while guys had to drop out for whatever reason: they got a job or, you know, you can't afford to have a babysitter take care of kids [so] you got to do it yourself, somebody's got to be home. So, situations like that we understood. But guys that didn't want to show up on the picket line because they didn't think it was worth it, they didn't want to be bothered by it, there's probably a few people – I mean, I won't mention any names – that I refuse to even associate with in any form. They would be the first ones lining up for the jobs if we got the place sold. They weren't there to help out to *try* get the place sold."

But the main reason their numbers ebbed was the loss of hope. As time went by, recalled Bruce Colquhoun, "we could see how useless it was. Nothing was happening. And they started hauling the machinery out. And that was it. Nobody went picketing anymore." At the time, some people told Marcel Boudreau that "we were wasting our time." Now he realized, "they were right. There was no hope there whatsoever, but we didn't know that. Our union, not our [local] union executive, but our union brass was telling us that 'there's things in the works here, there's things in the works.' And there was nothing." He explained: "We didn't accomplish what we wanted to accomplish, which was basically have them sell the mill. And they couldn't wait. They couldn't do it fast enough to tear that place down … I am pretty sure we won't see another paper mill in this town." That said, he "would have done it again."

There were also periodic rallies outside the mill, when the picketing workers were joined by union leaders and others. Speaking to a small rally in February 2003, with forty or so present, Local 7135 president Denis Senecal asked if the Ontario government was going "to let American companies dictate how to do business in Ontario? This is not only our fight … it's the province's fight."[98] Mill workers continued to wrap themselves in the Canadian flag, but it was not resonating in the ways it used to. A September 2003 article in the *Tribune*, with the headline, "Union rallies outside the mill," reveals that the picket line and the protests *belonged* to the union, rather than to the community.[99] For the most part, residents remained bystanders to the conflict.[100] Journalist Gord Young, who had closely covered the unfolding story for the North Bay *Nugget* since the beginning, wrote: "The fight to save the mill has been long and bitter."[101]

The national CEP also did what it could. It filed a complaint with the Canadian Competition Bureau that Weyerhaeuser was refusing to sell the mill as a going concern, which failed.[102] The union called on the Ontario government to intervene. It did not. If newspaper coverage outside Sturgeon Falls is any indication, the media campaign, such as it was, failed miserably. The union's rhetoric might have been militant, but its actions were feeble. At no time, outside the locality, was Weyerhaeuser under significant political pressure to sell. The national union sought new buyers, but despite the fog of rumours, none materialized. In February 2003, the

CEP told the press that a buyer was interested, but Weyerhaeuser was unwilling to provide access to the books.[103] Nothing happened. Similar announcements followed. Ultimately the union had promised something it could not deliver.

Controversially the national union also publicly challenged local community leaders to do more. In March 2003, for example, Joel Carr, the Ontario vice-president of the CEP, asked the town council to "take a more visible stand against the international company, and show leadership in helping the community find a way to reopen the mill."[104] He even urged council to do the "moral and right economic thing."[105] He said that the various actors needed more coordination, and called for a meeting between the union, council, the WNEDC and the CARC. He reminded them of the picket line outside the plant, which gave the union some moral author-ity in the room. It seems, however, that councillors did not appreciate the interven-tion, and defended their actions. Two of them told the union that they "did not approve of violent actions for any reason." Not surprisingly this comment "caused a murmur in the group of around 40 union members." Carr retorted that they were not doing anything close to violent. "Silence is golden," another councillor told the union. Mayor O'Connor said they were working on the situation and that the coun-cil was already working closely with the CARC and the WNEDC "to arrive at solu-tions not only for the Weyerhaeuser site, but also for the rest of the community."[106] The union was clearly the odd man out.

Yvon Marleau had a lot to say about the national union in his interview, sug-gesting that local workers were mistreated by both Weyerhaeuser and the CEP. At first he said, "The workers were glad to have their national union ... working for them. But then things got sour. And they quickly realized that the national union had another agenda. They were not interested in 140 people here. They were look-ing at the national picture." And this national picture required that they appear tough and take a hard line against Weyerhaeuser. As a result "they sort of flexed their muscles, and there was a lot of bad vibes." But it failed to deliver. Marleau noted that the CARC gave the local union $25,000 to prepare a business plan for the mill, with a promised second instalment of another $25,000, a necessary first step to find a buyer or go the route of employee ownership. The local union then handed this money over to the national CEP. But, Marleau insisted, "We never got any report. They never told us what they did with that money. All they'd say is that we had potential buyers, people who were willing to put up money. Okay, who are these people? They didn't say." The national union's failure to follow through led the CARC to refuse to pay the second instalment.

Mill workers eventually became disenchanted with their national union. Some thought that the union should have negotiated with Weyerhaeuser to win concessions on pensions or severance pay, instead of just focusing on reopening the mill. According to André Girard, "The union didn't give them a chance to do it, the union were just saying you can't close it … Sometimes you have to face facts and do the best you can with the situation. And I don't think they did." Girard's opinion is particularly telling, as he was one of the most active trade unionists in the mill. Daniel Olivier also thought that the union made a mistake trying to shame Weyerhaeuser: "They didn't know how to negotiate businesslike." Weyerhaeuser was under no obligation to sell it to them.

Others simply felt misled. One local union member noted that, when local members looked into buying the mill, their "national union got involved and told us to back off, they would take care of it all, for they supposedly had all the expertise and could be looking after all of it. To our dismay, the union got a consulting firm from Toronto that caused us nothing but grief."[107] One day, Percy Allary recalled, they came and said, "There is no more union, it's over." He sighed: "Nobody ever fought for us." Even Marcel Boudreau became disillusioned with the national CEP. "They are full of crap," he said bluntly, before adding a few other choice words. But Boudreau was also angry with others. He lamented that area residents "always blame it on the fact that Weyerhaeuser left town." In his mind, however, the politicians "*let* them leave town; they didn't do anything to prevent it! [For] crying out loud!" The sense of betrayal was palpable in the interviews, as mill workers lashed out at the company, their union, and the local community.

Conclusion

In March 2004, a little more than two months before the mill's demolition was slated to begin, Louis Benoit, representing former employees who were no longer identifying themselves as with the CEP, and Yvon Duhaime, vice-president of the West Nipissing Chamber of Commerce, made a final desperate plea to the town council to help purchase the mill.[108] Fifty-eight former employees had now agreed to contribute $10,000 each to finance the due diligence work needed to convince a financial backer to come on board. "We come before the Council of West Nipissing to ask for help," they began. Thanks to Duhaime, we have their presentation text, entitled "The Last Roll: Saving Our Local Economy, Preserving Our Environment, Building Partnerships." They called on council to join in a "last ditch effort to save the mill in Sturgeon Falls, a mill which has been part of this community for a century, a mill which is 100% viable, environmentally sound." They pleaded for a "joint venture" – using the language of the old partnership – with the town "to run the mill as it is, and further, to proceed with examining other product options."

It was, they insisted, "still an asset to the community." Although the mill was currently inoperative, the workforce was "ready and willing to go to work." They noted that Weyerhaeuser had already removed the skiving line, but otherwise everything was still intact. "The hour is late, and Weyerhaeuser had indicated that demolition will begin shortly. Once this demolition begins, all hope is lost." If there was any doubt about what decommissioning meant, "it means the total demolition of the mill. It will be flattened to the ground and all assets sold. All we will be left with is a field of rubble."[109]

Having established what was at stake, Louis Benoit went on to say that the mill workers now regretted their association with the national union, "which hurt us in our bid." Indeed, "Our local membership has been represented, in error, as argumentative and intractable." Benoit said that, at the time of the closure, the national CEP "told us they would take care of it," but this trust was broken: "It is the honest feeling of the local people that this was the biggest mistake we ever made. In all honesty, we had nowhere to go for leadership. The national directed us, and we followed suit, and this created animosity between workers, Weyerhaeuser, the municipality, and government officials." They now wished to "reverse this in any way possible." Benoit told the councillors that the CARC had given them $25,000 to develop a proper business plan, "which went to the national of the CEP to cultivate a letter of intent to purchase the mill. The national took that $25,000 and told the local they would take care of the matter. We were left looking like fools, and we accept and admit that. Consequently we've severed all ties with the national union and want nothing to do with them." Benoit ended this *mea culpa* with the realization that the municipality, not the national union, was truly "responsible for looking after all of West Nipissing."[110]

It was then left to Yvon Duhaime to make the case for belated action. Even now, the Chamber of Commerce saw the mill as an "entirely feasible opportunity."[111] Duhaime told those present: "It's almost as if everyone is hypnotized. The general public seems to believe that the mill is outdated, not viable, not environmentally sound, and that the employees are only self-interested. All these positions are untrue. We took it upon ourselves, fully realizing that the hour is extremely late, to make a last-ditch effort to throw our support behind this attempt at reconciliation and revitalization."[112] Duhaime thought that environmental groups in the province should be alerted to what was transpiring in Sturgeon Falls, as the mill's closure represented a blow against recycling. Finally, he told the town council that it was

> time we took charge of our own future. For too long we've been held to account by
> industry managed from outside the community ... We have a workforce which has

truly been humbled by current events, but still has the courage to come forward and petition for your help. The mindset is one of cooperation. We ask this council to look upon these people with a sympathetic heart. But more to the point, we ask this council to strike a committee to vigorously pursue the business potential which still exists, and which can be expanded upon. We are asking for your full partnership, your commitment to making every effort to maintain this industry.[113]

In his interview, councillor Yvon Marleau said: "We listened to their presentation, and we told them, 'well, okay.' They'd mentioned that they had potential backers and that they had potential buyers for the product." In response the council said it would help. For making this gesture of support, Marleau said, "Weyerhaeuser jumped on us." But time was short. In May the employee group filed its intention to purchase with Weyerhaeuser. "We don't know what else to do," Paul Couroux told the *Nugget*. "This is our last chance." On 28 May 2004 the news broke that the company had rejected the eleventh-hour bid, claiming that the decommissioning work was now too far along, with most of the equipment sold or transferred to other sites. A sale was no longer possible. "They never backed us," Couroux said.[114] And with that, "A lengthy battle to save this small town's largest industry has been lost."[115]

10

PROXIMITY AND DISTANCE

It was just like home. You know, you go to work … my brother was in the yard, my dad was in the hardboard … I had a cousin working with me in electrical, my brother, he used to work in the hardboard. I had uncles in the paint line … Every place you'd go in the mill, number one hardboard, number two hardboard, paint line… I had some relatives working there. So you'd stop here a couple of minutes, stop there a couple of minutes. Well, we could do that because we worked all over. Electrical can work all over, wherever you had to go … I mean, I saw everybody.

– Larry Shank, mill worker

For long-service workers, employment mobility or permanent relocation was understood to be a last resort in the months and years that followed the December 2002 closure of the Sturgeon Falls mill. This chapter offers both a sustained reflection on spatial and relational stances interviewees took in narrating their life stories in the immediate aftermath of deindustrialization and a contribution to the study of employment mobility in an increasingly post-industrial era. Among the dimensions of proximity and distance to be explored are the temporal proximity of the interview to the events being recounted, the perceived social proximity that prevailed before the mill closed, the remembered physical proximity of the mill in the narrated lives of residents, and, after the mill's closure, the spectre of forced relocation or distant daily commutes to new jobs in other towns and cities.

Forced employment mobility was a core concern for everyone we interviewed, not just for those who actually relocated or commuted to jobs found elsewhere.[1] Fear of having to move away in search of employment permeated the interviews, influencing how our interviewees understood and composed their life stories.[2] This fear had the disciplinary effect of lowering people's expectations not only of a good union wage but also a job nearby. As Jefferson Cowie notes in *Capital Moves*, capital's command of spatial relations is an important weapon in management's arsenal.[3] This advantage, however, extends beyond capital mobility to forced labour mobility as well. As sociologist Beverley Skeggs notes more generally, "[m]obility and control over mobility both reflects and reinforce power. Mobility is a resource to which not everyone has an equal relationship."[4]

The Proximity of the Interview

The close temporal proximity of the mill's closure – it had *just* happened – was evident throughout the interviews, as displaced workers and their families struggled to make sense of what was happening to them. Emotions were often raw, and some workers told us how they frantically searched the Internet looking for answers. Almost daily, rumours swept through the community about the company, the municipality, or about the appearance of a potential buyer for the mill. Would Weyerhaeuser even agree to sell the mill, or would it go ahead and demolish it? It was an emotional roller coaster. The oral history interviews we conducted recorded the changing moment, not some distantly remembered event. Interviewees often seemed uncertain if they should use the past or present tense in speaking of their recent experiences. When does the present end and the past begin? The vulnerability of the paper workers was most visible, perhaps, when they spoke of their current struggles to make ends meet and of their feelings of uncertainty and powerlessness. Working-class masculinity in Northern Ontario, like elsewhere, discourages men from showing their vulnerability.[5] Anger sometimes comes easier. As a result, their emotional fragility was often implied by the presence of spouses who hovered nearby ready to provide words of encouragement and support. Several couples were interviewed as part of this project. The close proximity of the interview to the events being recounted thus served to blur the usual distinctions in historical research between what is past and what is present.

Hot flashes of anger or anguish punctuated the interviews. Sometimes all it took was the mere mention of the name of the departing company: "Weyerhaeuser." Many interviewees still had to "get the anger out of their gut."[6] Here is an extract from our interview with Denis MacGregor:

Marcel Boudreau, who worked on the paper machine, 2005. Photograph by David W. Lewis.

What do I think about Weyerhaeuser, is that what you wanted to know? Hate them with a passion. They've changed my way of life. They don't give a shit about us. And like they said, it was a "corporate decision," and it's easy for a "corporate deci-sion" because it's in Washington. They don't want us. You're destroying somebody's livelihood, ah, get out ... I wear this [holding up his company ring with a big "W" inscribed on it] because I'm proud to wear it. Not because it's Weyerhaeuser, but because it's thirty years of service, good service. They made me live for thirty years, I can't take that away from them. Weyerhaeuser wasn't with us for very long, and I think that's why they did it that way. Had they been able to let us go within two months, they would have done it. But I think they couldn't. They were having a hard time. We were making money. We had a contract. It's not as if we were losing money. We were making five, six hundred thousand dollars a month. And we had a contract 'til September 2003 and they let us go December 2002. And that's one of the reasons we really hate them, because a lot of the guys, the average age at the mill was forty-seven or forty-eight. So the guys that would have gone for another year were that much closer to their pension. I was fifty-one when I got laid off. I had to go to fifty-five. Now I'm fifty-two ... my birthday's in March. So I have three years that I have to fill. How I'm going to fill it? Fifty-two I'm not moving. Fifty-two nobody wants you. I've got a bad leg, which I picked up at the mill. I'm a heart patient, I'm a diabetic. Who wants me? You know? I'm not complaining, I'm just saying that that's the way it is.[7]

Anger and hurt animated many of the other interviews as well. Bruce Colquhoun noted that there was a great deal of "doom and gloom and a lot of anger – anger toward Weyerhaeuser that will never go away."[8] Naturally these feelings led many to decline to be interviewed: nearly half, in fact – a far higher rate of "rejection" than I have encountered elsewhere. Some expressed fear that they might say something that could jeopardize the then-ongoing efforts to reopen the mill. Nobody wanted to be blamed for frightening away a potential investor or convincing Weyerhaeuser not to sell the closed mill. Mike Lacroix told us: "People are afraid to speak up. They're afraid to get into trouble for speaking up. I don't care. I don't care anymore. We've been screwed over enough there, I don't care anymore. What's gotta be said is gonna be said."[9]

Our university affiliation provided us with a certain level of legitimacy. Even so, there were small challenges. One former mill worker, who preferred to be interviewed in our university offices, checked to see if we were using Weyerhaeuser paper in our printer when he came into the room. He later admitted that he would have terminated the interview had he found any. Quite unusually the video recording of most of the interviews began with the signing of the consent form. The resulting recording captured some of the negotiations and "framing" conversations that usually occurred before the official *interview* even began. The recording of this pre-interview stage, lasting ten or fifteen minutes, revealed a great deal about the unfolding context. Interviewees repeatedly asked us questions: Who was behind the project? Did we have anything to do with the departing company? If we had, several made clear that they did not want to have anything more to do with us. The recording of pre-interview chit-chat and the signing of the consent form likewise allowed us to record the transition to the official interview. People often tensed up. André Cartier, for example, sat in an office chair with his legs crossed, sipping a cup of coffee. After some small talk with student-interviewer Kristen O'Hare, he glanced at the camera, took a deep breath, and asked: "What do you need?"[10] With this question, the formal interview began.

The Proximity of Everyday Lives before the Closure

In our life-story approach to interviewing, we asked our interviewees to frame their experience of job loss and factory closure within the *longue durée* of a life lived and remembered. This long view placed the closing within the context of the "before" and "after," as it was now remembered in the immediate aftermath of deindustrialization. Mill workers and their locally rooted managers thus spoke of growing up, attending school, applying for work, and getting hired on at the mill.

Despite its ups and downs, including a devastating sixteen-year closure between 1930 and 1946, the mill represented a relatively "stable workplace culture" that was "intelligible to both its established members and those being socialized into it."[11] As they struggled with present-day instability and future uncertainty, interviewees looked back on their working lives before the mill's closing "as settled, fixed, rounded, and intelligible."[12] This was to be expected. As Sean Field notes in another context, people who have experienced forced displacement or removal often "compress" their predisplacement memories into an "undifferentiated 'that time,' as opposed to the present. The memory strategies contribute to an exaggerated sense of community before forced removals."[13] From the vantage point of the deindustrialized present, the industrial past appeared to be – now more than ever – locally rooted and secure to our interviewees.

For the most part we interviewed people in their homes. This decision served to locate the past in close physical proximity to the present when people pointed next door, down the street, or across town to where they grew up. A few grew up in the very home in which they were being interviewed. Childhood memories were almost always nearby. Brian Laflèche told us that his mother lived so close that he "could throw a snowball at her house."[14] Marcel Boudreau's mother was born "two houses from here [points] … My uncle lives in the house, there, now … And my mother as a young child played in this house with the kids that used to live here, many, many years ago." Interviewees sometimes joked that they had not travelled far in their lifetime. Born in 1936 in a house just down the street from where he was being interviewed in 2004, Larry Shank laughed, "I didn't go very far, did I?"

When asked to recount their life "before" the closing, former mill workers emphasized the closeness of social relations and their own deep roots within the community. "Everybody knew everybody," recalled Percy Allary.[15] So, when a name came up in conversation, "you weren't talking about a stranger." Others made similar kinds of comments. Denis MacGregor, for example, said, "Everybody knows everybody's name, they know the dog's name." Those moving to Sturgeon Falls to work in the mill quickly recognized this reality. As a newly arrived manager, Gerry Stevens learned not to "say anything about anybody, because they're probably related." Geographic and social proximity thus animated people's memories of their life before the 2002 mill closure.

Many interviewees reminded us that they worked with friends and family. Percy Allary, for one, emphasized the many friendships he had in the mill: "Yeah, don't forget we were all out of high school when we went there, and we were all young, so we all hung out at the bars after and on days off. And, you know, you end up being [with] your friends, and you end up being the best man at their weddings.

And when their kids come along, he's your godchild, that's your godchild. So everybody had their own scene, like their own group. You had your friends." He noted that some friendship networks centred on hunting and fishing, others on sports. They grew up together, went to school together, and worked together. In fact, you "spent more time with the guys at work than you do with your own family. So you know them a lot better than, probably, your own family." For many, their working life inside the mill began in their late teens when they were first hired on as a summer student or upon graduation from high school.

The close physical proximity of the mill itself was evident in the recorded interviews, even as people recalled their childhood and school years. Asked what it meant for the town to lose its mill, Bruce Colquhoun responded that the mill had been there since 1898: "You know, you look all the way down John Street, you look west down John Street, and you see the mill. It's right … you see it there. Now it's gone. And while it was being torn down, there were a lot of guys from the mill watching that, sitting in the car looking at that. Couldn't believe it. It's like most of the town couldn't believe it. They're tearing it down? Why?"

The physical presence of the mill loomed particularly large for interviewees who grew up in "the Point," the neighbourhood that adjoined the mill, on the west side of the Sturgeon River. The rest of the town stands on the other side of the bridge. As a child, Larry Shank remembered playing clandestinely in the mill yard: "You played at night, there used to be big chip piles and stuff like that. You'd go climb the piles, but you weren't supposed to, it was dangerous. And there were log piles too, eh? Four-foot-long pulp [logs], great big piles of that. And we used to play in there. That was real dangerous. Like, in those days, the mill, the people at the mill, they were close knit. Everybody knew everybody, so there was no guy at the gate there with a gun. The mill was the town, and we were the town. It's changed. It did change during the years."[16] Lawrence Pretty played on the same chip pile in his youth, taking turns flipping off the top of it. In a way, he never left: "I went into work and stayed there. Thirty-eight years later I come out."[17]

If the mill's physicality loomed large in the memories of our interviewees, the sounds of the mill also resonated later in life. When the mill was still in operation, Marcel Boudreau could hear all kinds of mill sounds from his home in the Point – it was always in the background. He could hear mill operations especially at night: "You would be sitting here and you hear [the] alarm go off, it was a paper break. I would be here, [and] say 'Uh, they're losing money right now because they are not making paper, they gotta go and start over again.' … Now, obviously, you don't get any of these [sounds]." Boudreau also recalled that, for many years, the mill's whistle sounded the shift changes, but "then people complained" and they stopped the practice in the 1990s. The silencing of the whistle was not coincidental: by then, many of the people within earshot of the whistle no longer had a connection to the plant.

Former mill workers and their families measured the value of their job in various ways. First, it was the highest-paying job available for blue-collar workers. Consistently the point of comparison was with manual jobs that paid less. Second, the mill was said to offer workers greater security than did other jobs: it was unionized, so layoffs and promotions were governed by seniority. It also provided year-round employment. Third, the job was located in the town; many interviewees prized its geographic proximity. In speaking of his paper-making father, for example, André Cartier noted that the money was good – much more than other working-class jobs in the area paid: "That part was good. The only thing is, he was in shift work, [so] sometimes we missed him. But it wasn't far from home. It's not like having to travel, like being a trucker or being out of town for a week." We will return to the issue of employment mobility a little later.

As the town's major employer, and the one that paid the highest wages, the mill and its proximity made it difficult for young people *not* to follow older family members into the mill. The "hiring stories" our interviewees shared indicate that the gravitational force of the mill was considerable for the next generation of mill families. Working at the mill provided young people with the opportunity to stay in the community, according to Larry Shank: "Well. You were just happy to have a job … not to have to start looking. And, well, younger people, like I said, it didn't bother them. If you're young, you go. But once you're old enough, and you bought a house or you got this and you got that, and the kids are at school, well, you don't want to get up and leave. You know, you want to stay." Others concurred. Bruce Colquhoun "didn't want to go anywhere else." Nor did Denis MacGregor: "To tell you the truth, I've been here all my life, so that sort of shows you that I didn't want to leave. And [then] the opportunity of working at the mill came up [claps]. I was done for life, I thought." The caveat tucked in at the end reminded us that working lives are recalled with the knowledge of what followed.

For his part, Larry Shank remembered that he did not know where he wanted to work when he finished school in 1956. The mill was the best-paying job, locally, at least for those without a university degree. Shank had uncles working there, as well as his brothers, his father, and cousins. His wife's side of the family also worked there. "I didn't see them running away, so probably I figured, you know, it's gonna be all right. In June I got a job there, and if I wouldn't have liked it I would have moved on … But I didn't have to. I always liked what I did." When Shank was hired, he did not need to buy a car: "Two blocks, I'd walk over. You know, no expense."

Wages were relatively good, so Shank "never had to leave. That's why I stayed here forty-one years."

Asked if they wanted to work in the mill as a teenager, several interviewees expressed some ambivalence. For example, Harold Stewart laughed softly when he responded to our question:

> Well, to start off with, no. I thought I was going to get a job in some far-off place and make all kinds of money. But it didn't turn out like that. No, I started working at the mill when I was nineteen. And it was supposed to be temporary, I thought. But, you know, when you start to work and you start to gain a little bit of seniority, and you can start to get holidays, and then you buy a car, and you've got payments to make, and, hey, it's pretty hard to leave. And [nodding his head] for a small town, the mill paid pretty well. You know? About the best-paying job in town. And I was close to work ... I could be at work in ten minutes. And I knew a lot of the guys – well, pretty near all of them.

Larry Shank made a similar point in his interview: "These were steady, good-paying jobs with benefits ... year-round." Continuing, he noted: "We built this house in 1960 and the mill was always here, two blocks away. I worked there all my [life]. I liked my job. I liked the guys I worked with. I liked the guys I worked for. And when I was a little further up the line, I was trying to make sure that they liked me, too." Their relatively high wages and steady, year-round employment was sometimes a cause for jealousy in Sturgeon Falls on the part of those who earned less, worked seasonally, or had to commute to their job. As Harold Stewart observed, "They [the mill workers] were making good money, just ten minutes from home. They didn't know how lucky they were."

This belated realization was not necessarily the case for first-generation mill workers, who emphasized the fact that the mill offered wage rates far superior to anything they had seen previously. Karen Beaudette, for example, came from a family that could not afford to pay for her post-secondary education. "And that was understood," she recalled. "Then I got pregnant, got married, and [then] menial job, menial job, menial job. And then, '87, I went back to college [to become] an accountant."[18] After graduating, she handed out dozens of resumes in the area and found work in North Bay, a thirty-minute drive east of Sturgeon Falls. Four months later she got a phone call from her college teacher, who told her: "'Karen, there's a job in Sturgeon, I'm going to send your resume.' I didn't even send my resume. She sent it for me. And they phoned me and I had an interview the next week and got the job, started January 2nd." The new dream job, of course, was at the mill: "I hadn't ever seen money like that before, big money. I was working at nine dollars an hour, and then to start somewhere like sixteen was, like, 'wow,' and it's close to home. Yeah. It was great." Later in the interview, she spoke with real pride of how her mill wages helped put her own children through college.

Relocation and Employment Mobility

The spectre of forced relocation or long commuting times pervaded the interviews we conducted in Sturgeon Falls. Given all the uncertainty, the former proximity and solidity of the mill loomed large in the minds of the interviewees. Many commented that they could ill-afford to move: their spouses had a full- or part-time job, they owned their home, and their friends and families lived in Sturgeon Falls. Many spoke fondly of the pleasure they got from weekend hunting or fishing, and noted that this would be impossible if they moved "down south." Their regional identity as "Northerners" and as working-class men often asserted itself in these moments. In Northern Ontario, working-class masculinities are very much anchored in a persistent industrial culture as well as in outdoor recreation. The towns there are "workingmen's towns," where men wear work boots and drive pickup trucks.[19] Our interviews confirmed that work occupied a central part of our interviewees' lives, but, as Arthur McIvor found in the United Kingdom, work has changed in "complex and sometimes contradictory ways."[20]

The fear of forced relocation loomed over our conversations. Many interviewees noted that former mill workers were already leaving town, particularly skilled tradesmen who had found work elsewhere. These departure stories indicated that mill workers were intensely aware that some skills were more transferable than others. Pierre Hardy estimated that 90 per cent of the mill's tradesmen quickly found work out of town: "Whatever trade they were in, they found work out of town. But for the average mill worker, I can't really say, but I don't think [they have found work in the past year]." A number of interviewees mentioned two tradesmen who found work at Weyerhaeuser's sawmill in Wawa, on Lake Superior, northwest of Sault Ste Marie. The rest of them "could have submitted their applications, too," noted Percy Allary, "but then again, who was going to move?" Those who formerly tended the mill's paper machine had no illusions about finding another job as a paper maker: there was none.

Cautionary tales were also in circulation about the experience of these men in Wawa. Denis MacGregor, for one, noted that those who went to work for Weyerhaeuser in Wawa were

> blackballed there because they're from Sturgeon, and the people from Wawa want jobs and "my brother-in-law's not working because you're here." So, besides having to

work with the stress of being laid off and then having to move all the way over there, then the guys blackball you because you're taking their brother-in-law's job. And then your family's in Sturgeon, you're in Wawa, you're travelling back and forth to see your family, and you don't know if you're doing the right thing because you didn't buy at the other end and this and that ... And slowly, I guess, he integrated into the group, because time heals all sorts of [things] and the families moved up.

For his part, Raymond Marcoux noted that he bumped into one of those who moved to Wawa when he returned to Sturgeon Falls to sell his house. The man told Marcoux that Weyerhaeuser's Wawa sawmill was non-union, and that the company kept trying to "brainwash" employees there that unions were bad.[21] Most of the man's new co-workers were young men who did not know any better. In both of these stories, and others like it, we were given to understand that it was a difficult move for everyone involved. Such stories cautioned listeners about the perils of leaving, but also reassured them that staying was the right thing to do. Sturgeon Falls was where they belonged.

If the number of mill workers who actually relocated during the first two years was limited to a handful of skilled tradesmen, the fear of being forced to look for work elsewhere was intensely felt by those who could not yet retire. Asked if they saw themselves leaving Sturgeon Falls one day, Pierre and Jane Hardy answered in tandem:

> JANE: Oh, possibility's out there.
> PIERRE: We don't know.
> JANE: We don't know.
> PIERRE: We don't know what's going to happen.
> JANE: You know?

Jane noted that, in the year and three days since the mill closed, her husband had already applied for jobs elsewhere: "And if something was to come through he'd probably go to work out of town. Whether we would relocate, well, that would remain to be seen." Pierre then noted that he had only eight years left "to my pension ... I could tough it out." Many other long-service workers also spoke of toughing it out to retirement.

After the mill closed, Raymond Marcoux started to look for work in the area. He had received severance pay and was eligible for employment insurance benefits: "I lived on that for a while 'til I ran out." His wife, who worked part time for "many years" because "she wanted to," later "found a job, where she works full time now."

The mill under demolition, 2004. Photograph by David W. Lewis.

Actually, she now worked "full time and part time to make ends meet." He did not want to pick up and move, as he was "too old to relocate." He owned his own house and rented out a second one, which brought in some revenue. It would therefore be difficult to leave Sturgeon Falls. Shrugging, he added that, "my wife's working, she has a good job, so what do I do?" Yet to accept a likely drop to one-third or one-half of his former wage locally was hardly appealing: "There's no work in Sturgeon. Very little work," and what there is paid low wages. "I'm used to making big money," he admitted. Asked if it was easier for their wives to find employment than male mill employees, Marcoux replied in the affirmative: "Yes, yes. A lot of the spouses were working prior to the closure. Some of them part time, a few had good jobs working in North Bay … Some were working in town … So a lot of them were working – I'd say at least 60 to 75 per cent of the employees there, the spouses were working either part time or full time." Marcoux concluded: "It'd be too difficult for them to relocate. And it's very difficult to relocate once you've been living there so long … just pack up and leave. Most people had their house paid off. It's hard for them to sell and leave, because we're Northerners. You know, sure there's work down south, but it's hard, being [a] Northerner, to move south."

Unimpressed with these stark choices, nine of the mill workers – Raymond Marcoux included – registered for an "oil and gas" course at the local community college. Marcoux noted that Weyerhaueser had "something set up" a few months after the closure to "help people with their resumes, to find work and stuff like that." The union "got after Weyerhaeuser" to fund it, which is how he found out about the course. This was the first year that the college was offering the full course. At the time of his interview, Marcoux was taking two courses to get his certification as an oil and gas technician: "half my week is oil, the other half is gas," he said. Once certified, he hoped to start his own business and start contracting in the area. "At my age, I can start getting my reduced pension at fifty-five, which will be in four years … If I start contracting, stay small, and draw my pension for a few years, I should be all right." He preferred to stay small to reduce the red tape. He was hopeful once his course ended: "I'll start looking around North Bay, and Sturgeon Falls, and maybe Sudbury, but I won't relocate." Laughing, he also noted that he was an excellent carpenter, as his father had been. He had already done some carpentry jobs around town since the mill closed – it "kept us going, really."

André Cartier was another mill worker who sought retraining, this time as a nurse. Even getting into the program was a remarkable achievement, worthy of repeating here. On 11 October 2002, three days after the mill's closing was announced, Cartier signed up for adult education to finish high school in order to qualify for the nursing course. Laughing at the memory, he recalled that, in those last two months in the mill, he had to bring his homework in with him. Smiling, he repeated the date, 11 October, with real pride. He had just got into the nursing program at the community college: "I had grade 10 and I needed my grade 12, biology, chemistry, and all that, and the nursing course started in September, September 4th, and I got my grade 12 two weeks before that." To do this, "a lot of time I was doing homework before the sun come up." Eleven subjects had to be completed, starting in October – one per month: "Well, I worked!" Asked when he realized that he wanted to become a nurse, Cartier quickly replied: "I knew I wanted to do the nursing [because] every time … there was first aid, CPR, and all that, they always interested me. [I] always signed up for first aid, CPR, stuff like that … My wife's a [nurse]. Reading her books and all that. By the way, two of my buddies in '91, when they lost their jobs when they shut down the hardboard operation, they took the course and they worked at the site, doing good. So I just went."

Bruce Colquhoun quickly retooled, as a driving instructor. In August 2002 he foresaw that the mill was going to close from a Weyerhaeuser publication that promised major cuts in their division. As Colquhoun told it, he asked a co-worker whose wife once worked as a driving instructor if she had liked it:

He said, "Oh, she loved it." I asked him a question one day, a few weeks later I asked him another question. And then on October the 7th, I asked him, I said, "Why did she quit doing that job?" He told me why. And then he says, "Why are you asking me all these questions for?" I said, "'Cause you never know what's going to happen with this damn mill." An hour later, he's walking around giving everybody in the shop a paper. Show up at the Cache Bay community centre tomorrow, 'cause they're gonna make a big announcement. So they made the announcement. And I went home and told my wife. She went into a bit of a panic. Me too. Then, she said, "Well, call," … I said, "no, I don't want to be rejected anymore. I'm not in the mood for someone to say 'No, you're not getting it.'" Two weeks later my wife came up and said, "Here's the damn phone book. There's her number. Call her now!" "Fine. Get you off my back." My daughter's sitting here, my wife's here, and I'm here [indicates side by side with hands] on the couch. Got the cordless and I called. I said, "Hi, I'm Bruce Colquhoun, this is what's happening at the mill, and I'm wondering if you need a new driving instructor?" And she says, "Oh, perfect timing … the one we have now for West Nipissing wants to get back to North Bay." I said, "You're kidding." So we talked, I'm looking at my wife, I'm going like this [thumbs up]. Kathy and my wife, Sue, are just freaking out, eh? "Dad's got a job!" So then I had to meet with her that week. It was on the Friday, I met with her [at] eleven-thirty, we got out of there at two o'clock. And when we talked on the phone, at first she said, "I want to meet with you, I want to know that I can trust [you]." And I said, "When will I know?" She said, "You'll know the day of the meeting." Okay, so I went to North Bay. She said, "I feel like a coffee. What do you feel like? Do you want a coffee?" I said, "I've had nothing to eat or drink all day." She says, "Why not?" I said, "I'm too nervous." My first interview in thirty years, you know? I said, "I'm a nervous wreck." She says, "How are you feeling now?" "Oh, okay, I'll have a coffee." So we finished the coffee [and] she said, "You're hired. Go to school and take the course and you're hired. I'll hire you."

When he got back, Bruce Colquhoun had to prove to Weyerhaeuser that it was a real job offer in order to get them to pay for part of his training course. In January 2003 he took a month-long course in Ottawa, and started his new job: "And [I've] been doing it ever since. Two and a half years. And now I got a job I love." Even so, years later, he returned to the mill's hydroelectric power house, now operated by the city. There, mill seniority still prevails, and he was eventually called back to work.

Conclusion

Other interviewees were not as fortunate, and had to commute long distances to new jobs in other towns and cities. Before the mill closed, Karen Beaudette earned $25 or $26 per hour at the mill. "That's pretty good," she noted. "I'm making twelve dollars an hour now." She found work in Sudbury, but after eight months decided it was too far to drive each day, with winter coming: "I was getting stressed out, 'cause

I wasn't sleeping at night worrying about 'Can I get to work tomorrow?' Then at work I was stressed out about, 'Oh, I gotta drive home.'"

For his part, Marcel Boudreau was interviewed first in December 2003 and then again in June 2005. The two conversations allowed us to track his changing situation. He got hired on at the mill two or three years out of high school. In time, he went from earning seven dollars an hour to twenty dollars as a machine tender, "the top job on the paper machine." Asked in the first interview if he was considering moving away from Sturgeon Falls, he replied in the affirmative:

> Yes, I am. I've applied for a job up at Temagami. Temagami Forest Products. That new mill that, I guess, was announced, probably, about a month ago, month and a half ago … Made the front pages of the *Nugget*, there in North Bay. I've applied there. And if they hire me, I'll call my brother: "Get your ad in the window here and sell my house." He's told me there's some nice places for sale up in Temagami. And I've been up there probably four or five times, fishing. And Temagami's not a bad place to live. It's better than being down in that rat race down in Toronto, where you risk a chance of getting shot, you know? I don't want to live down south. It's too mental. I mean, I've lived in a small town most of my life … If I had to go down south, I think maybe it would be London or something like that. But there's no way I'm going to Toronto, Hamilton. Leave that for the freaks down there. I don't want nothing to do with that."

In our second interview, we learned that Boudreau had found work in the village of Sundridge, south of North Bay. They wanted him to start immediately, but he told them that he could not start that soon, as he had "to borrow a vehicle just to go down there for the interview." He had always worked in Sturgeon Falls, within walking distance. He had never needed a vehicle until then. They gave him a week to purchase one.

In his new job, Marcel Boudreau worked twelve-hour shifts from Friday through Sunday. He had to leave home at 4:20 a.m. to arrive at work at 6:00 a.m. It was a ninety-minute commute each way. It was tough work: "I hadn't had to do manual labour in a long, long time. It was a shock to my system." As he was about to be laid off, he found full-time factory work in North Bay, which was considerably closer. But the wage was only half what he made at the Sturgeon Falls mill. He liked the fact that the twelve-hour shifts reduced the amount of commuting, though it was sometimes difficult driving in the winter months: "I was fed up, but it's not a bad place to work. I mean it's [an] industrial setting, and I am used to that, and shift work doesn't bother me." But he had been "comfortable" at the Sturgeon Falls mill and "enjoying

Small reminders after the demolition: two tall shrubs stand in front of what once were the mill's main offices. Photograph by David W. Lewis.

what I was doing. I just entered my peak earning years – another ten years I would have been retired." In all, four of the mill workers were now at the North Bay factory. According to Boudreau, they "went from making rolls of paper to rolls of fabric. Do I like the job? No, not really. Prefer making paper, but ..." [trails off]. He also found his old job at the mill "a lot less stressful." "I am still not comfortable ... almost a year on and, well, I feel a lot better doing it. It took a long time." He did not want to move to North Bay as the payments on his house mortgage were less than what he would be paying for rent there. So he commuted. He then mentioned, again, how his mother used to play in his home when she was a child.

Reflecting further on his situation, Marcel Boudreau noted that it was hard not to think of "what ifs." He used to make $50,000 to $60,000 a year, "and I lived two minutes' walk from work. I didn't have to travel two hundred, three hundred miles to go to work." He also no longer felt secure in his employment: "No, no, I don't feel secure. It's an American-owned company, so anything can happen." In the face of rumours, he told his North Bay co-workers: "Just because you're making money doesn't mean a damn thing. If they say you're gonna shut down, you're gonna shut down ... Ain't a goddamn thing you can do about it." If the place shut down, there was "not a chance" that he would picket it as he had in Sturgeon Falls: "Not a chance; I am not driving to North Bay every day just to go to the picket line." The Sturgeon Falls mill closing had changed him. At one time he thought that he would spend his entire working life in the mill, and despite everything he still considered himself "a paper maker. I'm proud of it … Local 1735. CEP. And I make paper for a living."

SALVAGING HISTORY

You know what's too bad about the mill in Sturgeon? There's so much history. It's like taking a page out of history and closing the door, you know?

– Marc Côté

The demolition of the Sturgeon Falls mill began on 1 June 2004. Demolition crews started with the newest parts of the plant and worked towards the oldest, visibly turning back the clock. Restoration Environmental Contractors, based in Southern Ontario, got the contract to demolish the mill and provide environmental abatement.[1] Inside, the more modern equipment was sold off. The OCC facility, paid for by Ontario taxpayers and community investors, was shipped off to destination unknown – some said it was to the United States. The skiving line was also sold, probably to a buyer in the Caribbean. Other machinery was scrapped. A few weeks after the demolition began, the *Tribune* wrote that the "sounds of collapsing metal echoed through the streets of downtown Sturgeon Falls." It was a "chilling" noise to residents, "crushing any hopes of resurrecting the mill."[2] Paul Couroux told the *Tribune* that workers had "tossed around the idea" of "stopping the dismantling for one day, or going with signs, but I don't think the former employees are up to it anymore, they just want to walk away."[3] It had been a tough two years, a roller coaster of emotion and heightened anxiety.

The demolition also proved to be one of the most emotionally fraught topics broached in the oral history interviews. The reaction of mill workers was mixed. Once the mill closed, Hubert Gervais shifted his focus to documenting

The mill, demolished; Hubert Gervais generously allowed me to copy all of his more than one thousand photographs of the remains. Courtesy of Hubert Gervais.

the demolition with his own camera. Over the six months it took the company to demolish the mill completely, leaving the mill's hydroelectric plant and a big hole in the ground, Hubert took an astonishing 1,400 photographs of the mill.[4] He began taking pictures from outside the fence in July 2004, returning each day. One day he entered the mill property through the front gate. The security guard, who had been there while the mill was active, let him through after he explained that he was taking pictures for "the book" – the mill history binder. "Sure, go ahead, take all the pictures," she replied. As he walked onto the site, a contractor's truck came up to him and he was asked his business. He was then invited to trade access to the site for the right to use his images in company promotion.[5] He accepted: "I was there every day. From the [time] they started to the time they quit [in November 2004]." Gervais decided not to go the day they demolished the main office, but had someone take pictures for him. On the day the giant stack was toppled, Gervais took a piece of the rubble as a souvenir.

Marcel Labbé also watched the demolition crews at work, but from his parked car outside the fence. The mill's smokestack had special significance for him: "What we're watching is the chimney. You know, the tall chimney. When that goes down that will mean something because that's where we worked. It's bad."[6] Others likewise paid careful attention to areas of the plant where they had worked, but it was getting more and more difficult to pick them out among the wreckage. "All the memories are going," lamented Henri Labelle. When they were tearing it down, he and other former co-workers "were looking, saying, 'where was I before?' You even lose, it's so hard to comprehend where we were, where the shop was before, and everything else … I thought we would see it all the time. It would always be there." Ruth Thompson agreed: "It was like another era gone by. Now it is going to be torn down, just like part of your life is being ripped away. That's how I felt."

Not every former mill employee wished to witness the demolition. As can be imagined, the mill's demolition unleashed strong emotions. "When I stopped by on Ottawa Street on the far side of the mill and [took] some pictures," recalled Bruce Colquhoun, "I met with some of the older guys there who are retired. One guy looked up at me who was sitting in his car. I went over and talked to him, and he says, 'you know, Bruce, I never thought I'd live to see the day that they'd tear that mill down.' Then, tears are coming down. He says, 'I gotta go.' He took off. I never thought I'd see that place taken down either."[7] Most interviewees were repelled by the sight of the mill's demolition. Pierre Hardy, for one, avoided setting his eyes on the mill as it was being torn down. "I wanted to see the mill as it was," he confided. This was not an easy task in a town as small as Sturgeon Falls. Other workers looked, but did not like what they saw. Mike Lacroix told us his father still swore every time he passed the mill site, such was his anger. Randy Restoule also found it hard to watch. He recalled driving by the closed mill one time, talking "to this older gentleman, and he says 'back in the fifties,' he says, 'we built that.' It was hard for him to see that, and you could see that he was mad or frustrated … I didn't say too much to him."

In July 2004, in one final act of resistance, Mike Lacroix successfully halted demolition for a week when he filed a formal complaint that the demolition company was not following proper procedure in removing asbestos. The company's failure to install an air-monitoring system to detect asbestos dust was particularly troubling, as there were houses nearby.[8] The story was picked up by newspapers across the province.[9] To counter this bad-news story, Don Bremner, vice-president of operations of the demolition company, attributed the order to sour grapes: "There's a lot of negative public feeling and animosity about the closing and now demolition of this plant by former employees in the community."[10] The demolition soon restarted, however, and by November the mill had all but vanished. Marcel Boudreau remembered that, near the end, the old dryer cans from the paper machine were "just sitting there" in the empty field: "I mean I spent twenty-plus years working right *there*. The rest of the time I was in and out [of] different places in the mill, but most of my time [was] in that mill. I was right there at the paper machine – worked my way up from the bottom right to the top job." He still felt angry "at what was done to this town."

Despite its demolition, the mill's imprint on the land remains visible. The old chain-link fence continues to ring the site, now an empty field. There are also small reminders of what once stood there. Some of the landscaping undertaken by a former mill manager, a point of some derision in the interviews, outlasted the mill itself. There is also the guard hut at the main entrance, the employees' parking lot, and the access road on the property. The mill's hydro dam continues to operate. As Tim Edensor notes, the "attempted erasure of the past is incomplete and the hosts have now been consigned to dark corners, attics, and drawers, or been swept away, reinterpreted, and recontextualized."[11] If the main site has not yet been recontextualized, this is not the case across Cache Bay Road, where the North Yard once stood. Where they used to pile the pulp wood, there are now new suburban houses. Cheaper house values have encouraged people working in North Bay and Sudbury to reside in Sturgeon Falls. In the aftermath of the mill's closure and demolition, the town has become a bedroom community.

But there is more to this erasure than physical demolition. The departing company also shredded a century's worth of production records that were formerly housed in the "archive building" located at the base of the mill's water tower. Other documents were trucked away to destinations unknown – some said to Vancouver or Calgary, others thought that the boxes were sent to Weyerhaeuser's headquarters in Washington state. Not surprisingly, I got nowhere when I asked the company. Hubert Gervais told us there had been "boxes and boxes and boxes." He lamented that the company "should have come to us, the two [mill] historians, Bruce Colquhoun and myself, because there is a lot of files, old files, that they threw out, which was part of [our] history." For Gervais, "they threw out an awful lot when they closed the mill. I just couldn't believe it ... Why didn't they leave it here?" This is a very good question: Weyerhaeuser was there for three years of the mill's lifespan of 104 years – whose history was it? Perhaps the most evocative example of history's becoming a visible part of the struggle was when the company attempted to get its shredding van into the closed plant. As we heard, workers turned it away, but it returned, and all that history was shredded.

Enforced forgetting is an integral part of the deindustrialization process. Historian Jackie Clarke, who has studied deindustrialization in France, notes that invisibility can be understood not as "total disappearance, but [as] various forms of marginalisation, occlusion and disqualification from the mainstream political and media discourses."[12] As historian Robert Bevan reminds us, "[d]emolition has often been deployed to break up concentrations of resistance among the populace."[13] In

The building below the water tower apparently held the mill's century-old archive of production records, documents that were later shredded or shipped out to destinations unknown, 2004. Photograph by David W. Lewis.

such cases history itself is targeted. It is another way to dominate, terrorize, divide, or eradicate an enemy. Although Bevan is speaking in terms of ethnic cleansing, he does make the connection to deindustrialization. This, too, is an act of cultural erasure. Buildings gather meanings over time, and as long as they stand they represent a constant invitation to remember. Their demolition cuts this lingering connection. "To lose all that is familiar – the destruction of one's environment," Bevan writes, "can mean a disorienting exile from the memories they have invoked."[14]

This chapter considers the physical and historical erasure that accompanies deindustrialization. The mill's demolition and the shredding of its records, some dating back to the 1920s, were acts of enforced forgetting. Yet Weyerhaeuser was not entirely successful in erasing the mill's history. Although we found bits and pieces in public archives in Canada, the United States, and the United Kingdom, this book is based on the recounted working lives of our interviewees and the documentation *they* recovered: a box here, a file there – thousands of pages' worth. We have relied on this material throughout this study. One of my favourite stories came

Demolition workers; Hubert Gervais won access to the site to take his daily pictures by agreeing to take promotional photos for the demolition company as well. Photograph by Hubert Gervais.

from Hubert Gervais, who recounted how the employee newsletter was spirited out of the dying mill. It had to be done quietly, as the mill manager had forbidden its donation to the local museum. One day, when the manager was out of town, Gervais was told by another staff member to drive his vehicle up to the door, where the historical contraband was handed to him.

Much of the motivation for writing this book originated in my desire to respond to the company's wanton destruction of working-class memory, but I was also inspired by the historical labour of two former mill workers. Hubert Gervais and Bruce Colquhoun spent years researching the history of the mill for its 1998 centenary, gathering newspaper clippings, photographs, and facts into a mill history binder – the biggest binder I have ever seen. This giant memory book testifies to the strength of workers' attachment to the mill and to their sense of collective belonging. With the closure, however, the binder has become something more. In the aftermath of the closure, the binder circulated among former workers, enabling them to revisit their former lives in the mill or to show visiting relatives or a grandchild what it was like to work there. Much like a family photo album, it provides a continued connection to the past for this memory community.[15] To flip through its pages facilitates the social act of remembering and helps mill workers share their memories with others. The following pages thus tell the story of the historical agency of mill workers themselves. What is interesting here is how the two men and others have treated the binder in the months and years that followed the closure: it is spoken of with great reverence, in a whisper. It is as if the mill history binder has become a surrogate for the mill itself.[16]

The Making of the Mill History Binder

It should come as no surprise that mills and factories are highly meaningful places for those who toil there. This is particularly true of long-service workers who have spent twenty, thirty, or more years in a workplace. I cannot think of a single industrial worker whom I have interviewed in the past twenty years who has not used home and family metaphors to describe attachment to people, place, and product. Their intent is clear: the job meant more than a pay cheque. Other historians have found much the same thing. In their now classic study of the Amoskeag textile mill in New England published in the 1970s, Tamara Hareven and Randolph Langenback wrote that workers exhibited a "highly developed sense of place" and formed tightly knit groups.[17] Paper workers did, too. Place attachment is a complex phenomenon that involves affect, emotion, feeling, and memory.

My own thinking on place identity and attachment has been profoundly influenced by British geographer Doreen Massey. In her brilliant essay, "Places and their Pasts," which appeared in *History Workshop Journal* in 1994, Massey argues that place identity is constructed out of a particular constellation of social relations, meeting and weaving together. Places do not just exist on a map, but also *in time*. According to Massey, "places as depicted on maps are places caught in a moment; they are slices through time."[18] One might say that places are products of constantly shifting social relations. The identity of any place is thus temporary, uncertain, and in process.[19] For Massey the local is always a product of the global, at least in part. Larger social, economic, and political forces are thus integral to the making of places. Yet the past of a place is "as open to a multiplicity of readings as is the present. Moreover, the claims and counter-claims about the present character of a place depend in almost all cases on particular, rival interpretations of its past."[20] Places are thus products of history, and so exist in time and space.[21] What is largely missing from the scholarly discussion of place making, however, is its reverse: the unmaking or demolition of place. What happens when places are lost to us and these ties are forcibly broken?

The bonding of people with their workplace insures that periods of major economic and social change are periods of major spatial change as well.[22] The power of place was everywhere apparent in our conversations with displaced workers and their families. It infused their language and structured their stories. Mine, mill,

Trucking away parts of the mill. Photograph by Hubert Gervais.

and factory closings challenge our sense of place at the deepest level, as "workers lose a social structure in which they have felt valued and validated by their fellows."[23] The Sturgeon Falls mill's closure therefore hit interviewees hard. Randy Restoule spoke for many when he said: "I felt a deep loss. The fact that everyone else was leaving ... All your friends are gone. And ... the reason that you keep going [to] a job is because of friends."

For more than a century, the rising smoke from the stack offered a reminder of the jobs the mill provided. Smoke signalled prosperous times, and its absence was always a danger sign. We were told repeatedly that the mill's smokestack and water tower could be seen from anywhere in Sturgeon Falls.

It is not coincidental that, in the late 1990s, some workers sought to memorialize, commemorate, and make visible the history of the mill and those who worked there. The mill history binder emerged from the shop-floor renaissance discussed in Chapter 9. I first met Bruce Colquhoun in late 2003 at the "Action Centre," a job-assistance centre operated by the Paper Workers union. Dave Hunter, a local resident who assisted this research project in its early days, first told me about the "mill history binder" – the largest binder he had ever seen – I really *had* to see it. He also told me that everyone he approached to be interviewed told him to talk first to Colquhoun, one of its compilers. I of course agreed. We met one wintry day in the Action Centre, a big room with tables arranged end-to-end in long rows. There were three or four other men in the room when I was introduced to Colquhoun and his huge black binder.

Bruce Colquhoun and the others treated the mill history binder as a sacred text, spoken of with their voices lowered to a whisper, and Colquhoun turned the pages with loving care. I instinctively did the same, as it was immediately apparent that the binder meant a great deal to these men. It was like a giant memory book, with clippings of old news stories, photographs, and photocopied material on the mill found in the old *Abitibi Magazine*. Over the next two hours, Colquhoun told me stories as he slowly turned the pages. A soft-spoken man, he noted that the binder was treasured by the mill workers and their families. He related how he would sometimes get requests to borrow the binder to show a visiting family member or a grandchild. Sometimes former mill workers just wanted to revisit their old lives inside the mill.

Rereading my field notes from that day's meeting, I am reminded that this was a highly significant encounter in my own intellectual journey. It was the catalyst for my decision to write this book. At that moment I knew that the mill history binder would be the subject of a full chapter. The reader might wonder why it appealed to me. For one thing, it provided an opportunity to explore a personalized response to the economic crisis facing Canada's forest-dependent communities.[24] As well, the binder can be read as a deep expression of place attachment. Historians sometimes look down on "amateur" historians or "collectors": they are usually untrained – in the sense of not having a graduate degree in history – and are said to produce flawed research that is sentimental, celebratory, excessively detailed, or lacking in analysis. The mill history binder could be criticized on any of these counts. Yet to do so would be to ignore what it is: a storehouse of memories from and for a workplace community that was shattered by a decision taken far away. How displaced workers related to this memory book in the months and years following the closure tells us a great deal about the hold that the mill had on them.

The visual language of the mill history binder reminds me of a school yearbook, a family photograph album, or scrapbook: each image has a story attached to it. In her book *Suspended Conversations*, art historian Martha Langford asks what makes the photograph album so special: "Well, memories of course."[25] The album "preserves the life story of the departed within a concrete and bounded report."[26] The mill history binder serves much the same function: keeping its main protagonist, the mill itself, alive. In so doing the binder has come to symbolize their continuing connection with the past. People's attachments to specific places are not constant – we are most conscious of the sense of belonging that we derive from place when this connection is most at risk. Place attachment is often "activated retrospectively."[27] Yet the mill history binder differs from a yearbook or photograph album insofar as its very openness, the refusal to "close" the meanings or additions, suggests that the binder serves a very different function from that of Langford's albums.

We know a great deal about the making of the mill history binder from a series of interviews we conducted with Hubert Gervais and Bruce Colquhoun.

Bruce Colquhoun.
Photograph by David W. Lewis.

Gervais grew up in the nearby village of Field before starting to work at the mill on 29 April 1963 as an "office boy." He worked in the mill's offices for the next thirty-five years. Bruce Colquhoun, by contrast, followed his father, Ken – who had been one of the first hired when the mill reopened in 1947 after being shut for fifteen difficult years – onto the mill's shop floor. He worked in the maintenance department as an "oiler," oiling and greasing machines all over the plant. The job took him everywhere. The two men – one francophone and the other anglophone, one an office worker and the other a production worker – thus neatly mirrored the social structure of the mill, albeit in reverse. They were interviewed on several occasions, alone and together, between 2003 and 2006. In all there are probably ten hours of recorded conversations. We spent a great deal of time talking about the giant binder.

In an interview over lunch at Gervais's Restaurant, perhaps sitting at the same table where Mayor O'Connor met with Weyerhaeuser officials, I asked Bruce Colquhoun and Hubert Gervais why they undertook the mill history project. Why was it important to them? To this Colquhoun answered: "I like history, too, like Hubert. I wanted to know about the mill. I had always looked around and seen the old stuff in the mill. I don't know. I was doing my family history, too. Hubert would help me out at the time, and he showed me what he had done until 1976."[28] Colquhoun asked if he could take the story up to the present. At this juncture in the interview, Gervais interjected to say that Colquhoun had been after him for a few years to do so. Gervais explained: "I was retiring. I wanted to give it to somebody who was interested."[29] Colquhoun therefore became the mill's historian upon Gervais's retirement in 1998.

That year Bruce Colquhoun inserted a full-page tribute to Hubert Gervais and the making of the mill history project in the binder itself. He divided its development into three phases. It originated in Gervais's passion for the mill and its long history: "Like a few people working here," wrote Colquhoun, Gervais "wanted to know the history of our mill. So, he took it upon himself to find out what made our mill tick."[30] When asked, Gervais credited a co-worker for pushing him to put together the first mill history binder in time for the town's centenary in 1995. One of the women who worked with Gervais in the mill offices encouraged him to gather his historical materials in one place. "I had to put them someplace," he told me. The text that introduces each chapter of the binder was typed by her. She worked on it whenever she had fifteen or twenty minutes to spare. In this first effort Gervais provided a brief history of the mill from 1898 until 1976.

There were actually several versions of the mill history binder. The existence of the first was announced in the mill's newsletter, in a story entitled "Our Mill – Way Back Then." Employees were told that Hubert Gervais had "compiled a book of old photos and articles from the old *Abitibi* magazine dating from 1949–1969," and were advised that "anyone interested in looking at this book may do so in the main office lobby."[31] Only one or two copies appear to have been made. That month, the town's weekly newspaper, the *Tribune*, published a piece by Gervais entitled "1898–1947: A Bit of the Sturgeon Fall Mill's History."[32] It consisted of a chronology of the mill's development in its first half-century.

These efforts to tie the mill's history to the town's centennial were overshadowed, however, by the publication of *Sturgeon Falls, 1895–1995*, a book commissioned by the Sturgeon Falls Centennial Committee as a "salute to over 100 years of life in Sturgeon Falls." Authored by local journalist and historian Wayne LeBelle, this 173-page book, generously illustrated with over 500 photographs, was released to great fanfare.[33] All five hundred copies of the book were sold in four days. Asked why, LeBelle told me: "I think this is a family photo album of the Town of Sturgeon Falls." Centennial celebrations are "really family reunions," he said. Indeed, readers of the *Tribune* were informed that the book "portrays many of our families, special times, important events and interesting people who have made Sturgeon what it is today."[34] Although it celebrated the place identity of the town as a whole, the mill and the forest industry loomed large in LeBelle's narrative. "Wood has been the lifeblood of the community for the last 100 years," he wrote.[35] Yet the "constitutive narrative," or foundational myth, of the town – the founding families and so on – is largely missing from the mill history binder, which provides a surprisingly dispassionate description of the early years.[36]

If the first version of the mill history binder failed to reach much beyond those who flipped through its pages in the mill's offices, it still resonated with Bruce Colquhoun. Upon his retirement in 1998, Hubert Gervais agreed to let Colquhoun bring the history of the mill up to date. In August 1998 the two men were approached by the mill manager to finish the history in time for the mill's centenary later that year. For Colquhoun, "It was in August or September of that year that mill management approached [Gervais] and asked him if he would write a complete history of the mill, and if he could do it by October. It was on that date back in 1898 that our mill was born, and they wanted to put out a book to commemorate the first hundred years. It would be a monumental task to get the history written in time for the one hundredth anniversary, but Hubert took up the challenge. The result of his hard work is one extremely well written and documented history book, with lots of old photos included."[37] Twenty copies of this second version of the history binder were made, one for each department in the mill. "Hubert kept one, and since I am now the designated mill historian, I, too, received a copy," noted Colquhoun. "Everyone here loved it. He had done a wonderful job." Copies of the 1995 and 1998 binders were eventually donated to the local museum and to the public library by the mill manager as a lasting contribution to the history of the town.

After 1998 the mill history binder continued to evolve under the stewardship of Bruce Colquhoun, who explained its production this way:

Later that year, Hubert called me to say that he had about two hundred *Abitibi Magazines* ranging in years from 1947 to 1969. Each of them had a page or two on our division in them. He gave them to me, and what I saw was *fantastic*. Here was a pictorial and written history of our mill during some of the years that Abitibi owned it. I showed some of them to Marc Côté, mechanical superintendent. He was amazed with them. Marc and I photocopied each and every page that had something to do with Sturgeon Falls. Since there was twenty copies of Hubert's book, we decided to make twenty copies of each page. We put them in plastic sheet protectors, then in three-inch binders, and distributed them the same way as was done with Hubert's book. Everyone loved them. They saw pictures of their fathers, mothers, grandparents, aunts, uncles, brothers, sisters, and even some of themselves. There [are] well over two hundred pages of pictures and history. I combined Hubert's book and the *Abitibi* [*Magazine*] pages, and, together, they filled a five-inch binder. I am continuing on with the history, and Hubert is helping me with it. Every once in a while, he calls me to say that he has found another picture or a historical fact. If it wasn't for Hubert, we wouldn't know what we now know about our mill. I would like to take this opportunity to say, on behalf of everyone at the mill, a heart-felt *thank you* to Hubert.[38]

The mill history binder's very existence is an act of defiance in the face of the erasure that accompanied the mill's slow decline and final closing. Hubert Gervais had begun to collect historical and pictorial materials in the 1970s, and gathered them into an "archive" kept in the old transformer building that once stood at the base of the mill's water tower. By the time the mill closed, the space was filled with boxes dating back to Spanish River days. As noted earlier, the mill's records were shredded or shipped off to destinations unknown after the closure, but I managed to get into the mill on two occasions while the demolition company was "preparing the site" by stripping the interior. I saw hundreds of blueprints piled high on the floor in the engineering offices, ready for destruction. Some of these plans dated back to the 1920s. I asked the Weyerhaeuser official on-site if it would be possible to save this heritage, offering to go through the materials myself. He refused, albeit politely.

Narrating Place in the Mill History Binder

The mill history binder takes a biographical approach to the history of the mill. Its twenty-eight chapters closely follow the linear stages in its century-long development. The resulting meta-narrative can be divided into four periods: the early days from 1898 until 1930 (Chapters 1–5), the "depression years" from 1930 to 1947 (Chapter 6), the "good years" from 1947 until 1990 (Chapters 7–25), and the "trying years" from 1990 to 2002 (Chapters 26–28). Many chapters consist only of a few pages of text and a handful of photographs, others are longer. The visual and textual narrative provides a unifying image of the memory of place. The binder is a manifestation of "constitutive memory": it is both an expression of a shared history and identity and a builder of it. These proud memories were brought into question with the mill's closing in December 2002.

Hubert Gervais's original version of the binder focused on corporate ownership, work process, natural disasters, and the mill's physical structures. There are therefore chapters dedicated to the mill managers, sawmill waste utilization, the primary treatment plant, renovations to the main office, and the floods of 1928, 1951, and 1979.[39] The focus is resolutely on the mill buildings and machines, not on the mill workers themselves. It therefore resembles the kind of institutional history that one would expect to find from seeing the corporate logo of MacMillan Bloedel on the binder's front cover. This would be a mistake, however, as Gervais's narrative details the history of the mill itself, not the corporations that would claim it. It is the story of the making of the Sturgeon Falls paper mill – its industrial processes, production records, and other significant moments.

Foundations for the original grinders, 2004. Photograph by David W. Lewis.

After 1998 the binder becomes less a narrative history of the mill and more a yearbook peopled with mill workers and their families. An open invitation to the mill workforce produced photographs and documents, which are organized year-by-year within the existing chapter structure, with the years marked. These pages reveal the social world that existed in and around the mill. Many of the photographs mark ritualized moments: production records, retirement parties, service awards, scholarships to the children of employees, and the like. Anniversaries and other commemorative activities are also included, along with photographs of mill workers and their families.

Bruce Colquhoun also opened the binder to other workers, appealing for help in the *Insider* newsletter. The wording of the public call noted that Bruce was "compiling a historical book of the mill" and that he was looking for "pictures and or information about this division starting in 1976." He specifically asked for "old articles from newspapers or pictures about the people of the industry."[40] Other mill workers appear to have responded to the call. People submitted a variety of things: "I got guys with their moose in there. Little girls. New babies. One guy got mad at me. He says, 'How come my picture is not in there?' I said, 'Well, you didn't give it to me.'" Newly inserted documents included a photocopy of the "First Board Made No. 2 Hardboard Machine, October 16, 1963." The board had a number of signatures on it. Finally, Colquhoun included lists of local union executive members and shop stewards as well as other union milestones.

During one of our interviews, I asked Bruce Colquhoun and Hubert Gervais how they decided what to include in the binder. Both men insisted that everything went in: "It's all history. It's the past." For Colquhoun, "The mill is not just the mill. It is all of Sturgeon and West Nipissing." As a living memorial to the mill, the binder's evolving contents reflect the interests of the two co-authors. With the inclusion of visual and textual sources related to the mill workers and their families, the mill history binder changed substantially over the years, a shift that occurred during a period of heightened conflict within the workplace and the uncertainty that accompanied Weyerhaeuser's 1999 purchase of MacMillan Bloedel and with it the Sturgeon Falls mill.

It took Colquhoun hours to prepare each of the twenty copies of the binder. He asked Marc Coté, his superintendent, for permission to purchase the five-inch binders for the copies, which cost $35 apiece. "I was very shy about asking for stuff," he said. When the mill's communications officer later asked to see the binder, Colquhoun agreed to bring it in. The man then said he wanted to take a look at it, but Colquhoun refused. The man insisted, saying it was "mill property." Only then did Bruce relent and agree to show the binder to him.

Once recovered, these old stories were a hit on the shop floor. Several interviewees expressed fond memories of the binder: "Everybody likes to read about the mill. We photocopied all the Sturgeon papers there and brought them into the mill and guys were freaking out. 'Oh, my God, there is my dad.' 'There's my grandfather.' 'My aunt and uncle.'" While the mill still operated, Randy Restoule used to lug it into the operator's booth where he worked. He noted that the mill workers looked at it "when they could." The mill history resonated most with Ruth Thompson. One of the few women employed in the mill, she loved to look at the binder while on the job: "Something like that I related to because I love to hear stories of just things that happened, people's lives … what it was like ages ago. It showed the pictures of the logging operations and the old trucks. The clothes the old guys wore. I loved that book." Thompson particularly liked to see the photographs of her co-workers from "ages ago when they were young," and liked to see the clothes they wore in the fifties and sixties, especially during the "hippy times."

Family stories that risked being lost because few people had cameras in those days were now being recovered. Bruce Colquhoun explained his family's deep connection to the mill: "I worked [there] for twenty-nine years. My dad worked there for forty-one years. My grandfather worked there." In these comments, we see that the mill history binder was very much a family album like any other. One photograph shows Colquhoun's own father in 1952. But Colquhoun was amazed to find his grandfather there as well: "My dad's dad. He worked there as an electrician." Joseph Colquhoun was congratulated on the birth of a baby boy. Later he was honoured for saving the life of another worker in July 1924, for which he received a gold watch and a commendation. A proud grandson, Bruce included a copy of the Spanish River Medal for merit with blue ribbon and the certificate of commendation.

What are the politics of the mill history binder? Is it another case of "smokestack nostalgia"? The binder was institutionally sanctioned, but it differs in several ways from the slick corporate image making typically found in corporate publications of all kinds. The binder was never a public relations exercise; in fact, it was self-consciously produced by and for the mill workers themselves. Its loose format and the nature of its distribution within the mill insure that nobody could possibly confuse it with Weyerhaeuser's glossy commemorative book *Tradition Through the Trees*, published on its corporate centennial in 2000.[41] The binder therefore acts as a rearview mirror and a source of validation for mill workers and their families, relating the history of the place. These galleries of work and friendship offer a sense of pride in their work and in their shared history. The mill's production records are their collective achievements, as are the photographs of smiling retirees and service award recipients. There is none of the anger or loss that was so apparent in the interviews. Yet the binder is not a joyful history – the mass layoffs and eventual closure of the mill ensured that the mill workers flipping through its pages had a nostalgic reaction to its contents. Without question the two worker-historians felt empowered by the existence of the binder. Their special status within the mill community is widely acknowledged. People constantly advised us to "ask Hubert" or "go see Bruce" when we asked questions about the history of the mill. "Have you seen the binder?" was our constant companion.

During one of our meetings, I asked Colquhoun and Gervais if mill managers ever attempted to influence what went into the binder. It turns out they had. Both men, however, expressed some delight in recounting how they overcame these hurdles. For example, Colquhoun told us this story: "Scott Mosher [the mill manager at the time, said], 'I want to see everything before you put it in that book.

I want to approve it.' And I said, 'I work eight hours a day and I don't have time to run in here [to ask] is that okay? and next day, is that okay? We are not having classified secrets … I am not going to bad-mouth you … It is just the facts of the history of the mill.' He said, 'Don't go to extremes. We will pay for the ink and that for your cartridge, but don't go to extremes. Don't go out and buy a $500 printer.' I said, 'I got a printer.'" In the end Mosher agreed to pay for the paper and ink cartridges. With this Colquhoun shifted to a more conciliatory posture, adding, "He was good. I didn't like the idea that he wanted to control everything there for a while." This story was followed by another confrontation – this one with the mill's final manager, when Bruce was again told to hand over the binder: "He said, 'I've seen that binder.' He says, 'I want it.' 'No' [Hubert laughs]. He says, 'Why not? It's the mill property … That paper is my paper.' He says, 'Yes, we paid for the paper.' 'You didn't pay for the paper,' I said, 'that paper is my paper.' He said, 'We paid for the binder.' 'Fine, I'll give you the binder back.' He says, 'We paid for the ink.' I said, 'I'll buy you a cartridge. You're not getting that binder.' He says, 'That's mill property, Bruce.' I said, 'No, it isn't! It's at my place. You are going to need a court order to get it out of my yard' [laughs]. I said, 'You're not touching that binder.'" It was at this moment that the mill manager decided that Colquhoun and Gervais would not get their hands on the mill's newsletter, but as mentioned, the whole run of the *Insider* – which was produced throughout the 1990s – was rescued anyway. Both men took some satisfaction from their belief that an earlier plant manager now wanted "to see the binder bad." But it was not "*for him*" – it was theirs. The contents of the mill history binder are thus an expression of Gervais's and Colquhoun's profound attachment to the mill and the people who worked there. In many ways it is their personal response to the mill's long decline and final closure.

One question I had on my mind from my very first meeting with Bruce Colquhoun at the Action Centre was why they hadn't updated the binder to include the mill's closure and aftermath. Every time I asked the question, I got the same answer: to do so would have been to admit that the mill was dead and their workplace community with it. Both men feared this would signal the end of their efforts. It was still "too soon." They "weren't ready." Much the same thing happened when I asked if they intended to publish the binder in some way. Colquhoun told me that this would make it impossible for him to continue to add to its contents. It would freeze it forever. He did not want this – not now. It would stop being a living memorial to what was – to the mill and to the mill families. To my knowledge Colquhoun still has not inserted all the news stories, photographs, and other materials – such as a photocopy of the last roll of paper produced at the mill, signed by the workers – that he has collected.

Warehouse area in the closed plant as it was being dismantled. Photograph by David Lewis.

"Voices must be heard for memories to be preserved," notes art historian Martha Langford. For the family photograph album to fulfil its function, it must continue to live: "Ironically, the very act of preservation – the entrusting of an album to a public museum – suspends its sustaining conversation, stripping the album of its social function and meaning."[42] Langford's words made sense to me the first time I read them, largely because I had heard Bruce Colquhoun and Hubert Gervais make much the same point on several occasions. The mill history binder, like the photo albums Langford speaks of, has its roots in orality: workers remember by visual association. "The showing and telling of an album is a performance," writes Langford.[43] As long as the mill history binder continues to be interpreted for others, the conversation continues and the old connection to place remains. Yet, in not taking the story up to the mill's closing and the painful aftermath, Colquhoun and Gervais have detached the mill history binder from its present context. The conversation in the binder might not be "suspended," but it is certainly circumscribed.

We asked our interviewees about the memory book. Almost everyone knew what it was. It was a "great big binder," recalled Raymond Marcoux. Ray Lortie likewise remembered the book well, covering as it did the mill's entire lifespan. Several interviewees had their own copies – whisked away, no doubt, from the closing mill – "They showed them to me," said student interviewer Kristen O'Hare. Others had little to say about the memory book. A few had never heard of it. For his part, Lawrence Pretty told us that one of his children recently used the binder for a school project on the history of the mill. He was not alone.

Interviewing Ray Lortie at work at the now municipally owned dam, Kristen O'Hare asked him about the binder. He promptly got up and returned to his seat with it in hand: it is still being perused in what is left of the mill. Lortie then took O'Hare on an impromptu tour of the closed mill as it was being dismantled. He noted that the OCC facility and skiving line had already been stripped and sold off, leaving empty spaces behind. As they walked from one part of the closed plant to the next, Lortie explained each area's function, but then said what the area had been formerly: the finishing area's lunch room used to be the superintendent's office, the storage area used to have trains coming into it to unload, a warehouse area used to be the paint line, and so on. Lortie also pointed out small details that revealed the old age of the mill. "Look at the structure of this," he said at one point. "This is old. Any time you see that kind of cantilever setup, it's old." They also came across the manlift, a continuous belt with steps that took pulp makers from the basement to the top floor – something they had to do regularly. "It's better than a fireman's pole," Lortie explained.

The manlift, which took workers in the old pulping department from the basement to the upper floors, July 2004. Photograph by Kristen O'Hare.

Asked what it was like to be one of only eight mill workers still employed, Ray Lortie replied: "It's the same thing as reading a book. You turn the page and you flip it. Page number two, that's where we're going. You just can't stay there ... What's it like coming to work? Work is work." For Lortie, "life goes on." But he did not feel that his job was secure. He cited his grandfather's experience, laid off when the mill shut down in 1930: "He got recalled back in 1946. How do you like that one? And he did come back to work. Came back to work, and worked a little bit [before retiring]." History was repeating itself once again, as long displaced workers were eventually called back to work in the power house for a few years before finally reaching retirement age.

Conclusion

The mill history binder and my own desire to make sense of the carnage raise inevitable questions about nostalgia. In fact the study of deindustrialization has been preoccupied with the idea of "smokestack nostalgia" since it was introduced in 2003 by Jefferson Cowie and Joseph Heathcott in *Beyond the Ruins*. The "time is right," they declared, "to widen the scope of the discussion beyond prototypical plant shutdowns, the immediate politics of employment policy, the tales of victimization, or the swell of industrial nostalgia." Cowie and Heathcott suggested that researchers needed to "overcome 'smokestack nostalgia' in our scholarship, complicate the industrial legacy, and assist those communities most affected by these transformations."[44] But I wonder if simple nostalgia for an industrial past is what we are seeing here. Tim Strangleman has observed that people naturally "look back on the past as settled, fixed, rounded, and intelligible and compare that to the incomplete, flux, chaotic, unstable now."[45] A similar pattern can be seen in interviews with displaced workers.

The urge to reaffirm and celebrate industrial history in the face of the crisis in North American manufacturing and the resources sector is not limited to Sturgeon Falls, Ontario. In Pittsburgh, for example, the impulse to commemorate steelworkers – "to fix their historical identity forever in a didactic monument – arose from the demise of a living industrial culture that could nourish such memory from within."[46] What is different about the mill history binder is the insistence on keeping it open to additional materials and available to other mill workers. It serves to keep the mill alive in their memories, even as the mill itself has been erased from the physical landscape. A sense of place would be impossible without memory.[47]

Place is more than a static category, an empty container where things happen. It must be understood as a social and spatial process, undergoing constant change.[48]

Place is therefore contingent, fluid, and multiple. Like the piece of rubble Hubert Gervais picked up during the mill's demolition, the binder has become a last vestige, a remnant, of what was: a site of memory "in which a residual sense of continuity remains."[49] Yet the place being remembered is fixed to happier times before the mill's closing. Like the makers of other commemorative monuments, the co-creators of the mill history binder aim to "create a stable and coherent past sealed off from the vicissitudes of change."[50] The place that was the Sturgeon Falls mill, an active industrial site for more than a century until it closed in December 2002, is thus forever frozen in time.

CONCLUSION

Ruination is an act perpetrated, a condition to which one is subject, and a cause of loss ... But ruination is more than a process. It is also a political project that lays waste to certain peoples and places, relations and things.

– Anne Laura Stoler[1]

Deindustrialization has marked a crucial rupture in the lives of tens of millions of working-class families, including in Sturgeon Falls. The scale of the body count is staggering. The United States lost almost eight million manufacturing jobs between 1979 and 2010, representing 42 per cent of its manufacturing base.[2] Other countries have done as poorly. Between 1990 and 2003, manufacturing jobs declined 24 per cent in Japan, 29 per cent in the United Kingdom, and 14 per cent in France. For its part, Canada lost 278,000 manufacturing jobs, representing one in six industrial workers, from 2000 to 2007.[3] Moreover, unionized jobs in Canadian manufacturing vanished twice as fast as non-unionized jobs during this time. Unions have staggered from one tragedy to the next. As a result, the rate of unionization in Canadian manufacturing declined from 32.2 per cent in 1998 to 26.4 per cent in 2008.[4] Across Canada, seventy-six paper and sawmills closed between 2003 and 2007, with the loss of 40,000 forestry jobs.[5] The Sturgeon Falls story is therefore the story of towns and cities across the continent and the industrialized world. *One Job Town* reminds us that deindustrialization is not the story of a single emblematic place such as Detroit, but is part of a "much broader, more fundamental historical transformation."[6] Capitalism creates, or at least accentuates, difference and otherness "through the simple logic of uneven capital investment."[7] Old places are "devalued, destroyed and redeveloped" to make the new.[8]

The political isolation of displaced mill workers was largely confirmed in our interviews with elected officials and local economic development agents. But what made this closure different from so many others was that Weyerhaeuser could not rely on vague assertions that the closing mill was losing money. In fact, this was demonstrably false, as the financial standing of the mill was public knowledge. Otherwise communities faced with mill closures have "little choice but to accept the word of industry spokesmen and assume that the company has good reasons for what it is doing."[9] The Sturgeon Falls mill not only made money until the day it closed; it had a firm contract to purchase its entire output of corrugated medium for another nine months. Incredibly Weyerhaeuser cancelled its supply contract with MacMillan Bathurst, probably to reduce capacity to allow prices to rise. As one might expect, this action generated considerable bitterness and anger in the town. But so did the municipality's subsequent actions.

Sturgeon Falls's Community Adjustment and Recovery Committee (CARC) released its final report, entitled "Let's Grow Together," in 2004. It called on the amalgamated Town of West Nipissing to position itself as a bedroom community, or commuter suburb, for North Bay and Sudbury, as well as a family-oriented wilderness destination. The town was also considered "uniquely positioned" to build on its cultural identity as a Franco-Ontarian community,[10] and arts and cultural activities should be promoted to that end. But first the town's "industrial waterfront" and the downtown area had to be renovated to make them more attractive. The report lamented that travellers passing through Sturgeon Falls on the Trans-Canada Highway glimpsed only "the now derelict paperboard mill and the accompanying hydro dam. If a visitor stops in Sturgeon Falls and by chance finds the municipal pier – he or she will find an old abandoned shack on cracked concrete stretching out into one of the most beautiful rivers in Canada." Chaired by Royale Poulin, former chairman of the Ontario Northland Transportation Commission and a prominent local Progressive Conservative with good political connections in Toronto, the CARC concluded that the area's "traditional economic raison d'être has shifted." In effect, Sturgeon Falls had ceased to be "a northern mill town." For Poulin, "[a] lot of people thought the mill closure would spell doom for the area, but in fact it has served as a catalyst to get us working together at making West Nipissing prosper."[11]

In fact, suburbanization was already under way, as lower house prices proved attractive to young families living in nearby towns and cities.[12] By August 2004 some spoke of a booming local real estate market. Joanne Giroux, a realtor, was quoted in the *Tribune* as saying: "All the propaganda attached to Weyerhaeuser

Redeveloped marina, Sturgeon Falls, 2011. Photograph by David W. Lewis.

leaving town strangely enough actually worked in reverse for the real estate market. It encouraged people to come shopping for a home in West Nipissing, since
potential buyers expected to see attractive and competitive prices in this area, and
they were right. Prices are much more affordable than places like North Bay."[13] The
construction of a new hotel and another grocery store seemed to confirm this, as
did the subsequent building of a new residential area on what was once the mill's
North Yard. In many ways the town's geographic location has saved it from the cruel
fate of more remote former mill towns.

Nevertheless former mill workers entered an unforgiving job market. A CARC-
commissioned labour market survey provided a stark economic picture of West
Nipissing: officially, unemployment in 2002–3 stood at 12.3 per cent,[14] and the
services sector now employed two-thirds of the town's workforce, with no industrial employer in the top ten – the largest was Goulard Lumber, ranked fourteenth
overall, only slightly ahead of the local McDonald's restaurant.[15] The health and
educational sectors are now the largest employers in West Nipissing. But many people were being left behind. According to 2001 census figures, 26.3 per cent of the
residents of Sturgeon Falls over age twenty-five had less than a grade 9 education,
compared with 11.7 per cent across the province, while the average total annual
income was $19,498 compared with an Ontario average of $27,309. The situation
will have deteriorated further with the mill's final closure, as the mill had an annual
payroll of $7 million. The ripple (or multiplier) effect of the closure was estimated
to be a hefty $30 million per year.[16]

For those not directly tied to the Sturgeon Falls mill, there was a strong sense of
the inevitability of this shifting terrain. In some cases it was even understood as a

positive step forward for the community. Yvon Marleau, a town councillor interviewed in July 2004, said: "We realized that it's just another phase of our history.
Another page. It was going to happen sooner or later. So we had to go through this
transition." Many other Northern Ontario towns were undergoing the same meta-
morphosis, he continued: "If you go back years ago, Northern Ontario towns would
rely on [the] lumber industry or mines. Tourism was a second industry, but really
it was lumber and mines. Well, these have evolved, and a lot of them are closed
down, and the towns are still there and the towns have to look for something else
to survive. And most do, most do find something else ... So you have to adapt, you
got to change. And this is what's happening in Sturgeon Falls." Others agreed. Brian
Laflèche, another local councillor, who once worked inside the mill, told us: "'If the
mill closes the town is dead' – that used to be the saying." But the 2002 closing did
not have the expected negative impact. By then things had changed: "As the years
went on, the mill diminished." Mill employment slid from a high of 600 in the mid-
1960s to just 140 in 2002. In Sturgeon Falls, as elsewhere, deindustrialization was a
slow and uneven process. As historians Jefferson Cowie and Joseph Heathcott have
observed: "Disinvestment is not a one-time process. It has cumulative effects."[17]

Most of the elected officials we spoke to felt there was no going back. Locally,
industrialism was dead. Mayor Gary O'Connor believed that their only option was
to move on: "Poor Sturgeon Falls. Boo, hoo, hoo. That was never my attitude. And
I encouraged council: 'Let's move on, let's move forward. We can't stall here. This is
our wake-up call, and we have to get on with things.' And that's what's happening."
Other politicians and economic development leaders pointed to new housing construction and commercial development as positive signs for the future. "It's probably a good thing when you look at it," noted Denis Gauthier. "It forced people to
get jobs elsewhere. To look what we did, we definitely did not lose 125 residents."
By 2005 local leaders were becoming bullish again about the town's prospects. The
economic catastrophe many feared did not arrive. Mayor Joanne Savage, who had
replaced O'Connor by then, said she was excited about the future and "has no time
for people who say plans for its future won't work."[18]

Wayne LeBelle drew a similar conclusion. In our recorded conversation, he challenged me to "Drive around town and say, 'Okay, what is the legacy they [mill]
left behind? What did they leave behind?' They're going to leave behind some flat
territory. They are going to leave behind a big huge parking lot." The mill's closing "sounds like a huge tragedy, and it is for some individuals. It is a big smack. In
the bigger picture of West Nipissing, it's not. The world does not revolve around
Sturgeon Falls ... It does not. Ask all those questions in Verner, in Cache Bay." For
them the 2002 closing "is not even a blip." As a result, "You never saw a whole bunch

Main Street, Sturgeon Falls, 2011. Photograph by David W. Lewis.

of community people out there supporting them" on the picket line once the mill closed. Here, again we see the growing chasm between mill workers and the wider community. If residents quickly moved on, former mill workers were left to struggle on in private. And struggle they did.

Few mill workers we interviewed found work immediately. Mike Lacroix still had a month and a half of unemployment insurance benefits left when we interviewed him in November 2004. "It's going to get tough," he realized. "There's no work. I've looked. I've knocked on doors. And there's nothing. My son-in-law, you know, twenty-one years old, no problem. He's got work … But not a fifty-year-old. They don't want you. They know a lot of stuff, but they're not employable. They know that, at fifty, your booboos come out – you have a sore here, a sore there." For his part Raymond Marcoux lived on his severance pay until it ran out and then applied for employment insurance benefits. But there was no work in Sturgeon Falls. And what there was paid a very low wage, a third of what he earned at the mill. Nor was moving elsewhere an option, as they owned their house and his wife was working: "She has a good job, so what do I do?"

Denis MacGregor also spoke of this predicament. "Right now," he said, "I am doing nothing. The last place I applied was No-Frills [a grocery store] at $7.15 an hour for twenty to twenty-four hours a week. Like somebody said, it's better than nothing. But if you calculate $7.15 an hour for twenty, even if you put it at twenty-four hours a week, I have to sell the house, which is probably undervalued because of the [closure]. I've applied. Throughout the eighteen months, I've applied to at least eighteen places." As a result MacGregor's wife had to go back to work. He noted that "She's making money and I'm collecting unemployment. But what about when my unemployment finishes, there's zip coming in." He had one job offer, but after a week he realized that his injured leg would not let him continue: "I couldn't do it because of my leg … I was in charge of … walkers, chairs. Now, all that stuff is in the basement. It is landing, six stairs, landing, six stairs, landing, four stairs. Up and down, up and down. After three days I had to tell her, 'I'm sorry, I can't do this job.' Now that really sent me for a loop." Another time, he thought gender seemed to work against him for a new job: "If they took anybody over fifty, it was women, because they figured they could put them in as cashiers. And I guess women cashiers are more [shrugs] in vogue or whatever." The historic gendered division of labour, along with advancing age, now worked against the rapid re-employment of male production workers. Even before the closure, in 2001, the local unemployment rate was 14.7 per cent for men and 9.8 per cent for women.[19]

Despite their personal struggles, many mill workers were surprised that the closure did not visibly affect the town more. "At this moment," observed Marcel Labbé, "it doesn't appear to have affected the town too much." Life had gone on without them. Asked if Sturgeon Falls was still a "workingman's town," former mill workers replied that it used to be. "Not anymore," said Raymond Marcoux, "because there's very, very little industry there now." It was now a "retirement town," as young people left to find work elsewhere. Mike Lacroix believed that a town could not be run on tourism alone. Randy Restoule acknowledged that the town had teachers and a local hospital, "but the reason why they are there is because of this mill." Probably in response to the CARC report, Restoule added: "You can't just be a bedroom community for North Bay. We need an industry here, at least a base, a good tax base." The mill's closure cost the municipality $700,000 in annual revenue that it would otherwise have received from taxes ($350,000), garbage removal ($150,000), and water and sewerage services ($200,000).[20] Once the mill was demolished, mill workers had little choice but to accept the new reality. "The writing was on the wall," recalled Restoule. "We just didn't see it." He continued to feel a "deep loss" about the closure, but thought that "people have to stop wearing black now. It is over. Move on."

Work-life oral histories such as the ones found in this book offer a way into the shifting sands of culture and economy. Our Sturgeon Falls interviewees were born into what David Byrne calls a "culture of industrialism."[21] Industrialization produced a vibrant shop-floor culture in Sturgeon Falls that was "intelligible to both its established members and those being socialized into it."[22] Entire families were embedded in mill work. As sociologist Tim Strangleman has observed more generally, the relative stability of this industrial order, at least at a cultural level, allowed "a certain moral order to emerge and be reproduced."[23] In time the sedimentation

The old fence still rings the mill property, now an empty field, 2011. Photograph by David W. Lewis.

of experiences formed a dominant structure of feeling, or shared sensibilities and identity.[24] It was what people knew and understood. Although this culture survives, we see its precipitous decline within the lifetime of our interviewees. When the mill finally closed in December 2002, workers lost a social structure that had supported them. Once stripped of their culture of belonging, "dislocated workers face an external culture that no longer seems to value, or grant social legitimacy to, the kind of work they do." In a post-industrial era, industrial workers are usually assigned to the past, not to the present, and are thereby rendered invisible or irrelevant to others.

As we have seen, emotions were incredibly raw during the interviews. Many mill workers were still processing what was happening to them, and so had yet to settle on a stable narrative. For example, interviewees often searched for the right words, tone, or tense, and revealed their profound grief, anger, shame, mistrust, and what Andrew Sayer has called "moral-political rage" against the departing company.[25] In his fascinating book on *The Moral Significance of Class*, Sayer notes that emotions are not trivial, as they are invariably "about something."[26] Often produced spontaneously, without reflection, revealed emotions exhibit our deeper "ethical dispositions" and "moral sentiments." This was certainly the case in the interviews Kristen O'Hare and I conducted in 2003 and 2004.

The widespread revulsion concerning Weyerhaeuser that was expressed in the interviews originated in a deep-seated sense of injustice. The company had acted immorally in closing the mill when it did – after all, it had a firm order for its entire output of corrugated paper for another nine months. Nine more months might seem like a small thing, but it was significant for middle-aged workers who missed out on thousands of dollars of earnings. Some had children going to university and tuition fees to pay. Others had chronic health conditions, and so would lose their drug plan. A few might even have become eligible for early retirement by September 2003. Nine months is a long time when one is unemployed. But mainly, the company's actions offended workers – why would Weyerhaeuser do this to them? Mike Lacroix wished senior levels of governments would wake up to this injustice:

> They come over here, they cut all our trees down, they take 'em to the States, they sell us back the wood … They've destroyed – and when I say "they," I'm talking about American greed – they've destroyed the wood industry, it's been destroyed. They're destroying the paper industry in *this* community … They're destroying the whole of Canada, and nothing is being done about it. As you can see, I'm not too keen on Americans. I don't like to get screwed over, you know what I mean? I work like a dog, but I don't like to be screwed over. I don't like to see my friends get screwed over. I don't like to see my family get screwed over, nobody. People are people. You know, what's happening right now is that these big corporations, they don't care about people. That's one thing that I've seen. It's too bad, it's sad … You have to care about people! People are not animals, you know? We *are* people. And now there's no difference between animals and people. It's sad. You know, you look at TV and the news, you see it all over. So it's a sad thing to see.

When asked about the impact of the closure, Lacroix said, "It's gonna be a commuting town. That's all it's gonna be, a commuting town. North Bay, Sudbury, that's all it's gonna be … You can't base your economy, and you can't run your town, on fishing. You can't run your town on tourism. You *can't* do it! You *need* industry. You *have* to have some type of industry bringing in some fresh capital into your town."

Others revealed similar moral sentiments. The fury was not far beneath the surface, but ready to erupt. Bruce Colquhoun spoke of the rage he felt when he entered a local store and saw them selling Weyerhaeuser siding: "And I looked at that and I said, 'I'm gonna rip that sign off the wall!' I can't stand Weyerhaeuser because of what they did. I mean, they didn't have to tear the mill down. But it was a shock to a lot of people. I think a lot of people still find it hard to believe that the mill is down. They tore it down to the ground. Their parents worked there, they worked there. Now, nothing but grass" [shakes head and sighs]. Other vestiges of Weyer-haeuser's presence prompted similarly strong reactions. Ben Lajeunesse told us how he resented the Weyerhaeuser sign that still stood on the highway across from the town hall: "I don't know why that's still there, because there is no Weyerhaeuser in Sturgeon Falls. Get rid of the sign. I was bitter. I have to say I was bitter with Weyerhaeuser." Barbara Kerr, in a searing letter to the *Tribune*, told readers that she had "just finished hanging my Weyerhaeuser shares on the roll in the bathroom. On quiet reflection, I'm sure that's where they belong."[27] There were other such examples in the interviews. At one point Denis MacGregor tossed a ring over to interviewer Kristen O'Hare. It was an expensive ring, "white gold." He then related a story: "I usually wear that, and the guys at the mill sort of gave me a hard time, but I said, 'Hey, I earned that. So nobody's going to tell me if I can wear it or not.' I said, 'If I could take the [W] insignia off I would, because I really hate these guys.' And I'm not, I don't hate the States, I hate Weyerhaeuser."

For some this sense of bitterness extended to the community itself. Mike Lac-roix told us: "We had more backing from North Bay than we had from Sturgeon. I don't know why. Even the *Nugget*, they came over and covered the stories. Our own people … they wouldn't. 'Why aren't you backing us?'" In part, he thought that "people are afraid … People are afraid to speak up. They are afraid to get into trouble for speaking up. I don't care anymore. We've been screwed over enough. I don't care anymore." Lacroix told us that, when employees tried to buy the mill, "we got in a pile of crap. 'Ahh! They're stirring up *things* again.' Things! 'They're stirring up *things* again. The employees were stirring up things again.' We never stirred up nothing! We were just trying to buy the place. That's all we wanted to do." The bot-tom line, he said, was: "I can't accept the fact that they shut down. Never will. I'm going to take that to my grave. I can't accept it." Until the closure Marcel Boudreau thought he would work in the mill his entire working life. He therefore found job loss difficult, made worse by negative comments he heard in the community: "I know for a fact that there's a number of people who were quite happy to see that mill shut down and have us all lose our jobs: 'Welcome to the real world.' Jealous people."

For mill workers and their families, the town's indifferent response to the mill's closure came as a stunning blow. The growing isolation of mill workers can be seen in the pages of the local weekly newspaper. After the closure announcement, workers submitted a series of letters to the editor calling on residents to support their efforts to stop the closure or reopen the mill. After identifying himself as one of those losing his job and reminiscing with pride about how the "whole commu-nity" came together in 1991 to save the mill, Bruce Colquhoun noted that "there [were] a few people who [laughed] at us, because we've 'had it so good for so long.'"

Continuing, he wrote: "Laugh all you want, but what is this town without the mill? We will ALL soon find out, won't we."[28] Other comments were based on an assumed opposition between (US) capital and (Canadian or local) community. Jane Hardy wrote: "Shame, shame on you Weyerhaeuser! Is it because this is a multi-national American company, that they can just lock the door and pack up, return to the States and carry on their business as usual? Should they be allowed to operate in this manner? They have left their wreckage scattered all over Sturgeon Falls, Ontario, and areas and this will never be forgiven nor forgotten! Is this the American way of doing business in Canada? It sure looks like they hope to get away with this. Should we let them? Well, on October 8th 2002, those Americans might as well have dropped a bomb on Sturgeon Falls."[29]

By December 2002, however, some community members had had enough of these complaints. None was more uncompromising than Vera Charles, who wrote: "[T]here has been much boo-hoo-ing and feeling sorry for ourselves, which is mostly due to a big lack of understanding of how a business operates. The function of the mill is to produce a viable product for their customers and to generate profits for Weyerhaeuser. Period. The company owners do not owe it to us to create jobs, to give people life-time careers, to give out severance packages that permit laid-off employees to live happily ever after, or even to concern themselves with the economic effects on our town. Whether their actions are compassionate is irrelevant. They are not a charity!" She then went on to challenge Jane Hardy by name, who said it was a matter of corporate greed: "[T]hat's exactly right! That is what for-profit businesses in a free market are all about, and for that matter, most individuals as well." Charles agreed that it was difficult to relocate or find a new job, "but these are the realities of modern life. Compared to other workers, the mill workers should count their blessings. Not only were they employed for many years at salaries most of us can only dream about, they will actually receive severance pay, career counseling, and eventually, pensions! I bet any non-union workers, part-time workers, or small business owners would be thankful to receive such benefits when they are out of work."[30] Clearly on a roll, she added:

> Rather than whining, complaining, and shame shaming Weyerhaeuser like little children, we would do well to take our share of the responsibility and learn from this. Have we not watched as other single-industry towns suffered the same misfortune? Did we not know that plant closures, lay-offs, and cutbacks are common in our time, and that an individual now passes through about 5 careers in a lifetime? Why were we not proactive in developing other sources of revenue, rather than relying on this big, greedy, American company to feed our town? Instead of bemoaning what we lost,

we should think positively about where to go from here. Other towns have bounced back, so can Sturgeon Falls. It seems to me that the enormous amount of energy spent in outrage and grief could be channeled to better uses elsewhere.[31]

With such comments in circulation, it is hardly surprising that many mill families suddenly felt out of place in a town where they lived all their lives. Marcel Boudreau guessed that "Sturgeon will always be Sturgeon. But this town has been known as a paper mill town. It was always a situation when you pulled into town – didn't matter where you were coming from – you always saw steam coming out of the stacks there. When you saw steam coming out of those stacks, you knew you were making money." This was no longer the case. Percy Allary lived right across from the mill, and had looked out onto it for fifty-seven years, but "now it is just an open field." His father used to tell him about Sturgeon Falls in the 1930s, and would say that he hoped his son would never have to live through an economic depression. Arguably this was worse, as mill workers and their families struggled alone, since people, locally, were no longer in the same boat. Sturgeon Falls therefore stands out not for its uniqueness or prominence, but rather as a typical example of the marginalization of industrial workers and the accompanying culture of industrialism.

The signs of the wider societal post-industrial transformation are evident throughout the oral narratives recorded for this project. The sense of economic security at the mill did not last. Some now believed it never existed. For as long as Percy Allary could remember, people told him: "Oh, they're going to shut that down, or they're going to shut this down. Why are you applying here? Why did you come work here? You're not going to be here long, they're going to shut it down." These rumours were not empty. Gordon Jackson noted that the mill lost "jobs and jobs and jobs" throughout his decades working there: "You're losing all your boys, all your men. And then it comes to the point, 'Well, who's going to be gone?' You'd go down the line and follow your seniority lists. And you had people on the verge." By the early 1990s the tradition of intergenerational employment at the mill had largely broken down. Layoffs had insured that only high-seniority workers remained. No longer did the mill hire summer students. In any case, Percy Allary said, he would not want a child of his to work there, as it "wasn't stable … unless they were stuck." Others, such as Raymond Marcoux, lamented the changing times: "My father worked there before me. My kids were gonna work there, but not now." Although a key moment, the 2002 plant closing only confirmed the demise of the culture of industrialism in the town.

These changed circumstances were visible when we asked interviewees if they had wanted their children to follow them into the mill. But what they had wanted was no longer much of a factor – many of their sons and daughters had moved away. For Larry Shank,

> Well, I wanted to have a better job than my dad, [and] I wanted my children to have a better job than me. So I tried to give them the education they needed. But if they were to stay here in Sturgeon, if they had to stay in Sturgeon, well, that was the best-paying job and for benefits. Sure, I'd like them to work there. I never suffered. Why should they? It was a good job. My two sons worked there. Well, one son … Michael, he's the oldest son, he worked there for ten years 'til they shut it down in '90, '92, something like that. So he went to Tembec. But my other son, Brian, he's the youngest son, he worked there a little bit like, in the summertime.

Other interviewees went further, suggesting that they wanted something more for their children. When asked if he had wanted his children to follow him into the mill, André Cartier smirked: "Absolutely not." He explained that he wanted to see his kids "have a career, a challenging career." Whenever "career" was mentioned in the interviews, it was invariably used in reference to white-collar employment. Mill work was not viewed as a career per se, unless you were salaried staff or an engineer. Several interviewees spoke of how they pushed their children to go to university or college so they could "better themselves" or find a "better job." Jane and Pierre Hardy were also asked the question. Jane said "No" first, with Pierre saying "Not really, no" soon after. Jane continued: "I can't see any future in it for my kids." Others, such as Harold Stewart, hesitated before answering, eventually replying "No." Asked why not, he explained that the "times are changing, I couldn't see a future there for them." He went on to express his own relief that he managed to retire shortly "before they shut it down." His children had worked there as summer students, "which was great. But for a lifetime thing – no." Shaking his head, Stewart concluded: "As it's turned out, it's a good thing they didn't."

Notably, we had earlier asked these same interviewees if they thought they would end up working at the mill. More often than not, they emphasized that the mill paid considerably more than other blue-collar jobs in the area. The mill also provided year-round employment in close proximity to where they lived. Clearly their employment horizons were more bounded by class and locality than were those of their children. What is interesting here is the extent to which working people's expectations appeared to be changing. Randy Restoule was one who did not want his sons to follow him into the mill. Asked why not, he replied, after a long pause, "I wanted them to improve themselves. I found it was a kind of a dead-end place … There is monotony on the job because it's production, and the

The dam, now municipally owned, continues to operate, 2011. Photograph by David W. Lewis.

only way I guess that we went through all that is because you know the people in there, in the mill. I guess you could say they provided friendship and made the job interesting at times, but the job itself was pretty monotonous." Industrial work did not hold the same public value it once did.

For the most part, when faced with mill or factory closures, governments in Canada and elsewhere have had little choice but to accept vague corporate assurances that the job losses were unavoidable. Nobody is usually in a position to counter these claims, as the financial books are not open. The Sturgeon Falls closure was therefore different, as its books were open to its community partner in the recycling facility. Weyerhaeuser could not claim that the mill was losing money – it was not, as every mill worker we interviewed was quick to tell us. Since 1983, the mill had sold its entire output of corrugated paper to MacMillan Bathurst. Weyerhaeuser therefore relied on its claim that the plant would be uncompetitive once the evergreen contract expired, given the advanced age of its equipment. It was as though the mill had aged a century in its final decade of operation. In truth the mill was more modern in 2002 than it had been ten years earlier because of millions of dollars in public investment.

The Sturgeon Falls story is much more complicated than simply one of community versus capital, which has animated much of the US scholarship on deindustrialization. As we have seen, locality is a complicated and contested place. In his book *Rust Belt Resistance*, historian Perry Bush has challenged the assertion that local communities are no match for multinational corporations. He does so by highlighting a case in Lima, Ohio, where the community took on British Petroleum and won. In Lima it succeeded because of the "strenuous efforts of a range of dedicated people, both inside and outside the plant gates."[32] Bush suggests that this triumph offers "previously hidden possibilities in an era of deindustrialization." Although I agree that local leadership matters, it does not matter enough. Even Lima continued to hemorrhage jobs. Near the end of his book, Bush admits that, despite the victory against BP, Lima lost 23 per cent of its remaining industrial jobs to plant closures between 2000 and 2003.[33] So, do local communities have "effective sociocultural resources for challenging corporate power," as Perry suggests?[34] Or do local people have "limited capacity to act," as James J. Connolly has argued?[35] Although it pains me to do so, I would say the latter, as the balance of power is unfairly tilted towards corporations, with their high-priced lawyers and deep pockets. Capital's control over the spatial distribution of production is one of its chief advantages, allowing it to move production regularly from one region to the next, from one country to another.[36] Capital is now so mobile that even national governments struggle to regulate corporations, even when they want to.

Yet the local is not merely the product of the global; it also has agency.[37] One question we struggled with throughout the interviews was why the local community responded so differently to a possible mill closure in 1991–2 than it did to its actuality a decade later. The conclusion I have come to is that the key ingredients that made possible the effort to save the mill in the 1990s were no longer available a decade later. The old alliance between local management and the community, enabled by a provincial government committed to saving Northern Ontario industry, had been broken by retirements, new corporate ownership, a new laissez-faire government in Ontario, and municipal amalgamation. That the mill's union stood outside the effort in the 1990s and was ambivalent about being asked to "buy their own jobs" made it ill-placed to take a leadership role when it counted in 2002. There was also evident tension between two solidarities, one local (Sturgeon Falls) and the other national (CEP union membership). Nor was the local what it once was. The identity of the newly amalgamated Town of West Nipissing was no longer anchored in the industrial history of its predecessor. Besides, the mill's centrality in the economic, social, political, and cultural life of the community had receded over time. The days of mill colonialism were clearly numbered. Times had changed, as most local residents no longer had a connection to the mill. For all these reasons, then, the community largely failed to respond to the appeals of mill workers and their families.

To date much of the scholarship on deindustrialization has focused on the US Midwest or Northeast as that country's industrial heartland hollowed out and rusted. But what is its significance in other national or regional contexts? How do the politics of deindustrialization differ when industrialism was bound up in racial exclusion or Jim Crow racism? Historians working on the US South have had to consider this question, raising a troubling new dimension to often-expressed concerns about "smokestack nostalgia."[38] Historian Leon Fink, for example, has posed essential questions about "Southern milltown nostalgia" in his devastating critique of industrial heritage efforts in the former North Carolina textile town of Cooleemee. The "nostalgic recuperation of the 'old' days implicitly risked sentimentalizing a Jim Crow-ordered social world," he argues.[39] Local memory, he adds, serves a "self-protective function" when the history that is commemorated or otherwise publicly remembered "honors a single ethno-racial stream as the essential core of the community's achievements."[40] Is this what is happening in places such as Sturgeon Falls, too? How do we acknowledge the losses experienced by mainly white working people, while still recognizing settler colonialism and the exclusion of Indigenous people?

If deindustrialization "reorganizes our sense of place," as Kathryn Marie Dudley suggests, I am wary of being lumped in with those who celebrate mill and factory closures as a first step towards gender or racial equality or environmental sustainability.[41] Too often, white or male privilege is recognized only in working-class white men located on the geographic or social periphery, rather than in the central corridors of power or in urban cafés. In the United States, historian Judith Stein has likewise noted that rising environmental awareness has effectively anaesthetized the middle class to the pain inflicted on working people by deindustrialization.[42] Mill closures are thus viewed by some as a public good. Here in Canada, some scholars have similarly suggested that paper mill closures represent an opportunity to end the male domination of the forestry industry.[43] With the collapse of male wage earnings due to layoffs and mill closures, the statistical gap between men and women has narrowed and hard-pressed families have had to adapt to new economic realities.[44] To celebrate this loss, or to revel in industrial abandonment as unregulated or liberated spaces[45] that somehow exist outside of capitalism, strikes me as cynical abstraction or worse. We must remember that the capitalist processes behind mill colonialism and industrialization are the same ones responsible for the devastation that followed. The ruination of industrial areas is an "act perpetrated," not some kind of liberatory moment.[46]

The political aftershocks of deindustrialization were being felt even as I wrote this book. Deindustrialized areas helped push the United Kingdom out of the European Union with "Brexit" and pushed Donald Trump into the White House. Right-wing populism is also sweeping other parts of the deindustrialized world, as working people lash out furiously against perceived cultural and economic elites – liberal and conservative – for their indifference to the hardships faced by working-class communities. This moral-political outrage could be heard and felt in the interviews we conducted in Sturgeon Falls as well. If nothing else, these votes have demanded that middle-class people re-engage with those economically left behind and question our assumptions about societal progress. Race and gender matter. But so does class. In Sturgeon Falls, as elsewhere, we see the gradual erosion of the culture of industrialism – and the structure of feeling that it supported – and its eventual eclipse by an ascendant post-industrial order that values other things and other people.

It is fitting, perhaps, to end this journey where I began, with Bruce Colquhoun and the mill history binder. The last entry, entitled "Another Dark Day at Our Mill," dated two days after the Cache Bay meeting where the closure was announced, has Colquhoun saying that he could "write a book" on his "feelings about what has [just] happened." But for now, he was going to "end it here," as he still had "a lot of work to complete this history of our mill. It may take a while but I will do it and do it right." Colquhoun only hoped that

> we can save our mill from those American capitalists. This book is not finished. I will continue to add to it whatever I can, because now, it has more meaning … After 29 years, I will be out of a job. We will all be out of a job. Let's hope that someone will buy the place, and start it again. I know that whoever looks at this history, will be amazed at all the information it contains. It is not just a history of this mill, but, a history of our town. I made a lot of friends at the mill, and I will really miss them. I wish each and every one of them the best of luck in the future. Well, I've said enough, for now. Thanks everyone. It was fun while it lasted.[47]

NOTES

Preface

1 Steven High, "Placing the Displaced Worker: Narrating Place in Deindustrializing Sturgeon Falls, Ontario," in *Placing Memory and Remembering Place in Canada*, ed. James Opp and John Walsh, 159–86 (Vancouver: UBC Press, 2010).

2 Pierre Hardy, interview by Kristen O'Hare and Steven High, 5 December 2003 and 14 June 2005. All of the oral history interviews have been archived at the Centre for Oral History and Digital Storytelling (COHDS) at Concordia University in Montreal and are also available at the Sturgeon River House Museum in Sturgeon Falls.

3 Jane Hardy, interview by Kristen O'Hare and Steven High, 5 December 2003 and 14 June 2005.

4 William Boyd, *The Slain Wood: Papermaking and Its Environmental Consequences in the American South* (Baltimore: Johns Hopkins University Press, 2015), 172.

Introduction

1 Donald Creighton, *Dominion of the North: A History of Canada* (Toronto: Houghton Mifflin, 1944).

2 Ray D. Bollman, Rolland Beshiri, and Verna Mitura, "Northern Ontario's Communities: Economic Diversification, Specialization and Growth," Agricultural and Rural Working Paper Series 82 (Ottawa: Statistics Canada, 2006).

3 Ibid.

4 For example, Sudbury's "moonscape" is repeatedly invoked in J.R. McNeil, *Something New Under the Sun: An Environmental History of the Twentieth Century* (New York: W.W. Norton, 2000); and William Ashworth, *The Late, Great Lakes: An Environmental History* (Detroit: Wayne State University, 1986). On Temagami, see Bruce W. Hodgins, *The Temagami Experience: Recreation, Resources, and Aboriginal Rights in the Northern Ontario Wilderness* (Toronto: University of Toronto Press, 1989); and Bruce Hodgins, Ute Lischke, and David T. McNab, eds., *Blockades and Resistance: Studies in Actions of Peace and the Temagami Blockades of 1988–89* (Waterloo, ON:

Wilfrid Laurier University Press, 2003). On mercury poisoning at Grassy Narrows, see George Huchison and Dick Wallace, *Grassy Narrows* (Toronto: Van Nostrand Reinhold, 1977); Anastasia M. Shkilnyk, *A Poison Stronger than Love: The Destruction of an Ojibwa Community* (New Haven, CT: Yale University Press, 1985); and, C. Vecsey, "Grassy Narrows Reserve: Mercury Pollution, Social Disruption, and Natural Resources: A Question of Autonomy," *American Indian Quarterly* 11, no. 4 (1987): 287–314.

5 The phrase "forgotten places" comes from William W. Falk and Thomas A. Lyson, eds., *Forgotten Places: Uneven Development in Rural America* (Lawrence: University Press of Kansas, 1993). Today the provincial north might be the "poorest and least politically powerful region in the country"; see Kerry Abel and Ken S. Coates, eds., *Northern Visions: New Perspectives on the North in Canadian History* (Toronto: Broadview Press, 2001), 18.

6 A.R.M. Lower, "The Assault on the Laurentian Barrier, 1850–1870," *Canadian Historical Review* 10, no. 4 (1929): 294.

7 Donald Creighton, *The Commercial Empire of the St. Lawrence, 1760–1850* (Toronto: Ryerson Press, 1937). For more on historian Creighton and his view of Canada, see Donald Wright's insightful *Donald Creighton: A Life in History* (Toronto: University of Toronto Press, 2015).

8 W.A. Mackintosh wrote that westward expansion "met the impassable barrier of the Laurentian highlands, bordering the Upper Lakes on the north so closely that for half a century progress into the easily settled prairie region beyond was effectively blocked"; see W.A. Mackintosh, "Economic Factors in Canadian History," *Canadian Historical Review* 4, no. 1 (1923): 12–25.

9 Alex Himelfarb, "The Social Characteristics of One-Industry Towns in Canada," in *Little Communities and Big Industries: Studies in the Social Impact of Canadian Resource Extraction*, ed. Roy T. Bowles (Toronto: Butterworths, 1982), 16.

10 James E. Randall and R. Geoff Ironside, "Communities on the Edge: An Economic Geography of Resource-Dependent Communities in Canada," *Canadian Geographer* 40, no. 1 (1996): 21.

11 Roger Hayter, "Technological Imperatives in Resource Sectors: Forest Products," in *Canada and the Global Economy: The Geography of Structural and Technological Change*, ed. John N.H. Britton (Montreal; Kingston, ON: McGill-Queen's University Press, 1996), 107.

12 Rex Lucas, *Minetown, Milltown and Railtown: Life in Canadian Communities of Single Industry* (Toronto: Oxford University Press, [1971] 2008), 22.

13 For an overview of the field, see Steven High, "'The Wounds of Class': A Historiographical Reflection on the Study of Deindustrialization, 1973–2013," *History Compass* 11, no. 11 (2013): 994–1007.

14 For more on Indigenous labour history, see Steven High, "Native Wage Labour and Independent Production during the 'Era of Irrelevance,'" *Labour* 37 (Spring 1996): 243–64; John Sutton Lutz, *Makuk: A New History of Aboriginal-White Relations* (Vancouver: UBC Press, 2008); and Mary Jane Logan McCallum, *Indigenous Women, Work, and History, 1940–1980* (Winnipeg: University of Manitoba Press, 2014).

15 That said, this situation is now changing as Indigenous people move into the cities; see Suzanne E. Mills and Louise Clarke, "'We will go side-by-side with you': Labour Union Engagement with Aboriginal Peoples in Canada," *Geoforum* 40, no. 6 (2009): 991–1001.

16 Thomas Dunk, *A Working Man's Town: Male Working-Class Culture* (Montreal; Kingston, ON: McGill-Queen's University Press, 1991).

17 Adele Perry, *On the Edge of Empire: Gender, Race, and the Making of British Columbia, 1849–1871* (Toronto: University of Toronto Press, 2001), 194.

18 Kerry Abel, *Changing Places: History, Community, and Identity in Northeastern Ontario* (Montreal; Kingston, ON: McGill-Queen's University Press, 2006), 287.

19 Robert W. Wightman and Nancy M. Wightman, "Changing Patterns of Rural Peopling in Northeastern Ontario, 1901–1941," *Ontario History* 92, no. 2 (2000): 161–81.

20 For more on the corporate structure of Canadian forestry, see Barry Boothman, "High Finance/ Low Strategy: Corporate Collapse in the Canadian Pulp and Paper Industry, 1919–1932," *Business History Review* 74, no. 4 (2000): 611–56; Roger Hayter, "Corporate Strategies and Industrial Change in the Canadian Forest Product Industries," *Geographical Review* 66, no. 2 (1976): 209–28; and Mark Kuhlberg, "An Accomplished History, an Uncertain Future: Canada's Pulp and Paper Industry since the Early 1800s," in *The Evolution of Global Paper Industry 1800–2050: A Comparative Analysis*, ed. Juha-Antti Lamberg et al. (Dordrecht: Springer, 2012).

21 See Eileen Golz, "Espanola: The History of a Pulp and Paper Town," *Laurentian University Review* 6, no. 3 (1974): 75–104; and Anthony Winson and Belinda Leach, *Contingent Work, Disrupted Lives: Labour and Community in the New Rural Economy* (Toronto: University of Toronto Press, 2002), 70.

22 Himelfarb, "Social Characteristics," 16.

23 Trevor J. Barnes and Roger Hayter, "Economic Restructuring, Local Development and Resource Towns: Forest Communities in Coastal British Columbia," *Canadian Journal of Regional Science* 17, no. 3 (1994): 298.

24 Randall and Ironside, "Communities on the Edge," 21.

25 Glen Norcliffe, *Global Game, Local Arena: Restructuring in Corner Brook, Newfoundland* (St. John's: ISER Books, 2005), 11–12.

26 René Guénette, "Histoire de Sturgeon Falls (1878–1960)" (master's thesis, Laurentian University, 1966), chap. 1.

27 Ibid.

28 Claude Lortie, interview by Kristen O'Hare and Steven High, 7 September 2004 and 28 June 2005.

29 Harold Stewart, interview by Kristen O'Hare, 18 June 2004.

30 Mill towns often had a "highly developed sense of place and formed tightly knit societies around their kin and ethnic associations," noted Tamara Hareven and Randolph Langenback in *Amoskeag: Life and Work in an American Factory City* (New York: Pantheon, 1978), 12. See also Jacquelyn Dowd Hall, James Leloudis, and Robert Korstad, *Like a Family: The Making of a Southern Cotton Mill World* (Chapel Hill: University of North Carolina Press, 1987). For company towns in international perspective, see M. Borges and S. Torres, eds., *Company Towns: Labor, Space, and Power Relations across Time and Continents* (New York: Palgrave Macmillan, 2012).

31 See, for example, Naomi Krogman and Tom Beckley, "Corporate 'Bail-Outs' and Local 'Buyouts': Pathways to Community Forestry?" *Society and Natural Resources* 15, no. 2 (2002): 109–27; and Jack Quarter, *Crossing the Line: Unionized Employee Ownership and Investment Funds* (Toronto: Lorimer, 1995).

32 The financial reports were later submitted as part of a court challenge to Weyerhaeuser's decision to close the plant without any consultation or prior notice to the West Nipissing Economic Development Committee or the municipality, its partner in the recycling facility. These records were shared with us by Raymond Brouillette (hereafter cited as the Raymond Brouillette Collection); in the possession of the author.

33 This was how this moment was described by Christine J. Walley, the daughter of a Chicago-area steelworker, in her thought-provoking auto-ethnography, *Exit 0: Family and Class in Postindustrial Chicago* (Chicago: University of Chicago Press, 2013), 1–2.

34 Marcel Boudreau, interview by Kristen O'Hare and Steven High, 1 December 2003 and 23 June 2005.

35 Barry Bluestone and Bennet Harrison, *The Deindustrialization of America* (New York: Basic Books, 1982), 27.

36 Jefferson Cowie, *Capital Moves: RCA's 70-Year Quest for Cheap Labor* (Ithaca, NY: Cornell University Press, 1999).

37 The deindustrialization of New England's industry is a case in point. See David Koistinen, *Confronting Decline: The Political Economy of Deindustrialization in Twentieth-Century New England* (Gainesville: University Press of Florida, 2016); and Timothy Minchin, *Empty Mills: The Fight Against Imports and the Decline of the US Textile Industry* (Lanham, MD: Rowman and Littlefield, 2013). Other cross-national comparative works include Steven High, Lachlan MacKinnon, and Andrew Perchard, eds., *The Deindustrialized World: Confronting Ruination in Postindustrial Places* (Vancouver: UBC Press, 2017); Alice Mah, *Industrial Ruination, Community, and Place: Landscapes and Legacies of Urban Decline* (Toronto: University of Toronto Press, 2012); and Tracy Neumann, *Remaking the Rust Belt: The Postindustrial Transformation of North America* (Philadelphia: University of Pennsylvania Press, 2016).

38 Recent scholarship on the environmental and social legacies of mining in northern Canada, while not in direct conversation with the deindustrialization scholarship, has something valuable to offer this discussion. See Arn Keeling, "'Born in an Atomic Test Tube': Landscapes of Cyclonic Development at Uranium City, Saskatchewan," *Canadian Geographer* 54, no. 2 (2010): 228–9; see also Liza Piper and John Sandlos, "A Broken Frontier in Ecological Imperialism in the Canadian North," *Environment History* 12, no. 4 (2007): 759–95; and John Sandlos and Arn Keeling, "Claiming the New North: Development and Colonialism at the Pine Point Mine, Northwest Territories, Canada," *Environment and History* 18, no. 1 (2012): 5–34.

39 Roger Hayter, Trevor J. Barnes, and Michael J. Bradshaw, "Relocating Resource Peripheries to the Core of Economic Geography's Theorizing: Rationale and Agenda," *Area* 35, no. 1 (2003): 16; see also Trevor J. Barnes, "Retheorizing Economic Geography: From the Quantitative Revolution to the 'Cultural Turn,'" *Annals of the Association of American Geographers* 91, no. 3 (2001): 17.

40 Barnes, "Retheorizing Economic Geography," 18.

41 For example, see Jeffrey T. Manuel, *Taconite Dreams: The Struggle to Sustain Mining on Minnesota's Iron Range, 1915–2000* (Minneapolis: University of Minnesota Press, 2015); James Phillips, *Collieries, Communities and the Miners' Strike in Scotland, 1984–85* (Manchester, UK: Manchester University Press, 2012); and Gregory S. Wilson, *Communities Left Behind: The Area Redevelopment Administration, 1945–1965* (Knoxville: University of Tennessee Press, 2009).

42 Bob Russell, *More with Less: Work Reorganization in the Canadian Mining Industry* (Toronto: University of Toronto Press, 1999), 163.

43 Ibid., 11.

44 Gordon Hak, *Capital and Labour in the British Columbia Forest Industry, 1934–74* (Vancouver: UBC Press, 2007), 124.

45 E.P. Thompson, *The Poverty of Theory and Other Essays* (London: Marlin, 1978), 85.

46 John Kirk, *Class, Culture and Social Change: On the Trail of the Working Class* (London: Palgrave Macmillan, 2007), 2.

47 Stephen Meyer, *Manhood on the Line: Working-Class Masculinities in the American Heartland* (Urbana: University of Illinois Press, 2016), 1.

48 Ibid., 39–40.

49 Raymond Williams, *Marxism and Literature* (Oxford: Oxford University Press, 1977), 19.

50 Kirk, *Class, Culture and Social Change*, 9.

51 Williams, *Marxism and Literature*, 131.

52 Beverley Skeggs, *Class, Self, Culture* (London: Routledge, 2004), 45; see also Tim Strangleman, "Work Identity in Crisis? Rethinking the Problem of Attachment and Loss at Work," *Sociology* 46, no. 3 (2012): 411–25.

53 Skeggs, *Class, Self, Culture*, 54.

54 Richard Florida, *Ontario in the Creative Age* (Toronto: Prosperity Institute, 2009).

55 Skeggs, *Class, Self, Culture*, 50.

56 Luisa Passerini, *Fascism in Popular Memory: The Cultural Experience of the Turin Working-Class* (Cambridge: Cambridge University Press, 1987), 8.

57 Doreen Massey, *Spatial Divisions of Labour: Social Structures and the Geographies of Production* (London: Macmillan, 1984), 117.

58 Ibid., 177.

59 Kirk, *Class, Culture and Social Change*, 4.

60 Owen Jones, *Chavs: The Demonization of the Working Class* (London: Verso, 2011), 9.

1. The Industrial Frontier

1 Quoted in "Canada's pulpwood," *Globe* (Toronto), 7 October 1898.

2 Ibid.

3 H.V. Nelles, *The Politics of Development: Forests, Mines, and Hydro-Electric Power in Ontario, 1849–1941* (Toronto: Macmillan of Canada, 1974). This influential interpretation has been challenged by Mark Kuhlberg, who argues, I think persuasively, that the Ontario state gave pulp and paper companies only a "lukewarm reception at best." The government favoured the lumber interests. See Mark Kuhlberg, *In the Power of Government: The Rise and Fall of Newsprint in Ontario, 1894–1932* (Toronto: University of Toronto Press, 2015), 3.

4 R. Peter Gillis and Thomas R. Roach, *Lost Initiatives: Canada's Forest Industries, Forest Policy and Forest Conservation* (New York: Greenwood, 1986), 92; and Duncan McDowall, *Steel at the Sault: Francis H. Clergue, Sir James Dunn, and the Algoma Steel Corporation, 1901–1956* (Toronto: University of Toronto Press, 1984).

5 "The Sturgeon Falls Pulp Company," *Canadian Manufacturer and Industrial World* 37, no. 9 (1898): 33–4.

6 Agreement between Her Majesty and the Sturgeon Falls Pulp Company, 6 October 1898 (Toronto: Legislative Assembly, 1899), 3–5. For more, see Bruce W. Hodgins, *The Temagami Experience: Recreation, Resources, and Aboriginal Rights in the Northern Ontario Wilderness* (Toronto: University of Toronto Press, 1989), 55.

7 C.M. Wallace, "Communities in the Northern Ontario Frontier," in *At the End of the Shift: Mines and Single-Industry Towns in Northern Ontario*, ed. Matt Bray and Ashley Thomson (Toronto: Dundurn Press, 1992), 8.

8 "Canada's pulpwood," *Globe* (Toronto), 7 October 1898. The Occidental Syndicate comprised H.G. Sinclair of Tilley and Henderson (linen firm), H. Graham Lloyd of B.S. Lloyd & Co., and others.

9 Abel, *Changing Places*, 377–8.

10 Ibid., 378.

11 Wayne F. LeBelle, *Sturgeon Falls, 1895–1995* (Field, ON: WFL Communications, 1995), 1.

12 Massey, *Spatial Divisions of Labour*, 117.

13 Frederick Cooper, *Colonialism in Question: Theory, Knowledge, History* (Berkeley: University of California Press, 2005), 27.

14 Janet E. Chute, *The Legacy of Shingwaukonse: A Century of Native Leadership* (Toronto: University of Toronto Press, 1998).

15 See Nipissing First Nation, "History," available online at http://www.nfn.ca/historical/.

16 Lise C. Hansen, "Revocation of Surrender and Its Implications for a Canadian Indian Band's Development," *Anthropologica* 23, no. 2 (1981): 121–43.

17 "North Bay and Sturgeon Falls," *Globe* (Toronto), 8 May 1906.

18 Canada, Department of Indian Affairs, *Annual Report of the Department of Indian Affairs for the Year Ended, June 30, 1904 to 1918* (Ottawa, 1919).

19 Lise C. Hansen, "Thirty-five Dollars," *Canadian Journal of Native Studies* 2, no. 2 (1982): 271.

20 Nipissing First Nation, "History."

21 Hansen, "Thirty-five Dollars," 271–3.

22 Randy Restoule, interview by Kristen O'Hare, 5 August 2004.

23 "The News," *Canada Lumberman* 19, no. 2 (February 1898): 11.

24 R.S. Cassels, "A Paddler's Paradise," *Massey Magazine* 1, no. 6 (1896): 393, 399.

25 "The News," *Canada Lumberman* 12, no. 3 (1891): 8.

26 George Carruthers, *Paper-Making* (Toronto: Garden City Press, 1947), 663.

27 "Contracts Open," *Canadian Contract Record* 5, no. 43 (1894): 1; "Industrial Notes," *Canadian Engineer* 2, no. 11 (1895): 328.

28 "Industrial Notes," *Canadian Engineer* 4, no. 1 (1896): 24.

29 Certificate of Incorporation of the Sturgeon Falls Pulp Company, Limited, 28 July 1898, BT 31/8096/58387–58387, National Archives, London.

30 The Sturgeon Falls Pulp Company, Memorandum and Articles of Association, Incorporated 20 July 1898, BT 31/8096/58387–535466, National Archives, London.

31 Petition to the High Court of Justice of Harold Gilmore Campion, London Solicitor, 30 December 1904, File of Proceedings in the Matter of the Sturgeon Falls Pulp Co. Ltd., J1313821–535466, National Archives, London.

32 "Pulp Mill Information," *Monetary Times* 32, no. 21 (1898): 671.

33 "The News," *Canada Lumberman* 20, no. 6 (1899): 14; "The News," *Canada Lumberman* 21, no. 10 (1901): 15.

34 "The News," *Canada Lumberman* 20, no. 7 (1899): 15.

35 "Wood Pulp Department," *Canada Lumberman* 20, no. 8 (1899): 15.

36 "Big paper deal," *Globe* (Toronto), 22 February 1900.

37 "Pulp Concession Arbitration," *Canada Lumberman* 21, no. 10 (1900): 12.

38 Ibid.

39 "In the law of pulpwood," *Globe* (Toronto), 27 November 1902.

40 "The Sturgeon Falls Arbitration," *Canada Lumberman* (December 1901): 8.

41 "News," *Canadian Manufacturer and Industrial World* 43, no. 10 (1901): 20; and "Sturgeon Falls Arbitration," 8.

42 "Sturgeon Falls Arbitration," 10.

43 "In the law of pulpwood," *Globe* (Toronto), 27 November 1902.

44 Prospectus for SF Pulp Company, 7 July 1902, BT 31/8096/58387–535466, National Archives, London.

45 The Company Acts, File on Proceedings in the Matter of Sturgeon Falls Pulp Co Ltd. No 80 of 1906, in the High Court of Justice, Tuesday, 17 July 1906, J1314388–535466, National Archives, London. See also Prospectus for SF Pulp Company, Memorandum of Agreement, 22 July 1903, BT 31/8096/58387–535466, National Archives, London.

46 "Mr. C.W. Rantoul," *Canada Lumberman* 23, no. 6 (1902): 16.

47 "Pulp Notes," *Canada Lumberman* 24, no. 11 (1903): 25.

48 "The Pulp Industry in Ontario," *Canada Lumberman* 25, no. 5 (1904), 28. Imperial Mills expanded its Sturgeon Falls mill to such a degree that it could no longer be powered by the

existing water power. As a result, the company sought to dam Lake Temagami to better regulate seasonal water flow (and redirect water into the Sturgeon River), but ended up in a confrontation with cottage owners and recreationalists as well as the Ontario government; see Kuhlberg, *In the Power of Government*, 71.

49 "Sturgeon Falls booming," *Globe* (Toronto), 7 October 1904.

50 Canadian Pulp and Paper Association, *A Handbook of the Canadian Pulp and Paper Industry* (Montreal, 1920), 37.

51 Ibid.

52 The initial twenty-one-year agreement ended on 6 October 1919, but was then extended to 1932. See Ontario Timber Commission, *Interim Reports* (Toronto: Clarkson W. James, 1921), 62.

53 Ian Radforth, *Bushworkers and Bosses: Logging in Northern Ontario, 1900–1980* (Toronto: University of Toronto Press, 1987).

54 Canadian Pulp and Paper Association, *Handbook*, 2.

55 Guy Gaudreau has written extensively on the subcontracting system that was a vital part of rural life in francophone Ontario; see Guy Gaudreau, "La sous-traitance forestière dans le Nord-Est ontarien, 1900–1930," *Labour* 40 (Fall 1997): 95. For a New Brunswick example, see Bill Parenteau, "The Woods Transformed: The Emergence of the Pulp and Paper Industry in New Brunswick, 1918–1931," *Acadiensis* 22, no. 1 (1992): 5–43.

56 For a very useful chronology of these early years, see Chris Matthews, "The Sturgeon Falls Mill" (BA Honours thesis, Laurentian University, 1996), 30.

57 Hodgins, *Temagami Experience*, 126–8.

58 Boyd, *Slain Wood*, 13.

59 Henry W. Gill, Town Clerk, Sturgeon Falls, to Attorney General of Ontario, 23 August 1899, File 1526, RG 4–32, Office of the Attorney General of Ontario, Central Registry Files. Archives of Ontario, Toronto.

60 T.W. Ruddell, Sturgeon Falls, to Mr. Browning, Barrister, North Bay, 11 November 1903, File 1903, No. 1695, RG 4–32, Office of the Attorney General of Ontario, Archives of Ontario, Toronto.

61 Reverend J.G. Shearer, General Secretary, The Lord's Day Alliance of Canada, to J.R. Cartwright, Attorney General's Office, 19 November 1903, File 1903, No. 1695, RG 4–32, Office of the Attorney General of Ontario, Archives of Ontario, Toronto.

62 C.A. Rantoul, General Manager, The Imperial Paper Mills of Canada Limited. 23 November 1903, File 1903, No. 1695, RG 4–32, Office of the Attorney General of Ontario, Archives of Ontario, Toronto.

63 James A. Gross, "The Making and Shaping of Unionism in the Pulp and Paper Industry," *Labor History* 5, no. 2 (1964): 185.

64 Ibid.

65 Egil Schonning, "Union-Management Relations in the Pulp and Paper Industry of Ontario and Quebec" (PhD diss., University of Toronto, 1955), 46.

66 Matthews, "Sturgeon Falls Mill."

67 John Craig, Imperial Mills, 26 July 1907, Vol. 295, Strike 2960, RG 27, Canada, Department of Labour, Trade Disputes, Library and Archives Canada (hereafter cited as LAC), Ottawa.

68 Francis Reid, 25 July 1907, Vol. 295, Strike 2960, RG 27, Canada, Department of Labour, Trade Disputes, LAC.

69 John Craig, Imperial Mills, 10 August 1907, Vol. 295, Strike 2960, RG 27, Canada, Department of Labour, Trade Disputes, LAC.

70 Ibid.

71 Ibid.

72 For the evolution of labour law, see Judy Fudge and Eric Tucker, *Labour Before the Law: The Regulation of Workers' Collective Action in Canada, 1900–1948* (Toronto: Oxford University Press, 2001).

73 "Sturgeon Falls Division," *Abitibi Magazine* ([no month] 1958).

74 Ibid.

75 William H. Burnell, "On the Record," *Pulp, Sulphite and Paper Mill Workers Journal* (March–April 1963): 8.

76 "The Loyalty of the French Canadians to Our International Union," *Canadian Paperworker PS&PMU Journal* (November-December 1952).

77 Gross, "The Making and Shaping of Unionism," 192.

78 A. Wagner, Secretary, Sturgeon Falls Local No. 71 Pulp, Sulphite and Paper Mill Workers, to John P. Burke, International President-Secretary (Fort Edward, NY), 24 February 1921, File Local 71–1921, International Brotherhood of Pulp, Sulphite and Paper Mill Workers Records, Kheel Center for Labor-Management Documentation & Archives, Cornell University Library (hereafter cited as Kheel Center, CUL), Ithaca, NY.

79 Ibid.

80 John P. Burke to A. Wagner, 26 February 1921, Local 71–1921, International Brotherhood of Pulp, Sulphite and Paper Mill Workers Records, Kheel Center, CUL.

81 Western Union telegram from Wagner to Burke, Local 71–1921, International Brotherhood of Pulp, Sulphite and Paper Mill Workers Records, Kheel Center, CUL.

82 Wagner to Burke, 22 April 1921, Local 71–1921, International Brotherhood of Pulp, Sulphite and Paper Mill Workers Records, Kheel Center, CUL.

83 Ibid.

84 Burke to Wagner, 25 April 1921, Local 71–1921, International Brotherhood of Pulp, Sulphite and Paper Mill Workers Records, Kheel Center, CUL.

85 Burke to Wagner, 7 May 1921, Local 71–1921, International Brotherhood of Pulp, Sulphite and Paper Mill Workers Records, Kheel Center, CUL.

86 Ibid.

87 Wagner to Burke, Western Union telegram, 11 May 1921, Local 71–1921; Burke to Wagner, 12 May 1921, Local 71–1921, International Brotherhood of Pulp, Sulphite and Paper Mill Workers Records, Kheel Center, CUL.

88 Burke to Wagner, 13 May 1921, Local 71–1921, International Brotherhood of Pulp, Sulphite and Paper Mill Workers Records, Kheel Center, CUL.

89 Ibid.

90 Burke to Wagner, 23 June 1921, Local 71–1921, International Brotherhood of Pulp, Sulphite and Paper Mill Workers Records, Kheel Center, CUL.

91 C.H.L. Jones, "The Spanish River Pulp & Paper Mills Ltd.," *Bulletin No. 7*, Sault Ste Marie, 22 June 1921, Local 71–1921, International Brotherhood of Pulp, Sulphite and Paper Mill Workers Records, Kheel Center, CUL.

92 Ibid.

93 Wagner to Burke, 24 June 1921, Local 71–1921, International Brotherhood of Pulp, Sulphite and Paper Mill Workers Records, Kheel Center, CUL.

94 Ibid.

95 Wagner to Burke, 27 June 1921, Local 71–1921, International Brotherhood of Pulp, Sulphite and Paper Mill Workers Records, Kheel Center, CUL.

96 Wagner to Burke, 19 July 1921; Burke to Wagner, 21 July 1921, Local 71–1921, International Brotherhood of Pulp, Sulphite and Paper Mill Workers Records, Kheel Center, CUL.

97 Wagner to Burke, 1 August 1921, Local 71–1921, International Brotherhood of Pulp, Sulphite and Paper Mill Workers Records, Kheel Center, CUL.

98 Ibid.

99 Burke to Wagner, 18 August 1921, Local 71–1921, International Brotherhood of Pulp, Sulphite and Paper Mill Workers Records, Kheel Center, CUL. See also Schonning, "Union-Management Relations," 157.

100 Union Headquarters to Wagner, 23 August 1921, Local 71–1921, International Brotherhood of Pulp, Sulphite and Paper Mill Workers Records, Kheel Center, CUL.

101 Burke to Wagner, 24 August 1921, Local 71–1921, International Brotherhood of Pulp, Sulphite and Paper Mill Workers Records, Kheel Center, CUL.

102 Wagner to Burke, 21 August 1921, Local 71–1921, International Brotherhood of Pulp, Sulphite and Paper Mill Workers Records, Kheel Center, CUL.

103 Wagner to Burke, 6 September 1921, Local 71–1921, International Brotherhood of Pulp, Sulphite and Paper Mill Workers Records, Kheel Center, CUL.

104 Ibid.

105 Burke to Wagner, 8 September 1921, Local 71–1921, International Brotherhood of Pulp, Sulphite and Paper Mill Workers Records, Kheel Center, CUL.

106 Burke to Wagner, 4 November 1921, Local 71–1921, International Brotherhood of Pulp, Sulphite and Paper Mill Workers Records, Kheel Center, CUL.

107 Burke to Wagner, 8 September 1921, Local 71–1921, International Brotherhood of Pulp, Sulphite and Paper Mill Workers Records, Kheel Center, CUL.

108 Schonning, "Union-Management Relations," 107.

109 Quoted in ibid., 115.

110 The other companies were the Manitoba Paper Company (with a newsprint mill at Pine Falls), the Fort William Power Company (a newsprint mill in Thunder Bay), the Ste. Anne Paper Company (a newsprint mill at Beaupré, Quebec), and the Murray Paper Company (a mill at Murray Bay, Quebec). See Ontario, Royal Commission Inquiring into the Affairs of Abitibi Power & Paper Company Limited, *Report* (Toronto, March 1941), G-6.

111 Ibid.

2. A Town on Trial

1 LeBelle, *Sturgeon Falls*, 94

2 Ken Colquhoun, interview by Steven High, 23 June 2005.

3 *Labour Gazette* 33 (1933): 56.

4 Fully 27.8 per cent were still on poor relief in 1940, far more than other hard-hit Northern Ontario towns such as Blind River (19.2 per cent) and Mattawa (14.3 per cent). See Ontario, Department of Municipal Affairs, *Annual Report of Municipal Statistics for the Year 1940* (Toronto, 1941), 25; and Lara Campbell, *Respectable Citizens: Gender, Family, and Unemployment in Ontario's Great Depression* (Toronto: University of Toronto Press, 2009), 3.

5 Ben Lajeunesse, interview by Kristen O'Hare, 22 June 2004.

6 P.G. Masterson, "The Sturgeon Falls Operations of Abitibi Power and Paper Company, Limited" (manuscript, October 1956), in the author's possession.

7 Town of Sturgeon Falls, "Remember Sturgeon Falls Yesterday," centennial booklet, personal collection of Hubert Gervais.

8 Ibid.

9   "The History of the Town of Sturgeon Falls and Its Masonic Temple" (West Nipissing, ON: West Nipissing Public Library, n.d.), 5.

10 LeBelle, *Sturgeon Falls*, 95.

11 Barry Broadfoot, *Ten Lost Years, 1929–1939* (Toronto: McClelland & Stewart, 1973). For Broadfoot's impact on the field of oral history, see Steven High, "Sharing Authority in the Writing of Canadian History: The Case of Oral History," in *Contesting Clio's Craft: New Directions and Debates in Canadian History*, ed. Michael Dawson and Christopher Dummitt (London: Institute for the Study of the Americas, 2009).

12 Ed Fortin, interview by Kristen O'Hare, 5 August 2004.

13 Merna Nesbitt, interview by Kristen O'Hare, 10 August 2004.

14 "Sturgeon Falls Division," *Abitibi Magazine* (April 1930), 29.

15 "Sturgeon Falls Division," *Abitibi Magazine* (May 1930), 29.

16 "Sturgeon Falls Division," *Abitibi Magazine* (July 1930).

17 At the time of its closing in 1930, the mill employed 195 people; see In the Matter of Abitibi Power & Paper Company, Limited, Compilation of Statements and Information obtained by The Bondholders' Representative Committee, Toronto, 21 July 1937, G-6, Sault Ste Marie Public Library.

18 In the three years following the mill's closing, Abitibi's receivers reported that the total cost of caretaking the property was $63,769 (to 31 December 1933) and it had paid $52,260 in local taxes; see Abitibi Power & Paper Company Limited, *Second Report of Receiver and Manager* (April 1934), G-6, Sault Ste Marie Public Library.

19 G.T. Clarkson, Receiver and Manager, In the Matter of Abitibi Power & Paper Company Limited, *Report for 1932*, G-6, Sault Ste Marie Public Library.

20 Ibid.

21 In 1929–30, the last year of production, the mill purchased 26,199 cords from farmers and jobbers, and cut another 43,469 from the Sturgeon Falls Concession; see In the Matter of Abitibi Power & Paper Company, Limited, Compilation of Statements and Information obtained by The Bondholders' Representative Committee, Toronto, 21 July 1937, G-6, Sault Ste Marie Public Library.

22 Ibid.

23 The archival records of the International Brotherhood contain no reports from the Sturgeon Falls local after the mill closed. They do include a February 1938 letter from George Denault, acting president of Local 74 at Espanola, that reveals some of the challenges faced by those trying to keep union locals alive at closed mills. In 1938, Denault reported that there were only seven union members left on payroll at the mothballed plant. No regular meeting could be organized, as the handful of surviving members worked different shifts. The union responded that it was no longer necessary to send monthly reports "because I know your mill is not running and you only have a few members left. I do appreciate the manner in which you are keeping the local alive at Espanola. Let us hope the day will come when the mill at Espanola will run again." John P. Burke to George Denault, Acting President, Local 74, 28 February 1938, File Local 71–1938, International Brotherhood of Pulp, Sulphite and Paper Mill Workers Records, Kheel Center, CUL.

24 Quoted in Gross, "Making and Shaping of Unionism," 195.

25 Ibid., 197.

26 "The voucher system," *Globe* (Toronto), 16 February 1933.

27 James Struthers, "How Much Is Enough? Creating a Social Minimum in Ontario, 1930–44," *Canadian Historical Review* 72, no. 1 (1991): 39.

28 During the first two years, "municipalities scrambled to put in place structures for dispensing aid on a mass scale with only the vaguest guidance from the province or federal government" (ibid., 42).

29 Jonathan A. Rodden and Gunnar S. Eskeland, "Constraining Subnational Fiscal Behavior in Canada," in *Fiscal Decentralization and the Challenge of Hard Budget Constraints*, ed. Richard M. Bird and Almos Tassanyi (Cambridge, MA: MIT Press, 2003), 102.

30 "Sturgeon Falls facing anarchy, say petitioners," *Globe* (Toronto), 15 April 1931.

31 "Intimates relief of pulp mill town," *New York Times*, 7 May 1931.

32 This was even mentioned in *Pulp and Paper Magazine of Canada* 31 (1931).

33 "Destitute Ontario children can go to school barefoot," *New York Times*, 19 April 1931.

34 "Sturgeon Falls facing anarchy, say petitioners," *Globe* (Toronto), 15 April 1931; Ontario, Royal Commission on the Enquiry as to the Handling of Unemployment and Direct Relief at Sturgeon Falls, Ontario, *Report* (Toronto, 1933), RG 18, Series B-81, Archives of Ontario, Toronto (hereafter cited as Hall Report).

35 Ibid.

36 Ontario, Department of Municipal Affairs, *Annual Report of Municipal Statistics for the Year 1937* (Toronto, 1938).

37 Ontario, Department of Municipal Affairs, *Annual Report of Municipal Statistics for the Year 1938* (Toronto, 1939); idem, *Annual Report of Municipal Statistics for the Year 1939* (Toronto, 1940).

38 Ontario, Department of Municipal Affairs, *Annual Report of Municipal Statistics for the Years 1937–1941* (Toronto, 1942).

39 Hall Report.

40 Ibid.

41 Ibid.

42 Ibid.

43 "Padded accounts cut town's costs, judge suggests," *Globe* (Toronto), 13 January 1933.

44 Ibid.

45 "Sharing in relief, wife of merchant uses maiden name," *Globe* (Toronto), 14 January 1933.

46 "Figures incorrect for relief rentals, probers informed," *Globe* (Toronto), 24 January 1933.

47 Hall Report.

48 Ibid.

49 Ibid.

50 Ibid.

51 "Even horses paid in Sturgeon Falls, evidence reveals," *Globe* (Toronto), 12 January 1933.

52 "Many irregularities at Sturgeon Falls are cited by judge," *Globe* (Toronto), 21 April 1933.

53 "Sturgeon Falls to ask one hundred per cent relief," *Globe* (Toronto), 23 January 1933.

54 Ibid.

55 "Threaten to kill cows," *Globe* (Toronto), 27 January 1933.

56 Ibid.

57 J.A. Ellis, Secretary, Unemployment Relief Fund, to Premier George S. Henry, 5 May 1933, Memorandum on Sturgeon Falls, RG 3-8-0-404, Archives of Ontario, Toronto.

58 W.L. Fortier, Clerk and Treasurer, Town of Sturgeon Falls, to Ontario Premier George S. Henry, 13 February 1933, Sturgeon Falls: Financial Position, RG 3-8-0-404 (1933), Archives of Ontario, Toronto.

59 Ibid.

60 Ibid.

61 Unsigned (probably Premier's Office), 15 February 1933, Sturgeon Falls – Financial Position, RG 3–8-0–404, (1933), Archives of Ontario, Toronto.

62 W.L. Fortier, Clerk and Treasurer, Sturgeon Falls, to J.D. Monteith, Minister of Public Works and Labour, 9 May 1933, RG 3–8-0–404, Archives of Ontario, Toronto. The town's deteriorating financial position can be tracked in the records kept by the Department of Municipal Affairs. In a March 1933 letter to local MPP A.Z. Aubin, Fortier notes that $46,986.58 in town debentures were set to mature in 1933. The list of the town's debentures maturing in 1933 included a 1905 issuance for the municipal building (1905), sewers (1906–7, 1921, 1924), waterworks (1921, 1923, 1924, 1925), water purification (1924), sidewalks (1921), electric light plant (1921), fire hall (1923), fire protection (1924), spur tracks (1924), House of Refuge (1925), and a public school (1925). Clearly, the early 1920s was a period of economic prosperity and civic optimism in Sturgeon Falls. This standard mechanism for the financing of local improvements now meant paying down commitments made in the best of times in the worst of times. See W.L. Fortier, Clerk and Treasurer, Town of Sturgeon Falls, to A.Z. Aubin, MPP, Summary of Debenture Debt Annuities Paid in 1932 and Maturing, 1933, 13 March 1933, File: Sturgeon Falls, Town of, RG 19–33, No. 3, Archives of Ontario, Toronto.

63 Clerk of Sturgeon Falls to J.E. Arpin, Controller, La Banque Canadienne Nationale, Montreal, File: Sturgeon Falls, Town of, RG 19–33, No. 3, Archives of Ontario, Toronto.

64 Ontario, Department of Municipal Affairs, *Annual Report of Municipal Statistics for the Year 1934* (Toronto, 1935).

65 "Sturgeon relief strike lasts for only a day," *Sudbury Star*, 2 December 1933.

66 "Three run relief in Sturgeon Falls," *Globe* (Toronto), 3 February 1933.

67 "Relief workers refuse to toil when food cut," *Toronto Telegram*, 1 December 1933.

68 Ibid.

69 "Relief cut, men strike, 'not enough to live on' – 2,734 people affected," *Toronto Star*, 2 December 1933.

70 "Men strike when relief is reduced by Ontario government," *Toronto Worker*, 9 December 1933.

71 "Relief cut, men strike, 'not enough to live on' – 2,734 people affected," *Toronto Star*, 2 December 1933.

72 "Relief workers refuse to toil when food cut," *Toronto Telegraph*, 1 December 1933.

73 "Sturgeon relief strike settled," *North Bay Nugget*, 14 December 1933.

74 "Cut postponed and strikers return to work," *Toronto Worker*, 9 December 1933.

75 "Strike forces withdrawal of relief cuts," *Toronto Worker*, 30 December 1933.

76 Robert Verdun, Unemployed and Workers Union of Sturgeon Falls, 9 April 1936, in William Lyon Mackenzie King Papers, 197119–20, MG 26J1, C3695, LAC.

77 Madeleine Parks, "Sturgeon agog over mill rumor," *North Bay Nugget*, 13 May 1944.

78 Ibid.

79 "Sturgeon Falls Division," *Abitibi Magazine* (1948). These pages from the *Abitibi Magazine* were accessed in Hubert Gervais and Bruce Colquhoun, "The Mill History Binder," available at the West Nipissing Public Library.

80 "Sturgeon Falls Division," *Abitibi Magazine* (March–September 1948).

81 "Sturgeon Falls Division," *Abitibi Magazine* (September 1948).

82 Ibid.

83 "Sturgeon Falls Division," *Abitibi Magazine* (December 1947).

84 "Sturgeon Falls Division," *Abitibi Magazine* (July 1949).

85 "Sturgeon Falls Division," *Abitibi Magazine* (June 1953).

86 "Sturgeon Falls Division," *Abitibi Magazine* ([no month], 1956).

87 "Sturgeon Falls Division," *Abitibi Magazine* (January 1958).
88 "Sturgeon Falls Division," *Abitibi Magazine* ([no month], 1958).
89 "Sturgeon Falls Division," *Abitibi Magazine* ([no month], 1959).
90 "Sturgeon Falls Division," *Abitibi Magazine* ([no month], 1953).
91 "Sturgeon Falls Division," *Abitibi Magazine* (December 1950).

3. Working Lives

 1 Lionel Sarazin, interview by Kristen O'Hare, 6 April 2005.
 2 "It's official now: Sturgeon mill will re-open," *North Bay Nugget*, 2 October 1946.
 3 Schonning, "Union-Management Relations," 9.
 4 Ibid., 15.
 5 "Sturgeon Falls Mill," *Abitibi Magazine* (May 1947).
 6 For more on the "political apparatus of production," and a good discussion of Fordist and post-Fordist practices, see Russell, *More with Less*, 163.
 7 Nelson Lichtenstein, quoted in Hak, *Capital and Mobility*, 8.
 8 Strangleman, "Work Identity in Crisis?" 419.
 9 Thompson, *Poverty of Theory*, 85.
10 Kirk, *Class, Culture and Social Change,* 39–40.
11 Andrew Sayer, *The Moral Significance of Class* (Cambridge: Cambridge University Press, 2005), 22.
12 Benny Haarsma, interview by Kristen O'Hare, 30 June 2004.
13 Hubert Gervais, interview by Kristen O'Hare, 12 March 2004.
14 Henri Labelle, interview by Kristen O'Hare, 9 December 2004.
15 Looking back, however, Mike Lacroix now thought it ironic that he was in such a rush to leave school: "The first thing you know, you wind up in a job and it's mostly a dead end job." Continuing, "If I [had] known back then what I know today, I would have went to school. That's the difference between myself and my wife. She's still working, she's got a good job, she went to school and a university degree, [shrugs] no problem getting work. My daughter's a graduate from Canadore [College] in North Bay. She's got a good job. So that's the difference."
16 Gaudreau, "Sous-traitance forestière dans le Nord-Est Ontarien"; idem, "Importance du cadre juridique," 229; Bruce W. Hodgins and Jamie Benidickson, "Resource Management Conflict in the Temagami Forest, 1898 to 1914," *Historical Papers* 13, no. 1 (1978): 148–75; J. David Wood, *Places of Last Resort: The Expansion of the Farm Frontier into the Boreal Forest in Canada, 1910–1940* (Montreal; Kingston, ON: McGill-Queen's University Press, 2006), 7.
17 Vic Laberge, "Find new uses for Abitibi hardboard," *North Bay Nugget*, 3 September 1953.
18 Receipts for 1952, untitled folder (ink stained), in the possession of Claude Lortie, who salvaged a box of mill records found in a neighbour's garage (hereafter cited as the Claude Lortie Collection), Sturgeon Falls, ON.
19 J.E. Gracie to Mrs Florence Hainer, Mount Forest, 16 October 1959, File H-1, "H" Misc., Claude Lortie Collection.
20 J.J. Kearns, Provincial Sanitary Inspector, to W.O. Cooke, Department of Industrial Hygiene. Re Mr Pierre Aubin, Field, ON, 7 October 1959, File A-2, "A" Misc., "Pulpwood suppliers 1950s and early 1960s," Claude Lortie Collection.
21 Abitibi Pulp and Paper, File "Oscar Rivet, Season 1952–3: Purchase wood program (pulpwood purchase prices, volume)," Claude Lortie Collection.
22 Radforth, *Bushworkers and Bosses*.

23 Carl Backstrom, Verner, to Dwyer, buyer, 9 September 1958, File B-1, "B" Misc., Claude Lortie Collection.

24 Reverend W. Bradley, Paroisse Ste-Rose-de-Lima, River Valley, ON, to Abitibi, 12 April 1956, File B-1, "B" Misc., Claude Lortie Collection.

25 J.M. Becking to J.E. Gracie, 5 April 1957, File B-1, "B" Misc., Claude Lortie Collection.

26 Marc Côté, interview by Kristen O'Hare, 30 January 2004.

27 Thomas Dunk, "Remaking the Working Class: Experience, Class Consciousness, and the Industrial Adjustment Process," *American Ethnologist* 29, no. 4 (2002): 878–900.

28 For more on the organization of industrial work under Fordism, see David M. Gordon, Richard Edwards, and Michael Reich, *Segmented Work, Divided Workers: The Historical Transformation of Labor in the United States* (Cambridge: Cambridge University Press, 1982); and Peter S. McInnis, *Harnessing Labour Confrontation: Shaping the Postwar Settlement in Canada, 1943–1950* (Toronto: University of Toronto Press, 2002).

29 Ruth Thompson, interview by Kristen O'Hare, 22 June 2004.

30 John Dillon, interview by Kristen O'Hare, 19 May 2004.

31 Ron Demers, interview by Kristen O'Hare, 6 May 2004.

32 Frank Gerbasi, interview by Kristen O'Hare, 23 January 2004.

33 Gerry Stevens, interview by Kristen O'Hare, 2 July 2004.

4. Accident Stories

1 A complete run of the *Insider* newsletter, published in the 1990s, was saved from the shredding machine by salaried employees who secreted it out of the closing mill.

2 Almost all the injured workers Robert Storey interviewed across Ontario emphasized their own strong work ethic. "In each narrative," Storey concludes, "one can find a close association between work and a personal sense of integrity and independence." See Robert Storey, "'They Have All Been Faithful Workers': Injured Workers, Truth, and Workers' Compensation in Ontario, 1970–2008," *Journal of Canadian Studies* 43, no. 1 (2009): 161; see also idem, "Pessimism of the Intellect, Optimism of the Will: Engaging with the 'Testimony' of Injured Workers," in *Beyond Testimony and Trauma: Oral History in the Aftermath of Mass Violence*, ed. Steven High, 56–87 (Vancouver: UBC Press, 2015).

3 Kirk, *Class, Culture and Social Change*, 5–8.

4 Arthur McIvor, "Economic Violence, Occupational Disability and Death: Oral Narratives of the Impact of Asbestos-Related Diseases in Britain," in High, *Beyond Testimony and Trauma*, 247.

5 Ibid., 266.

6 Joy Parr, *Sensing Changes: Technologies, Environments and the Everyday, 1953–2003* (Vancouver: UBC Press, 2010), 1.

7 Marcel Labbé, interview by Kristen O'Hare and Steven High, 18 August 2004 and June 2005.

8 In the United Kingdom, workers were ten times less likely to be killed on the job in the early 2000s than they had been in the 1950s; see Arthur McIvor, *Working Lives: Working Britain since 1945* (London: Palgrave Macmillan, 2013), 178.

9 *Insider–Weyerhaeuser Bulletin*, 29 September 2002.

10 Appendix – General Instructions Covering Mills Employees, 1 May 1923, File 6178–01785F11, Local 71, International Brotherhood of Pulp, Sulphite and Paper Mill Workers Records, Kheel Center, CUL.

11 Vol. 1, File 1, 1956 Memorandum of Agreement, MG 28 I484, LAC.

12 Vol. 1, Abitibi (Main File), File 1, 1961 Memorandum of Settlement, MG 28 I484, LAC.

13 Vol. 1, Abitibi (Main File), File 1, 1975 Memorandum of Agreement, MG 28 I484, LAC.

14 Wally Shisko, interview by Kristen O'Hare, 8 May 2004.

15 Andy Cull to J.M. Buchanan, 15 April 1980, File: Local 7135 – 1972 to 1981, Box 14, MG 28 I484, Accession 1994/0028, LAC.

16 On one wall in the OCC area, workers were warned to "chock wheels before loading" and to avoid using air hoses to blow out trailers, and reminded that they were required to wear eye protection in this area of the mill.

17 Tim Edensor, *Industrial Ruins: Space, Aesthetics, and Materiality* (New York: Berg, 2005), 67.

18 Ibid.

19 Due to the sensitivity of this story, the interviewee is anonymous.

20 See, for example, Jeremy Milloy, *Blood, Sweat, and Fear: Violence at Work in the North American Auto Industry* (Vancouver: UBC Press, 2017).

21 Ontario, Ministry of Labour, *Improving Health and Safety in the Pulp and Paper Industry: Report of the Provincial Inquiry into Health and Safety of Worker in the Pulp and Paper Industry* (Toronto: April 1990).

5. Upstairs, Downstairs

1 Wayne Pigeau, interview by Kristen O'Hare, 19 May 2004.

2 David Harvey has called on us to treat spaces as relational and relative rather than absolute; see *Spaces of Global Capitalism* (London: Verso, 2006), 77.

3 Workers are spatial as well as economic or social actors, even within the mill itself; see Andrew Herod, "Workers, Space and Labor Geography," *International Labor and Working Class History* 64 (Fall 2003): 112–38.

4 André Girard, interview by Kristen O'Hare, 29 July 2004.

5 Gordon Jackson, interview by Kristen O'Hare, 9 June 2004.

6 Cam Barrington, interview by Steven High, March 2004; Barrington was one of only two interviewees who asked not to be recorded electronically. His comments are therefore based on my rapid note taking.

7 For more on the history of women workers in Canada, see Joan Sangster, *Transforming Labour: Women and Work in Postwar Canada* (Toronto: University of Toronto Press, 2010); and Katrina Srigley, *Breadwinning Daughters: Young Working Women in a Depression-Era City, 1929–1939* (Toronto: University of Toronto Press, 2009).

8 McInnis, *Harnessing Labour Confrontation*, 187.

9 Ibid.

10 Hak, *Capital and Labour,* 190.

11 Triggered as it was by the promotion of an unpopular union member, this wildcat posed a dilemma for me: should I reveal the identity of the individual? After all, his name appeared in the media as well as in union records. Earlier I named Denis Ladouceur, who died tragically in a workplace accident, but this seemed different: this man sued the union and the company for damages to his reputation and lost earnings, winning a substantial sum of money. In the end, I decided against naming him here.

12 "Abitibi workers return to work," *Port Arthur News Chronicle*, 15 May 1967.

13 James M. Buchanan to Executive Board Members, January 1974, File: Correspondence and Documents Leading to Merger, Vol. 16, MG 28 I484, LAC.

14 L.A. MacLean, of MacLean & Caley Barristers and Solicitors, to J.M. Buchanan, 7 June 1974, File: Local 7135 – 1972 to 1981, Box 14, MG 28 I484, LAC.

15 Andrew Cull, Michael Goss, and André Girard of Local 7135, 10 July 1975, File: Local 7135 – 1972 to 1981, Box 14, MG 28 I484, LAC.

16 James M. Buchanan to Andy Cull, 20 November 1984, File: Local 7135 – 1982 to 1988, Box 14, MG 28 I484, Accession 1994/0028, LAC.

17 At this point, it had 427 union members; Union Dues Remittance Form, UPIU 71–135, 10 August 1974, File: Local 7135 – 1972 to 1981, Box 14, MG 28 I484, Accession 1994/0028, LAC.

18 *Canadian Pulp and Paper Workers Journal* 9, no. 6 (1971), Box 64, MG 28 I 484, Accession 1995/0011, LAC.

19 President's Conference Report of the Canadian Identity Committee Appointed by First VP and Canadian Director L. H. Lorrain at the Request of the First Canadian Conference of the International Brotherhood of Pulp, Sulphite and Paper Mill Workers. February 1974. File: Canadian Identity Committee. Volume 19. MG 28 I484. Library Archives Canada.

20 "Identity Report Adopted," *Canadian Pulp and Paper Workers Journal* 6, no. 4 (1968); see also "Merger Convention Called," *Canadian Pulp and Paper Workers Journal* 10, no. 2 (1972).

21 Robert H. Ziegler, *Rebuilding the Pulp and Paper Workers' Union, 1933–1941* (Knoxville: University of Tennessee Press, 1984), 219; and Bob Bull, "Delegates eye US labor envoy with distrust," *Winnipeg Free Press*, 17 May 1976.

22 Resumé of Events in Area XIII, Beginning mid-February 1973, File: 1973 Conference, Vol. 16, MG 28 I484, LAC.

23 The other companies included American Can, Domtar, E.B. Eddy, Great Lakes Paper, Kimberly-Clark (Terrace Bay), Ontario-Minnesota, and Spruce Falls; ibid.

24 For more on Lorrain's long association with the union, see Frank Slover, "Lorrain: 'Born with union label,'" *Gazette* (Montreal), 20 June 1974.

25 Resumé of Events in Area XIII, Beginning mid-February 1973, File: 1973 Conference, Vol. 16, MG 28 I484, LAC.

26 "Eleventh Hour Agreement Averts Major Strike at Abitibi Mills," *Canadian Paperworkers Journal* 1, no. 10 (1973).

27 Analysis of Exchange of Letters between J.M. Buchanan and J.P. Tonelli, compiled by Buchanan, File: Papermakers – UPP, 1957–72, Vol. 16, MG 28 I 484, LAC.

28 Ibid.

29 Resumé of Events in Area XIII, Beginning mid-February 1973, File: 1973 Conference, Vol. 16, MG 28 I484, LAC.

30 Resolution – Canadian Local Unions, File: Local 7135 – 1972 to 1981, Box 14, MG 28 I484, LAC.

31 Resumé of Executive Board Session, 29 January 1974, San Juan, Puerto Rico, File: 1973 Conference, Vol. 16, MG 28 I484, LAC.

32 "Vote on Independence," *Canadian Paperworkers Journal* 1, no. 13 (1974).

33 Ronald Rumball, "Paperworkers ignite union powderkeg," *Financial Post*, 2 March 1974.

34 President's Conference, Report of Proceedings of the Special Local Union Presidents Conference, UPIU, Montreal, 19 February 1974, File: Canadian Identity Committee, Vol. 19, MG 28 I484, LAC.

35 Richard Gwyn, "Nationalist fervour hits the labour unions," *Toronto Star*, 9 March 1974.

36 "Canadians Vote to Separate," *Canadian Paperworkers Journal* 1, no. 14 (1974).

37 These included local unions representing workers at paper mills in Pine Falls (Manitoba), Rivière-du-Loup (Quebec), and Thorold, Georgetown, Marathon, and Terrace Bay (Ontario); UPIU Summary of Ballot Results, File: Canadian Identity Committee, 1974 Referendum Vote on Separation from UPIU, Vol. 19, MG 28 I484, LAC.

38 "A vote for Canada," *Gazette* (Montreal), 23 April 1974; see also "Nationalism main force in UPIU autonomy drive," *Thunder Bay Times-News*, 5 March 1974.

39 L.H. Lorrain to Joseph P. Tonelli, President, UPIU, 15 August 1974, File: Property Owned by UPIU, Vol. 19. MG 28 I484, LAC.

40 A. Peden, Vice-President, Local 122, and Pete Richardson, President, Local 122, To all UPIU Locals, 17 June 1974, Vol. 20, MG 28 I484, LAC.

41 The other two unions were the Communication and Electrical Workers of Canada and the Energy and Chemical Workers Union; see James McCrostie, *Just the Beginning: The Communications, Energy and Paperworkers Union of Canada* (Ottawa: Communications, Energy and Paperworkers Union of Canada, 1996). Today the old CEP is now part of Unifor after its 2013 merger with the Canadian Auto Workers.

42 "Vice-President Louis H. Lorrain Makes Stirring Address to Quebec and Eastern Canada Council of Pulp and Paper Mill Union's Delegates," *Canadian Paperworkers Journal* (July-August 1965), Box 64, MG 28 I 484, Accession 1995/0011, LAC.

43 Winson and Leach, *Contingent Work, Disrupted Lives*, 70–1.

44 "Lumber men strike at all Abitibi mills in Ontario," *Gazette* (Montreal), 18 July 1975.

45 J.E. Murphy. Report on Industrial Dispute Commencement, 15 July 1975, T 3467, Vol. 3637, RG 27, Department of Manpower and Immigration, Canada Manpower Division, LAC; see also "4,300 Abitibi workers can strike July 6," *Gazette* (Montreal), 26 June 1975.

46 Abitibi/Provincial Negotiations, 1975–76, Vol. 1, Abitibi (Main File), MG 28 I 484, LAC.

47 Fred Rose, "Abitibi talks fail again," *Gazette* (Montreal), 14 June 1975.

48 J.E. Murphy, Report on Industrial Dispute Commencement, 15 July 1975, T 3467, Vol. 3637, RG 27, Department of Manpower and Immigration, Canada Manpower Division, LAC.

49 Harvey Schachter, "A strange strike," *Toronto Star*, 4 October 1975.

50 This was confirmed in media articles; see, for example, Wayne Major, "Abitibi strikers off jobs 11 weeks at Sturgeon Falls," *North Bay Nugget*, 30 September 1975.

51 Fred Rose, "Abitibi's 4,500 workers holding new contract vote," *Gazette* (Montreal), 17 February 1976.

52 Thomas H. Curley to President L.H. Lorrain, 20 February 1976, File 1, Vol. 1, Abitibi (Main File), MG 28 I484, LAC.

53 Rod Mickleburgh, "Angry CLC delegates walk out on speaker," *Vancouver Sun*, 18 May 1976; Léonce Gaudreault, "Les travailleurs de papier boudent l'union americaine," *Le Soleil* (Quebec City), 19 May 1976.

54 L.H. Lorrain to Joseph P. Tonelli, 29 August 1975, File: 1975 Correspondence, Vol. 19, MG 28 I484, LAC.

55 Ibid.

56 "US union chief booed," *Toronto Sun*, 19 May 1976.

57 Bull, "Delegates eye US labor envoy with distrust."

58 McCrostie, *Just the Beginning*.

59 Particularly useful were two correspondence files that detail the communications between Local 7135 and the union's leadership over a sixteen-year time frame from 1972 to 1988; see A.D. Moon, Recording-Secretary, Notice, File: Local 7135 – 1972 to 1981, MG 28 I484, Box 14, Accession 1994/0028, LAC.

60 For more on this wider context, see Roger Hayter, *Flexible Crossroads: The Restructuring of BC's Forest Industry* (Vancouver: UBC Press, 2000); idem, "High-Performance Organizations and Employment Flexibility: A Case Study in In-Situ Change at the Powell River Paper Mill, 1980–1994," *Canadian Geographer* 41, no. 1 (1997): 26–40; and John Holmes, "In Search of

Competitive Efficiency: Labour Process Flexibility in Canadian Newsprint Mills," *Canadian Geographer* 41, no. 1 (1997): 7–25.

61 An Open Letter to All Our Brothers in Local 7135 CPU, 30 January 1985, File: Local 7135 – 1982 to 1988, Box 14, MG 28 I484, Accession 1994/0028, LAC.

62 Ibid.

63 Andy Cull to Don McLauchlin, 3 May 1985, File: Local 7135 – 1982 to 1988, Box 14, MG 28 I484, Accession 1994/0028, LAC.

64 Submitted to Company Management and Supervision on April 26, 1985, by Officers of Local 7135, File: Local 7135 – 1982 to 1988, Box 14, MG 28 I484, Accession 1994/0028, LAC.

65 Andy Cull to Don McLauchlin, 30 September 1985, File: Local 7135 – 1982 to 1988, Box 14, MG 28 I484, Accession 1994/0028, LAC.

66 Telegram to Denis Tremblay, Recording Secretary, Local 7135, October 1985, File: Local 7135 – 1982 to 1988, Box 14, MG 28 I484, Accession 1994/0028, LAC.

67 Madeleine A. Martel to Don Holder, 23 April 1987, File: Local 7135 – 1982 to 1988, Box 14, MG 28 I484, Accession 1994/0028, LAC.

68 Ibid.

6. The Raised Fist

1 Casey explained his artistic approach in an *Abitibi Magazine* (1968) article found in Gervais and Colquhoun, "Mill History Binder."

2 Monica Heller examines the educational struggles of the 1960s and 1970s – specifically, the fight for a parallel system of unilingual French-language schools at the primary and secondary levels – in "La sociolinguistique et l'éducation franco-ontarienne," *Sociologie et sociétés* 26, no. 1 (1994): 156. See also Robert Dickson, "La 'révolution culturelle' en Nouvel-Ontario et le Québec: Opération Ressources et ses consequences," in *Produire la culture, produire l'identité*, ed. Andrée Fortin, 183–97 (Quebec City: Les Presses de l'Université Laval, 2000). Lucie Hotte similarly identifies the early 1970s as a turning point, as Quebec nationalism had rendered the older notion of French Canada obsolete; see Lucie Hotte, "Litterature et conscience identitaire heritage de CANO," in Fortin, *Produire la culture, produire l'identité*, 53–68. See also Michel Bock, "Le sort de la memoire dans la construction historique de l'identité franco-ontarienne," *Francophonies d'Amerique* 18 (Autumn 2004): 119–26. Franco-Ontarians now had to define themselves as a distinct community with its own history, institutions, and imagined geographies (such as Nouvel-Ontario). French-language schools were thus viewed as the primary bulwark against assimilation in an overwhelmingly English-speaking province.

3 Michael D. Behiels, *Canada's Francophone Minority Communities: Constitutional Renewal* (Montreal; Kingston, ON: McGill-Queen's University Press, 2005), 92; Matthew Hayday, *Bilingual Today, United Tomorrow* (Montreal; Kingston, ON: McGill-Queen's University Press, 2005). See also Don Cartwright, "The Expansion of French Language Rights in Ontario, 1968–1993: The Uses of Territoriality," *Canadian Geographer* 40, no. 3 (1996): 238–57; and Lucie Hotte, "Un pays à soi: construction d'une territoire franco-ontarienne," in *Frontières flottantes/ Shifting Boundaries: lieu et espace dans les cultures francophones du Canada*, ed. Jaap Lintvelt and François Paré, 217–28 (Amsterdam: Rodopi, 2001).

4 Wayne LeBelle, interview by Steven High, 6 September 2004.

5 John Hinshaw and Judith Modell, "Perceiving Racism: Homestead from Depression to Deindustrialziation," *Pennsylvania History* 63, no. 1 (1996): 17–52.

6 Raymond Brouillette, interview by Kristen O'Hare, 11 June 2004.

7   Gaétan Gervais, "Le règlement XVII (1912–1927)," *Revue du Nouvel Ontario* 18 (1996): 123–92.

8   "A question of ethics," *Globe* (Toronto), 1 April 1904.

9   "A question of ethics," *Globe* (Toronto), 6 April 1904.

10 Ibid.

11 "A question of ethics," *Globe* (Toronto), 8 April 1904.

12 Ibid., 8.

13 "By a majority of one," *Globe* (Toronto), 12 April 1904.

14 *Globe* (Toronto), 9 June 1904.

15 "School tax dispute," *Globe* (Toronto), 20 August 1909.

16 "Sturgeon Falls taxes," *Globe* (Toronto), 10 September 1909.

17 "Teachers on strike," *Globe* (Toronto), 4 December 1909.

18 "Sturgeon Falls school opened," *Globe* (Toronto), 19 January 1910.

19 Yvon Marleau, interview by Kristen O'Hare, 15 July 2004.

20 Pietro Carello, interview by Kristen O'Hare, 9 August 2004.

21 "L'Abitibi Paper and Power ne contribue pas à nos écoles," *Le Droit* (Ottawa), 29 March 1962.

22 Wayne LeBelle, "Sturgeon students protest," *North Bay Nugget*, 7 April 1970.

23 Claude Picher, "Les francophones du Nipissing ignores par le Conseil scolaire," *Le Droit* (Ottawa), 8 April 1970.

24 "Here's Bill 141 in full," *North Bay Nugget*, 13 April 1970.

25 Francophones, however, were not unanimously in favour of this. Working-class francophones had to be convinced that an exclusively French-language education was in their economic interest; see Heller, "Sociolinguistique et l'éducation franco-ontarienne," 157.

26 LeBelle, "Sturgeon students protest."

27 Wayne LeBelle, "French school protest gathers steam in Nipissing district," *North Bay Nugget*, 8 April 1970.

28 LeBelle, "Sturgeon students protest."

29 Ibid.

30 LeBelle, "French school protest gathers steam."

31 Picher, "Francophones du Nipissing ignores par le Conseil scolaire."; idem, "Nouvelle manifestation à Sturgeon Falls," *Le Droit* (Ottawa), 9 April 1970; and "Sturgeon Falls plant demonstration target by students, parents," *Sudbury Star*, 8 April 1970.

32 Marc Cazabon, president of AEON, was principal of d'Youville primary school in Verner.

33 "Appui de l'ACFO," *Le Droit* (Ottawa), 9 April 1970.

34 "Sturgeon Falls students get support here," *Sudbury Star*, 9 April 1970.

35 "Sturgeon school issue still hotly disputed," *North Bay Nugget*, 10 April 1970.

36 Marsha Scott, "1,000 students in protest march," *North Bay Nugget*, 9 April 1970.

37 Marsha Scott, "To split Sturgeon HS in French, English units," *North Bay Nugget*, 14 April 1970.

38 Ibid.

39 Rapport du voyage du secrétaire général à Sturgeon Falls, 11–12 August 1971, C2/584/6, Centre de recherche en civilisation canadienne-française, University of Ottawa.

40 Brief to the Nipissing Board of Education for Michael Sullivan, President, English Section, Student Council, Sturgeon Falls Secondary School, C2/584/6, Centre de recherche en civilisation canadienne-française, University of Ottawa.

41 Brief, Jean St-Louis, President, Conseil d'étudiants, section française, C2/584/6, Centre de recherche en civilisation canadienne-française, University of Ottawa.

42 Paul-André Rochon and Gilbert Belisle, "Sturgeon Falls blues," *La Rotonde* (Ottawa), 1 October 1971.

43 "Sturgeon Falls facing school 'powder keg,'" *Sudbury Star*, 14 August 1971.

44 Rochon and Belisle, "Sturgeon Falls blues."
45 Wayne LeBelle's interview notes with Jean St-Louis, conducted in 1972–3, in the author's possession.
46 ACFO-Nipissing, *Étude du milieu et statistiques sur la situation des francophones de la région du Nipissing dans les localités suivantes: North Bay, Sturgeon Falls, Mattawa* (Ottawa: ACFO-Nipissing, 1988); see also Louis-Gabriel Bordeleau, Raymond Lallier, and Aurèle Lalonde, *Les écoles secondaires de langue françaises en Ontario: dix ans après* (Toronto: Ministry of Colleges and Universities, 1980).
47 "Sturgeon Falls facing school 'powder keg,'" *Sudbury Star*, 14 August 1971.
48 Declaration de Monsieur André Roy, président général de la Société Saint-Jean-Baptiste de Québec, 18 September 1971, C2/584/7, Centre de recherche en civilisation canadienne-française, University of Ottawa.
49 ACFO, "Memoire présente au conseil scolaire de Nipissing par l'Association canadienne-française de l'Ontario," C50/107/7, Centre de recherche en civilisation canadienne-française, University of Ottawa.
50 Rapport du voyage du secrétaire général à Sturgeon Falls, 11–12 August 1971, C2/584/6, Centre de recherche en civilisation canadienne-française, University of Ottawa.
51 "Sturgeon Falls mayor explains his views on school languages," *North Bay Nugget*, 3 August 1971.
52 Brief to the Nipissing Board of Education from Our Lady of Sorrows Parent Teacher Association, Sturgeon Falls, 1971, C2/584/15, Centre de recherche en civilisation canadienne-française, University of Ottawa.
53 Mrs Ruth Couchie, Educational Committee of the Nipissing Band, C2/584/6, Centre de recherche en civilisation canadienne-française, University of Ottawa.
54 B.C. Barrington to Nipissing Board of Education, 25 June 1971, C2/584/15, Centre de recherche en civilisation canadienne-française, University of Ottawa.
55 Rapport du voyage du secrétaire général à Sturgeon Falls, 11–12 August 1971, C2/584/6, Centre de recherche en civilisation canadienne-française, University of Ottawa.
56 Ibid.
57 Ibid.
58 Donald Dennie, "Nouveau refus du Conseil," *Le Droit* (Ottawa), 8 September 1971.
59 Jacques Deschênes, Direction Jeunesse, letter, 10 September 1971, C50/107/7, ACFO, Centre de recherche en civilisation canadienne-française, University of Ottawa.
60 Rémy M. Beauregard aux amis de la francophonie ontarienne, 23 February 1972, C2/325/6, Centre de recherche en civilisation canadienne-française, University of Ottawa.
61 Wayne LeBelle, "Will use means necessary – student leaders," *North Bay Nugget*, 7 September 1971.
62 "L'ACFO, l'ACEBO et le journal Le Droit sont-ils attaches?" *Le Voyageur* (Sudbury), 15 September 1971.
63 "Le poing fermé: emblème revolutionnaire 'politique,'" *Le Voyageur* (Sudbury), 15 September 1971.
64 Ibid.
65 Ibid.
66 LeBelle, "Will use means necessary."
67 Ibid.
68 "Menace de violence à Sturgeon Falls," *Le Droit* (Ottawa), 18 September 1971.
69 Ontario, Department of Education, News Release, n.d. [1971]. C50/107/7, ACFO, Centre de recherche en civilisation canadienne-française, University of Ottawa.

70 Normal Hartley, "Professor answers call," *Globe and Mail*, 18 September 1971.

71 Rochon and Belisle, "Sturgeon Falls blues."

72 Marsha Scott, "Approve 2 high schools at Sturgeon," *North Bay Nugget*, 8 December 1971; "Sturgeon Falls aura son école française," *Le Voyageur* (Sudbury), 15 December 1971.

73 Wayne LeBelle, interview notes with Jean St-Louis, conducted in 1972–3, in the author's possession.

74 Ibid.

7. Managing Decline

1 Barrington, interview.

2 "Abitibi regards Sturgeon Falls as prime example of industrial research benefits," *North Bay Nugget*, 30 June 1964.

3 J.I. McGibbon to W.C. Harrison, Abitibi Paper, Toronto, 15 March 1968; see also inter-office memorandum from W.G. Lang, Durham Mill Manager, to J. Ian McGibbon, 10 April 1968, and Dr M.M. Yan, Sheridan Park, to J.I. McGibbon, Toronto, 17 April 1968, Sturgeon River House Museum.

4 J.G. Sullivan to J. I. McGibbon, Abitibi Paper, 19 April 1968, Sturgeon River House Museum.

5 Thirty-eight workers in the platewood mill eventually would lose their jobs, along with twenty-seven in hardboard fabricating, four in the control division, nine in the mechanical department, two in electrical, and ten who worked in wood handling and outside in the mill's North Yard; Abitibi Power & Paper, Platewood Mill Shutdown Draft, Sturgeon River House Museum.

6 J.I. McGibbon to B.C. Barrington, Abitibi Power & Paper, 26 September 1968, Sturgeon River House Museum.

7 Jefferson Cowie, *The Great Exception: The New Deal and the Limits of American Politics* (Princeton, NJ: Princeton University Press, 2016).

8 A.G. Mackie, Toronto, to Cam Barrington, Mill Manager, Sturgeon Falls, 1 October 1968, Sturgeon River House Museum.

9 Confidential "Appreciation," no date or author, but clearly developed by Abitibi's central office for the closure of the platewood mill in 1968–9, Sturgeon River House Museum.

10 Ibid.

11 Handwritten notes from management meeting, likely mid-September 1968, Sturgeon River House Museum.

12 Significantly, the correspondence – which Barrington would have seen – included an assessment of wage rates at Sturgeon Falls compared with those at one of these newer mills (which were treated as a kind of benchmark rate); Sturgeon Falls workers were paid less in almost every job category.

13 J.I. McGibbon to B.C. Barrington, Abitibi Power & Paper, 30 October 1968, Sturgeon River House Museum.

14 Labbé, interviews.

15 "Abitibi Forest Products phases out hardboards and panelling; mothballs plant," *Globe and Mail*, 25 March 1975.

16 Holmes, "In Search of Competitive Efficiency," 8.

17 Ibid., 11.

18 Hayter, *Flexible Crossroads*, 108.

19 "Mill workers vote to accept contract," *Tribune* (Sturgeon Falls), 24 April 1991.

20 In his interview, Wally Shisko blamed the 1991 closure on the declining market for exterior wood siding. He suggested that the mill's market "was a low-end market in the States."

21 MacMillan Bloedel, "Decade of Losses: Finally Closes MB Hardboard Siding Plant," Press release, 8 October 1991, copy received from Megan Moholt, Research Assistant, Weyerhaeuser, Federal Way, WA, 6 July 2004, in author's possession.

22 Isabel Mosseler, "Workers fear lay-offs at MacMillan Bloedel," *Tribune* (Sturgeon Falls), 9 October 1991.

23 Ibid.

24 Isabel Mosseler, "Union upset over handling of lay-offs," *Tribune* (Sturgeon Falls), 16 October 1991.

25 Handwritten notes from labour-management Industrial Adjustment Committee meeting, 15 October 1991, André Girard Collection.

26 "Union upset over mill tactics," *Tribune* (Sturgeon Falls), 20 November 1991. In terms of the layoff of 162 mill workers, local readers were told that the ripple effect would mean 2.7 full-time jobs and five part-time jobs would be lost elsewhere in town; Isabel Mosseler, "Spin-off of lay-offs could mean 600 jobs," *Tribune* (Sturgeon Falls), 16 October 1991

27 Editorial, "It's past due the time to develop new interests," *Tribune* (Sturgeon Falls), 16 October 1991.

28 Ibid.

29 Isabel Mosseler, "West Nipissing Action Committee formed to combat spin-offs of lay-offs," *Tribune* (Sturgeon Falls), 30 October 1991.

30 These loans financed new vehicles, recreational equipment, household appliances, medical expenses, and educational fees; MacMillan Bloedel Employees' (Sturgeon Falls) Credit Union Limited, Directors, André Girard Collection.

31 MacMillan Bloedel Employees' (Sturgeon Falls) Credit Union Limited, *Annual Report of the Board of Directors for Year Ended March 31, 1994*, André Girard Collection.

8. Recycled Dreams

1 Boyd, *Slain Wood*, 149.

2 David Sonnenfeld, "Social Movements and Ecological Modernization: The Transformation of Pulp and Paper Manufacturing," *Development and Change* 33, no. 1 (2002): 4.

3 Ibid., 1.

4 William F. Sinclair, "Controlling Effluent Discharges from Canadian Pulp and Paper Manufacturers," *Canadian Public Policy* 17, no. 1 (1991): 87–90.

5 Ontario Water Resources Commission, *Water Pollution Survey of the Town of Sturgeon Falls* (Toronto: Ministry of Environment, 1965), 3.

6 George Hendry and Susan Janhurst, *The Bacteriological Water Quality of the Sturgeon River at Sturgeon Falls, 1977; Effects of Wastewater from the Abitibi Paper Mill* (Toronto: Ministry of Environment, June 1978).

7 Isabel Mosseler, "Rotten odor temporary," *Tribune* (Sturgeon Falls), 20 June 1990; idem, "Smell from mill should no longer be a problem," *Tribune* (Sturgeon Falls), 5 December 1990.

8 Isabel Mosseler, "MoE testing fish in Sturgeon River," *Tribune* (Sturgeon Falls), 15 June 1991.

9 Ibid.

10 Isabel Mosseler, "Test reveals Mac-Bloe is the cause of tainted fish," *Tribune* (Sturgeon Falls), 25 March 1992.

11 Sturgeon Falls Partnership, *The Construction and Operation of a Mill to Recycle Old Corrugated Cardboard* (Toronto: Ministry of Environment and Energy, February 1995).

12 Handwritten notes from labour-management Industrial Adjustment Committee meeting, 12 October 1991, André Girard Collection.

13 Mosseler, "Union upset over handling of lay-offs."

14 Sturgeon Falls Partnership, *Construction and Operation of a Mill.*

15 John Schreiner, "Has forest industry hit rock bottom yet?" *Financial Post*, 18 November 1991.

16 "Mills Invest in Their People," *Northern Ontario Business* 12, no. 7 (1992): 1; see also Laura Fowlie, "Union blamed for pulp mill closing," *Financial Post*, 5 February 1992.

17 "Report predicts massive job losses in pulp and paper industry in next six years," *Gazette* (Montreal), 21 June 1994.

18 Krogman and Beckley, "Corporate 'Bail-Outs' and Local 'Buyouts,'" 116.

19 The Ontario New Democratic Party also initiated the Ontario Training and Adjustment Board to further assist worker and community adjustment; see Stephen McBride, "The Continuing Crisis of Social Democracy: Ontario's Social Contract Perspective," *Studies in Political Economy* 50 (Summer 1996): 65–78.

20 Lachlan Mackinnon, "Deindustrialization on the Periphery: An Oral History of Sydney Steel, 1945–2001" (PhD diss., Concordia University, 2016).

21 Krogman and Beckley, "Corporate 'Bail-Outs' and Local 'Buyouts,'" 113.

22 Corey Rosen and Karen M. Young, eds., *Understanding Employee Ownership* (Ithaca, NY: ILR Press, 1991). They might also have found inspiration in the public bailout of Chrysler in the early 1980s; see Steven High, *Industrial Sunset: The Making of North America's Rust Belt* (Toronto: University of Toronto Press, 2003), chap. 6.

23 Quarter, *Crossing the Line*, 1.

24 Ibid.

25 Jeremy Brecher, *Banded Together: Economic Democratization in the Brass Valley* (Chicago: University of Illinois Press, 2011), xiii.

26 Quarter, *Crossing the Line*, 11; "Saving Ont. pulp mill a smart investment," *Edmonton Journal*, 1 April 1997.

27 Brecher, *Banded Together*, 203. Some have also suggested that these buyouts furthered the goal of community control over the resource base; see Krogman and Beckley, "Corporate 'Bail-Outs' and Local 'Buyouts,'" 109.

28 Steven Chase, "Town dodges kiss of death," *Globe and Mail*, 8 September 1992.

29 Sturgeon Falls Partnership, *Construction and Operation.*

30 Wally Shisko, quoted in Isabel Mosseler, "Official launch of OCC to be held tomorrow," *Tribune* (Sturgeon Falls), 15 April 1992.

31 Ibid.

32 Chase, "Town dodges kiss of death."

33 Isabel Mosseler, "One good used dam for sale?" *Tribune* (Sturgeon Falls), 17 July 1991.

34 Ray Hudson and David Sadler, "Contesting Works Closures in Western Europe's Old Industrial Regions: Defending Place or Betraying Class?" in *Production, Work, Territory: The Geographical Anatomy of Industrial Capitalism*, ed. Allen J. Scott and Michael Storper, 182–5 (Boston: Allen and Unwin, 1986).

35 Chase, "Town dodges kiss of death."

36 Ibid.

37 Ibid.

38 The WNEDC was a non-profit corporation managed by the five municipalities in West Nipissing. It was governed by a board that included Denis Lafrèniere, Jean-Guy Lefebvre, Guy Rochon, and Wayne LeBelle. The economic development officer was Denis H. Gauthier. All of these men were interviewed for this project.

39 A.N. Grunder, Senior VP, MacMillan Bloedel, Finance and Administration, to Wally Shisko and Guy Rochon, 13 March 1992, André Girard Collection, in the author's possession.

40 The measure enjoyed cross-party support, as the sponsor of the private member's bill was the Progressive Conservative Party's Mike Harris, the local MPP (and future Ontario premier). Harris had a close relationship with Mike DeCaen, the mayor of Sturgeon Falls, as well as with J.P. Charles.

41 Chase, "Town dodges kiss of death."

42 Exhibit 10, Container Board Supply Contract, 1 July 1983, MacMillan Bloedel and MacMillan Bathurst, part of Ontario Supreme Court Exhibits filed by Denis H. Gauthier, Raymond Brouillette Collection, in the author's possession.

43 Denis Gauthier, interview by Kristen O'Hare, 31 May 2004.

44 Alan Korell, interview by Kristen O'Hare, 29 October 2004.

45 Minutes, Sturgeon Falls Partnership, 24 March 1994, Raymond Brouillette Collection.

46 J.P. Charles, interview by Kristen O'Hare, 10 August 2004.

47 "Fund kick-off nets $224,500," *Tribune* (Sturgeon Falls), 15 December 1992.

48 Isabel Mosseler, "West Nipissing Investment Fund proceeding to plan," *Tribune* (Sturgeon Falls), 12 January 1993.

49 Quoted in "Fund goes over half-way mark," *Tribune* (Sturgeon Falls), 2 March 1993.

50 Rod Blais, quoted in Isabel Mosseler, "Fund for OCC is presented at annual Chamber meeting," *Tribune* (Sturgeon Falls), 8 December 1992.

51 Isabel Mosseler, "Sturgeon Chamber asked to help EDC raise $1 million," *Tribune* (Sturgeon Falls), 8 April 1992.

52 Quoted in "Fund goes over half-way mark," *Tribune* (Sturgeon Falls), 2 March 1993.

53 Minutes, West Nipissing Recycling Company – Sturgeon Falls Partnership, Raymond Brouillette Collection.

54 Minutes, West Nipissing Recycling Company – Sturgeon Falls Partnership, 26 May 1994, Raymond Brouillette Collection.

55 Guy Ethier, interview by Kristen O'Hare, 17 June 2004.

56 Isabel Mosseler, "Recycling does nothing for wood chip suppliers," *Tribune* (Sturgeon Falls), 15 April 1992.

57 Ken Landry, interview by Kristen O'Hare, 28 July 2004.

58 Gary O'Connor, interview by Kristen O'Hare, 5 August 2004.

59 Quoted in Isabel Mosseler, "Martel announced $4 million loan, $4 million grant," *Tribune* (Sturgeon Falls), 22 April 1992.

60 Ibid.

61 Bruce Macfarlane, "Sturgeon 'success story' officially opened Friday," *North Bay Nugget*, June 1993; see also Chase, "Town dodges kiss of death."

62 Isabel Mosseler, "West Nipissing – a supportive community," *Tribune* (Sturgeon Falls), 4 May 1993.

63 Quoted in Macfarlane, "Sturgeon 'success story.'"

64 Sturgeon Falls Partnership, *Construction and Operation*; Limited Partnership Agreement, 17 March 1992, Exhibit 13, Ontario Supreme Court, Motion Record, Exhibits to the Affidavit of Denis. H. Gauthier, Raymond Brouillette Collection.

65 Minutes, Sturgeon Falls Partnership, 24 March 1994, Present: Gerry Stevens, Wally Shisko, Guy Rochon, Denis Lafrèniere, Denis H. Gauthier, and Lynn Duhaime, Raymond Brouillette Collection.

66 Intervenor Cecil Makowski on behalf of the Communications, Energy and Paperworkers Union of Canada, 7135, Superior Court of Justice, *WNEDC v. Weyerhaeuser*, 29 November 2002, Raymond Brouillette Collection.

67 David Montgomery, *The Fall of the House of Labor: The Workplace, the State, and American Labor Activism, 1865–1925* (Cambridge: Cambridge University Press, 1987), chap. 1.

68 Minutes, West Nipissing Recycling Company – Sturgeon Falls Partnership, 26 May 1994, Raymond Brouillette Collection.

69 Minutes, West Nipissing Recycling Company – Sturgeon Falls Partnership, 22 November 1996, Raymond Brouillette Collection.

70 Minutes, West Nipissing Recycling Company – Sturgeon Falls Partnership, 17 December 1996, Raymond Brouillette Collection.

71 Hodgins, *Temagami Experience*, 264.

72 Judith Stein, *Running Steel, Running America: Race, Economic Policy, and the Decline of Liberalism* (Chapel Hill: University of North Carolina Press, 1998), 318. A similar point is made in Jennifer Foster and L. Anders Sandberg, "Post-Industrial Urban Greenspace: Justice, Quality of Life and Environmental Aesthetics in Rapidly Changing Urban Environments," *Local Environment* 19, no. 10 (2014): 1043; and in Steven High and David Lewis, *Corporate Wasteland: The Landscape and Memory of Deindustrialization* (Ithaca, NY: Cornell University Press, 2007). For more on hipster commodification, see Sharon Zukin, *Naked City: The Death and Life of Authentic Urban Places* (New York: Oxford University Press, 2010).

73 Minutes, West Nipissing Recycling Company – Sturgeon Falls Partnership, 28 June 1995, Raymond Brouillette Collection.

74 *Insider*, 30 May 1995.

75 *Insider*, 9 July 1995.

76 *Insider*, 12 February 1996.

77 *Insider*, 19 November 1996.

78 "Plenty of corrugated medium coming out of recycling facility after one year of operation," *Tribune* (Sturgeon Falls), 31 May 1994.

79 "Recycling program arrives," *Tribune* (Sturgeon Falls), 31 October 1995.

80 "Recycling workshop," *Tribune* (Sturgeon Falls), 5 December 1995.

81 MacMillan Bloedel, Sturgeon Falls Division, "The Inside Story of Recycling at Sturgeon Falls," in the author's possession.

82 *Insider*, 3 April 1996; "Recycling bins arrive in Verner," *Tribune* (Sturgeon Falls), 7 May 1996.

83 *Insider*, 17 May 1995.

84 N. Shivgulam, "Environmental Update," *MacMillan Bloedel Limited*, 16 March 1993, in the author's possession.

85 Cindy Laundry, "Costs now decreasing for Sturgeon Falls mill," *Tribune* (Sturgeon Falls), 16 August 1994; idem, "Safest Mill in Canada," *Tribune* (Sturgeon Falls), 22 November 1994.

86 *Insider*, 1 August 1996, 17 July 1995.

87 *Insider*, 25 April 1995.

88 *Insider*, 12 May 1995.

89 *Insider*, 14 August 1995.

90 *Insider*, 22 August 1995.

91 *Insider*, 8 May 1995.

92 *Insider*, 31 October 1995.

93 Ibid.

94 *Insider*, 23 May 1995.

95 *Insider*, 1 August 1996.

96 *Insider*, 13 July 1995.

97 Wally S. Shisko to All Employees, Inter-Office Memo, 3 December 1993, André Girard Collection.

98   R.T. Hawkins to All Employees, MacMillan Bloedel, Inter-Office Memo, 30 May 1994, André Girard Collection.

99   "MacMillan Bloedel news," *Tribune* (Sturgeon Falls), 20 December 1994.

100 Editorial, "Applause should go to MacMillan Bloedel," *Tribune* (Sturgeon Falls), 4 April 1995; see also "Study to review mill's operations," *Tribune* (Sturgeon Falls), 20 December 1994.

101 Minutes, West Nipissing Recycling Company – Sturgeon Falls Partnership, 1 May 1996, Raymond Brouillette Collection.

102 *Insider*, 19 September 1995.

103 *Insider*, 14 December 1995; "MacMillan Bloedel puts new paper machine plans on hold," *Tribune* (Sturgeon Falls), 16 January 1996.

104 *Insider*, 25 January 1996; *Insider*, 8 December 1998.

105 Wally Shisko, quoted in Mosseler, "Official launch of OCC to be held tomorrow."

106 "MacMillan Bloedel welcomes new resident manager," *Tribune* (Sturgeon Falls), 16 July 1996.

107 Ron Beauchamp, interview by Kristen O'Hare, 8 July 2004.

108 Guy Robichaud, "Mill looks toward future as it enters its 100th year in Sturgeon Falls," *Tribune* (Sturgeon Falls), 21 April 1998.

109 *Insider*, 3 December 1997.

110 Len Barton, "MacMillan Bloedel hopes Sturgeon 2000 plan will identify a market niche," *Tribune* (Sturgeon Falls), 10 June 1997.

111 Tom Stephens, quoted in "Macmillan Bloedel Restructuring," *News for Employees*, 21 January 1998, MacMillan Bloedel Public Affairs (Vancouver), André Girard Collection.

112 Newsletter Editors Conference Call with Tom Stephens, President and CEO of MacMillan Bloedel, 21 January 1998, André Girard Collection.

113 Tom Stephens, transcript of interview by Bill Good, CKNW Radio, 28 January 1998, André Girard Collection.

114 "Macmillan-Bloedel Restructuring," *News for Employees*, 21 January 1998, MacMillan Bloedel Public Affairs (Vancouver), André Girard Collection; and Kathryn Leger, "Stone delays sale of Abitibi stake, mulls MacBlo deal," *Financial Post*, 3 September 1998.

115 *Insider*, 28 April 1998.

116 *Insider*, 24 July 1998.

117 Kathryn Leger, "MacBlo pulls trigger, Stone wins shootout," *Financial Post*, 5 September 1998; *Insider*, 3 June 1999; Exhibit 10, Container Board Supply Contract, 1 July 1983, MacMillan Bloedel and MacMillan Bathurst, part of Ontario Supreme Court Exhibits filed by Denis H. Gauthier, Raymond Brouillette Collection.

118 *Insider*, 21 June 1999.

9. Betrayal

1   Anonymous mill worker, interview by Steven High, 2 December 2003.

2   Ibid.

3   Ron Demers, quoted in Gord Young, "Province loosens purse strings," *North Bay Nugget*, 8 November 2002.

4   See High, *Industrial Sunset*, 188–9.

5   Ontario Superior Court of Justice, Affidavit of Denis Senecal, WNEDC (Plaintiff) and Weyerhaeuser Company Limited (Defendant), Court File No. 2528–02, Motion Record, Raymond Brouillette Collection.

6   Demers quoted in Young, "Province loosens purse strings."

7 High, *Industrial Sunset*, 175.

8 Anonymous mill worker, interview.

9 Ibid.

10 Dean Pigeau, quoted in Dean Lisk and Susanne Gammon, "West Nipissing marches," *Tribune* (Sturgeon Falls), 10 December 2002.

11 "Lives 'ripped away' by shutdown – workers," *North Bay Nugget*, 30 November 2002.

12 Dean Pigeau, quoted in Phil Novak, "Mill employees punch out for good," *North Bay Nugget*, 6 December 2002.

13 *Insider*, 15 November 2002.

14 Thomas Dunk, Stephen McBride, and Randle W. Nelsen, "Introduction," in *The Training Trap: Ideology, Training and the Labour Market*, ed. Thomas Dunk, Stephen McBride, and Randle W. Nelsen (Toronto: Society for Socialist Studies, 1996), 2–3.

15 Thomas Dunk, "Culture, Skill, Masculinity and Whiteness: Training and the Politics of Identity," in Dunk, McBride, and Nelsen, *Training Trap*, 102.

16 Dunk, McBride, and Nelsen, "Introduction," 7.

17 Ibid.

18 Anonymous mill worker, interview.

19 *Weyerhaeuser Bulletin* 2071, 20 March 2002.

20 *Weyerhaeuser Bulletin* 2072, 27 March 2002.

21 *Weyerhaeuser Bulletin* 2076, 24 April 2002.

22 *Weyerhaeuser Bulletin* 2096, 11 September 2002.

23 *Weyerhaeuser Bulletin* 2098, 25 September 2002.

24 *Weyerhaeuser Bulletin* 2102, 23 October 2002.

25 Anonymous office worker, interview by Kristen O'Hare, 10 March 2004.

26 Minutes, Sturgeon Falls Limited Partnership, 4 May 1999, Raymond Brouillette Collection.

27 Ontario Superior Court of Justice, Affidavit of Denis Gauthier, Raymond Brouillette Collection.

28 Scott Mosher and Ronald Beauchamp to West Nipissing Transition Board, 29 June 1998, shared by an anonymous local source, in the author's possession.

29 Daniel Olivier, interview by Kristen O'Hare, 21 November 2004.

30 Dan Olivier, "Blame and shame not exclusive to Weyerhaeuser," *Tribune* (Sturgeon Falls), 26 August 2003.

31 Minutes, Sturgeon Falls Limited Partnership. 13 December 2000, Raymond Brouillette Collection.

32 Ontario Superior Court of Justice, Affidavit of Denis Gauthier, Raymond Brouillette Collection.

33 Olivier, "Blame and shame not exclusive to Weyerhaeuser."

34 Ibid.

35 Ibid.

36 Ibid.

37 Dean Lisk, "Council reacts to impending closure of Weyerhaeuser," *Tribune* (Sturgeon Falls), 15 October 2002.

38 Dean Lisk, "Struggling to find solution," *Tribune* (Sturgeon Falls), 22 October 2002.

39 West Nipissing Economic Development Committee, Press release, 8 November 2002, Raymond Brouillette Collection.

40 WNEDC board, on 27 October 2002.

41 Anne Giardini, Assistant General Counsel to WNEDC, 6 November 2002, Raymond Brouillette Collection.

42 Ontario Superior Court of Justice, WNEDC (Plaintiff) and Weyerhaeuser Company Limited (Defendant), Court File No. 2528–02, Motion Record, Raymond Brouillette Collection.

43 Ibid.

44 Ibid.

45 Statement of Claim submitted to Ontario Superior Court of Justice, WNEDC (Plaintiff), Weyerhaeuser Company (Defendant), 8 November 2002, Raymond Brouillette Collection.

46 Ontario Superior Court of Justice, Affidavit of Denis Gauthier, Raymond Brouillette Collection.

47 Gord Young, "Injunction battle underway," *North Bay Nugget*, 21 November 2002.

48 J.P. Charles, quoted in Gord Young, "EDC takes legal action," *North Bay Nugget*, 9 November 2002.

49 Ibid.

50 Ontario Superior Court of Justice, WNEDC and Weyerhaeuser Factum of the Responding Party, WNEDC (Plaintiff) and Weyerhaeuser Company Limited (Defendant), Court File No. 2528–02, Motion Record, Raymond Brouillette Collection.

51 Ibid.

52 "Weyerhaeuser says Sturgeon Falls lawsuit lacks merit," *Sault Star*, 12 November 2002.

53 Ontario Superior Court of Justice, Affidavit of Paul Whyatt, Finance and Planning Manager, Weyerhaeuser, Raymond Brouillette Collection.

54 Ibid.

55 Ibid.

56 Ontario Superior Court of Justice, Affidavit of Naraine Shivgulam, Finance and Planning Manager, Weyerhaeuser, Raymond Brouillette Collection.

57 *Tribune* (Sturgeon Falls), 26 November 2002.

58 Ontario Superior Court of Justice, WNEDC (Plaintiff) and Weyerhaeuser Company Limited (Defendant), Court File No. 2528–02, Motion Record, Raymond Brouillette Collection.

59 Ontario Superior Court of Justice, *WNEDC v. Weyerhaeuser*, 29 November 2002, Raymond Brouillette Collection.

60 "No reprieve for paper mill," *Toronto Star*, 30 November 2002.

61 Anne Giardini, Assistant General Consul, Weyerhaeuser, to Sturgeon Falls Repulping Limited, 18 November 2002, Raymond Brouillette Collection.

62 WNEDC, Press release, 8 November 2002, Raymond Brouillette Collection.

63 Douglas J. Wray, labour lawyer, to Robert J. Arcand, 3 December 2002, Raymond Brouillette Collection.

64 Denis Senecal, President, CEP Local 7135, to J.P. Charles, Chair, WNEDC, 2 December 2002, Raymond Brouillette Collection.

65 Naraine Shivgulam, Mill Manager, Weyerhaeuser, to WNEDC, 9 December 2002, Raymond Brouillette Collection; Jay Barbeau, General Manager, WNEDC, to Naraine Shivgulam, Weyerhaeuser, 13 December 2002, Raymond Brouillette Collection.

66 Minutes of Meeting of Shareholders of Sturgeon Falls Repulping Limited, 7 January 2003, Raymond Brouillette Collection.

67 Jay Barbeau, General Manager, WNEDC, to Anne Giardini, Assistant General Counsel, Weyerhaeuser, 11 February 2003, Raymond Brouillette Collection.

68 Ibid.

69 Ibid.

70 "Dam purchase gives town big boost," *North Bay Nugget*, 11 July 2003; Municipality of West Nipissing, Press release, 9 July 2003.

71 In June 2004 the Ontario government announced that it would invest $4.5 million in the West Nipissing Hydro Electric Power Plant (or the mill's dam); see Ontario, Ministry of Northern Development and Mines, "McGuinty Government to Invest $4.5 Million in West Nipissing Hydro Electric Power Plant," Press release, 21 June 2004.

72 Sharon Paquette, "Municipality celebrates purchase of power dam," *Tribune* (Sturgeon Falls), 29 June 2004.

73 Olivier, "Blame and shame not exclusive to Weyerhaeuser."

74 Ibid.

75 High, *Industrial Sunset*, 170–2.

76 Jamie Swift, *Walking the Union Walk: Stories from CEP's First Ten Years* (Toronto: Between the Lines, 2003), vii.

77 Lucy Taksa, "Like a Bicycle, Forever Teetering between Individualism and Collectivism: Considering Community in Relation to Labour History," *Labour History* 78 (May 2000): 7–32; John Walsh and Steven High, "Re-thinking the Concept of 'Community,'" *Social History* 17, no. 64 (1999): 255–74.

78 Unfortunately I was unable to find the local union records for the 1990s or early 2000s. The union did connect me to the staff member who serviced Local 7135 at the time of the closure. It was a very open (but informal) conversation about the challenges confronting trade unions faced with closures.

79 "Readers back union's bid for mill," *North Bay Nugget*, 19 October 2002.

80 Gord Young, "Employees explore purchase of paper mill," *Sudbury Star*, 13 October 2002.

81 Joel Carr, CEP Ontario, to Weyerhaeuser Locals, 8 October 2002, in author's possession.

82 CEP, "Weyerhaeuser abandons Sturgeon Falls," Press release, 8 October 2002.

83 Memorandum, Joel Carr, Ontario Region, CEP, to various National/Regional Officers, 19 November 2002, in author's possession.

84 CEP, "Union 'more determined than ever' after injunction to stop Sturgeon Falls closure denied," Press release, 29 November 2002.

85 Novak, "Mill employees punch out for good."

86 "Mill workers protest," *North Bay Nugget*, 7 December 2002.

87 Ibid.

88 Pierre Hardy, Text of a speech given at the rally in New Brunswick, in the author's possession.

89 Ibid.

90 The term "plant gate" is used to describe the leafleting of incoming and outgoing workers at the front gate of a mill during a shift change. My first experience of plant gating was at age sixteen, when I helped my local New Democratic Party candidate distribute leaflets at the (now closed) paper mill in Red Rock. I was there with Jim Foulds and Jack Stokes, two veteran area MPPs, who regaled me with stories. Stokes, in particular, had the ability to connect with workers in these rushed moments. Foulds was similarly impressive, instructing me on the political importance of plant gating in the region.

91 "Members Across Canada Rally to Save Ontario Mill," *CEP Journal* (Winter 2003).

92 Marcel Boudreau, quoted in Gord Young, "Former employees fight to reopen closed plant," *Timmins Daily Press*, 15 May 2003.

93 Mike Lacroix, "Weyerhaeuser still bullying protesters," *Tribune* (Sturgeon Falls), 16 September 2003.

94 Ibid.

95 CEP, "CEP stops Weyerhaeuser from shredding mill documents," Press release, 27 February 2003.

96 Gord Young, "Former Weyerhaeuser employees want province to join fight," *North Bay Nugget*, 7 February 2003.

97 Brendan Anthony Sweeney, "Comparing Employment Relations in a Cross-Border Region: The Case of Cascadia's Forest Products Industry" (PhD diss., Queen's University, 2010).

98   Denis Senecal, quoted in Young, "Former Weyerhaeuser employees want province to join fight."

99   Dean Lisk, "Union rallies outside mill," *Tribune* (Sturgeon Falls), 9 September 2003.

100 Gord Young, "Union blockades Sturgeon mill," *North Bay Nugget*, 4 September 2003.

101 Ibid.

102 Young, "Former Weyerhaeuser employees want province to join fight."

103 Dean Lisk, "Weyerhaeuser cooperating says union," *Tribune* (Sturgeon Falls), 11 February 2003.

104 Dean Lisk, "Union wants council involvement to save mill," *Tribune* (Sturgeon Falls), 11 March 2002.

105 Ibid.

106 Ibid.; notice, however, that he did not say "for the employees."

107 "Former Employee Group," text of speech, provided by an anonymous mill worker, in the author's possession.

108 Gord Young, "Time running out for mill purchase: Plea made for municipality to get involved," *North Bay Nugget*, 5 March 2004.

109 "The Last Roll: Saving Our Mill, Saving Our Local Economy, Preserving Our Environment, Building Partnerships," presentation by former employees of Weyerhaeuser and West Nipissing Chamber of Commerce, 15 July 2004, in author's possession.

110 Ibid.

111 Ibid. Because Sturgeon Falls is a small town, there were many points of connection between the mill workers and local economic development officials, elected politicians, and the Chamber of Commerce.

112 Ibid.

113 Ibid.

114 Gord Young, "Sturgeon Falls mill's fate sealed," *North Bay Nugget*, 28 May 2004.

115 Ibid.

10. Proximity and Distance

1   According to the 2006 census, nearly 32 per cent of Canadians worked outside their census subdivision. This statistic is taken from the grant application for On the Move: Employment-related Geographic Mobility in the Canadian Context, a pan-Canadian research project headed by Barb Neis, of which I am part. See http://www.onthemovepartnership.ca/.

2   For more on composure, see Alistair Thomson, *Anzac Memories: Living with the Legend* (Oxford: Oxford University Press, 1994); see also Kirk, *Class, Culture and Social Change*, 149–50.

3   Cowie, *Capital Moves*, 185.

4   Skeggs, *Class, Self, Culture*, 49; and Doreen Massey, "Power-Geometry and a Progressive Sense of Place," in *Mapping the Futures: Local Cultures, Global Change*, ed. Jon Bird et al. (London: Routledge, 1993), 61.

5   For a good example of this, see McIvor, "Economic Violence."

6   Kathryn Marie Dudley, *The End of the Line: Lost Jobs, New Lives in Postindustrial America* (Chicago: University of Chicago Press, 1994), 158.

7   Denis MacGregor, interview by Kristen O'Hare, 26 November 2012.

8   Bruce Colquhoun, interview by Kristen O'Hare and Steven High, 18 December 2004, 23 June 2005, and 19 July 2005. I also interviewed Bruce's father, Ken Colquhoun on 26 May 2005.

9   Mike Lacroix, interview by Kristen O'Hare, 12 November 2004, and by Steven High, December 2005.

10 André Cartier, interview by Kristen O'Hare, 12 November 2004.

11 This supports the UK findings of Strangleman, "Work Identity in Crisis?"; see also idem, *Work Identity at the End of the Line? Privatisation and Culture Change in the UK Rail Industry* (London: Palgrave Macmillan, 2004).

12 Strangleman, "Work Identity in Crisis?" 422.

13 Sean Field, *Oral History, Community and Displacement: Imagining Memories in Post-Apartheid South Africa* (New York: Palgrave Macmillan, 2012), 11.

14 Brian Laflèche, interview by Kristen O'Hare, 3 June 2004.

15 Percy Allary, interview by Kristen O'Hare and Steven High, 9 June 2004 and June 2005.

16 Larry Shank, interview by Kristen O'Hare, 17 August 2004.

17 Lawrence Pretty, interview by Kristen O'Hare, 22 June 2004.

18 Karen Beaudette, interview by Kristen O'Hare, June 2004; her husband, Jean-Guy, was also interviewed.

19 Dunk, *Working Man's Town.*

20 McIvor, *Working Lives,* 1, 280; see also Marina Chauliac and Pascal Raggi, eds., *Le dire pour le fer* (Aumetz, France: Éditions Serpenoise, 2010), esp. chap. 2.

21 Raymond Marcoux, interview by Kristen O'Hare, 20 May 2004.

11. Salvaging History

1   "Weyerhaeuser Pulp and Paper demolition," *Canada News Wire,* 17 June 2004.

2   *Tribune* (Sturgeon Falls), 22 June 2004.

3   Dean Lisk, "Dismantling of mill begins," *Tribune* (Sturgeon Falls), 8 June 2004.

4   Hubert Gervais, interview by Kristen O'Hare and Steven High, 22 June 2005.

5   The photographs can be found on the demolition company's website, http://www.environmentalhazards.com/demolition/weyerhaeuser.htm.

6   In a second interview conducted months later, Marcel Labbé told us that he had been tipped off about the demolition of the stack by the guard at the gate, a local woman. It was a cold day and the town had not been notified beforehand. He took photographs of the demolition crew cutting the base of the stack – "like a tree" – and the rising dust after the stack hit the earth. Marcel Labbé, interview, June 2005.

7   For more on former workers watching the demolition of their factories, see High and Lewis, *Corporate Wasteland,* chap. 1.

8   "Ministry puts brakes on mill demolition," *Sault Star,* 13 July 2004.

9   Ibid.; Maria Calabrese, "Mill demolition will go on: Air-quality monitors focus of concern," *Sudbury Star,* 15 July 2004.

10 W.D. Lighthall, "Demolition of Former Mill Back on Track After Delay," *Daily Commercial News and Construction Record* 77, no. 144 (2004): 1.

11 Edensor, *Industrial Ruins.*

12 Jackie Clarke, "Closing Moulinex: Thoughts on the Visibility and Invisibility of Industrial Labour in Contemporary France," *Modern & Contemporary France* 19, no. 4 (2011): 446.

13 Robert Bevan, *The Destruction of Memory: Architecture of War* (London: Reaktion Books, 2006), 11.

14 Ibid., 12–13.

15 Martha Langford, "Introduction," in *Suspended Conversations: The Afterlife of Memory in Photographic Albums* (Montreal; Kingston, ON: McGill-Queen's University Press, 2001).

16 Social psychologist Setha Low suggests that we treasure these memories all the more; see "Symbolic Ties that Bind: Place Attachment in the Plaza," in *Place Attachment*, ed. Irwin Altman and Setha M. Low (New York: Plenum Press, 1992), 167.

17 Hareven and Langenback, *Amoskeag*, 12; see also Hall, Leloudis, and Korstad, *Like a Family*.

18 Doreen Massey, "Places and Their Pasts," *History Workshop Journal* 39 (1995): 188.

19 Ibid., 189.

20 Ibid., 183.

21 In her study of the working-class Hillesluis district of Rotterdam, sociologist Talja Blokland asks how place making includes and excludes; see Talja Blokland, "Bricks, Mortar, Memories: Neighbourhood and Networks in Collective Acts of Remembering," *International Journal of Urban and Regional Research* 25, no. 2 (2001): 279.

22 Massey, *Spatial Divisions of Labour*, 11. Scholars increasingly view spatiality as actively produced; see Harvey, *Spaces of Global Capitalism*, 77. Henri Lefebvre's tripartite division of space as material (space as experience and perception), as conceptual (space as conceived or represented), and as lived (sensation, imagination, emotion) has been particularly influential in this regard. See Henri Lefebvre, *The Production of Space*, trans. Donald Nicholson-Smith (Oxford: Blackwell, 1991); and idem, *The Survival of Capitalism: Reproduction of the Relations of Production*, trans. Frank Bryant (London: Allison and Busby, 1976).

23 Dudley, *End of the Line*, 47.

24 For more on vernacular heritage, see Robert Summerby-Murray, "Interpreting Personalized Industrial Heritage in the Mining Towns of Cumberland County, Nova Scotia: Landscape Examples from Springhill and River Hebert," *Urban History Review* 35, no. 2 (2007): 51–9.

25 Langford, *Suspended Conversations*, 3.

26 Ibid., 63.

27 Low, "Symbolic Ties that Bind," 167.

28 Bruce Colquhoun and Hubert Gervais, interview by Steven High and Kristen O'Hare, 18 December 2004.

29 Ibid.

30 Colquhoun's full-page tribute to Gervais is found in the binder itself, in the part that deals with 1998.

31 *Insider*, May 1995, in the author's possession. My copies of these documents will be donated to the Sturgeon Falls House Museum at the project's conclusion.

32 Hubert Gervais, "1898–1947: A bit of the Sturgeon Falls mill's history," *Tribune* (Sturgeon Falls), 30 May 1995.

33 The activities can be followed in the town's weekly newspaper, the *Tribune*: 14 March 1995, 4 April 1995, 11 April 1995, 25 April 1995, 2 May 1995, 30 May 1995, and 15 August 1995.

34 LeBelle, *Sturgeon Falls*, 1.

35 Ibid., 23.

36 For more on the founding myths of industrial towns and cities, see Sherry Lee Linkon and John Russo, *Steeltown USA: Work and Memory in Youngstown* (Lawrence: University Press of Kansas, 2002), 2; and James, *Doña María's Story*, 186.

37 Bruce Colquhoun and Hubert Gervais, "The Mill History Binder" (2005 version). The original is in the possession of Bruce Colquhoun; a copy is in the author's possession.

38 Ibid. The mother of Lawrence Pretty had served as the magazine's editor, so he had the originals. It took Bruce Colquhoun three nights, staying late, to make all the photocopies: "I put them all in binders and plastic sleeves. We made twenty copies of each page."

39 For more on photographic image worlds, see David E. Nye, *Image Worlds: Corporate Identities at General Electric, 1890–1930* (Cambridge, MA: MIT Press, 1985).

40 *Insider*, 18 September 1998.

41 Joni Sensel, *Tradition Through the Trees: Weyerhaeuser's First 100 Years* (n.p.: Documentary Book Publishers, 2000).

42 Langford, *Suspended Conversations*, 5.

43 Ibid.

44 Jefferson Cowie and Joseph Heathcott, *Beyond the Ruins: The Meaning of Deindustrialization* (Ithaca, NY: Cornell University Press, 2003), 15. Since then, scholars in the field have largely examined the cultural representation of industrial abandonment across North America and Europe, culminating in a special theme issue of *International Labor and Working Class History* in 2013 on "Crumbling Cultures."

45 Strangleman, "Work Identity in Crisis?" 422.

46 Kirk Savage, "Monuments of a Lost Cause: The Postindustrial Campaign to Commemorate Steel," in Cowie and Heathcott, *Beyond the Ruins*, 248.

47 Joan M. Schwartz makes precisely this point in "Constituting Place of Presence: Landscape, Identity and the Geographical Imagination," in *Places of Presence: Newfoundland Kin and Ancestral Land, Newfoundland 1989–1991*, ed. Marlene Creates, 9–17 (St. John's: Killick Press, 1997).

48 Walsh and High, "Rethinking the Concept of Community."

49 Pierre Nora, "General Introduction: Between Memory and History," in *Realms of Memory: The Construction of the French Past*, vol. 1, ed. Pierra Nora and Lawrence D. Kritzman, 1–20 (New York: Columbia University Press, 1998).

50 Savage, "Monuments of a Lost Cause," 238.

Conclusion

1 Anne Laura Stoler, *Imperial Debris: On Ruins and Ruination* (Durham, NC: Duke University Press, 2013), 8.

2 Harold Wolman, Eric Stokan, and Howard Wial, "Manufacturing Job Loss in U.S. Deindustrialized Regions – Its Consequences and Implications for the Future: Examining the Conventional Wisdom," *Economic Development Quarterly* 29, no. 2 (2015): 102.

3 Statistics Canada, *Canada Yearbook, 2011* (Ottawa, 2011); available online at: http://www.statcan .gc.ca/pub/11-402-x/2011000/chap/man-fab/man-fab-eng.htm, accessed 18 November 2016.

4 Ibid.

5 Anne Howland, "Financial health of paper products sector 'precarious,'" *Telegraph-Journal* (Saint John, NB), 10 May 2007. Five thousand pulp and paper mill workers lost their jobs in Ontario between 2002 and 2006; see Keith Leslie, "Ontario's tax rebate won't save forest industry, critics say," *Vancouver Sun*, 21 November 2006.

6 Cowie and Heathcott, *Beyond the Ruins*, 1–2.

7 David Harvey, "From Space to Place and Back Again: Reflections on the Conditions of Postmodernity," in Bird et al., *Mapping the Futures*, 5.

8 Ibid., 7.

9 Dudley, *End of the Line*, 43.

10 Chaired by Royale Poulin, the CARC had seventeen members, including Mayor Gary O'Connor, Denis Senecal (local union leader), Ron Demers (mill worker), Ray Brouillette, and others. See Dean Lisk, "CARC releases road plan for West Nipissing," *Tribune* (Sturgeon Falls), 24 June 2003; Gord Young, "Plan unveiled to help survive mill closure," *Sault Star*, 21 June 2003; and idem, "Weyerhaeuser to respond next week to bid," *North Bay Nugget*, 7 May 2004.

11 Suzanne Gammon, "West Nipissing rises above," *Tribune* (Sturgeon Falls), undated, available on the website of the West Nipissing Economic Development Authority, http://www

.westnipissingouest.ca/en/growing.html, accessed August 2009. In his interview, Tom Sayer raised questions about the money spent by the CARC on out-of-town consultants and the negligible results that followed. Patricia and Tom Sayer, interview by Kristen O'Hare, 24 June 2004.

12 Town of West Nipissing, "West Nipissing Positioning Plan" (May 2003).

13 Sharon Paquette, "Real estate boom creates optimism in West Nipissing," *Tribune* (Sturgeon Falls), 10 August 2004.

14 The local population had contracted 2.7 per cent between 1996 and 2001, a reflection of the mill's declining importance as a local employer. This decline was less, however, than the regional rate for Northern Ontario, as Franco-Ontarians and Indigenous people have proved far less likely to leave. Indigenous people then accounted for 11.6 per cent of the local population.

15 For the employment list, see the website of the Town of West Nipissing, at http://www .westnipissingouest.ca/en/demographics.html, accessed August 2009.

16 Ontario Superior Court of Justice, Affidavit of Denis Gauthier, Raymond Brouillette Collection.

17 Cowie and Heathcott, *Beyond the Ruins*, 157.

18 "West Nipissing Family of Businesses," *North Bay Nugget*, 2 July 2005, advertising insert.

19 Dean Lisk, "2001 Census shows unemployment over 12% in West Nipissing," *Tribune* (Sturgeon Falls), 4 March 2003.

20 Anna Piekarski, "Loss of mill has cost town $1.4 million," *Sudbury Star*, 20 July 2004.

21 David Byrne, "Industrial Culture in a Post-Industrial World: The Case of the North East of England," *City* 6, no. 3 (2002): 279–81.

22 Strangleman, "Work Identity in Crisis?" 419.

23 Ibid.

24 Ibid., 8.

25 Sayer, *Moral Significance of Class*, 13.

26 Ibid., 42.

27 Barbara Kerr, "Weyerhaeuser shows total lack of concern," *Tribune* (Sturgeon Falls), 29 October 2002.

28 Bruce Colquhoun, "Mill closure will affect us all," *Tribune* (Sturgeon Falls), 22 October 2002.

29 Jane Hardy, "Weyerhaeuser's not fooling anyone," *Tribune* (Sturgeon Falls), 10 December 2002.

30 Vera Charles, "Time for action, not whining," *Tribune* (Sturgeon Falls), 17 December 2002.

31 Ibid.

32 Perry Bush, *Rust Belt Resistance: How a Small Community Took on Big Oil and Won* (Kent, OH: Kent State University Press, 2012), 8.

33 Ibid., 250.

34 Ibid., 227.

35 James J. Connolly, *After the Factory: Reinventing America's Industrial Small Cities* (New York: Lexington Books, 2010), 2.

36 Cowie, *Capital Moves*.

37 Doreen Massey, "Geographies of Responsibility," *Geografiska Annaler* 86B, no. 1 (2004): 10.

38 Cowie and Heathcott, *Beyond the Ruins*, 15; see also Tim Strangleman, "'Smokestack Nostalgia,' 'Ruin Porn,' or Working-Class Obituary: The Role and Meaning of Deindustrial Representation," *International Labor and Working Class History* 84 (Fall 2013): 23–37.

39 Leon Fink, "When Community Comes Home to Roost: The Southern Milltown as Lost Cause," *Journal of Social History* 40, no. 1 (2006): 125.

40 Ibid., 136.

41 Dudley, *End of the Line*, 28.

42 Stein, *Running Steel*.

43 Brian Egan and Suzanne Klaussen, "Female in a Forest Town: The Marginalization of Women in Port Alberni's Economy," *BC Studies* 118 (1998): 35.

44 For more on the gendered division of labour in forestry towns, see Maureen G. Reed, "Reproducing the Gender Order in Canadian Forestry: The Role of Statistical Representation," *Scandinavian Journal of Forest Research* 23, no. 1 (2008): 78, 81; and Suzanne E. Mills, "Restructuring in the Forest Sector and the Re-Shaping of Women's Work Identities," *Canadian Geographer* 56, no. 1 (2012): 39–57.
45 See, for example, Bradley L. Garrett, *Explore Everything: Place-Hacking the City* (London: Verso, 2013).
46 Stoler, *Imperial Debris*, 11.
47 Gervais and Colquhoun, "Mill History Binder."

BIBLIOGRAPHY

Oral History Interviews

Production Workers (organized by mill seniority)

Ken Colquhoun (18 September 1947). Interviewed by Steven High, 23 June 2005.

Harold Stewart ([later management] 3 November 1954). Interviewed by Kristen O'Hare, 18 June 2004.

Marcel Labbé ([later management] 21 May 1957). Interviewed by Kristen O'Hare and Steven High, 18 August 2004 and June 2005.

André Girard (8 October 1959). Interviewed by Kristen O'Hare, 29 July 2004.

Claude Lortie ([later management] 23 June 1962). Interviewed by Kristen O'Hare and Steven High, 7 September 2004 and 28 June 2005.

Lawrence Pretty (23 July 1962). Interviewed by Kristen O'Hare, 22 June 2004.

Marc Côté ([later management] 21 September 1962). Interviewed by Kristen O'Hare, 30 January 2004.

Frank Gerbasi (8 July 1964). Interviewed by Kristen O'Hare, 23 January 2004.

Wayne Pigeau (14 August 1971). Interviewed by Kristen O'Hare, 19 May 2004.

Randy Restoule (14 August 1971). Interviewed by Kristen O'Hare, 5 August 2004.

Henri Labelle (20 August 1971). Interviewed by Kristen O'Hare, 9 December 2004; plant tour with Steven High, July 2004.

Ron Demers (20 August 1971). Interviewed by Kristen O'Hare, 6 May 2004.

Percival (Percy) Allary (20 August 1971). Interviewed by Kristen O'Hare and Steven High, 9 June 2004 and June 2005.

Raymond Marcoux (8 September 1971). Interviewed by Kristen O'Hare, 20 May 2004.

Denis MacGregor (11 November 1972). Interviewed by Kristen O'Hare, 17 June 2004.

Benny Haarsma ([later management] 28 August 1972). Interviewed by Kristen O'Hare, 30 June 2004.

Raymond Lortie ([later management] 27 August 1974). Interviewed by Kristen O'Hare, 7 September 2004.

Bruce Colquhoun (13 January 1975). Interviewed by Steven High and Kristen O'Hare, 18 December 2004, 23 June 2005, and 19 July 2005.

Pierre Hardy (25 December 1975). Interviewed by Kristen O'Hare and Steven High, 5 December 2003 and 14 June 2005.

Marcel Boudreau (5 September 1978). Interviewed by Kristen O'Hare and Steven High, 1 December 2003 and 23 June 2005.

André Cartier (5 September 1978). Interviewed by Kristen O'Hare, 12 November 2004.

Mike Lacroix (5 September 1978). Interviewed by Kristen O'Hare, 12 November 2004, by Steven High, December 2005.

Gordon Jackson (seniority date unknown). Interviewed by Kristen O'Hare, 9 June 2004.

Lionel Sarazin (seniority date unknown). Interviewed by Kristen O'Hare, 6 April 2005.

Anonymous mill worker (seniority date confidential). Interviewed by Steven High, 2 December 2003.

Mill Office Workers, Union and Salaried

Anonymous. Interviewed by Kristen O'Hare, 10 March 2004.

Karen Beaudette. Interviewed by Kristen O'Hare, 7 June 2004.

Hubert Gervais. Interviewed by Kristen O'Hare and Steven High, 12 March 2004, 18 December 2004, and 22 June 2005.

Ben Lajeunesse. Interviewed by Kristen O'Hare, 22 June 2004.

Merna Nesbitt. Interviewed by Kristen O'Hare, 10 August 2004.

Ruth Thompson. Interviewed by Kristen O'Hare, 22 June 2004.

Spouses and Children of Mill Workers

Jean-Guy Beaudette. Interviewed by Kristen O'Hare, 7 June 2004.

Pietro Carello. Interviewed by Kristen O'Hare, 9 August 2004.

Jane Hardy. Interviewed by Kristen O'Hare and Steven High, 5 December 2003 and 14 June 2005.

Managers

Cam Barrington. Interviewed by Steven High, March 2004.

John Dillon. Interviewed by Kristen O'Hare, 19 May 2004.

Ed Fortin. Interviewed by Kristen O'Hare, 5 August 2004.

Ed Hatton. Interviewed by Kristen O'Hare, 29 July 2004.

Larry Shank. Interviewed by Kristen O'Hare, 17 August 2004.

Wally Shisko. Interviewed by Kristen O'Hare, 8 May 2004.

Gerry Stevens. Interviewed by Kristen O'Hare, 2 July 2004.

Economic and Political Leaders

Ron Beauchamp. Interviewed by Kristen O'Hare, 8 July 2004.

Raymond Brouillette. Interviewed by Kristen O'Hare, 11 June 2004.

J.P. Charles. Interviewed by Kristen O'Hare, 10 August 2004.

Guy Ethier. Interviewed by Kristen O'Hare, 17 June 2004.

Denis Gauthier. Interviewed by Kristen O'Hare, 31 May 2004.
Alan Korell. Interviewed by Kristen O'Hare, 29 October 2004.
Brian Laflèche. Interviewed by Kristen O'Hare and Steven High, 3 June 2004.
Ken Landry. Interviewed by Kristen O'Hare, 28 July 2004.
Wayne LeBelle. Interviewed by Steven High, 6 September 2004.
Robert Marier. Interviewed by Kristen O'Hare, 9 July 2004.
Yvon Marleau. Interviewed by Kristen O'Hare, 15 July 2004.
Guy Robichaud. Interviewed by Kristen O'Hare, 18 July 2004.
Gary O'Connor. Interviewed by Kristen O'Hare, 5 August 2004.
Daniel Olivier. Interviewed by Kristen O'Hare, 21 November 2004.
Patricia and Tom Sayer. Interviewed by Kristen O'Hare, 24 June 2004.

Public Archives Consulted

Archives of Ontario. Toronto.
Centre de recherche en civilisation Canadienne-française. University of Ottawa.
Kheel Center for Labor-Management Documentation and Archives. Cornell University, Ithaca, NY.
Library and Archives Canada. Ottawa.
Laurentian University Archives. Sudbury, ON.
National Archives. London.
National Archives and Records Administration. Washington, DC.
Nipissing University Library. North Bay, ON.
Sault Ste. Marie Public Library.
Sturgeon River House Museum. Sturgeon Falls, ON.
Personal collections, Sturgeon Falls: Ray Brouillette, André Cartier, Bruce Colquhoun, André Gervais, Hubert Gervais, Claude Lortie, and anonymous workers.

Newspapers and Magazines

Abitibi Magazine
Canadian Engineer
Canada Lumberman
Canadian Manufacturing and Industrial World
Canadian Paperworkers Journal
Canadian Pulp and Paper Workers Journal
La Cause
CEP Journal
Le Droit (Ottawa)
Financial Post
Gazette (Montreal)
Globe (Toronto)
Globe and Mail
Insider
Labour Gazette
Monetary Times

New York Times
North Bay Nugget
Port Arthur News Chronicle
Pulp and Paper Magazine of Canada
La Rotonde (Ottawa)
Sault Star
Le Soleil (Quebec City)
Sudbury Star
Telegraph-Journal (Saint John)
Thunder Bay Times-News
Timmins Daily Press
Toronto Star
Toronto Telegraph
Toronto Worker
Tribune (Sturgeon Falls)
Vancouver Sun
Le Voyageur (Sudbury)
Weyerhaeuser Bulletin
Winnipeg Free Press

Secondary Sources

Abel, Kerry M. *Changing Places: History, Community, and Identity in Northeastern Ontario.* Montreal; Kingston, ON: McGill-Queen's University Press, 2006.
Abel, Kerry, and Ken S. Coates, eds. *Northern Visions: New Perspectives on the North in Canadian History.* Toronto: Broadview Press, 2001.
ACFO-Nipissing. *Étude du milieu et statistiques sur la situation des francophones de la région du Nipissing dans les localités suivantes: North Bay, Sturgeon Falls, Mattawa.* Ottawa: ACFO-Nipissing, 1988.
Ashworth, William. *The Late, Great Lakes: An Environmental History.* Detroit: Wayne State University Press, 1986.
Barnes, Trevor J. "Retheorizing Economic Geography: From the Quantitative Revolution to the 'Cultural Turn.'" *Annals of the Association of American Geographers* 91, no. 3 (2001): 546–65.
Barnes, Trevor J., and Roger Hayter. "Economic Restructuring, Local Development and Resource Towns: Forest Communities in Coastal British Columbia." *Canadian Journal of Regional Science* 17, no. 3 (1994): 289–310.
Behiels, Michael D. *Canada's Francophone Minority Communities: Constitutional Renewal.* Montreal; Kingston, ON: McGill-Queen's University Press, 2005.
Bevan, Robert. *The Destruction of Memory: Architecture of War.* London: Reaktion Books, 2006.
Blokland, Talja. "Bricks, Mortar, Memories: Neighbourhood and Networks in Collective Acts of Remembering." *International Journal of Urban and Regional Research,* 25, no. 2 (2001): 268–83.
Bluestone, Barry, and Bennet Harrison. *The Deindustrialization of America.* New York: Basic Books, 1982.
Bollman, Ray D., Rolland Beshiri, and Verna Mitura. "Northern Ontario's Communities: Economic Diversification, Specialization and Growth." Agricultural and Rural Working Paper Series 82. Ottawa: Statistics Canada, 2006.

Bock, Michel. "Le sort de la memoire dans la construction historique de l'identité franco-ontarienne." *Francophonies d'Amerique* 18 (Autumn 2004): 119–26.

Boothman, Barry. "High Finance/Low Strategy: Corporate Collapse in the Canadian Pulp and Paper Industry, 1919–1932." *Business History Review* 74, no. 4 (2000): 611–56.

Bordeleau, Louis-Gabriel, Raymond Lallier, and Aurèle Lalonde. *Les écoles secondaires de langue françaises en Ontario: dix ans après*. Toronto: Ministry of Colleges and Universities, 1980.

Borges, M., and S. Torres, eds. *Company Towns: Labor, Space, and Power Relations across Time and Continents*. New York: Palgrave Macmillan, 2012.

Boyd, William. *The Slain Wood: Papermaking and Its Environmental Consequences in the American South*. Baltimore: Johns Hopkins University Press, 2015.

Brecher, Jeremy. *Banded Together: Economic Democratization in the Brass Valley*. Chicago: University of Illinois Press, 2011.

Broadfoot, Barry. *Ten Lost Years, 1929–1939*. Toronto: McClelland & Stewart, 1973.

Burnell, William H. "On the Record." *Pulp, Sulphite and Paper Mill Workers Journal* (March–April 1963): 8.

Bush, Perry. *Rust Belt Resistance: How a Small Community Took on Big Oil and Won*. Kent, OH: Kent State University Press, 2012.

Byrne, David. "Industrial Culture in a Post-Industrial World: The Case of the North East of England." *City* 6, no. 33 (2002): 279–81.

Campbell, Lara. *Respectable Citizens: Gender, Family, and Unemployment in Ontario's Great Depression*. Toronto: University of Toronto Press, 2009.

Canada. Department of Indian Affairs. *Annual Report of the Department of Indian Affairs for the Year Ended, June 30, 1904 to 1918*. Ottawa, 1919.

Canadian Pulp and Paper Association. *A Handbook of the Canadian Pulp and Paper Industry*. Montreal, 1920.

Carruthers, George. *Paper-Making*. Toronto: Garden City Press, 1947.

Cartwright, Don. "The Expansion of French Language Rights in Ontario, 1968–1993: The Uses of Territoriality." *Canadian Geographer* 40, no. 3 (1996): 238–57.

Cassels, R.S. "A Paddler's Paradise." *Massey Magazine* 1, no. 6 (1896): 393, 399.

Chauliac, Marina, and Pascal Raggi, eds. *Le dire pour le fer*. Aumetz, France: Éditions Serpenoise, 2010.

Chute, Janet E. *The Legacy of Shingwaukonse: A Century of Native Leadership*. Toronto: University of Toronto Press, 1998.

Clarke, Jackie. "Closing Moulinex: Thoughts on the Visibility and Invisibility of Industrial Labour in Contemporary France." *Modern & Contemporary France* 19, no. 4 (2011): 443–58.

Connolly, James J. *After the Factory: Reinventing America's Industrial Small Cities*. New York: Lexington Books, 2010.

Cooper, Frederick. *Colonialism in Question: Theory, Knowledge, History*. Berkeley: University of California Press, 2005.

Cowie, Jefferson. *Capital Moves: RCA's 70-Year Quest for Cheap Labor*. Ithaca, NY: Cornell University Press, 1999.

Cowie, Jefferson. *The Great Exception: The New Deal and the Limits of American Politics*. Princeton, NJ: Princeton University Press, 2016.

Cowie, Jefferson, and Joseph Heathcott. *Beyond the Ruins: The Meaning of Deindustrialization*. Ithaca, NY: Cornell University Press, 2003.

Creighton, Donald. *Dominion of the North: A History of Canada*. Toronto: Houghton Mifflin, 1944.

Creighton, Donald. *The Commercial Empire of the St. Lawrence, 1760–1850*. Toronto: Ryerson Press, 1937.

Dickson, Robert. "La 'révolution culturelle' en Nouvel-Ontario et le Québec: Opération Ressources et ses consequences." In *Produire la Culture, Produire l'identité*, edited by Andrée Fortin, 183–97. Quebec City: Les Presses de l'Université Laval, 2000.

Dudley, Kathryn Marie. *The End of the Line: Lost Jobs, New Lives in Postindustrial America*. Chicago: University of Chicago Press, 1994.

Dunk, Thomas. "Culture, Skill, Masculinity and Whiteness: Training and the Politics of Identity." In *The Training Trap: Ideology, Training and the Labour Market*, edited by Thomas Dunk, Stephen McBride, and Randle W. Nelsen, 101–23. Toronto: Society for Socialist Studies, 1996.

Dunk, Thomas. "Remaking the Working Class: Experience, Class Consciousness, and the Industrial Adjustment Process." *American Ethnologist* 29, no. 4 (2002): 878–900.

Dunk, Thomas. *A Working Man's Town: Male Working-Class Culture*. Montreal; Kingston, ON: McGill-Queen's University Press, 1991.

Dunk, Thomas, Stephen McBride, and Randle W. Nelsen. "Introduction." In *The Training Trap: Ideology, Training and the Labour Market*, edited by Thomas Dunk, Stephen McBride, and Randle W. Nelsen, 1–12. Toronto: Society for Socialist Studies, 1996.

Edensor, Tim. *Industrial Ruins: Space, Aesthetics, and Materiality*. New York: Berg, 2005.

Egan, Brian, and Suzanne Klaussen. "Female in a Forest Town: The Marginalization of Women in Port Alberni's Economy." *BC Studies* 118 (Summer 1998): 5–40.

Falk, William W., and Thomas A. Lyson, eds. *Forgotten Places: Uneven Development in Rural America*. Lawrence: University Press of Kansas, 1993.

Field, Sean. *Oral History, Community and Displacement: Imagining Memories in Post-Apartheid South Africa*. New York: Palgrave Macmillan, 2012.

Fink, Leon. "When Community Comes Home to Roost: The Southern Milltown as Lost Cause." *Journal of Social History* 40, no. 1 (2006): 119–45.

Florida, Richard. *Ontario in the Creative Age*. Toronto: Prosperity Institute, 2009.

Foster, Jennifer, and L. Anders Sandberg. "Post-Industrial Urban Greenspace: Justice, Quality of Life and Environmental Aesthetics in rapidly changing urban environments." *Local Environment* 19, no. 10 (2014): 1043–8.

Fudge, Judy, and Eric Tucker. *Labour Before the Law: The Regulation of Workers' Collective Action in Canada, 1900–1948*. Toronto: Oxford University Press, 2001.

Garrett, Bradley L. *Explore Everything: Place-Hacking the City*. London: Verso, 2013.

Gaudreau, Guy. "La sous-traitance forestière dans le Nord-Est ontarien, 1900-1930." *Labour* 40 (Fall 1997): 75–112.

Gaudreau, Guy. "L'importance du cadre juridique dans les approvisionnements de bois: le bassin de la rivière Sturgeon, 1898–1918." In *La nature et la loi: le pluralisme juridique dans la gestion de la nature*. Edited by François-Xavier Ribordy, 227–42. Sudbury, ON: Presses de l'Université Laurentienne, 1999.

Gervais, Gaétan. "Le Règlement XVII (1912–1927)." *Revue du Nouvel Ontario* 18 (1996): 123–92.

Gillis, R. Peter, and Thomas R. Roach. *Lost Initiatives: Canada's Forest Industries, Forest Policy and Forest Conservation*. New York: Greenwood, 1986.

Golz, Eileen. "Espanola: The History of a Pulp and Paper Town." *Laurentian University Review* 6, no. 3 (1974): 75–104.

Gordon, David M., Richard Edwards, and Michael Reich. *Segmented Work, Divided Workers: The Historical Transformation of Labor in the United States*. Cambridge: Cambridge University Press, 1982.

Gross, James A. "The Making and Shaping of Unionism in the Pulp and Paper Industry." *Labor History* 5, no. 2 (1964): 183–208.

Guénette, René. "Histoire de Sturgeon Falls (1878–1960)." Master's thesis, Laurentian University, 1966.

Hak, Gordon. *Capital and Labour in the British Columbia Forest Industry, 1934–74.* Vancouver: UBC Press, 2007.

Hall, Jacquelyn Dowd, James Leloudis, and Robert Korstad. *Like a Family: The Making of a Southern Cotton Mill World.* Chapel Hill: University of North Carolina Press, 1987.

Hansen, Lise C. "Revocation of Surrender and Its Implications for a Canadian Indian Band's Development." *Anthropologica* 23, no. 2 (1981): 121–43.

Hansen, Lise C. "Thirty-five dollars." *Canadian Journal of Native Studies* 2, no. 2 (1982): 269–83.

Hareven, Tamara, and Randolph Langenback. *Amoskeag: Life and Work in an American Factory City.* New York: Pantheon, 1978.

Harvey, David. "From Space to Place and Back Again: Reflections on the Conditions of Postmodernity." In *Mapping the Futures: Local Cultures, Global Changes*, edited by Jon Bird, Barry Curtis, Tim Putnam, George Robertson, and Lisa Tickner, 2–29. London: Routledge, 1993.

Harvey, David. *Spaces of Global Capitalism.* London: Verso, 2006.

Hayday, Matthew. *Bilingual Today, United Tomorrow.* Montreal; Kingston, ON: McGill-Queen's University Press, 2005.

Hayter, Roger. "Corporate Strategies and Industrial Change in the Canadian Forest Product Industries." *Geographical Review* 66, no. 2 (1976): 209–28.

Hayter, Roger. *Flexible Crossroads: The Restructuring of BC's Forest Industry.* Vancouver: UBC Press, 2000.

Hayter, Roger. "High-Performance Organizations and Employment Flexibility: A Case Study in In-Situ Change at the Powell River Paper Mill, 1980–1994." *Canadian Geographer* 41, no. 1 (1997): 26–40.

Hayter, Roger. "Technological Imperatives in Resource Sectors: Forest Products." In *Canada and the Global Economy: The Geography of Structural and Technological Change*, edited by John N.H. Britton, 101–22. Montreal; Kingston, ON: McGill-Queen's University Press, 1996.

Hayter, Roger, Trevor J. Barnes, and Michael J. Bradshaw. "Relocating Resource Peripheries to the Core of Economic Geography's Theorizing: Rationale and Agenda." *Area* 35, no. 1 (2003): 15–23.

Heller, Monica. "La sociolinguistique et l'éducation franco-ontarienne." *Sociologie et sociétés* 26, no. 1 (1994): 155–66.

Hendry, George, and Susan Janhurst. *The Bacteriological Water Quality of the Sturgeon River at Sturgeon Falls, 1977; Effects of Wastewater from the Abitibi Paper Mill.* Toronto: Ministry of Environment, June 1978.

Herod, Andrew. "Workers, Space and Labor Geography." *International Labor and Working Class History* 64 (Fall 2003): 112–38.

High, Steven. *Industrial Sunset: The Making of North America's Rust Belt.* Toronto: University of Toronto Press, 2003.

High, Steven. "Native Wage Labour and Independent Production during the 'Era of Irrelevance.'" *Labour* 37 (Spring 1996): 243–64.

High, Steven. "Placing the Displaced Worker: Narrating Place in Deindustrializing Sturgeon Falls, Ontario." In *Placing Memory and Remembering Place in Canada*, edited by James Opp and John Walsh, 159–86. Vancouver: UBC Press, 2010.

High, Steven. "Sharing Authority in the Writing of Canadian History: The Case of Oral History." In *Contesting Clio's Craft: New Directions and Debates in Canadian History*, edited by Michael Dawson and Christopher Dummitt, 21–46. London: Institute for the Study of the Americas, 2009.

High, Steven. "'The wounds of class': A Historiographical Reflection on the Study of Deindustrialization, 1973–2013." *History Compass* 11, no. 11 (2013): 994–1007.

High, Steven, and David Lewis. *Corporate Wasteland: The Landscape and Memory of Deindustrialization*. Ithaca, NY: Cornell University Press, 2007.

High, Steven, Lachlan Mackinnon, and Andrew Perchard, eds. *The Deindustrialized World: Confronting Ruination in Post-Industrial Places*. Vancouver: UBC Press, 2017.

Himelfarb, Alex. "The Social Characteristics of One-Industry Towns in Canada." In *Little Communities and Big Industries: Studies in the Social Impact of Canadian Resource Extraction*, edited by Roy T. Bowles, 16–43. Toronto: Butterworths, 1982.

Hinshaw, John, and Judith Modell. "Perceiving Racism: Homestead from Depression to Deindustrialziation." *Pennsylvania History* 63, no. 1 (1996): 17–52.

Hodgins, Bruce W. *The Temagami experience: Recreation, Resources, and Aboriginal Rights in the Northern Ontario Wilderness*. Toronto: University of Toronto Press, 1989.

Hodgins, Bruce W., and Jamie Benidickson. "Resource Management Conflict in the Temagami Forest, 1898 to 1914." *Historical Papers* 13, no. 1 (1978): 148–75.

Hodgins, Bruce, Ute Lischke, and David T. McNab, eds. *Blockades and Resistance: Studies in Actions of Peace and the Temagami Blockades of 1988–89*. Waterloo, ON: Wilfrid Laurier University Press, 2003.

Holmes, John. "In Search of Competitive Efficiency: Labour Process Flexibility in Canadian Newsprint Mills." *Canadian Geographer* 41, no. 1 (1997): 7–25.

Hotte, Lucie. "Littérature et conscience identitaire: l'héritage de CANO." In *Produire la culture, Produire l'identité*, edited by Andrée Fortin, 53–68. Quebec City: Les Presses de l'Université Laval, 2000.

Hotte, Lucie. "Un pays à soi: construction d'une territoire franco-ontarienne." In *Frontières flottantes/Shifting Boundaries: lieu et espace dans les cultures francophones du Canada*, edited by Jaap Lintvelt and François Paré, 217–28. Amsterdam: Rodopi, 2001.

Howland, Anne. "Financial health of paper products sector 'precarious.'" *Telegraph-Journal* (Saint John), 10 May 2007.

Hudson, Ray, and David Sadler. "Contesting Works Closures in Western Europe's Old Industrial Regions: Defending Place or Betraying Class?" In *Production, Work, Territory: The Geographical Anatomy of Industrial Capitalism*, edited by Allen J. Scott and Michael Storper, 172–93. Boston: Allen and Unwin, 1986.

Huchison, George, and Dick Wallace. *Grassy Narrows*. Toronto: Van Nostrand Reinhold, 1977.

James, Daniel. *Doña María's Story: Life History, Memory, and Political Identity*. Durham, NC: Duke University Press, 2000.

Jones, Owen. *Chavs: The Demonization of the Working Class*. London: Verso, 2011.

Keeling, Arn. "'Born in an Atomic Test Tube': Landscapes of Cyclonic Development at Uranium City, Saskatchewan." *Canadian Geographer* 54, no. 2 (2010): 228–52.

Kirk, John. *Class, Culture and Social Change: On the Trail of the Working Class*. London: Palgrave Macmillan, 2007.

Koistinen, David. *Confronting Decline: The Political Economy of Deindustrialization in Twentieth-Century New England*. Gainesville: University Press of Florida, 2016.

Krogman, Naomi, and Tom Beckley. "Corporate 'Bail-Outs' and Local 'Buyouts': Pathways to Community Forestry?" *Society and Natural Resources* 15, no. 2 (2002): 109–27.

Kuhlberg, Mark. "An Accomplished History, An Uncertain Future: Canada's Pulp and Paper Industry since the Early 1800s." In *The Evolution of Global Paper Industry 1800–2050: A Comparative Analysis*, edited by Juha-Antti Lamberg, Jari Ojala, Mirva Peltoniemi, and Timo Särkkä, 101–33. Dordrecht: Springer, 2012.

Kuhlberg, Mark. *In the Power of Government: The Rise and Fall of Newsprint in Ontario, 1894–1932*. Toronto: University of Toronto Press, 2015.

Langford, Martha. *Suspended Conversations: The Afterlife of Memory in Photographic Albums.* Montreal; Kingston, ON: McGill-Queen's University Press, 2001.

LeBelle, Wayne. *Sturgeon Falls, 1895–1995.* Field, ON: WFL Communications, 1995.

Lefebvre, Henri. *The Production of Space.* Translated by Donald Nicholson-Smith. Oxford: Blackwell, 1991.

Lefebvre, Henri. *The Survival of Capitalism: Reproduction of the Relations of Production.* Translated by Frank Bryant. London: Allison and Busby, 1976.

Lighthall, W.D. "Demolition of Former Mill Back on Track After Delay." *Daily Commercial News and Construction Record* 77, no. 144 (2004): 1.

Linkon, Sherry Lee, and John Russo. *Steeltown USA: Work and Memory in Youngstown.* Lawrence: University Press of Kansas, 2002.

Low, Setha M. "Symbolic Ties that Bind: Place Attachment in the Plaza." In *Place Attachment,* edited by Irwin Altman and Setha M. Low, 165–86. New York: Plenum Press, 1992.

Lower, A.R.M. "The Assault on the Laurentian Barrier, 1850-1870." *Canadian Historical Review* 10, no. 4 (1929): 294–307.

Lucas, Rex. *Minetown, Milltown and Railtown: Life in Canadian Communities of Single Industry.* Toronto: Oxford University Press, [1971] 2008.

Lutz, John Sutton. *Makuk: A New History of Aboriginal-White Relations.* Vancouver: UBC Press, 2008.

Mackinnon, Lachlan. "Deindustrialization on the Periphery: An Oral History of Sydney Steel, 1945-2001." PhD thesis, Concordia University, 2016.

Mackintosh, W.A. "Economic Factors in Canadian History." *Canadian Historical Review* 4, no. 1 (1923): 12–25.

Mah, Alice. *Industrial Ruination, Community, and Place: Landscapes and Legacies of Urban Decline.* Toronto: University of Toronto Press, 2012.

Manuel, Jeffrey T. *Taconite Dreams: The Struggle to Sustain Mining on Minnesota's Iron Range, 1915-2000.* Minneapolis: University of Minnesota Press, 2015.

Massey, Doreen. "Geographies of Responsibility." *Geografiska Annaler* 86B, no. 1 (2004): 5–18.

Massey, Doreen. "Places and Their Pasts." *History Workshop Journal* 39 (1995): 182–92.

Massey, Doreen. "Power-Geometry and a Progressive Sense of Place." In *Mapping the Futures: Local Cultures, Global Change,* edited by Jon Bird, Barry Curtis, Tim Putnam, and Lisa Tickner, 60–70. London: Routledge, 1993.

Massey, Doreen. *Spatial Divisions of Labour: Social Structures and the Geographies of Production.* London: Macmillan, 1984.

Masterson, P.G. "The Sturgeon Falls Operations of Abitibi Power and Paper Company, Limited." Manuscript, October 1956.

Matthews, Chris. "The Sturgeon Falls Mill." BA Honours thesis, Laurentian University, 1996.

McBride, Stephen. "The Continuing Crisis of Social Democracy: Ontario's Social Contract Perspective." *Studies in Political Economy* 50, no. 1 (1996): 65–93.

McCallum, Mary Jane Logan. *Indigenous Women, Work, and History, 1940–1980.* Winnipeg: University of Manitoba Press, 2014.

McCrostie, James. *Just the Beginning: The Communications, Energy and Paperworkers Union of Canada.* Ottawa: Communications, Energy and Paperworkers Union of Canada, 1996.

McDowall, Duncan. *Steel at the Sault: Francis H. Clergue, Sir James Dunn, and the Algoma Steel Corporation, 1901–1956.* Toronto: University of Toronto Press, 1984.

McInnis, Peter S. *Harnessing Labour Confrontation: Shaping the Postwar Settlement in Canada, 1943-1950.* Toronto: University of Toronto Press, 2002.

McIvor, Arthur. "Economic Violence, Occupational Disability and Death: Oral Narratives of the Impact of Asbestos-Related Diseases in Britain." In *Beyond Testimony and Trauma: Oral History in the Aftermath of Mass Violence*, edited by Steven High, 257–84. Vancouver: UBC Press, 2015.

McIvor, Arthur. *Working Lives: Working Britain Since 1945*. London: Palgrave Macmillan, 2013.

McNeil, J.R. *Something New Under the Sun: An Environmental History of the Twentieth Century*. New York: W.W. Norton, 2000.

Meyer, Stephen. *Manhood on the Line: Working-Class Masculinities in the American Heartland*. Urbana: University of Illinois Press, 2016.

Milloy, Jeremy. *Blood, Sweat, and Fear: Violence at Work in the North American Auto Industry*. Vancouver: UBC Press, 2017.

Mills, Suzanne E. "Restructuring in the Forest Sector and the Re-Shaping of Women's Work Identities." *Canadian Geographer* 56, no. 1 (2012): 39–57.

Mills, Suzanne, and Louise Clarke. "'We will go side-by-side with you': Labour Union Engagement with Aboriginal Peoples in Canada." *Geoforum* 40, no. 6 (2009): 991–1001.

Minchin, Timothy. *Empty Mills: The Fight Against Imports and the Decline of the US Textile Industry*. Lanham, MD: Rowman and Littlefield, 2013.

Montgomery, David. *The Fall of the House of Labor: The Workplace, the State, and American Labor Activism, 1865–1925*. Cambridge: Cambridge University Press, 1987.

Murton, James, Dean Bavington, and Carly Dokis, eds. *Subsistence Under Capitalism: Historical and Contemporary Perspectives*. Montreal; Kingston, ON: McGill-Queen's University Press, 2016.

Nelles, H.V. *The Politics of Development: Forests, Mines, and Hydro-Electric Power in Ontario, 1849–1941*. Toronto: Macmillan of Canada, 1974.

Neumann, Tracy. *Remaking the Rust Belt: The Postindustrial Transformation of North America*. Philadelphia: University of Pennsylvania Press, 2016.

Nora, Pierre. "General Introduction: Between Memory and History." In *Realms of Memory: The Construction of the French Past*, vol. 1, edited by Pierre Nora and Lawrence D. Kritzman, 1–20. New York: Columbia University Press, 1998.

Norcliffe, Glen. *Global Game, Local Arena: Restructuring in Corner Brook, Newfoundland*. St. John's: ISER Books, 2005.

Nye, David E. *Image Worlds: Corporate Identities at General Electric, 1890–1930*. Cambridge, MA: MIT Press, 1985.

Ontario. Department of Municipal Affairs. *Annual Report of Municipal Statistics for the Year 1934*. Toronto, 1935.

Ontario. Department of Municipal Affairs. *Annual Report of Municipal Statistics for the Year 1937*. Toronto, 1938.

Ontario. Department of Municipal Affairs. *Annual Report of Municipal Statistics for the Year 1938*. Toronto, 1939.

Ontario. Department of Municipal Affairs. *Annual Report of Municipal Statistics for the Year 1939*. Toronto, 1940.

Ontario. Department of Municipal Affairs. *Annual Report of Municipal Statistics for the Year 1940*. Toronto, 1941.

Ontario. Department of Municipal Affairs. *Annual Report of Municipal Statistics for the Years 1937–1941*. Toronto, 1935.

Ontario. Ministry of Labour. *Improving Health and Safety in the Pulp and Paper Industry: Report of the Provincial Inquiry into Health and Safety of Worker in the Pulp and Paper Industry*. Toronto: April 1990.

Ontario. Royal Commission Inquiring into the Affairs of Abitibi Power & Paper Company Limited. *Report*. Toronto, March 1941.

Ontario. Royal Commission on the Enquiry as to the Handling of Unemployment and Direct Relief at Sturgeon Falls, Ontario. *Report of Judge James McNairn Hall*. Toronto, 1933.

Ontario Timber Commission. *Interim Reports*. Toronto: Clarkson W. James, 1921.

Ontario Water Resources Commission. *Water Pollution Survey of the Town of Sturgeon Falls*. Toronto: Ministry of Environment, 1965.

Parenteau, Bill. "The Woods Transformed: The Emergence of the Pulp and Paper Industry in New Brunswick, 1918–1931." *Acadiensis* 22, no. 1 (1992): 5–43.

Parr, Joy. *Sensing Changes: Technologies, Environments and the Everyday, 1953–2003*. Vancouver: UBC Press, 2010.

Passerini, Luisa. *Fascism in Popular Memory: The Cultural Experience of the Turin Working-Class*. Cambridge: Cambridge University Press, 1987.

Perry, Adele. *On the Edge of Empire: Gender, Race, and the Making of British Columbia, 1849–1871*. Toronto: University of Toronto Press, 2001.

Phillips, James. *Collieries, Communities and the Miners' Strike in Scotland, 1984–85*. Manchester, UK: Manchester University Press, 2012.

Piper, Liza, and John Sandlos. "A Broken Frontier in Ecological Imperialism in the Canadian North." *Environment History* 12, no. 4 (2007): 759–95.

Quarter, Jack. *Crossing the Line: Unionized Employee Ownership and Investment Funds*. Toronto: Lorimer, 1995.

Radforth, Ian. *Bushworkers and Bosses: Logging in Northern Ontario, 1900–1980*. Toronto: University of Toronto Press, 1987.

Randall, James E., and R. Geoff Ironside. "Communities on the Edge: An Economic Geography of Resource-Dependent Communities in Canada." *Canadian Geographer* 40, no. 1 (1996): 17–35.

Reed, Maureen G. "Reproducing the Gender Order in Canadian Forestry: The Role of Statistical Representation." *Scandinavian Journal of Forest Research* 23, no. 1 (2008): 78–91.

Rodden, Jonathan A., and Gunnar S. Eskeland. "Constraining Subnational Fiscal Behavior in Canada." In *Fiscal Decentralization and the Challenge of Hard Budget Constraints*, edited by Richard M. Bird and Almos Tassanyi, 85–132. Cambridge, MA: MIT Press, 2003.

Rosen, Corey, and Karen M. Young, eds. *Understanding Employee Ownership*. Ithaca, NY: ILR Press, 1991.

Russell, Bob. *More with Less: Work Reorganization in the Canadian Mining Industry*. Toronto: University of Toronto Press, 1999.

Sandlos, John, and Arn Keeling. "Claiming the New North: Development and Colonialism at the Pine Point Mine, Northwest Territories, Canada." *Environment and History* 18, no. 1 (2012): 5–34.

Sangster, Joan. *Transforming Labour: Women and Work in Postwar Canada*. Toronto: University of Toronto Press, 2010.

Savage, Kirk. "Monuments of a Lost Cause: The Postindustrial Campaign to Commemorate Steel." In *Beyond the Ruins: The Meaning of Deindustrialization*, edited by Jefferson Cowie and Joseph Heathcott, 237–56. Ithaca, NY: Cornell University Press, 2003.

Sayer, Andrew. *The Moral Significance of Class*. Cambridge: Cambridge University Press, 2005.

Schonning, Egil. "Union-Management Relations in the Pulp and Paper Industry of Ontario and Quebec." PhD diss., University of Toronto, 1955.

Schumpeter, Joseph A. *Capitalism, Socialism and Democracy*. Toronto: Harper Torchbooks, [1942] 1975.

Schwartz, Joan M. "Constituting Place of Presence: Landscape, Identity and the Geographical Imagination." In *Places of Presence: Newfoundland Kin and Ancestral Land, Newfoundland 1989–1991*, edited by Marlene Creates, 9–17. St. John's: Killick Press, 1997.

Sensel, Joni. *Tradition Through the Trees: Weyerhaeuser's First 100 Years*. N.p.: Documentary Book Publishers, 2000.

Shkilnyk, Anastasia M. *A Poison Stronger than Love: The Destruction of an Ojibwa Community*. New Haven, CT: Yale University Press, 1985.

Skeggs, Beverley. *Class, Self, Culture*. London: Routledge, 2004.

Sinclair, William F. "Controlling Effluent Discharges from Canadian Pulp and Paper Manufacturers." *Canadian Public Policy* 17, no. 1 (1991): 86–105.

Sonnenfeld, David. "Social Movements and Ecological Modernization: The Transformation of Pulp and Paper Manufacturing." *Development and Change* 33, no. 1 (2002): 1–27.

Srigley, Katrina. *Breadwinning Daughters: Young Working Women in a Depression-Era City, 1929–1939*. Toronto: University of Toronto Press, 2009.

Statistics Canada. *Canada Yearbook, 2011*. Ottawa, 2011. Available online at http://www.statcan.gc.ca/pub/11-402-x/2011000/chap/man-fab/man-fab-eng.htm.

Stein, Judith. *Running Steel, Running America: Race, Economic Policy, and the Decline of Liberalism*. Chapel Hill: University of North Carolina Press, 1998.

Stoler, Anne Laura. *Imperial Debris: On Ruins and Ruination*. Durham, NC: Duke University Press, 2013.

Storey, Robert. "Pessimism of the Intellect, Optimism of the Will: Engaging with the 'Testimony' of Injured Workers." In *Beyond Testimony and Trauma: Oral History in the Aftermath of Mass Violence*, edited by Steven High, 56–87. Vancouver: UBC Press, 2015.

Storey, Robert. "'They Have All Been Faithful Workers': Injured Workers, Truth, and Workers' Compensation in Ontario, 1970–2008." *Journal of Canadian Studies* 43, no. 1 (2009): 154–85.

Strangleman, Tim. "'Smokestack Nostalgia,' 'Ruin Porn,' or Working-Class Obituary: The Role and Meaning of Deindustrial Representation." *International Labor and Working Class History* 84 (Fall 2013): 23–37.

Strangleman, Tim. *Work Identity at the End of the Line? Privatisation and Culture Change in the UK Rail Industry*. London: Palgrave Macmillan, 2004.

Strangleman, Tim. "Work Identity in Crisis? Rethinking the Problem of Attachment and Loss at Work." *Sociology* 46, no. 3 (2012): 411–25.

Struthers, James. "How Much Is Enough? Creating a Social Minimum in Ontario, 1930–44." *Canadian Historical Review* 72, no. 1 (1991): 39–83.

Sturgeon Falls Partnership. *The Construction and Operation of a Mill to Recycle Old Corrugated Cardboard*. Toronto: Ministry of Environment and Energy, February 1995.

Summerby-Murray, Robert. "Interpreting Personalized Industrial Heritage in the Mining Towns of Cumberland County, Nova Scotia: Landscape Examples from Springhill and River Hebert." *Urban History Review* 35, no. 2 (2007): 51–9.

Sweeney, Brendan Anthony. "Comparing Employment Relations in a Cross-Border Region: The Case of Cascadia's Forest Products Industry." PhD diss., Queen's University, 2010.

Swift, Jamie. *Walking the Union Walk: Stories from CEP's First Ten Years*. Toronto: Between the Lines, 2003.

Taksa, Lucy. "Like a Bicycle, Forever Teetering between Individualism and Collectivism: Considering Community in Relation to Labour History." *Labour History* 78 (May 2000): 7–32.

Thompson, E.P. *The Poverty of Theory and Other Essays*. London: Marlin, 1978.

Thomson, Alistair. *Anzac Memories: Living with the Legend*. Oxford: Oxford University Press, 1994.

Vecsey, C. "Grassy Narrows Reserve: Mercury Pollution, Social Disruption, and Natural Resources: A Question of Autonomy." *American Indian Quarterly* 11, no. 4 (1987): 287–314.

Wallace, C.M. "Communities in the Northern Ontario Frontier." In *At the End of the Shift: Mines and Single-Industry Towns in Northern Ontario*, edited by Matt Bray and Ashley Thomson, 5–18. Toronto: Dundurn Press, 1992.

Walley, Christine J. *Exit 0: Family and Class in Postindustrial Chicago*. Chicago: University of Chicago Press, 2013.

Walsh, John, and Steven High. "Rethinking the Concept of 'Community.'" *Social History* 17, no. 64 (1999): 255–74.

Wightman, Robert W., and Nancy M. Wightman. "Changing Patterns of Rural Peopling in Northeastern Ontario, 1901–1941." *Ontario History* 92, no. 2 (2000): 161–81.

Williams, Raymond. *Marxism and Literature*. Oxford: Oxford University Press, 1977.

Wilson, Gregory S. *Communities Left Behind: The Area Redevelopment Administration, 1945–1965*. Knoxville: University of Tennessee Press, 2009.

Winson, Anthony, and Belinda Leach. *Contingent Work, Disrupted Lives: Labour and Community in the New Rural Economy*. Toronto: University of Toronto Press, 2002.

Wolman, Harold, Eric Stokan, and Howard Wial. "Manufacturing Job Loss in U.S. Deindustrialized Regions – Its Consequences and Implications for the Future: Examining the Conventional Wisdom." *Economic Development Quarterly* 29, no. 2 (2015): 102–12.

Wood, J. David. *Places of Last Resort: The Expansion of the Farm Frontier into the Boreal Forest in Canada, 1910–1940*. Montreal; Kingston, ON: McGill-Queen's University Press, 2006.

Wright, Donald. *Donald Creighton: A Life in History*. Toronto: University of Toronto Press, 2015.

Ziegler, Robert H. *Rebuilding the Pulp and Paper Workers' Union, 1933–1941*. Knoxville: University of Tennessee Press, 1984.

Zukin, Sharon. *Naked City: The Death and Life of Authentic Urban Places*. New York: Oxford University Press, 2010.

INDEX

Printed and bound by CPI Group (UK) Ltd, Croydon, CR0 4YY

23/04/2025

14660954-0005